BUSINESS INFORMATION SOURCES

BUSINESS INFORMATION SOURCES

LORNA M. DANIELLS

Head, Reference Department, Baker Library
Harvard University Graduate School
of Business Administration

UNIVERSITY OF CALIFORNIA PRESS
Berkeley   Los Angeles   London

CENTER FOR BUSINESS INFORMATION
Paris

University of California Press
Berkeley and Los Angeles, California

University of California Press, Ltd.
London, England

ISBN 0-520-02946-1
Library of Congress Catalog Card Number: 74-30517
Printed in the United States of America

2 3 4 5 6 7 8 9 0

CONTENTS

v

Chapter 5   INDUSTRY STATISTICS, 53

Chapter 6   FOREIGN STATISTICS AND ECONOMIC TRENDS, 79

Chapter 7   INVESTMENT SOURCES, 92

Chapter 8 U.S. BUSINESS AND ECONOMIC TRENDS, 122

Chapter 9 BUSINESS IN AMERICAN SOCIETY, 137

Chapter 10 MANAGEMENT, 149

Chapter 11 MANAGEMENT OF PUBLIC AND NONPROFIT
ORGANIZATIONS, 172

Chapter 16   INTERNATIONAL MANAGEMENT, 244

Chapter 17   MANAGEMENT SCIENCE AND STATISTICAL METHODS, 264

Chapter 18   MARKETING, 275

Chapter 19   PERSONNEL MANAGEMENT AND INDUSTRIAL
                 RELATIONS, 306

Chapter 20   PRODUCTION AND OPERATIONS MANAGEMENT, 331

Chapter 21   A BASIC BOOKSHELF, 351

INDEX, 357

FOREWORD

The advent of the computer, the development of the multinational company and increasing government regulation of business have brought about rapid changes in business operations and a need for the latest published information. It has been a satisfaction to know that my *Sources of Business Information* has met this need in the past, and that there is now a demand for a new edition.

Since I left the field of business librarianship some years ago to become a university librarian, it was not possible to consider undertaking a revision when the University of California Press approached me several years ago about preparing a third edition. Despite this fact, I suppose one never passes a book on to another to write without a certain emotional response akin to giving a child out for adoption. This was surely true in my case. However, I have no qualms at all about the ability and qualifications of the present compiler and am impressed by the depth and breadth of her knowledge of business literature. As I read Miss Daniells' manuscript I was struck by the many excellent approaches she used. Her format and contents are good; the introductory paragraphs to each chapter provide succinct information on the coverage that follows; the annotations are clear and helpful. It is with great pleasure that I think about the many people who, because of this new work, will continue to benefit from a source book of business information.

EDWIN T. COMAN, JR.

PREFACE

Obtaining up-to-date business information in this complex computerized age is imperative, yet there are many businessmen who either do not know what is available or do not understand how to find it. This book is intended as a guide to the vast and varied sources of business information for three types of users: (1) the practicing businessman — both to provide possible sources for solving particular business problems or information needs and to suggest a few books for professional reading; (2) the business student — as a general introduction to the literature of business; and (3) the librarian — as a basic reference tool.

Although this was begun as a revision of Edwin T. Coman's *Sources of Business Information* (2d ed., University of California Press, 1964), two facts soon became clear: first, that no one could hope to write the same sort of book Mr. Coman did, with his interesting discussions about each topic and his insightful annotations; and second, the business world of today is so changed that a different approach is required. Consequently, although the purpose of this book is much the same as that of Mr. Coman's indispensable guide and covers some of the same material, it is, in fact, a completely different work.

Some general comments are necessary to set the scope and limitations of this volume. It is a selected, annotated list of business books and reference sources, with an emphasis on recent material in the English language. The selection was based on several factors: my experience as a business reference librarian; the accessibility of material, principally in Baker Library at the Harvard Business School but also in a few other Boston libraries; some personal preferences; and my endurance in what turned out to be a concentrated year-long effort. There is an admitted emphasis on books published in the United States, since these are the ones with which I am most familiar. Thus, because many good books necessarily are omitted, readers are urged to consult bibliographies mentioned throughout when researching any business topic.

Since it was not possible to read all of the books cited or the many other volumes examined during the course of making these selections, the annotations, for the most part, are descriptive rather than critical. The fact that a value judgment may have been made in describing some books and not others should be of little significance in one's decision about which of several books to consult. All of the books, I hope, are of high quality, but the reader will want to look at several titles before deciding which will suit a particular need. It should be noted here that a few annotations for reference books were adapted from my *Business Reference Sources: A Guide for Harvard Business School Students* (Baker Library, 1971).

Two kinds of books are not covered in this work. Published proceedings of association conferences, with but a few exceptions, are not included even though they often contain useful information on new developments and new research. Business casebooks also are omitted unless they have a substantial percentage of text.

This book is arranged roughly in two parts. Chapters 1 through 8 describe the basic kinds of business reference sources, such as bibliographies, indexes and abstracts, directories, statistical and financial sources, and data on current business and economic trends. Beginning with Chapter 9 the emphasis shifts to management and to each specific management function, so the arrangement of material is different. In this latter part, handbooks and basic textbooks are usually of most importance, so their descriptions appear first, followed in each chapter by the reference works relating to the particular subject (bibliographies and abstracts, dictionaries, loose-leaf services, statistics, periodicals, directories and names of associations). Chapter 21 lists a few important reference works indispensable for almost any small office library. A detailed author/title/subject index is at end.

Within each list of books I have attempted to include examples of textbooks, books written especially for the practicing manager and collections of readings. Textbooks, although written for course work, usually are intended also for management training programs and for general reading by business executives, although this fact is not mentioned in every instance. Selected readings are useful in amplifying concepts discussed in textbooks and in providing a broad and varied view of professional thinking not always found in a textbook.

Each book entry contains all bibliographical data except for pagination. Special note is made when a book contains a bibliography or has suggested reading lists. Only the U.S. publisher is given unless a book was originally published in another country, in which case the foreign publisher is cited along with the U.S. publisher when it is known. Most of the books listed can be purchased through any bookstore, from a book agent, directly from the publisher, or through a subscription agent. Complete names and addresses of publishers can be found in any library. Potential buyers abroad will find that many publishers have branches in several large foreign cities.

Frequency of periodicals is given in abbreviated form, for example, "5/wk." refers to a daily newspaper consisting of five issues each week; "10/yr." refers to a journal published ten times a year. Notation is made with each periodical when its articles are indexed in one of the important commercial indexes, since this fact is of interest to many researchers. The names of these indexes are cited in abbreviated form (for example, "BPI"), and abbreviations are explained at the end of this preface. Other abbreviations are explained in the Index.

However much an author tries to avoid errors and inaccuracies, there are bound to be some in a work as comprehensive as this, where every bibliographic detail is so important. I hope there are few and will appreciate having them called to my attention along with any serious omissions or suggestions for improvement. The intent has been to provide information believed to be accurate as of October 1975. It is an unfortunate fact that publishers make changes almost daily, and this possibility should be kept in mind as one searches for the publications listed here.

In this day when women are finally being accepted into the ranks of management, I feel it important to add a comment about my consistent use of the word "businessman." In every case I intend this word (as well as any other related words) to refer in the broadest sense to any person, regardless of sex, who holds a responsible business position. Early in this research I made the decision that I would not attempt to word sentences in order to acknowledge that there are both men and women executives. To me this is obvious.

It has been a long-time ambition of mine to undertake a bibliographic project that might make a significant professional contribution in my field of expertise. I hope this is that book. It would never have been possible without the enthusiastic approval and support of the Harvard Business School, which granted me a research leave from my duties in Baker Library. I am deeply grateful to Dean Lawrence E. Fouraker, to Senior Associate Dean George F. F. Lombard and to Baker's librarian, Laurence J. Kipp, for giving me this opportunity. Many people gave help and encouragement. In fact, in some ways this could be considered a Baker Library team effort, since almost everyone on the staff was involved in one way or another — a few very actively by shifting jobs or assuming added responsibilities during my absence, and others in the day-to-day routines of helping to find the books and checking serial title changes, as well as in countless expressions of interest and enthusiasm. A number of faculty members gave freely of their time to talk with me about specific chapters. Company librarians in Boston and several publishers were most cordial in making their facilities available. I am also grateful to Mr. Coman for passing his "child" on to me, for his friendly interest throughout the preparation of this work, and for his willingness to write the Foreword. Lastly, I wish to thank the several persons who helped type the manuscript, principally Pamela Hickman, who remained cheerful and patient during this long and difficult process.

Boston, Massachusetts
October 1975

ABBREVIATIONS USED
FOR PERIODICAL INDEXES

ASTI   *Applied Science and Technology Index*
BPI   *Business Periodicals Index*
F&S   *F & S Index of Corporations & Industries*
F&SI   *F & S International*
PAIS   *Public Affairs Information Service Bulletin*
RGPL   *Readers' Guide to Periodical Literature*
SSI   *Social Sciences Index*

1

METHODS OF LOCATING FACTS

**Business Services of Public Libraries — University Libraries —
Company Libraries — Other Special Libraries and Information
Sources — Directories of Libraries and Information Centers —
Encyclopedic Sources of Information**

Since this book is to serve as a guide to business information, it
must first indicate where to go to look for material that may provide answers to
an information need. Therefore Chapter 1 will discuss briefly the kinds of
libraries and information centers of use to businessmen, and then it will
describe several broad encyclopedic sources that are often good first places to
check on almost any topic.

The *American Library Directory* listed over 28,000 libraries in the United
States in 1974. This is an awesome figure when one contemplates what vast
storehouses of information must then be available for anyone to use. These
libraries come in all sizes and varieties — some are general, serving all people
and covering all subjects, others concentrate on a particular subject or are
limited to a specialized clientele. An understanding of these differences can be
useful.

BUSINESS SERVICES OF PUBLIC LIBRARIES

Today public libraries in almost every city with manufacturing and commercial
interests have well-rounded collections of the books and reference tools that are
most useful to the businessman. Some are in special departments of the main
library, occasionally combined with materials on economics or the social
sciences; others are in separate branches located near the business and financial
district. The emphasis in these libraries is on *current* information — a large part
of it in nonbook sources such as company and city directories, financial
manuals, statistical sources, tax and other legal services and current journals.
Any businessman who makes the initial effort to visit his local business library,
introduce himself to the reference librarian, and ask for guidance in unraveling
the mysteries of its systems and procedures, will be amply rewarded by dis-

covering the proverbial gold mine of information that can be of immense value to him in his work. He will discover a staff that is eager and ready to help him, sources he never dreamed existed, useful guides, bibliographies or booklists the library prepares, and new surprises on almost every visit. Not only will much of the material he needs be immediately accessible, but he will find also that librarians have at their fingertips a whole network of other information sources either via the telephone or through a cooperative system among libraries called "interlibrary loan" whereby books not located in one library may be borrowed by mail or messenger service for use in any other library. And all of this service is usually free of charge! Once this contact with a business library is established, assistance in answering specific inquiries for data or statistics is often no farther away than one's telephone, since public libraries also offer prompt and efficient telephone service. Several of the largest, best known business libraries in the United States are located in Brooklyn, Cleveland and Newark, but there are many others in cities such as Boston, Chicago, Dallas, Detroit, Los Angeles and Philadelphia, to name just a few. It should not be inferred, however, that only large cities have good business libraries. On the contrary, many small cities with industrial interests have excellent library facilities, adequately financed and staffed with enthusiastic and service-minded librarians.

UNIVERSITY LIBRARIES

Every accredited business school has a good collection of materials needed to support its teaching program. The scope of its library reflects the nature of the courses, the extent of its research activities, and also whether it is a school for management or business administration exclusively or is combined with schools in such related departments as economics or public administration. Many of these libraries are located within the main university library building, while others, particularly the large ones, are in separate buildings or even on separate campuses. Business school collections tend to be more extensive than those in public libraries and to emphasize both the importance of maintaining a good collection of current materials and also the need to preserve essential retrospective, scholarly and theoretical publications that any first-rate permanent research collection must have. Several of the leading business school libraries are at Harvard University Graduate School of Business Administration, Stanford University Graduate School of Business, the University of Pennsylvania's Wharton School, Cornell University Graduate School of Business and Public Administration, the Graduate Schools of Management at both Northwestern University and the University of California in Los Angeles, Purdue University Krannert Graduate School of Industrial Administration, and the Graduate Schools of Business at both Indiana University and the University of California in Berkeley. These institutions necessarily are all concerned primarily with their own students, faculty and graduates, but they do arrange in varying degrees to assist any businessman who has a serious need. Those libraries that are part of state universities make their facilities freely available to everyone as far as is possible; some of those in private universities have found it necessary to charge an annual fee for continuous use of their facilities by local businessmen. Thus, it is usually wise to exhaust the resources of a public library first and then to turn to college and university libraries should the need arise.

COMPANY LIBRARIES

Many large progressive business firms have well-established libraries to serve their organizations. These specialized libraries are found not only in various manufacturing concerns but also in financial firms such as banks, insurance companies and investment management firms; service firms such as those of accountants, consultants, market research and advertising specialists; and businesses such as publishers, transportation companies, and engineering, technical and scientific companies. The executive who works for one of these firms is fortunate indeed because he has all of his informational needs taken care of quickly and thoroughly by staffs of well-trained information specialists who concentrate their entire effort in his behalf. These specialized librarians make it their business to know the information needs and interests of each individual in the company. They compile tailor-made bibliographies, do in-depth indexing and abstracting, route journals, alert individuals to new developments and publications, maintain clipping files for up-to-date subject retrieval and perform many other related tasks. Since their book collections are often relatively small and highly concentrated from a subject point of view, company librarians are experienced in knowing where to go or whom to telephone for speedy answers to questions, and they will usually take over the responsibility for research themselves rather than expect the executive to do his own searching. Although company libraries are usually not open to the general public it is important to know of their existence, and, for the lucky businessman who is employed by one, this is obviously the first and usually the only library he needs to contact to satisfy all of his information needs.

OTHER SPECIAL LIBRARIES AND INFORMATION SOURCES

The federal government is a prime source of information and advice. Many of its departments maintain libraries to collect materials in the area with which each is concerned. Although these libraries are most accessible to people living in the Washington, D.C., area there are other services of government agencies that anyone can take advantage of. The many excellent statistical publications of such agencies as the Department of Commerce and its Bureau of the Census, the Department of Agriculture and the Bureau of Labor Statistics are well known, and several are discussed elsewhere in this book. Periodic catalogs of government publications help to locate the wide range of material available either free or at a modest cost. These are described in Chapter 2. If one does not find answers to problems through published documents he can always write or telephone the agency involved or contact its regional office if there is one. A good example of one federal agency whose sole purpose is to give both financial assistance and management advice to small businessmen is the Small Business Administration. Anyone can obtain a list on request of their various published management aids or bibliographies. Many state and municipal agencies and groups are also useful information sources that the businessman can tap. State departments of commerce and development, local chambers of commerce, for instance, can often supply information on local economic conditions, plans and trends.

For information on particular industries or professions, many large trade and professional associations maintain excellent libraries. Although these are often restricted to use only by their own members, the librarians are usually willing to answer legitimate outside inquiries. A few trade associations publish short factbooks that are available free or at a nominal cost. Several examples of associations with good research and library facilities are the American Bankers Association, the Conference Board, the American Iron and Steel Institute, the Institute of Life Insurance, and the National Association of Realtors. An excellent directory of associations (which includes statements on the scope of each association and the names of its publications) is described in Chapter 3.

DIRECTORIES OF LIBRARIES AND INFORMATION CENTERS

The following directories will suggest many other libraries and information centers, both those located in individual cities and those covering specific subject specialties.

American Library Directory. New York, R. R. Bowker (annual).

> This is a geographic list of libraries in the United States and Canada, including for each the names of top personnel, total volumes, specific subject interests. It covers public libraries, college and university libraries and many of the best known special libraries.

Special Libraries Association. New York Chapter. *Special Libraries Directory of Greater New York.* 13th ed. New York, 1974.

> There are probably more good business and other special libraries in New York City than in any other metropolitan area. This is a descriptive directory, arranged by broad subject.
>
> Several other SLA chapters with recently published directories are those in Boston, New Jersey, Philadelphia. Directories are also available for several SLA divisions, e.g., Business/Finance, and Transportation.

Subject Directory of Special Libraries and Information Centers. Vol. 1: Business and Law Libraries, Including Military and Transportation Libraries. 1st. ed. Ed. by Margaret L. Young, Harold C. Young and Anthony T. Kruzas. Detroit, Mich., Gale Research Co., 1975.

> Kruzas' excellent directory, formerly in one volume and published triennially, is now divided into 5 volumes along subject lines, and this first one includes U.S. and Canadian business libraries. It covers "special libraries, research libraries, information centers, archives, and data centers maintained by government agencies, business, industry, newspapers, educational institutions, nonprofit organizations and societies." For each, the data includes subject specialty, special collections; holdings in total books, periodicals, microfilms, microfiche, etc.; publications; what services are offered (whether library is open to the public, whether it accepts interlibrary loans, etc.).

ENCYCLOPEDIC SOURCES OF INFORMATION

With a brief description of various libraries as background, we can now turn to the principal task at hand, which in the first part of this book is to describe different kinds of reference works used for finding information. Probably those works that are most familiar to the largest number of people regardless of age or interest are compilations such as almanacs and encyclopedias, so full of information on almost any topic that they often can answer one's need for concise data without recourse to other more specialized publications.

Almanacs

The one-volume almanacs listed below are each almost portable reference libraries in themselves and are well worth the modest paperback price for persons who like to keep a copy close at hand either on an office desk or at home for the whole family to use. Each of the first three are worldwide in scope, are revised annually, and can answer all sorts of factual and statistical questions about nations, states, people, dates, events of the year, education, sports, the arts, awards, weather, geography, business, government, and on and on. The *World Almanac* is the best known and most comprehensive, but the others are also very detailed and good. *Whitaker's* is the British counterpart of the *Almanac,* concentrating on factual data, organizations and events in Commonwealth countries but also including a section on other countries.

Information Please Almanac: Atlas and Yearbook. New York, Simon and Schuster (annual).

Official Associated Press Almanac. Successor to the *New York Times Encyclopedic Almanac.* Maplewood, N.J., Hammond Almanac (annual).

World Almanac & Book of Facts. New York, Newspaper Enterprise Association (annual).

Whitaker's Almanac. London, J. Whitaker & Sons (annual).

Yearbooks

Yearbooks differ from almanacs in that they usually give fuller information but concentrate either on a broad subject area, a country, or current trends and events (as in the case of yearly supplements to encyclopedias). One good example of a yearbook covering the governments of the world is:

Statesman's Year-Book. New York, St. Martin's Press (annual).

This yearbook is in 4 sections: the first contains factual data about important international organizations; this is followed by sections giving information about Commonwealth countries and about the United States. The last section provides concise, descriptive data and a few statistics on other countries and includes history, constitution and government, area and population, religion, education, social welfare, industries, commerce, transportation, communications, diplomatic representatives.

Europa Year Book gives much the same type of information, and it is also worldwide in scope despite the title. It is more strictly a list of names, organizations, etc., for each country and is especially useful for that information. A description of this important yearbook is included in both Chapters 6 and 16.

Yearbooks published for individual countries permit a more detailed review of the economic, social and political developments in the particular country. Some yearbooks include brief statistics even though many governments also publish separate statistical annuals, a few examples of which are mentioned in Chapter 6. Following are typical yearbooks for three countries:

Canada Year Book. Ottawa, Ministry of Industry, Trade and Commerce.

Denmark: An Official Handbook. Copenhagen, Royal Danish Ministry of Foreign Affairs (annual).

India: A Reference Annual. New Delhi, Ministry of Information and Broadcasting.

Encyclopedias

While almanacs and yearbooks serve a vital function in providing factual data, there are times when one wants to delve into a subject in somewhat more depth, so he will turn instead to an encyclopedia for help. Here can be found excellent, signed articles on every imaginable subject and on important personalities, each written in a concise but easy-to-understand style. Useful features include frequent illustrations, plates, diagrams and maps. Good, short bibliographies accompany most entries for persons interested in pursuing a topic further. There is also a detailed index volume as well as yearbook supplements essential for providing up-to-date information on current trends and events.

Even though only two of the leading encyclopedias are described in this book it is important to realize that there are other good encyclopedias on the market today. Most libraries purchase more than one set so that they can be compared for completeness and accuracy on any topic. Persons considering which encyclopedia to purchase for either business or home use would be advised to consult with a professional librarian who can supply the name of a current article or book giving comparative evaluations.

Encyclopedia Americana. International ed. New York, Americana Corp. 30 volumes.

> A top-ranking encyclopedia with special emphasis on the sciences, social sciences and humanities. There are some 60,000 signed articles, good illustrations, plates, diagrams, maps. Bibliographies accompany the long articles, and glossaries are sometimes included. A detailed index appears as Vol. 30. This encyclopedia is continuously revised, and there is also an *Americana Annual* that contains the year's major political, economic, scientific and cultural developments.

The New Encyclopaedia Britannica. 15th ed. Chicago, 1975. 30 volumes.

> This newest edition of the oldest, perhaps most widely known, encyclopedia offers a completely new concept in encyclopedias based on a division of its 30 volumes into 3 sections. Readers are expected to turn first to the "Micropaedia" (10 volumes) because it serves both as a ready reference and as an index. This section contains over 100,000 short, factual articles and includes references to topics to be found in the "Macropaedia." The Macropaedia (19 volumes) contains over 4,200 major articles written by experts and treating each subject in much greater depth. Bibliographies accompany all articles for persons wanting to study a topic further. There are maps with articles on countries and their leading cities; many illustrations, plates, diagrams

appear throughout. The last section is a one-volume "Propaedia," a systematic out-line of the whole of human knowledge. Thus the new encyclopedia is an exciting departure, designed to serve 2 functions: a reference function for quick answers and basic facts; an educational function, with longer articles that discuss and interpret the more important subjects.

A number of encyclopedias are published on specific subjects, although most are of a technical or scientific nature and so are of little interest to businessmen. One that is not technical and is of great interest is the following:

International Encyclopedia of the Social Sciences. Ed. by David L. Sills. New York, Macmillan and the Free Press, 1968. 17 volumes.

This excellent encyclopedia covers all important areas of social science, industrial economics, psychology, sociology, statistics; also biographies of prominent persons in these fields. Each article is written by a qualified social scientist, and bibliographies refer to relevant information on each subject. A detailed index is in the last volume.

Dictionaries

English-language dictionaries serve an important function when one needs to check the meaning, spelling or pronunciation of words, terms or phrases. It is not essential to have an unabridged dictionary, but in most cases it is preferable to use one if it is available. The two best unabridged dictionaries are:

Funk & Wagnalls Comprehensive Standard International Dictionary. New York, Funk & Wagnalls Publishing Co.

Webster's Third New International Dictionary of the English Language Unabridged. Springfield, Mass., G. & C. Merriam Co.

There are many abridged collegiate and desk dictionaries from which to choose, and it may be wise to look at a number before deciding which one to purchase for one's personal use. Checking a sample of the definitions may be helpful as may looking for added features such as illustrations, a style manual, a gazetteer, a list of signs and symbols, etc. Paperback editions are often not as complete as clothbound dictionaries, but they are inexpensive and may serve the purpose. If searching for a "Webster's," care should be taken not to select one of the several imitations that may use this name. Several good collegiate dictionaries are:

Funk & Wagnalls Standard College Dictionary. Updated ed. New York, Funk & Wagnalls Publishing Co.

Webster's New World Dictionary of the American Language. 2d college ed. New York, World Publishing Co.

Webster's Seventh New Collegiate Dictionary. Springfield, Mass., G. & C. Merriam Co. This is especially recommended for its added features.

Comprehensive Booklists

There are several comprehensive, periodic lists of all in-print books (*not* government publications, services or pamphlets) published by commercial publishing firms and university presses. These are excellent for identifying titles and prices of all books on a particular subject or by an individual author. Every library, regardless of size, and most bookstores will have at least one of these bibliographies. If it is not in evidence, persons should feel free to ask for it, because librarians and bookstore personnel usually keep these close by for checking purposes.

Books in Print. New York, R. R. Bowker. 4 volumes (annual); and *Subject Guide to Books in Print.* 2 volumes (annual).

The 1974 volumes of *Books in Print* listed approximately 418,000 titles available from 3,600 U.S. publishers, with 2 volumes indexing the books by author, and 2 volumes by title. A publishers' index is at the back of the last title volume. The information includes publication date (usually) and price. *Subject Guide to Books in Print* is a companion series that lists all books by specific subject. A mid-year author/title/subject supplement to *Books in Print* gives updated information with price and other major changes, out-of-print titles and new and forthcoming books.

Cumulative Book Index. New York, H. W. Wilson (monthly, except August, with quarterly and annual cumulations).

This is a continuing worldwide author/title/subject index of English-language books, including publication date and price for each.

Forthcoming Books. New York, R. R. Bowker (bimonthly); and *Subject Guide to Forthcoming Books* (bimonthly).

The first of these reference works is an author/title list of U.S. books due to be published within the coming 5 months of each issue. *The Subject Guide* is a companion volume containing the same books in a subject arrangement.

Paperbound Books in Print. New York, R. R. Bowker (3/yr.).

This gives complete coverage for paperback books and is arranged by subject, with an author index.

British Books in Print. London, J. Whitaker & Sons, 2 volumes (annual).

An author/title/subject index of over 260,000 books in print and for sale in the United Kingdom, from 7,700 publishers. There is also a quarterly list with annual cumulations called *Whitaker's Cumulative Book List* that is arranged by author and subject.

There are periodic booklists compiled in other countries. Persons interested in checking these can consult with a librarian about their availability.

2

BASIC TIME-SAVING SOURCES

Bibliographies of Business Literature — Indexes and Abstracts — Government Publications — Computerized Information Services — Handbooks — Loose-leaf Services — Microforms and Cassettes — Doctoral Dissertations — Business Dictionaries

There are many aids available to help businessmen locate useful information. A familiarity with some of these can be advantageous in carrying out a successful library search with the least expenditure of time. This chapter discusses several of the principal kinds of time-saving sources.

BIBLIOGRAPHIES OF BUSINESS LITERATURE

In undertaking any literature or statistical search the first step is to determine whether or not the information needed is already available. For statistics this is a matter of using basic bibliographies of statistics (mentioned in Chapters 4 and 6) and also statistical data base directories (listed later in this chapter). For literature searches this can be ascertained by checking in card catalogs, in books and in indexes, looking for recent bibliographies that may cover the subject. Today more and more bibliographies are being compiled on a wide range of subjects. Those that are annotated are preferable because the inclusion of descriptive notes often helps in deciding which citations are most pertinent.

Every chapter in this book includes the names of bibliographies on specific topics. In the section below are a few that cover all business literature or business reference sources and also several examples of booklists and bibliographies prepared by libraries or other organizations. A few lists on management in general are in Chapter 10, while the basic bibliographies of economic literature are included in Chapter 8.

Bibliography of Publications of University Bureaus of Business and Economic Research. Denver, published for the Association for University Business and Economic Research by the Business Research Division, University of Colorado (annual).

This useful 2-part bibliography (by subject and by name of institution) lists the books, series, working papers, articles, etc., that are published by each business school. An author index is at end.

Brown, Barbara E. *Canadian Business and Economics: A Guide to Sources of Information.* Ottawa, Canadian Library Association, 1975.

This guide, scheduled for publication in fall 1975, promises to be a useful annotated list of publications and services on Canadian business and economics. It is arranged by province and under each province by subject, and it covers primarily material published since 1960. Both English and French titles are included, and there is an author/title index.

A short guide (32 pages) to basic reference books, periodicals, government publications and statistics is *Sources of Information for the Canadian Businessman* by Brian Land (Montreal, Canadian Chamber of Commerce, 1972).

Business Books in Print. New York, R. R. Bowker (annual).

A fairly complete annual list of all books available from major U.S. publishers and university presses on business, finance and economics. It is arranged by author/title/subject, and for each book it gives publication date (usually) and price. Bowker's annual *Books in Print* (4 volumes) and *Subject Guide to Books in Print* (2 volumes) also list these same books along with novels and books on all nonbusiness topics.

Campbell, Malcolm J., ed., *Manual of Business Library Practice.* London, C. Bingley; Hamden, Conn., Linnet Books (Shoe String Press), 1975.

A short introduction for new British business librarians, with contributions by 7 British librarians or information specialists. Over half of the book consists of bibliographical essays on the principal kinds of business information: directories and company information, statistical guides and indexes, basic statistical publications, management literature sources, periodicals and newspapers. The rest briefly discusses the structure, organization and services of British libraries. An earlier book by Campbell, also written primarily for British librarians, is *Business Information Services: Some Aspects of Structure, Organisation and Problems* (C. Bingley, 1974, distributed in U.S. by Linnet Books).

Grant, Mary M. and Norma Cote, eds. *Directory of Business and Financial Services.* 7th ed. New York, Special Libraries Association, 1976.

This is the latest edition of an excellent directory that describes business, economic and financial services that are published periodically or with regular supplements. It is arranged by title, with indexes by subject and by name of publisher.

Johnson, H. Webster. *How to Use the Business Library, With Sources of Business Information.* 4th ed. Cincinnati, Ohio, South-Western, 1972.

A very handy guide that provides brief instruction on how to use a library, followed by 15 chapters describing the various categories of business information, such as handbooks, almanacs, dictionaries, encyclopedias, directories, services, government publications, audio-visual aids. This is recommended as a good, short introduction to business sources.

Mechanic, Sylvia. *Outline for the Course in Business and Economics Literature* (LS K8252y). New York, School of Library Service, Columbia University (annual).

This is a well-organized list of those important business reference works that all prospective business information specialists should know about, and thus it is a good list for any library to have. It is arranged in 16 units according to the sequence of this course, e.g., general reference books, periodicals and newspapers, statistics, etc. Copies can be purchased at a nominal cost ($3.00) from the SLS at Columbia. Some of these same sources are briefly discussed in an informative chapter on "Key Reference Sources," which the author wrote for *Financial Analyst's Handbook,* edited by S. N. Levine (Homewood, Ill., Dow Jones-Irwin, 1974, Vol. 2, pp. 859–880).

SIE Guide to Business and Investment Books. New York, Select Information Exchange, 1974.

A descriptive list of over 8,100 business and investment books arranged by specific topic. This is a broad list of books that can be useful as long as one realizes it may not include some good books unavailable through this subscription clearinghouse.

Vernon, K. D. C., ed. *Use of Management and Business Literature.* London and Boston, Butterworths, 1975.

A bibliographical guide to published information in the English language on business and management. Its 17 chapters are in 3 parts. Part 1, written by Vernon who is librarian at the London Business School, covers "the literature, the library and the bibliographical tools." The emphasis is on British publications and library practices, and it includes a core list of books and periodicals as well as separate chapters describing abstracts and indexes, periodicals, reference works. Part 2 deals with "business information in three different forms" — research materials, statistical publications, company information — each written by an information specialist. Part 3 consists of bibliographical "surveys of the literature" written by subject specialists in each of 6 important areas (corporate finance and management accounting, organizational behavior, manpower management and industrial relations, marketing, computers and management, quantitative methods and production).

Beginning in 1976 a new loose-leaf *European Directory of Business Information Sources and Services* will be published in Paris, France, by the Center for Business Information. This will consist of monthly packets of 4-page descriptive analyses for new or standard information sources. Eventually this service will be expanded on an international basis, with separate directories for the other three major geographic areas.

Booklists Compiled by Libraries and Organizations

To keep informed about newly published business books, it is worthwhile to review, on a regular basis, one or more of the various booklists, checklists or bibliographies compiled by many libraries and organizations. These may be periodic lists of selected books added to the business section of a public library or those in a business school library, a company library or an association or government agency library. Public libraries almost always have guides or lists distributed free or at a very small cost to users. Those lists prepared by specialized institutions and organizations are not always available to outsiders, but this is well worth investigating if an especially pertinent list is found.

A number of business schools prepare good lists of their current acquisitions, but unfortunately these usually are available only on a limited basis outside the school. There are several exceptions. The University of Chicago publishes a short subject list of books that appears in each issue of its *Journal of Business*. Baker Library at the Harvard Business School publishes two periodic bibliographies that are widely available, since they are priced publications. These are:

Core Collection: An Author and Subject Guide. Boston (annual).
This is a computer-produced list of a selection of about 4,000 recent English-language business books collected on open shelves to encourage HBS students to browse among a relatively small group of recent books that is constantly changing. It is not meant as a purchasing guide but does attempt to include a few representative books in each subject field. As the subtitle indicates the books are arranged both by author and by subject, and the guide is revised annually. Current additions to the collection are noted in the following booklist.

New Books in Business and Economics: Recent Additions to Baker Library. Boston (10/yr.).
A periodic list (not annotated) of most of the books and substantial pamphlets added to Baker Library. Each issue is arranged by subject, and special notation is made for those books located in Baker's Core Collection.

A number of libraries publish series of short bibliographies, with each issue concentrating on a different topic of current interest. Three of the best known business public libraries have good examples.

Brooklyn Public Library. Business Library. *Service to Business and Industry.* New York (10/yr.).
Annotated lists, with recent issues covering such topics as "The Energy Crisis," "Periodical Special Issues," "Business Books, 1974," "Statistics! Statistics!" This series is published jointly with the library's Science and Industry Division.

Cleveland Public Library. Business Information Department. *Business and Technology Sources.* Cleveland, Ohio (quarterly).
Useful lists, although not all are annotated. Recent titles include "Energy," "Going Metric," "Business Books, 1974," "Occupational Safety and Health." This series is published jointly with the library's Science and Technology Department.

Public Library of Newark. Business Library. *Business Literature.* Newark, N.J. (quarterly).
Good, annotated lists on such topics as "Women and Work," "Investment Companies," "Multinational Corporations," "The Problem Employee in Industry."

Several business school libraries compile very short subject reference guides meant as handy pickups on topics of special interest to students. Those prepared by the Graduate School of Management Library, University of California at Los Angeles, are 2-page *Library Reference Guides;* Harvard Business School's are 2-to-6-page *Baker Library Mini-Lists*. Both of these series can be purchased at a nominal cost to cover mailing. Other business school libraries prepare useful lists primarily for internal use, although a few, such as the University of Rochester's *Rochester Management Bibliographies,* can sometimes be found in other business school libraries.

Examples of student guides to the reference resources of two business schools are:

Barker, William L. *Business Student's Guide to Selected Library Sources.* Bowling Green, Ohio, Bowling Green State University Library (annual).

This is a good annotated guide to the business and economic reference resources of the BGSU library, revised annually. There are 13 subject sections, each listing pertinent dictionaries, encyclopedias and handbooks, laws and regulations, services, biographies, statistical sources, bibliographies. A limited number of copies are available to interested libraries.

Daniells, Lorna M., comp. *Business Reference Sources: An Annotated Guide for Harvard Business School Students* (Reference List, No. 27). Boston, Baker Library, Harvard Business School, 1971.

An annotated guide in 13 sections. This is now quite old but a new edition is planned for 1977.

The libraries of many business firms and other organizations prepare excellent acquisitions lists and other current awareness services, but these unfortunately are usually available only within the firm. Following are three exceptions:

Chase Manhattan Bank. *What's New in Business Publications.* New York (monthly).

This is a selected list compiled by the bank's library to give the busy banker and businessman a continuing source for keeping up to date on some of the best material being written in books, pamphlets and journal articles both in finance and business. It is arranged by subject and contains descriptive notes about each item. Plans call for a change in this publication by the end of 1975. It will be expanded; the title and perhaps the frequency will change. It will be offered on a subscription basis, with an annual index, and there will be an added bibliographical service offered to subscribers who want cumulated, annotated lists on specific topics covered in the bibliography.

Conference Board. *Library Acquisitions List.* New York (quarterly).

The Conference Board is interested in a broad range of business topics and this is reflected in their short acquisitions list, which is arranged by subject.

Continental Illinois Bank and Trust Co. *Coband: Continental Bank Annotated Digest.* Chicago (weekly).

This useful service is meant for the busy executive who wants to keep informed about a few current articles (also several books and pamphlets) on banking, finance and business, selected from a wide range of business, management, finance and economic journals. It is arranged by subject and there are informative digests with each citation. The lists are short (about 8 pages) so they do not take long to scan each week. There are quarterly and annual indexes that are actually cumulated lists without the digests. Subscribers can request literature searches and specially prepared bibliographies from Coband's computerized data base.

INDEXES AND ABSTRACTS

There are many occasions when a book is not what is needed — the subject being researched may be either too new a development or much too specific a

topic to expect to find a full-length published study. In such cases one will turn
to periodical indexes and abstracting services. Both are valuable sources for
current information on a wide variety of subjects — abstracts are of special interest because of their descriptive notes, but they usually do not index any one
journal in its entirety as most indexes do.

Several excellent indexes and abstracts covering specific fields such as accounting, economics, operations research and personnel are described elsewhere in this book with other material on these subjects. Unless otherwise
noted the basic indexes described below cover U.S. periodicals only. (The newly
published *Canadian Business Periodicals Index* and the established U.K.
Research Index are the only two foreign works of this kind.) Files of *Business
Periodicals Index* and *Public Affairs Information Service* will be found in most
libraries of average size; larger public and university libraries will probably
have most of these indexes. For a complete listing of "Abstracting and Indexing
Services" refer to the latest annual volume of *Ulrich's International Periodicals
Directory*. To discover which of these indexes will best suit a particular need it
may be helpful to check the list of periodicals indexed in each, usually found at
the front of any bound volume. As an aid in learning which of 7 important U.S.
indexes cover articles in any one magazine, this fact is mentioned with each
journal cited in this book, for example, with the entry for *Harvard Business
Review* there is the notation "Indexed in BPI, F&S, PAIS, RGPL."

Applied Science & Technology Index (ASTI). New York, H. W. Wilson
(monthly except July, with periodic cumulations).
Subject index to over 200 selected journals in the fields of aeronautics and space
science, automation, chemistry, construction, earth sciences, electricity and electronics, engineering, industrial and mechanical arts, materials, mathematics,
metallurgy, physics, telecommunication, transportation, and related subjects.

Business Periodicals Index (BPI). New York, H. W. Wilson (monthly except July, with periodic cumulations).
This is probably the best known index for its overall subject coverage of selected
periodicals in the following fields of business: accounting, advertising and public
relations, automation, banking, communications, economics, finance and investments, insurance, labor, management, marketing, taxation, and also specific
businesses, industries and trades. A recent feature is its inclusion of reviews of books
appearing in the journals it indexes, listed together under the heading "Book
Reviews."

Canadian Business Periodicals Index. Toronto, Information Access (monthly,
with annual cumulations).
A new index to Canadian periodicals in business, administrative studies, industry,
economics, industrial relations and related fields, scheduled for publication in fall
1975. It will index about 100 periodicals by subject and corporate and personal
authors, and will include also the *Financial Post, Financial Times* and *Globe and Mail
Report on Business*.

Engineering Index. New York, Engineering Index, Inc. (monthly, with annual
cumulation in 3 volumes).
Subject listing of abstracts covering significant technological journals (both U.S. and

foreign) encompassing all engineering disciplines. This index is also available on computer tapes as *COMPENDEX.*

F & S Index of Corporations & Industries (F&S). Cleveland, Ohio, Predicasts, Inc. (weekly, with monthly and annual cumulations).

This is the best index for current information on companies and industries. It covers a wide selection of business, industrial and financial periodicals and also a few brokerage house reports. The yellow pages in the weeklies and the green pages in cumulated issues list articles (or data in articles) on all SIC (Standard Industrial Classification) industries; the white pages list articles on companies. Since many of the entries refer to very brief citations it is important to note that major articles are designated by a black dot, which precedes the abbreviated title of the journal. This index can also be accessed via *Predicasts Terminal System.*

F & S Index International (F&SI). Cleveland, Ohio, Predicasts, Inc. (monthly, with quarterly and annual cumulations).

A companion to the index above, covering articles on foreign companies and industries that have appeared in some 1,000 foreign and domestic periodicals and other documents. It is arranged in 3 parts: (1) by SIC number or product; (2) by region and country; (3) by company. This index can also be accessed via *Predicasts Terminal System.*

Public Affairs Information Service Bulletin (PAIS). New York (weekly, with periodic cumulations).

This is a selective subject listing in the areas of economic and social conditions, public administration and international relations, published in English throughout the world. The important differences in this index are that: (1) it only selectively indexes journals, to cover those articles pertinent to its subject coverage; (2) it covers not only periodical articles but also selected books, pamphlets, government publications, reports of public and private agencies. There is a companion index called *Public Affairs Information Service: Foreign Language Index,* which is described in Chapter 6.

Readers' Guide to Periodical Literature (RGPL). New York, H. W. Wilson (semi-monthly, with periodic cumulations).

An author and subject index to selected U.S. general and nontechnical periodicals.

Research Index. Wallington, Surrey, England, Business Surveys, Ltd. (fortnightly).

This is an index to articles on British industries and companies, covering over 100 British business, trade and economics journals as well as several newspapers. Each issue is in 2 parts: an index to articles by subject; an index to articles on companies, arranged alphabetically. This is rather similar in type of entry to the U.S. *F & S Index of Corporations and Industries,* but unfortunately it does not include periodic cumulations.

Social Sciences Index (SSI). New York, H. W. Wilson (quarterly, with annual cumulations).

A subject and author index to articles in over 260 journals that cover the fields of anthropology, area studies, economics, environmental science, geography, law and criminology, medical sciences, political science, psychology, public administration, sociology and related subjects. At the back of each issue is an author listing of book reviews that appear in the indexed journals.

Three more specialized indexes are:

Conference Board. *Cumulative Index.* New York (annual).

A useful subject index to the wide range of studies, pamphlets and articles that this business research firm has published in the areas of business economics, corporate administration, finance, marketing, personnel, international operations and public affairs. Covers material published during the past 20 years, with special emphasis on the most recent 10 years.

Current Contents: Social & Behavioral Sciences. Philadelphia, Pa., Institute for Scientific Information (weekly).

A pocket-sized weekly that reproduces the tables of contents for almost 1,000 periodicals in the social and behavioral sciences. Includes business and finance, communications, computer applications, environmental sciences, industrial relations and labor, international relations, management science, psychology, social issues, statistics, transportation, urban studies, as well as other areas of less interest, such as anthropology, criminology. A subject (key-word) index is in each issue as are an author index and address directory for persons who want to request reprints of articles. Full text for articles not easily accessible in one's library can be obtained by using ISI's "Original Article Tear Sheet" (OATS) service.

Management Contents. Skokie, Ill., G. D. Searle & Co. (biweekly).

This new service, begun in Fall 1975, reproduces the tables of contents for a selection of about 150 of the best business/management journals. It may prove to be more popular with the busy executive than the more comprehensive weekly noted above, since it takes so little time to scan each issue for significant articles. Subscribers can request reprints of any article for an additional fee.

Social Sciences Citation Index. Philadelphia, Pa., Institute for Scientific Information (3/yr., with last issue an annual cumulation in 10 volumes).

This new (1972) international citation index is based on the concept that an author's references to previously published material indicate subject relationships, and so it provides a good means of locating information on specific topics. It covers all articles in over 1,000 social sciences journals and selected articles relevant to the social sciences that have appeared in 2,200 journals in other areas. There are 3 parts: (1) "Source Index," which indexes all articles by author and gives bibliographic details; (2) "Citation Index," listing under each author the names of other authors who have cited each book or article (the citation could be in an abstract, book review, editorial, letter, or in a book, article, technical paper, etc.); (3) "Permuterm Subject Index," an alphabetical index of the important words in each article title. ISI publications are all computer-produced, making it possible for them to offer various individualized alerting services in any area of interest.

Newspaper Indexes

New York Times Index. New York (semi-monthly, with annual cumulations).

This is an excellent and very detailed index, arranged alphabetically and including many helpful cross-references. Indexing is based on the Late City Edition.

A new development in indexing is the computerized *New York Times Information Bank,* which provides full text coverage of almost all news and editorial matter from the Late City Edition, the Sunday feature sections and daily and Sunday regional material not distributed within New York City. Indexing extends back to January 1969. In addition, this new data bank includes a selection of material from over 60 periodicals and other newspapers including the *American Banker, Barron's, Business Week, Economist, Financial Times* of London, *Fortune, Journal of Commerce, Los Angeles Times, Washington Post*. The kind of material selected usually includes significant news items, biographical material, business and financial news, editorials, surveys of general interest. This data base is likely to expand in the future and bears watching as a potential comprehensive business storage and retrieval system.

Wall Street Journal Index. New York, Dow Jones and Co. (monthly, with annual cumulations).

Each issue is in 2 parts: corporate news and general news. Indexing is based on the Final Eastern Edition. Includes list of book reviews.

GOVERNMENT PUBLICATIONS

The publications of various governments are excellent sources for authoritative studies and official information on all sorts of subjects. The many departments, bureaus, ministries, agencies, and committees publish a wide variety of reports, statistical publications, bibliographies, periodicals, etc., and much of this is of vital importance to the businessman. The U.S. government probably stands at the top in total volume of publications. Since its various departments and bureaus shift their responsibilities frequently, it is especially important to have well-indexed, easily understood manuals, bibliographies and catalogs of publications. This section describes a few of the most important lists and catalogs as well as two indexes covering current legislation and congressional news. Examples of the catalogs of other governments are also listed. Bibliographies and catalogs that describe the many U.S. government statistical publications are described in Chapter 4; directories of U.S. government agencies and of Congressmen are in Chapter 3.

Andriot, John L., ed. *Guide to U.S. Government Publications.* McLean, Va., Documents Index, 1973 to date. 3 volumes (Vols. 1 and 2 are loose-leaf, with periodic supplements).

An annotated guide to publications of the various U.S. government agencies. Vol. 1 contains a list of those publications in existence as of January 1973; Vol. 2 covers publications of abolished agencies and discontinued publications; Vol. 3 explains and outlines the Superintendent of Documents classification scheme (by which Vols. 1 and 2 are arranged), and it also contains an agency and title index.

U.S. Department of Commerce. *Business Service Checklist.* Washington, D.C., U.S. Government Printing Office (weekly).

A 4-page weekly checklist of Department of Commerce publications, arranged by specific bureau or office. Includes a table of "key business indicators."

U.S. Superintendent of Documents. *Monthly Catalog of United States Government Publications.* Washington, D.C., U.S. Government Printing Office.

A continuing list of federal government publications, some of which are free. It is arranged alphabetically by agency, with an index in each issue and a cumulated index in the December issue each year. The February issue includes a "Directory of United States Government Periodicals and Subscription Publications" (a similar list appears as GPO's *Price List* 36). There is a newly published *Cumulative Subject Index to the Monthly Catalog of United States Government Publications, 1900–1971* (Washington,

D.C., Carrollton Press, 15 volumes) that is useful for making retrospective subject searches.

U.S. Superintendent of Documents. *Price Lists.* Washington, D.C., U.S. Government Printing Office.

This is a series of sales catalogs in specialized subject areas, e.g., No. 28, Finance; No. 33, Labor; No. 37, Tariff and Taxation; No. 59, Interstate Commerce; No. 62, Commerce; No. 70, Census.

Foreign Government Publications

The governments of other countries also publish detailed catalogs. Those for Canada and Great Britain are especially noteworthy for locating their many excellent statistical publications.

Canadian Government Publications: Catalogue. Ottawa, Information Canada (monthly, with annual cumulations).

A bilingual (French and English) catalog of Parliamentary publications and all department publications, with a section at the end for important international publications. Each issue contains an index.

Great Britain. *Government Publications.* London, H. M. Stationery Office (monthly, with annual cumulations).

Each issue of the catalog of British government publications is in 3 parts: Parliamentary publications; publications arranged by name of government department; periodicals. An index is in each issue.

Congressional Legislation and News

Commerce Clearing House. *Congressional Index.* Chicago. 2 loose-leaf volumes for each 2-session Congress.

This loose-leaf service provides quick access to the status of all legislation pending in Congress by listing and indexing all public bills and resolutions and reporting their progress from introduction to final disposition.

Congressional Quarterly. *Washington, D.C. (weekly).*

An excellent weekly service for up-to-date news on all activities of Congress, the Federal government and politics. Each issue includes the status of legislation and Congressional voting charts. There is a quarterly cumulated index; also an annual CQ *Almanac,* which is a compendium of legislation for one session of Congress. A record of the government for one presidential term is published every 4 years as *Congress and the Nation.*

United States Code Congressional and Administrative News. St. Paul, Minn., West Publishing Co. (monthly with annual cumulations).

Text of all Public Laws enacted by Congress, arranged by Public Law number, with a subject index that cumulates in each monthly issue. Includes also Legislative History, Proclamations, Executive Orders, popular names of acts.

COMPUTERIZED INFORMATION SERVICES

Recent rapid advances in computer technology have resulted in the development of much more efficient and faster methods of storing and retrieving information, and this is revolutionizing the whole information business. There are in operation today computer-based search services using well-established machine-readable files and data bases to provide: (1) indexing and abstracting of articles, books, etc., on a much greater scale than was ever previously possible and so flexible that they can meet almost any individual request in a matter of minutes; (2) access to in-depth statistics that also can be easily adapted to meet widely varying specifications; and (3) mailing lists and other directories of companies variously arranged according to such factors as geographic location, type of business, and size of company. These computer services are offered by commercial search firms, by regional information centers, and also by a growing number of large university libraries where computer terminals have been leased and computer-based search services are offered for a number of different data bases. (The term "data base" is used by computer people to refer to any organized collection of information or data in a particular subject area or bearing some relationship one to another.)

Machine searches are still very expensive and are used as of spring 1975 more by companies and researchers than by individuals. However, there is a growing group of individuals who are turning to the computer for bibliographic searches while still using traditional search procedures for most of their relatively simple statistical needs. In the near future, as computer services are used with more frequency, these high costs are likely to be substantially reduced. In the meanwhile, there is no doubt that most users of computer search services find them well worth the cost in terms of staff time saved and in making possible high-speed access to the massive data now on tapes. These developments warrant continual monitoring in the coming years by business and economic researchers and by information specialists because of their important implications for both the availability and adaptability of data at one's command.

Bibliographical Data Bases

There are two principal companies that provide on-line interactive search access to various bibliographic data bases: Lockheed Aircraft Corporation's Lockheed Information Service (Palo Alto, California) and System Development Corporation's On-Line Bibliographic Search Service (Santa Monica, California). Both firms offer the following data bases in the social sciences: CAIN, for agriculture and related areas; ERIC covering the field of education; and INFORM (see below). Lockheed also offers the *Predicasts Terminal System* (see below) and bibliographical data bases for *Psychological Abstracts, Social Sciences Citation Index,* and *Sociological Abstracts.*

Of special interest to business are the following two data bases:

INFORM. Louisville, Ky., Abstracted Business Information, Inc. (ABI).
This is an individualized management SDI (selective dissemination of information) service based on a data bank of selected major articles that appear in about 240 periodicals specializing in management, finance, statistics, marketing, personnel, etc. A subscriber receives weekly abstracts of selected articles in those specialized subject areas he has indicated an interest in. (He can also request a complete copy of any article.) Not only can this file be used as a continuing current awareness service, but it is also possible to have direct access to the whole data base through several on-line searching services that are available in libraries and organizations that have com-

puter terminals. As of early 1975 this data base only selectively indexes major articles in these 240 periodicals, but it will probably expand in the near future to offer more complete coverage.

Predicasts Terminal System. Cleveland, Ohio, Predicasts, Inc.

This is a very useful, comprehensive file that is a combination bibliographical and statistical data base, and which provides access to Predicasts publications that are both indexes and sources for market data, statistics and forecasts. It covers: *Chemical Market Abstracts; Equipment Market Abstracts; F & S Index to Corporations and Industries; F & S International;* the quarterly forecasting service, *Predicasts;* the Predicasts' *Basebook* and their *Source Directory;* and *Worldcasts,* the quarterly for international statistics and forecasts. Persons familiar with these publications (all described elsewhere in this book) will appreciate the possibility of having instant access to this data when they need to cover many business journals and other special reports in searching for current articles and statistics on an industry, a geographic location or a company.

One other bibliographical data base of possible interest is the *New York Times Information Bank,* which is described earlier in this chapter.

Statistical Data Bases

Widely used by professionals and researchers for in-depth and complex searches, statistical data bases are usually one of three basic types: (1) economic time series (such as Bureau of the Census tapes, National Bureau of Economic Research data bank for economic and cyclical indicators, Bureau of Labor Statistics data bank for labor and price statistics); (2) marketing data (*Sales and Marketing Management's* "Survey of Buying Power" estimates, for example); or (3) financial data (such as the Investors Management Sciences' *Compustat* magnetic tapes).

Lists of Companies

The computer has made it possible to provide directories of companies and mailing-list labels that can take into account a number of marketing or financial factors. One of the most extensive data files for compiling such lists is that of the Marketing Services Division of Dun & Bradstreet. These files include their *Dun's Market Indentifiers* service, which covers all U.S. and Canadian companies in their *Reference Book* and which can retrieve up-to-date information instantly in any sequence desired, such as lists by location, branch plant, number of employees, sales size, industry, telephone area code, year business was started, and (for subscribers of its Credit Service) credit rating.

Directories of Computer Information Services

There are many other sources for computerized information systems and services, which can be identified by using one of several published directories.

Directory of Computerized Data Files & Related Software Available from Government Agencies. Washington, D.C., National Technical Information Service, U.S. Department of Commerce, 1974.

This guide to over 500 machine-readable data files available from 60 federal agencies is arranged by subject field and includes descriptive notes about each.

Encyclopedia of Information Systems and Services. 2d International ed. Ed. by Anthony T. Kruzas. Ann Arbor, Mich., A. T. Kruzas Associates, 1974.

"An international guide to information storage and retrieval systems, computerized data bases, SDI services, data base publishers, clearinghouses and information centers, library and information networks, data collection and analysis centers, micrographic systems and services; and consulting, research and coordinating agencies." This is a comprehensive directory covering about 1,750 organizations, including 225 in countries other than the United States. The listing is arranged alphabetically by the organization or service, and the one page of data for each includes description of the system or service, input or data sources, holdings or storage media, publications, microform or computer applications and services, computer and information processing equipment, use restriction. There are 13 indexes at end, by type of service, by location, etc.

International Directory of Computer and Information System Services. 3d ed. Published for the Intergovernmental Bureau of Informatics, Rome. London, Europa Publications, 1974.

Describes the computer services for almost 3,000 institutions in about 100 countries. It is arranged by country and is subdivided into national centers, educational and training institutions, government agencies, research institutions, consultants and service bureaus. Information for each includes type of computer installations, language and equipment; details of services, restrictions on use, fields of application, etc. There are 2 indexes: by institutions and by computer installations.

Sessions, Vivian S., ed. *Directory of Data Bases in the Social and Behavioral Sciences.* New York, Science Associates/International, 1974.

An international directory of nonbibliographic data bases in the social sciences, arranged by name of sponsoring organization (including governments, universities, associations). Information for each includes data sources, storage media, hardware, software, output media, documentation, publications, access. Includes subject, institution, personnel and geographic indexes.

U.S. Bureau of the Census. *Catalog.* Washington, D.C., U.S. Government Printing Office.

The quarterly and annual cumulations of this catalog contain a section at the end describing Census "Data Files and Special Tabulations." These files include materials not available in printed form but rather stored on computer tapes or punch cards, thus making it possible for the bureau to prepare special tabulations to meet an individual customer's need.

HANDBOOKS

Business handbooks are often excellent first places to check for a good, short introduction on the concepts, procedures, and techniques of specific management functions, such as accounting, finance, industrial management, marketing, personnel, public relations and purchasing. These useful compendiums are comprehensive yet concise; most chapters are written by experts; many include valuable supplementary reference data, such as glossaries, bibliographies, directories, statistics and legal forms. In addition, they are well organized and well indexed for easy access to the precise facts or explanations needed, since they are meant more as handy reference volumes than as books to be read from cover to cover. Ronald Press handbooks are especially noteworthy for their distillations of the best that has been written on any subject, with frequent quotations from the works of authorities scattered throughout.

Individual handbooks are described in Chapters 9 through 20 with the basic books in each subject area. They may also be located by consulting the index.

LOOSE-LEAF SERVICES

The increased complexities and frequent changes in federal and state laws regulating business make it imperative for the businessman to have an efficient, up-to-date method for keeping informed about all legal matters that affect his day-to-day operations and decisions. Topical law reports provide such a service by bringing together all of the laws, regulations, rules, orders and decisions (along with explanations and interpretations) on a specific topic, arranged in loose-leaf volumes that are constantly revised and thoroughly indexed for quick and easy access. Their weekly or biweekly supplementary packets of newly revised, prepunched pages include instructions for removing all pages that have become obsolete.

The two principal business law and tax service publishers are Commerce Clearing House (Chicago) and Prentice-Hall, Inc. (Englewood Cliffs, N.J.). The Bureau of National Affairs (Washington, D.C.) is another excellent publisher, perhaps best known for its labor information services. Today each of these firms maintains a large and expert staff to prepare these complex and highly specialized services. They are important reference works, widely used and highly regarded by lawyers, accountants, government officials and businessmen, and files of the most important ones can usually be found in large business or law libraries or in libraries specializing in each subject area.

There is a great similarity in the arrangement of CCH and P-H services, and a general explanation may be helpful. First, every service contains an introductory section explaining its scope and giving instructions on how to use it. Second, each service contains several indexes and tables that are detailed and easy to use. There is a topical, or master, index; a current index (for the most recent changes); an index of court cases; and a "Finding List" (for locating the paragraph number that corresponds to the official section number of the statute, regulation or ruling). With tax services there is also a "Citator Table" that lists federal tax decisions and refers to other decisions that have cited them. Supplementary data of value often includes official forms, law review articles, special pamphlets with texts of new bills and statutes, reports or studies undertaken by congressional committees, and brief summaries of current news accompanying the packages of revised pages.

In using any CCH or P-H service it is important to understand that the numbers in the index refer to a paragraph numbering system (at the bottom of each page) rather than to a page number (at the top of each page). This is essential in publications such as these where pages are continually changing but paragraph numbers remain constant.

Descriptions of individual loose-leaf services are scattered throughout this book with other material on each subject. The index lists these under both publisher and title. Brochures containing complete lists of all services are available directly from each publisher. CCH also has a separate pamphlet explaining how to use services, called *Todays Tax and Business — And How to Find It.*

MICROFORMS AND CASSETTES

Micropublishing and microcopying provide a new form for information that has many advantages, probably the greatest being a saving of large blocks of shelf space, which is a perennial problem in most libraries. The two principal types of microforms are microfilm and microfiche.

Microfilms are films of published works that are stored on reels. The material can be read by putting the reel onto a special microfilm reader that projects an enlarged image of the page on a screen in front of the viewer. Hand-operated levers are used to turn from page to page and to sharpen the focus. Those reading machines that are combined reader/printers have the advantage of making it possible to copy any page needed for one's personal file simply by pushing a copy button. Most libraries today have large and growing collections of microfilm — principally for back files of important newspapers, for many lesser-used periodicals, and for such materials as doctoral dissertations purchased from Xerox University Microfilms.

A new form of microcopying used today with increasing frequency is the microfiche. These are 4 × 6 sheets of film containing photographically reduced pages of books, documents, serial publications, and other works. Most of these sheets (or cards) contain around 70 pages each, but there have been successful efforts at much greater photographic reductions, making it feasible to reproduce complete sets of works on just one small sheet. Documents on microfiche are read by placing the card in a special fiche reader and manipulating it by hand until the pages wanted appear on the viewing screen. These machines are easy to operate, and some have combined features of reader and printer.

Many U.S. government reports and studies are now available on microfiche as are back files of periodicals, scholarly collections, and clipping files of such newspapers as the *Wall Street Journal.* A good example of a large body of material now being distributed on microfiche is U.S. corporate disclosure documents, such as annual reports, 10-K reports, and prospectuses (discussed in Chapter 7).

The micropublishing business has grown so dramatically in the past few years that there are now a number of complete catalogs listing the various publications available in these new formats. In the near future, reading certain types of books and serial publications on a screen will be common practice in most libraries, and, eventually, with the aid of portable lap-sized readers, in homes and offices as well.

A somewhat different development in nonbook information sources is the audio cassette tape. These are usually tapes of speeches, articles, or summaries of current information in a particular subject area that can be played on any tape recorder at the listener's convenience. One such service offered commercially is the Continental Illinois Bank and Trust Company's *BankerTape,* monthly 15-minute summaries of current economic forecasts plus an additional 15-minute practical discussion on various current bank management topics. Some companies prepare their own informative or instructional tapes that are routed to interested persons just as books and journals are.

DOCTORAL DISSERTATIONS

Often overlooked sources for finding in-depth, original research are the many unpublished dissertations required for completion of a doctoral degree at all universities. These are easily identifiable, and many are readily accessible as a result of the two publications noted below, both of which are published by a firm that specializes in making available unpublished research and out-of-print books via microfilm and Xerographic copies.

American Doctoral Dissertations. Ann Arbor, Mich., compiled for the Association of Research Libraries by Xerox University Microfilms (annual).
A complete listing of all doctoral dissertations accepted at American and Canadian universities. It is arranged by broad subject classification, and, under each heading, alphabetically by name of university. Includes an author index. Publication is slow, with the latest volume, as of 1975, covering 1971–1972.

Dissertation Abstracts International. Section A: The Humanities and Social Sciences. Ann Arbor, Mich., Xerox University Microfilms (monthly).
These contain informative abstracts of those dissertations submitted to XUM by more than 345 cooperating institutions, so it provides a good cross section but is not a complete listing as is the preceding annual. These abstracts are arranged in the same broad subject categories, but each issue also has a detailed "Keyword Title Index," and there is an annual cumulative index as well. XUM publishes a companion abstracting service as *Section B: The Sciences.* A cumulative subject and author index is *Dissertation Abstracts International, 1938–1969* (29 volumes). *Section C* (quarterly) covering European dissertations will begin publication in spring 1976.
    A complete retrospective index covering ALL dissertations and mentioning which ones are abstracted in DAI is *Comprehensive Dissertation Index, 1861–1972.* This is a subject index in 37 volumes, with Vols. 25–26 covering "Business & Economics." Supplements to this comprehensive index are published annually, with the set for 1973 in 5 volumes. Since this index has been computerized the publisher is now offering a new personalized search service, *Datrix II,* which can search all past and current dissertations on any subject requested.
    In the United Kingdom there is also an annual list of British theses called *Index to Theses Accepted for Higher Degrees by the Universities of Great Britain and Ireland,* published annually in London by the Association of Special Libraries and Information Bureaux (ASLIB) and the Council for National Academic Awards. These theses are available only on interlibrary loan in the United Kingdom through the Lending Division of the British Library at Boston Spa, Wetherby, Yorks, England.

Specialized Dissertations Lists

The broadest lists appearing in journals are those in the January issue each year of the *Journal of Business* of the University of Chicago, called "Doctoral Dissertations Accepted," and arranged in 18 subject categories; and a "List of Doctoral Dissertations in Political Economy" in the December issue of the

American Economic Review, which covers U.S. dissertations in 10 subject categories, two of which are business administration and industrial organization, and public policy. Several other more specialized lists are in:

American Journal of Agricultural Economics (May), "Doctoral Degrees in Agricultural Economics Conferred in [year], by Subject Area."

Doctoral Dissertations on Transportation: A Bibliography. Evanston, Ill., Library of the Transportation Center, Northwestern University (annual).

Financial Review. "Abstracts of Doctoral Dissertations" is included in each issue of this annual, which is published by the Eastern Finance Association.

Industrial Relations Theses and Dissertations. Ottawa, Ontario, Canada Department of Labour (annual). For description see listing in Chapter 19.

Journal of Creative Behavior. Since 1972 occasional issues include "Bibliography of Recent Theses on Creativity and Problem-Solving."

Journal of Economic History (March), "Summaries of Doctoral Dissertations."

Journal of Finance. "Abstracts of Doctoral Dissertations" are in most issues.

Further specialized lists can be located by checking under the subject heading "Dissertations — Bibliography" in any annual volume of *Public Affairs Information Service Bulletin.*

BUSINESS DICTIONARIES

Most dictionaries concentrate on just one area of business, such as accounting, finance, data processing, or marketing. These are described with other reference material in each subject. Of special interest are the several excellent economics dictionaries listed in Chapter 8. There are two good, recent business and management dictionaries:

French, Derek and Heather Saward. *Dictionary of Management.* New York, International Publications Service, 1975.

Contains definitions of nearly 4,000 management and economic terms and techniques chosen for inclusion because of their use by managers and writers about management. It is meant to be equally useful to American and British readers and so distinguishes varying usage in the 2 countries. Includes abbreviations and short descriptions of important associations and organizations.

Johannsen, Hano and G. Terry Page. *International Dictionary of Management: A Practical Guide.* Boston, Houghton Mifflin, 1975.

This is an up-to-date dictionary covering the whole area of business and management. Its 5,000 entries define terms, concepts, initials and acronyms in international usage, and it also gives concise data on institutions such as government and non-government agencies, associations, trade unions, stock exchanges. Includes many useful cross-references.

Also worth mentioning, although it is now too old to be used for more than the older, time-tested terms and concepts, is *University Dictionary of Business and Finance* by Donald T. Clark and Bert A. Gottfried (New York, Apollo

Editions, T. Y. Crowell, 1957). A much shorter but more recent dictionary containing about 3,000 of the most common business terms is *Lexicon of American Business Terms* by James F. Filkins and Donald L. Caruth (New York, Simon and Schuster, 1973).

Dictionaries of Acronyms and Abbreviations

Crowley, Ellen T. and Robert C. Thomas, eds. *Acronyms and Initialisms Dictionary*. 4th ed. Detroit, Mich., Gale Research Co., 1973. And Supplement, 1975.

"A guide to alphabetic designations, contractions, acronyms, initialisms, and similar condensed appellations." This includes initials for groups, agencies, processes, equipment, projects, etc. The 1975 supplement is titled "New Acronyms and Initialisms." A companion volume was *Reverse Acronyms and Initials Dictionary,* 1971.

De Sola, Ralph. *Abbreviations Dictionary*. New International 4th ed. New York, American Elsevier, 1974.

Covers abbreviations, acronyms, anonyms, contractions, initials and nicknames, short forms and slang shortcuts, signs and symbols. Includes supplementary abbreviations of airlines, railroads, chemical element symbols, weather symbols, etc.

3

LOCATING INFORMATION ON COMPANIES, ORGANIZATIONS AND INDIVIDUALS

Basic U.S. Company Directories — Basic International and Foreign Directories — U.S. Regional, State and Local Directories — Directories of Industries — Directories of Trade Names — Directories of Associations — Directories of Consultants — Directories of Foundations — Directories of Government Organizations — Directories of Periodicals — Directories of Research Centers — Biographical Dictionaries — Guides to Directories

Directories are another important time-saving source when one seeks brief data on companies, organizations or individuals. They are used for varied purposes: to find out who manufactures a specific product; to check companies located in a particular area; to verify company names, addresses, and telephone numbers; and to identify company officers or directors.

This chapter describes a selection of basic business directories, those for specific industries or geographic locations and those covering government agencies, organizations, periodicals and individuals. Company directories that include financial information are described in Chapter 7, as are the best known lists of largest companies. Several bibliographies of company histories and biographies of businessmen are mentioned in Chapter 9. Many other specialized directories are scattered throughout this book with other material on each subject, for example, accountants, advertising agencies, banks, brokers, insurance companies, labor unions, market research agencies, public relations firms, real estate companies, and venture capital companies.

It is assumed that all directories give addresses and that most include the company's telephone number, so these facts are not given with each entry in this chapter.

BASIC U.S. COMPANY DIRECTORIES

Dun & Bradstreet. *Million Dollar Directory.* New York (annual, with semi-annual cumulated supplements).

Lists approximately 39,000 U.S. companies with an indicated worth of $1 million or more. For each it gives officers and directors, products or services, SIC (Standard Industrial Classification) number, approximate sales and number of employees. Includes an index by division, a list of companies appearing for the first time, an alphabetical list of officers, and indexes by geographic location and by industry. A companion volume is their *Middle Market Directory* (annual), which lists about 31,000 companies with an indicated worth of from $500,000 to $999,999. Coverage and information are similar except that it contains only the geographic and industry indexes. The data from these and from other D & B directories are available on magnetic tape, punch cards and as mailing labels, which makes a variety of personalized services possible.

Standard & Poor's Register of Corporations, Directors and Executives. New York, Standard & Poor's Corp. 3 volumes (annual, with 3 cumulated supplements).

Vol. 1 is an alphabetical listing of over 36,000 U.S. and Canadian companies, and for each it gives officers, products or line of business, SIC number, sales range and number of employees. Vol. 2 is a list of executives and directors, with brief data about each. Vol. 3 contains the following indexes and lists: index of companies by SIC and by location; list of companies added for the first time; list of officers included for the first time; an obituary section.

Standard Directory of Advertisers. Skokie, Ill., National Register Publishing Co. (annual, with monthly cumulated supplements).

Directory of 17,000 companies that advertise nationally, arranged by industry, with an alphabetical index. Gives officers, products, advertising agency, advertising appropriations (in some cases), media used. Includes a "Trademark Index," and also a "Geographic Index" in a separate volume. This is especially useful for its listing of top sales personnel, which is usually not given in the two big directories above.

The "Marketing Reports" issue of *Advertising Age* (4th or last August issue each year) contains a directory of the 100 top U.S. national advertisers, with the names of marketing personnel and advertising agency account executives, both for parent company and for principal divisions.

Thomas Register of American Manufacturers and Thomas Register Catalog File. New York, Thomas Publishing Co. 11 volumes (annual).

This is a comprehensive listing of American manufacturing firms and is the best place to look after an unsuccessful check in either of the first two directories above. Vols. 1–6 list manufacturers by each specific product; Vol. 7 is the alphabetical list, usually giving the address, branch offices, subsidiaries, products, assets classification, and occasionally, principal officers. Vol. 8 is an "Index" to product classifications and includes a list of leading trade names. Vols. 9–11 are "Catalogs of Companies."

U.S. Industrial Directory. Denver, Colo., Cahners Publishing Co. 4 volumes (annual).

This gives similar information to that in *Thomas* above but is not as comprehensive. Vol. 1 is an alphabetical list of manufacturers giving address, product line, code for employee size; it also contains a list of trade names. Vols. 2–3 have the listing by individual product; Vol. 4, "Industrial Literature Directory," lists catalogs and other brochures. This directory is perhaps better known under its former title, *Conover-Mast Purchasing Directory.*

Probably the most complete geographic list of U.S. and Canadian business firms of all types is the 4-volume, bimonthly *Reference Book* compiled by Dun & Bradstreet for customers of its *Business Information Reports,* a long-time, highly regarded credit rating service. It is not available to libraries, but persons employed by companies or organizations that are subscribers will find in the *Reference Book* a very detailed listing of firms, by state and then by city, and giving for each the SIC number, an abbreviation for line of business, a code for estimated financial strength and for composite credit appraisal. The list for Canada is in the back of Vol. 4. There is no index.

Other Lists of Companies

American Register of Exporters and Importers. New York (annual).

A comprehensive list of exporters and importers, arranged by product, and usually giving only the address and products handled.

Directory of American Firms Operating in Foreign Countries. 8th ed. Ed. by Juvenal L. Angel. New York, Simon & Schuster, 1975.

This is a very useful directory of over 3,500 companies, in 2 parts: Section 1 is an alphabetical list, giving name of officer in charge of foreign operation and countries of operation; Section 2 lists the companies by geographic location. A companion volume is the *Directory of Foreign Firms Operating in the United States* (2d ed., 1975), in 3 parts: a list by country; an alphabetical list of foreign parent companies with the name of the corresponding American subsidiary; an alphabetical list of American subsidiaries, branches and affiliates.

The U.S. Bureau of International Commerce published a list of *Foreign Direct Investors in the United States* (1973, with annual supplements), which is arranged by country, but lacks a company index.

Directory of Corporate Affiliations. Skokie, Ill., National Register Publishing Co. (annual, with bimonthly supplements).

A "who own whom" volume, listing about 3,000 American parent companies, with their divisions, subsidiaries and affiliates. A complete index is at end. The supplements are called *Corporate Action.*

Dun & Bradstreet. *Metalworking Directory.* National ed. New York (annual).

This is a comprehensive and expensive directory of U.S. metalworking and metal-producing plants and distributors in 4 sections: Section 1 is a geographic list of plants giving for each the names of end products, the SIC, number of employees, principal processes performed, key plant personnel in charge of production, engineering and purchasing. For distributors this includes metals distributed, square feet of warehouse space. Sections 2 and 3 are product and company indexes. Section 4 is a "statistical summary" consisting of total plants and total employees for each SIC by county, as well as statistics for 3 employee size categories. This directory is also available in 5 regional editions that contain only Sections 1 and 4 above. All of this data can be purchased on magnetic tape, punch cards and as mailing labels.

Marketing Economics Institute. *Marketing Economics: Key Plants.* New York, 1973.

A directory of 40,000 plants with 100 or more employees, in 2 parts. Part 1 is a geographic listing by state and county, and within each county the plants are arranged by SIC number. Part 2 lists the companies by SIC and, within each industry, by state and county.

Who Owns Whom: North American Edition. London, O. W. Roskill (annual).

A directory of U.S. and Canadian parent companies with their subsidiaries and associate companies outside the United States (or Canada). Includes an index for subsidiaries and associates.

A similar directory for American companies is *Directory of Inter-Corporate Ownership,* compiled by Juvenal Angel for the World Trade Academy Press (New York, Simon and Schuster, 1974, 2 volumes).

Several good lists of the largest companies ranked either by sales or by assets are described in Chapter 7.

BASIC INTERNATIONAL AND FOREIGN DIRECTORIES

Bottin International: International Business Register. Paris, Société Didot-Bottin (annual).

The main part of this comprehensive international directory is a listing of manufacturers, distributors, importers and exporters arranged by product or service and under each, by country. The second part gives brief data on "countries of the world," and for important cities it includes a selective list of banks, hotels, importers, exporters, customs agents, consulates, chambers of commerce, etc.

Dun & Bradstreet. *Principal International Businesses.* New York (annual).

Section 1 lists over 44,000 companies, arranged alphabetically by country, and for each it gives chief officer, line of business, SIC number, approximate sales and number of employees. Sections 2 and 3 are indexes by SIC number and by company.

Kelly's Manufacturers and Merchants Directory. Kingston Upon Thames, Surrey, England. 2 volumes (annual).

This is probably the most used world directory of merchants and manufacturers. Vol. 1 provides comprehensive coverage for the United Kingdom and for Ireland, with an alphabetical list for U.K. companies, a list classified by trades and by exporters and importers. There are separate alphabetical and classified lists for companies in both London and Ireland. Vol. 2 is a listing by major product and then by country, for companies in all other countries of the world. There is also a "Trades & Services Index."

Who Owns Whom: Continental Edition. London, O. W. Roskill. 2 volumes (annual).

These 2 volumes are arranged by country and list parent companies, with the associates and subsidiaries for each.

Dun & Bradstreet publishes several regional directories in connection with their international credit rating service. These are *International Market Guide*

— *Continental Europe* (annual, with two intervening supplements) *and International Market Guide* — *Latin America* (semi-annual). Each lists the firms by geographic location and gives for each a trade classification code as well as financial strength and a composite credit appraisal.

British Directories

See also *Kelly's* directory above.

Dun & Bradstreet, Ltd. *Guide to Key British Enterprises.* London. 2 volumes (annual).

Vol. 1 is a guide to over 11,000 large public and private companies in the United Kingdom, giving for each the nature of business, names of subsidiaries and affiliate companies, number of employees, capital or sales turnover range, names of officers, trade names. Includes an index of companies by SIC number, a list of products and services, and a list of subsidiaries of parent companies. Vol. 2 is a companion volume listing companies with sales of from ±100,000 to ±750,000; its former title was *British Middle Market Directory.* Dun & Bradstreet (Australia) Pty., Ltd., publishes *The Australian Key Business Directory,* a list of 10,000 businesses; Dun & Bradstreet of Ireland, Ltd., publishes a *Guide to Irish Manufacturers,* a biennial list of 4,000 companies.

Who Owns Whom: U.K. Edition. London, O. W. Roskill. 2 volumes (annual).

Vol. 1 is a list of companies showing subsidiaries for each, as well as a list of Irish companies; Vol. 2 is the index of subsidiaries and associate companies.

Canadian Directories

See also *Who Owns Whom: North American Edition* and *Standard & Poor's Register* in the first section of this chapter.

Canadian Trade Index. Toronto, Canadian Manufacturers' Association (annual).

An alphabetical directory of over 13,000 Canadian manufacturing companies, giving products, officers, subsidiaries, brand name, number of employees. There is a geographic index, a list of products and a list of trade names and brands.

Dun and Bradstreet of Canada, Ltd. *Canadian Key Business Directory.* Toronto (annual).

The alphabetical section gives for each company its products or services, chief officer, SIC number, sales range, number of employees, subsidiaries. There are geographic and industry indexes.

Fraser's Canadian Trade Directory. Toronto (annual).

The largest part of this directory is a list of over 22,000 companies arranged by product. There is also an alphabetical list, a list of trade names and a list of foreign firms with agents or distributors in Canada.

National List of Advertisers. Toronto, Maclean-Hunter (annual).

Section 1 contains the top national advertisers in Canadian media, showing personnel (including sales, advertising and account executives), products, advertising agency, approximate budget appropriation and media used. This is followed by a brand name index, a list of Canadian advertising agencies with accounts handled and a direct mail directory.

Directories of Other Foreign Countries

There are directories published for almost every country. See the "Guides to Directories" at the end of this chapter for bibliographies of directories. Several examples are:

Japan Directory. Tokyo, Japan Press. 3 volumes (annual).

Kompass Register of Selected German Industry and Commerce. 3d ed. Freiberg i Breisgau, Kompass Deutschland Verlag, 1974. 3 volumes.

Who Owns Whom: Australasia and Far East. London, O. W. Roskill (annual).

U.S. REGIONAL, STATE AND LOCAL DIRECTORIES

There are directories of manufacturing companies published for every state. Most of them are arranged by geographic location (giving top officers, SIC number, products, number of employees), and they usually have both alphabetical and product indexes. A complete list of these is included in several of the "Guides to Directories" at the end of this chapter. A few examples are:

California Manufacturers Register. Sponsored by the California Manufacturers Association. Los Angeles, Times Mirror Press (annual).

Classified Directory of Wisconsin Manufacturers. Milwaukee, Wisconsin Manufacturers Association (annual).

Directory of New England Manufacturers. Boston, G. D. Hall (annual).

Missouri Directory of Manufacturing and Mining. Jefferson City, Missouri Division of Commerce and Industrial Development (annual).

Pennsylvania State Industrial Directory. New York, State Industrial Directories (annual).

Directories for Local Areas

(1) Chamber of Commerce Publications

The chambers of commerce in a number of cities publish annual lists of the industrial firms in their metropolitan areas. Two examples are: *Metropolitan Chicago Major Employees* (Chicago Association of Commerce and Industry); and *St. Louis Commerce,* "Roster Issue" (published as the April issue each year by the St. Louis Regional Commerce & Growth Association).

(2) City Directories

City directories are useful for checking names, addresses and telephone numbers of residents and business firms. The *Boston (Suffolk County, Massachusetts) City Directory* (Boston, R. L. Polk & Co., annual) is a typical city directory in 4 parts: a classified list of all business and professional firms, associations, etc.; an alphabetical list of the names of residents (with occupation and name of wife) and names of businesses (giving nature of business and chief officers); a directory of householders and businesses arranged by street or avenue; and a numerical telephone directory.

(3) Telephone Directories

The classified sections of telephone directories are useful for identifying local firms in any industry, and the author sections for checking correct name, address or telephone number. Most public libraries have a selection of telephone books for the region; many large libraries have a good collection covering all important U.S., and some foreign, cities.

DIRECTORIES OF INDUSTRIES

Directories for many specific industries are published by either a trade association or a commercial publisher. These usually include names of officers and products; some also give data such as subsidiaries, capacity, or trade names. For a complete list arranged by industry, consult the "Guides to Directories" at the end of this chapter. Several examples of trade directories for U.S. and Canadian companies are:

American Iron and Steel Institute. *Directory of Iron and Steel Works of the United States and Canada.* Washington, D.C. (annual).
Gives officers, subsidiaries, assets, and for specific plants it also gives number of furnaces, capacity, equipment, etc.

Lockwood's Directory of the Paper and Allied Trades. New York, Vance Publishing Corp. (annual).
A directory of U.S. and Canadian pulp, paper and allied companies, arranged geographically. It includes officers, products, subsidiaries, plants. There is an alphabetical list of mill officials and a list of trademarks, trade names and trade associations.

Thomas Grocery Register. New York, Thomas Publishing Co. (annual).
This covers not only supermarket chains, wholesale grocers, exporters, importers, brokers, canners, frozen food processors, but it also lists manufacturers and packers by line of business. It includes officers, buyers, a code for capital ratings and an index of brand names at front.

Some trade journals publish annual "Buyers' Guide" issues, usually just giving names and addresses of companies. Two examples are:

Chemical Week. "Buyers' Guide Issue," Part 2 of October issue.
Electronics. "Buyers' Guide." A separate issue published in January each year.

DIRECTORIES OF TRADE NAMES

Trade names and brand names are given in a number of the directories above, with an especially long list in *Thomas Register of American Manufacturers.* There is also a separate guide to consumer product trade names:

Crowley, Ellen T., ed. *Trade Names Dictionary.* Detroit, Mich., Gale Research Co., 1975. 2 volumes.
A guide to over 100,000 consumer product trade names, brand names, and product names, with addresses of their manufacturers, importers, marketers and distributors. A list of sources is at front.

DIRECTORIES OF ASSOCIATIONS

Since trade associations are such valuable sources for statistics and other information about industries it is especially important to have access to a good, up-to-date directory.

Encyclopedia of Associations. Detroit, Mich., Gale Research Co. 3 volumes (biennial).

Vol. 1 is a comprehensive list of all types of national associations arranged in the following broad categories: trade, business and commercial; agricultural and commodity; governmental; public administration; scientific; educational; religious; athletic; labor unions; chambers of commerce; Greek letter societies. There is an alphabetical and a key-word index. For each association this directory provides name of chief officer, brief statement of activities, number of members, names of publications, etc. Vol. 2 is a "Geographic and Executive Index" to Vol. 1; Vol. 3 is a quarterly listing of "New Associations and Projects."

National Trade and Professional Associations of the United States and Canada and Labor Unions. Washington, D.C., Columbia Books, Inc. (annual).

An alphabetical list of more than 4,700 national trade and professional associations; also labor unions with national memberships. For each it gives chief officer, approximate number of members, annual budget, names of publications, date of annual meeting. Four indexes are at end: key word, geographic, executive, and budget size.

Yearbook of International Organizations. Brussels, Union of International Associations.

A computer-produced directory available either in an English or a French edition, covering politics, religion, professions, trade unions, economics, science, education, arts, finance, health, commerce, industry. For each international organization this gives year founded, aim, structure, finance, activities, congresses, publications, countries in which there are members.

World Guide to Trade Associations. 1st ed. New York, R. R. Bowker, 1973. 2 volumes.

A list of national and international trade associations and professional associations, chambers of commerce, etc., arranged by country. Vol. 1 covers Europe; Vol. 2 is for Africa, America, Asia, Oceania. It also contains a key-word index and a classified list.

Directory of European Associations. Part 1, National Industrial, Trade & Professional Associations. Beckenham, Kent, England, CBD Research Ltd., 1971. (Now distributed in the U.S. by Gale Research Co., Detroit, Mich.). New edition scheduled for publication in 1976.

This directory is arranged by industry, with indexes in English, French and German. For each association it gives sphere of interest, number of members, publications, etc. Part 2 covers *National Learned, Scientific and Technical Societies* (1975). A companion volume is *Directory of British Associations & Associations in Ireland* (4th ed., 1974). It includes trade unions and chambers of commerce and is arranged alphabetically with a subject index.

Directory of Associations in Canada. Toronto, University of Toronto Press, 1974.

An alphabetical list giving address and chief officer, with a subject index.

DIRECTORIES OF CONSULTANTS

Association of Consulting Management Engineers. *Directory of Membership and Services.* New York (annual).

This is a directory of the largest, best known consulting firms, with a one-page description of the services of each.

Consultants and Consulting Organizations Directory. Detroit, Mich., Gale Research Co. (triennial, with semi-annual supplements).

Lists over 5,000 consulting firms, giving top officers and type of service offered. Includes subject index of firms, arranged by state, and an alphabetical index of individuals. The supplements are called *New Consultants.*

Who's Who in Consulting: A Reference Guide to Professional Personnel Engaged in Consultation for Business, Industry and Government. 2d ed. Detroit, Mich., Gale Research Co., 1973.

Factual data on over 7,500 individuals doing consulting work, with a subject index by location, using the same subjects as the preceding directory.

DIRECTORIES OF FOUNDATIONS

Foundation Directory. 5th ed. New York, Foundation Center, 1975.

A directory of U.S. foundations arranged by state and including the following data for each: date of incorporation, donors, purpose and activities, financial statistics (total assets, gifts, expenditures, grants), officers, directors and trustees. There are indexes by field of interest, by location, by donor, and one by name of foundation. The Foundation Center also offers complete sets of foundation annual reports on microfiche.

DIRECTORIES OF GOVERNMENT ORGANIZATIONS

Book of the States. Lexington, Ky., Council of State Governments (biennial).

Authoritative source for information on the structure, working methods, financing and functional activities of state governments. Includes data on major state services such as education, law enforcement, health and welfare; also names of top officials. One supplement lists elective officials and legislators, and a second supplement contains names of administrative officials classified by function.

U.S. Congress. *Official Congressional Directory.* Washington, D.C., U.S. Government Printing Office (annual).

An annual containing biographical data on each member of Congress, the composition of each Congressional committee, Capitol staff, top officers and staff of all federal departments and agencies, foreign and U.S. diplomats, press galleries.

United States Government Manual. Washington, D.C., U.S. Office of the Federal Register, General Services Administration (annual). Purchase from U.S. Government Printing Office.

This is the indispensable official handbook of the federal government that describes the purposes and programs of most government agencies and lists top personnel for each. "Appendix A" lists defunct or transferred agencies.

DIRECTORIES OF PERIODICALS

Ayer Directory of Publications. Philadelphia, Pa., Ayer Press (annual).

This geographic list of newspapers, magazines and trade publications has been in existence for over 100 years, and it covers not only the United States but Puerto Rico, Virgin Islands, Canada, Bahamas, Bermuda, Republic of Panama and the Philippines. For each publication it gives editor, year founded, frequency, circulation, subscription and advertising rates. There are maps for each state and brief descriptions of each state and city. Several classified indexes are at back, including a list of "Trade, Technical and Class Publications"; there is also a general alphabetical index.

Standard Periodical Directory. New York, Oxbridge Publishing Co. (annual).

A subject listing of over 62,000 U.S. and Canadian periodicals, giving data similar to the directory above. An alphabetical index is at end.

Standard Rate & Data Service: Business Publication Rates and Data. Skokie, Ill. (monthly).

Lists U.S. trade journals by industry groupings, with an alphabetical index. Includes subscription rate, analysis of circulation, as well as advertising rates and specifications. SRDS publishes companion monthlies for *Consumer Magazine and Farm Publication Rates & Data* and *Newspaper Rates & Data;* a semi-annual for *Weekly Newspaper Rates & Data;* an annual for *Newspaper Circulation Analysis.* There are also several international editions that list periodicals and newspapers in one volume along with other types of media. These are: *British Rates & Data* (monthly); *Canadian Advertising Rates & Data.* (monthly); and foreign language editions for France, Italy, Mexico and West Germany.

Ulrich's International Periodicals Directory. New York, R. R. Bowker (biennial).

A list, by subject, of about 55,000 in-print periodicals, both domestic and foreign. It gives the usual data such as frequency, subscription rate, circulation, and is especially useful for noting which journals include book reviews, statistics, which have indexes or are indexed in a regular indexing service. One section contains quite a complete list of "Abstracting and Indexing Services." There is a title and subject index at end. A companion volume is their *Irregular Serials and Annuals: An International Directory,* which covers proceedings, transactions, annual reviews, handbooks, monographic series.

Willings Press Guide. Croyden, England, T. Skinner Directories; New York, IPC (America), Inc. (annual).

An alphabetical list of periodicals and newspapers published in the United Kingdom of Great Britain, Northern Ireland and the Irish Republic; as well as the principal European publications, arranged by country. There is a classified index at end; also a geographic index of U.K. newspapers and a list of news agencies.

Several other specialized lists of periodicals are:

Grant, Mary M., and Norma Cote, eds. *Directory of Business and Financial Services.* 7th ed. New York, Special Libraries Association, 1976. (For descriptive note see Chapter 2.)

Devers, Charlotte M., Doris B. Katz and Mary M. Regan. *Guide to Special Issues and Indexes of Periodicals.* 2d ed. New York, Special Libraries Association (forthcoming).

This new edition, scheduled for publication in late 1975 or early 1976, should prove to be as useful as its predecessor for identifying annual issues, annual feature articles and annual statistical issues of consumer, trade and technical periodicals.

Harvard University. Graduate School of Business Administration. Baker Library. *Current Periodical Publications in Baker Library.* Boston (annual).

This is a computer-produced list of all periodicals and serials currently received in Baker Library. For each it gives publisher, frequency, whether it has its own index or is indexed in a commercial indexing service. The list is in 3 parts: by title or author; by subject; by geographic region.

Industrial Marketing. Chicago, Crain Communications, Inc. (monthly).

A continuing feature of this periodical is its "Guide to Special Issues of Business Publications," listing journals by primary market classification. Unfortunately there is no index or annual cumulation.

DIRECTORIES OF RESEARCH CENTERS

A directory of industrial research laboratories is described in Chapter 20.

Research Centers Directory. 5th ed. by Archie M. Palmer. Detroit, Mich., Gale Research Co., 1975. And quarterly supplements.

A directory of over 6,000 research institutes, centers, foundations, laboratories, bureaus, and other nonprofit research facilities in the United States and Canada. It is arranged in 14 broad subject sections, including "Business, Economics and Transportation," "Labor and Industrial Relations." For each this provides data on when the center was established, present fields of research, sources of support, total number of staff, names of directors, publications, seminars, library facilities. The supplements are called *New Research Centers*.

The World of Learning. London, Europa Publications. 2 volumes (annual).

For every country this directory lists academies, learned societies, research institutes, libraries and archives, museums, universities — giving purpose, officers, publications for each organization. A section on international organizations is at the front of Vol. 1.

BIOGRAPHICAL DICTIONARIES

Collections of biographies are called biographical dictionaries. These usually follow a standard format for giving important facts about prominent individuals: when and where born, parents, education, marital status, names of children, career (itemized in chronological order), career related activities, civic activities, political activities, nonprofessional directorships, military record, decorations and awards, political affiliation, religion, lodges, clubs, publications, home and office addresses.

The various directories of directors give much less information about each individual, usually only the current position and other organizations with which each is associated. A troublesome problem in searching for biographical information about businessmen is the fact that only the top and most successful executives can be found in most biographical dictionaries. For the executive in middle management it is often more difficult to find published biographical data; one must check the more specialized directories and consider other possibilities, such as associations and newspapers.

United States

American Men and Women of Science: The Social & Behavioral Sciences. 12th ed. New York, R. R. Bowker, 1973. 2 volumes.

Contains full-length biographical data about leading American social and behavioral scientists. There are 2 companion series: *American Men and Women of Science: Economics* (1974) and *American Men and Women of Science: The Physical and Biological Sciences* (12th ed., 1971, 6 volumes).

Dun& Bradstreet Reference Book of Corporate Managements. New York (annual).

This directory of top executives is arranged by company, and for each executive it gives date of birth, college attended, past and present employment.

Who's Who in America. Chicago, Marquis Who's Who (biennial).

Biographical data on prominent living Americans. A companion series, *Who Was Who in America,* contains biographical sketches of prominent Americans who are now deceased. Marquis also publishes a series of 4 regional "who's whos" for men and women whose achievements are better known in one particular region. These are *Who's Who in the East* (which covers also the eastern part of Canada); *Who's Who in the Midwest*; *Who's Who in the South and Southwest*; *Who's Who in the West.*

Who's Who in Finance and Industry. Chicago, Marquis Who's Who (biennial).

Career sketches of leading businessmen and others noteworthy in the fields of finance and industry. A selected index of principal businesses is at back.

Webster's American Biographies. Springfield, Mass., G. & C. Merriam Co., 1974.

Full-scale biographies of over 3,000 notable living and deceased Americans. A geographic index and an index of careers and professions is at end.

Standard & Poor's Register of Corporations, Directors and Executives includes a section listing officers and directors, with brief data about each. There are also several local directories of directors: *Directory of Directors in the City of New York* (New York, Directory of Directors Co., annual) and *Directory of Directors in the City of Boston and Vicinity* (Boston, Bankers Service Co., annual). Each of these is an alphabetical list of executives, directors and trustees, giving present job of each as well as other directorships, and each contains a list of leading firms, with officers, at end.

For the names of specialized "who's whos" in advertising, banking, consulting, economics, insurance, public relations, railroading, securities, refer to the chapters covering each of these subjects.

International

International Businessmen's Who Who. 2d ed. London, Burke's Peerage Ltd., 1970.

A biographical dictionary that covers international business persons who made notable achievements prior to 1970.

International Who's Who. London, Europa Publications (annual).

This covers almost all countries and contains biographical information about important living persons in every sphere of human activity.

Many foreign countries publish their own biographical dictionaries, and a selection of the most important ones can usually be found in large public or university libraries.

United Kingdom

The Business Who's Who. London, Leviathan House in Association with the Daily Telegraph, 1974.

"A biographical dictionary of chairmen, chief executives and managing directors of over 3,000 key British-registered companies, together with the boards of directors of the top 200 companies." A company index is at end.

Who's Who. London, A. & C. Black; New York, St. Martin's Press (annual).

Biographical data on prominent living British men and women, with a few leaders of other nations also included. A companion series for deceased persons is *Who Was Who.*

Who's Who in British Finance. New York, R. R. Bowker, 1972.

Biographical information about individuals who make or influence the key decisions in the British financial community. Gives primary job, secondary positions, career history, personal details.

There are also directories of directors for the United Kingdom and for Canada: *Directory of Directors* (Croydon, England, T. Skinner Directories, annual), which lists directors of the principal public and private companies in the United Kingdom, giving the names of companies with which each is associated; and the Financial Post's *Directory of Directors* (Toronto, Maclean-Hunter, annual), which is a list of Canadian executives and directors with their positions and directorships, and a second part arranged by company.

GUIDES TO DIRECTORIES

American

Guide to American Directories. 9th ed. Rye, N.Y., B. Klein Publications, 1975.

This is a useful directory of over 5,200 major industrial, professional and mercantile directories. It is arranged by subject and includes a description and the price of each directory. Under the heading "Manufacturers" there is a listing of the industrial directories for each state. An alphabetical index is at end. A companion volume is their *Guide to American Scientific and Technical Directories* (1972). It covers the social sciences, physical sciences and all industrial and technical areas, and to a certain extent it duplicates the guide above. These 2 guides occasionally list the various "Buyer's Guide" issues that are published annually by some trade journals.

Chamber of Commerce of the United States. *Sources of State Information & State Industrial Directories.* Washington, D.C., 1974.

A handy little brochure, arranged by state, that lists state directories of manufacturers and a few other sources for state information.

Public Affairs Information Service Bulletin. New York (weekly, with periodic cumulations).

The cumulated issues of this useful index contain a selection of directories listed under the heading "Directories."

Foreign

Henderson, G. P., comp. and ed. *Current European Directories.* Beckenham, Kent, England, CBD Research Ltd., 1969. (Now distributed in the U.S. by Gale Research Co., Detroit, Mich.). Second ed. scheduled for publication late in 1975.

Section 1 is an annotated guide, arranged by country in Europe, to commercial directories, telephone directories, directories of associations, city directories, as well as general yearbooks, research organizations, biographical dictionaries, gazetteers. Section 2 is an alphabetical list of more specialized industry directories, incorporating references to directories in Section 1.

CBD Research Ltd. has also published 2 other directories; *Current British Directories* edited by Henderson and Ian G. Anderson (7th ed., 1973), which describes about 2,500 directories and lists published for Great Britain, Ireland, the Commonwealth and South Africa; *Current African Directories,* edited by Ian G. Anderson (1972), a guide that covers all countries of Africa. A guide covering Asia and Australasia is scheduled for publication in 1977.

International Bibliography of Directories. 5th rev. ed. New York, R. R. Bowker, 1973.

This is a list of over 6,000 directories, arranged by subject. Over half of the book covers commerce, industry, business and special industry directories. For each directory this usually gives only year started and price. There is a subject and geographic index.

Trade Directories of the World. Queens Village, N.Y., Croner Publications (loose-leaf,) with monthly supplementary pages).

This annotated list of business and trade directories is arranged by continent and then by country. There is an index to "Trades and Professions" and a country index.

The annual volume of *Public Affairs Information Service: Foreign Language Index* contains a selection of directories listed under the heading "Directories."

4

BASIC U.S. STATISTICAL SOURCES

Comprehensive Statistical Compilations — Basic Specialized Sources — Census Statistics — Standard Industrial Classification Scheme — Foreign Trade Statistics — Monthly Government Statistical Periodicals — Statistics on Government Finance — Guides to Statistics

Statistics are such an absolute necessity to business that three chapters in this book are devoted to describing the most important published sources available from such organizations as government agencies, trade associations, universities, corporations, publishers and private organizations. In addition, other statistical publications are scattered throughout this book: banking and monetary statistics in Chapter 14; corporate and investment statistics in Chapter 7; industrial research expenditures in Chapter 20; insurance and real estate statistics in Chapter 15; labor statistics in Chapter 19; marketing statistics in Chapter 18; plant and equipment expenditures in Chapter 14; and U.S. regional trends and statistics in Chapter 8.

This first of the three statistics chapters describes those publications that one will usually turn to first because they are so comprehensive and so basic for locating U.S. business and economic statistics. At the end of the chapter are several bibliographical guides to suggest other useful works. Chapter 5 covers sources that provide data on specific industries, including compilations of operating ratios for industries. Chapter 6 concentrates on the important international and foreign statistics and foreign economic trends, including also indexes and bibliographies. Fundamental to all of this vast statistical data is knowing how to use it. There are many books devoted entirely to the study of the techniques, tools and theories of statistical analysis in decision-making, and a selection of these appears in Chapter 17.

COMPREHENSIVE STATISTICAL COMPILATIONS

The following three publications form the backbone of any statistical reference collection and are often the compilations to use first if one is not familiar with a more specialized source that may contain the data needed.

Handbook of Basic Economic Statistics. Economics Statistics Bureau of Washington, D.C. (annual, with monthly supplements).

Current and historical statistics on industry, commerce, labor and agriculture, with more than 1,800 statistical series included.

Standard & Poor's Corp. *Standard & Poor's Trade and Securities: Statistics.* New York (loose-leaf, with monthly supplements).

Current and basic statistics in the following areas: banking and finance; production and labor; price indexes (commodities); income and trade; building and building materials; transportation and communications; electric power and fuels; metals; autos, rubber and tires; textiles, chemicals, paper; agricultural products; security price index record.

U.S. Bureau of the Census. *Statistical Abstract of the United States.* Washington, D.C. U.S. Government Printing Office (annual).

This is probably *the* most important statistical reference work because it serves both as the prime source for U.S. industrial, social, political and economic statistics and as a bibliographical guide. The majority of tables are for the United States as a whole, but there is a short section for regional, state and metropolitan area statistics. Source notes are at the foot of each table; a useful "Guide to Sources of Statistics" lists important statistical publications arranged by subject and includes a descriptive list of recent Census publications. A biennial paperback *Pocket Data Book, USA* contains summary statistics as well as graphs.

Although the figures in the *Statistical Abstract* usually cover just 1 or 2 years, there are 2 historical supplements, now out of print but available for use in most libraries. These are *Historical Statistics of the United States, Colonial Times to 1957,* and *Historical Statistics of the United States, Continuation to 1962 and Revisions.*

BASIC SPECIALIZED SOURCES

Commodity Year Book. New York, Commodity Research Bureau (annual).

A useful statistical compilation covering about 99 commodities and giving production, prices, stocks, exports and imports. A quarterly *Commodity Year Book Statistical Abstract Service* is also available to supplement statistics in the yearbook.

Federal Reserve Bank of St. Louis. *National Economic Trends.* St. Louis (monthly).

Although this perhaps is not as basic a source as most of the other publications in this section, it is still a very useful monthly compilation of charts and statistics to show recent rates of change for important economic indicators. This bank also compiles a companion *Rates of Change in Economic Data for Ten Industrial Countries.*

Predicasts. Cleveland, Ohio, Predicasts, Inc. (quarterly).

This useful quarterly service gives short- and long-range forecast statistics both for basic economic indicators and for individual products (by SIC number). Accompanying each forecast is the date and page reference of the current journal, government report or special study from which the statistics were taken. "Composite Forecasts," at front, present historical data for 500 key series. Statistics from *Predicasts* are also available via their on-line *Predicasts Terminal System* (see Chapter 2). Predicasts publishes a *Basebook,* giving annual data from 1960, for over 16,000 statistical series. A companion abstracting service to *Predicasts,* covering foreign countries and industries and called *Worldcasts,* is described in Chapter 6.

U.S. Board of Governors of the Federal Reserve System. *Industrial Production.* 1971 ed. Washington, D.C., 1972.

The first half of this publication describes and discusses the newly revised production index and makes analytical comparisons of production with related data. The last 249 pages contain retrospective statistical tables for this index. Monthly averages of industrial production (seasonally adjusted) for major industry groups and for industry subtotals are quoted from 1954 to 1972; similar tables with figures that are not seasonally adjusted are also quoted, with the beginning date varying. Current statistics appear in the monthly *Federal Reserve Bulletin* and also in a monthly statistical release on "Industrial Production," which the board publishes.

U.S. Bureau of Economic Analysis, Department of Commerce. *Long Term Economic Growth, 1860–1970.* Washington, D.C., U.S. Government Printing Office, 1973.

Long-term charts and statistics for basic economic indicators. Sections cover: aggregate output, input, and productivity; processes related to economic growth; regional and industry trends (including national income, GNP, etc.); international comparisons, growth rate triangles. Appendix 3, pp. 181–303, contains basic statistics used in the charts and tables. For current charts and statistics analyzing short-term business conditions see the bureau's monthly *Business Conditions Digest.*

U.S. Department of Commerce. *Business Statistics.* Washington, D.C., U.S. Government Printing Office (biennial).

This provides an historical record of the statistical series (about 2,500) that appear currently in the important monthly *Survey of Current Business,* and it is published as a supplement to the *Survey.* Tables give annual averages, beginning with the year 1947, and monthly figures for the most recent years. An appendix contains monthly or quarterly statistics for over 400 series back to 1947 when such data are available. Includes source references and good explanatory notes.

U.S. Department of Commerce. *Survey of Current Business.* "National Income Issue" (annual, July issue).

The monthly *Survey* itself is described with other statistical periodicals. This special issue is important enough to list by itself, since it is the prime source of national income and account statistics. Figures in this annual issue cover: gross national product and national income (including GNP, GNP in constant dollars, GNP by major type of product; national income by type of income, by industry and by sector; gross corporate dollar; gross product by industry); personal income and outlay (including personal consumption expenditures by type of product); government receipts and expenditures (including expenditures by type of function); foreign transactions; saving and investment; income and employment by industry (includes corporate profits both before and after taxes, by industry). These statistics usually cover a 4-year period; the most recent totals are in each monthly issue of the *Survey.*

U.S. Department of Commerce. *U.S. Industrial Outlook.* Washington, D.C., U.S. Government Printing Office (annual).

A very handy volume for information on recent trends and outlook (for about 5 years) in over 200 individual industries. The short narrative with statistics usually contains discussions of changes in supply and demand for each industry, developments in domestic and overseas markets, price changes, employment trends, capital investment.

U.S. Internal Revenue Service. *Statistics of Income: Corporation Income Tax Returns.* Washington, D.C., U.S. Government Printing Office (annual).

Balance sheet and income statement statistics derived from a sample of corporate income tax returns. Includes tables by major industry, by asset size, etc. Historical summaries are at end. This is issued first as a short preliminary report and then as this final. more detailed, report.

The IRS also publishes several other annuals in their *Statistics of Income* series. One covers *Business Income Tax Returns,* giving financial and economic data about proprietorships, partnerships and small business corporations; another covers *Individual Income Tax Returns* and includes statistics by income size, deductions and exemptions, tax rates, data by state and SMSAs (standard metropolitan statistical areas).

U.S. Office of Management and Budget, Executive Office of the President. *Social Indicators.* Washington, D.C., U.S. Government Printing Office, 1973.

Selected statistics and charts on U.S. social conditions and trends, covering health, public safety, education, employment, income, housing, leisure and recreation, population. Sources for statistics are at foot of each table. This is the first volume to be published, and it will probably be continued annually.

U.S. President. *Economic Report of the President. Transmitted to the Congress, February* (each year); *Together with the Annual Report of the Council of Economic Advisers.* Washington, D.C. U.S. Government Printing Office (annual).

The Annual Report of the CEA comprises the major portion of this publication. It discusses economic policy and outlook, economic trends of the year and includes statistical tables relating to income, employment and production.

Various marketing guides provide useful regional estimates for population, households, income, buying power and retail sales. These are described in Chapter 18.

CENSUS STATISTICS

The Bureau of the Census is by far the largest publisher of comprehensive statistical data. Their *Catalog* (monthly, with quarterly and annual cumulations) contains good, descriptive lists of all Census publications. Only the most important series are listed below. The economic censuses (retail, wholesale, selected service industries, construction, manufactures, mineral industries, transportation, outlying areas and enterprise statistics) are all taken every 5 years in the years ending with the numbers 2 and 7; the censuses of population and housing are taken every 10 years in the year ending with zero; the agriculture census is also taken every 5 years in the years ending with the numbers 4 and 9.

The Census Bureau publishes only their most widely used censuses and surveys, but much more information is available, most of it on computer tapes or in punch card files. All of this provides almost limitless possibilities for subject cross-classifications or area tabulations, any of which can be processed (except for confidential records) according to a customer's specifications. For further information and a listing of "Data Files and Special Tabulations" consult Part

II in any cumulated issue of their *Catalog* or contact the Data User Services Bureau, U.S. Bureau of the Census, Washington, D.C. 20233.

Census of Agriculture.

Complete information on farms and farming, in 6 volumes. Vol. 1 has separate reports for each state with statistics by county, giving size of farms, tenure and characteristics of farm operators, farm income and sales, farm production and expenses, etc. The other volumes comprise a general report, agricultural services, irrigation, special reports, drainage of agricultural lands.

Census of Construction Industries (Series CC).

In 2 volumes, this reports statistics by industry and by state, including number of construction establishments, receipts, employment, payrolls, capital expenditures, payments for materials and for renting equipment — all for construction establishments operating as contractors, special trade contractors, land subdividers and developers.

Census of Governments (Series G).

Although not of as much continual interest to business researchers, this is an important source for detailed statistics on government finance. The census is taken every 5 years in years ending with the numbers 2 and 7. The titles of its 8 volumes are listed later in this chapter under "Statistics on Government Finance."

Census of Housing (Series MC).

Very detailed tabulations on the number and characteristics of houses. Includes volumes for metropolitan housing characteristics, and also "Subject Reports" on such topics as mobile homes, cooperative and condominium housing, housing of senior citizens and selected racial groups. The titles of the 7 series volumes are listed in Chapter 15 under "Housing and Real Estate Statistics."

Census of Manufactures (Series MC).

This census is probably used more than any of the others by businessmen, since it reports, in 5 volumes, on 450 manufacturing industries in every state, including for each: number of establishments, value of shipments, cost of materials, capital expenditures, assets, rents, inventories, employment and payrolls. Vol. 2 covers industry statistics arranged by SIC number; Vol. 3, area statistics; Vol. 4, data on locations of manufacturing plants, including tabulations by state and county; Vol. 5, indexes of production for both manufacturing and mining industries. Vol. 1 contains summary figures and special subject reports on such topics as employment and labor costs, expenditures for plant and equipment.

In the years between each census the bureau publishes an *Annual Survey of Manufactures,* which gives statistics for broad industry groups and selected products. In addition, the bureau publishes a continuing series of over 100 monthly, quarterly or annual *Current Industrial Reports.* These contain detailed statistics on about 5,000 manufactured products, generally including from 2 to 8 tables in each report on production, shipments, stocks and inventories, foreign trade.

Census of Mineral Industries (Series MIC).

Statistics on establishments engaged in extracting minerals for 42 4-digit SIC industries, with one volume covering summary and industry statistics, and the other covering area statistics. Data given is similar to that in the *Census of Manufactures.*

Census of Population (Series PC).

Detailed characteristics of the population for states, counties, cities and towns in a series of reports (PC[1]A-D) that give data on number of inhabitants, general population characteristics (age, sex, race, etc.), general social and economic characteristics. Separate "Subject Reports," Series PC[2], cover statistics on ethnic groups, migration, fertility, marriage and living arrangements, education, employment, occupation and industry, income, low income.

In addition, the bureau publishes several series of short *Current Population Reports,* the most useful of which are: *Current Population Reports: Consumer Income* (Series P-60); *Current Population Reports: Population Estimates* (Series P-25).

Census of Population and Housing (Series PHC).

The joint population/housing reports are in 3 series: "Census Tract Reports" for each SMSA (Standard Metropolitan Statistical Area); reports for each state and the District of Columbia on "General Demographic Trends for Metropolitan Areas," with those for 1970 comparing 1960 and 1970 population data on age, race, and housing data on such subjects as tenure, plumbing facilities; a series of "Employment Profiles of Selected Low-Income Areas."

Census of Retail Trade (Series RC).

Another important census for the business researcher, this provides statistics by state, SMSA, and areas outside SMSAs for about 100 different kinds of retail enterprises. The data includes number of establishments, sales, payroll, employment. A special report on size provides data based on sales and employment size and legal form of organization. There are 4 volumes, with 2 separate reports on "Retail Merchandise Line Sales" and on "Major Retail Center Statistics."

Census of Selected Service Industries (Series SC).

This contains similar tabulations to the retail census, but covers more than 150 kinds of service industries, such as hotels, laundries, automotive services, amusement and recreation services, law firms, engineering firms, etc., in 2 volumes.

Census of Transportation (Series WC).

Consists of 3 independent surveys. The *Truck Inventory and Use Survey* of 1972 collected data on a sample of 114,000 trucks, including number of vehicles, major use, vehicle miles, characteristics such as body type; the *National Travel Survey* provides statistics on volume and characteristics of nonlocal travel, based on a sample of households; the *Commodity Transportation Survey* reports on a sampling of characteristics of intercity commodity shipments originated by manufacturers, including ton-miles, means of transport, etc.

Census of Wholesale Trade (Series WC).

Statistics for 118 kinds of wholesale businesses by area, in 2 volumes. Data includes number of establishments, sales, payroll, employment, operating expenses, size, legal form of organization, type of operation, and a special report on "Wholesale Commodity Line Sales."

County Business Patterns (annual).

This is a separate and very useful annual compilation of first-quarter and annual employment and payroll statistics by county and by industry. For each 4-digit SIC industry this gives county totals in number of employees, taxable payrolls and total establishments; also number of establishments by employment size, and 2-digit SIC figures for SMSAs. Includes finance, insurance and real estate SIC categories that are not covered in the census. Excludes government employees, self-employed, farm and domestic workers, etc. Beginning with the 1974 annual (to be published in 1976) the reporting will all be on an establishment basis rather than a reporting unit basis. A title change is being considered for the volumes to be published in 1977.

Enterprise Statistics (Series ES).

This is a regrouping of the data from the economic censuses (construction, manufacturing, mineral, wholesale, retail and selected service industries) to provide tabulations by company organization, size and industry classification. There are 3 reports: "General Report on Industrial Organization"; "Central Administrative Offices and Auxiliaries"; "Link of Census Establishment and Internal Revenue Service Corporation Data."

A separate *Censuses of the Outlying Areas* (Series OAC) provides economic census statistics for Puerto Rico, Virgin Islands and Guam.

STANDARD INDUSTRIAL CLASSIFICATION SCHEME

In order to facilitate the collection and presentation of statistical data on so many industries, the federal government some years ago developed a standard industrial classification (SIC) scheme, which is a 4-digit classification of all manufacturing and nonmanufacturing industries. Not only are all the Census industry statistics arranged by this scheme, but it has also been widely adopted by many nongovernment sources for use in such publications as market guides, directories of companies, and indexes. Following is the name of the manual that is an important guide to the kinds of establishments included within each SIC number:

U.S. Office of Management and Budget, Executive Office of the President. *Standard Industrial Classification Manual.* Washington, D.C., U.S. Government Printing Office, 1972.

FOREIGN TRADE STATISTICS

The Bureau of the Census publishes a Foreign Trade (FT) series consisting of a number of monthlies and annuals containing detailed export and import statistics. The two principal monthlies are:

FT 410: *U.S. Exports: Schedule B Commodity Groupings, Schedule B Commodity by Country*
FT 135: *U.S. General Imports: Schedule A Commodity by Country*

These give quantity and value for individual Schedule B (or A) commodities exported (or imported), by country of destination (or origin). For an alphabetical index to the commodity classification system used in these monthlies refer to *Commodity Indexes for the Standard International Trade Classification, Revised* published by the United Nations Statistical Office 1963, as their "Statistical Papers," Series M, No. 38, Vol. 1.

The three principal annuals are:

FT 610: *U.S. Exports: Domestic Merchandise SIC-Based Products by World Area*

FT 210: *U.S. Imports — SIC-Based Products*
FT 246: *U.S. Foreign Trade: Imports — TSUSA Commodity by Country*

FT 610 and FT 210 give net quantity and value of exports (or imports) for consumption, by SIC-based export (or import) product code, arranged by commodity and world area of destination (or origin). FT 246 contains quantity and value of imports for consumption by individual TSUSA (Tariff Schedules of the United States Annotated) commodity and country of origin. For an alphabetical index of TSUSA commodities consult *Tariff Schedules of the United States Annotated* published by the U.S. International Trade Commission.

MONTHLY GOVERNMENT STATISTICAL PERIODICALS

The most important of many government periodicals for current American business statistics are the following monthlies:

U.S. Board of Governors of the Federal Reserve System. *Federal Reserve Bulletin.* Washington, D.C.
This is the best single source for current U.S. banking and monetary statistics. It also includes some international financial statistics, and basic business statistics such as construction, employment, prices, national income and the well-known Federal Reserve Board's index of industrial production. This bulletin is indexed in BPI, PAIS. The board also publishes a *Federal Reserve Monthly Chart Book,* which provides graphic trends for many of these statistics.

U.S. Bureau of Economic Analysis, Department of Commerce. *Business Conditions Digest.* Washington, D.C., U.S. Government Printing Office.
Charts and back-up statistical tables for those leading economic time series of most use to business analysts and forecasters. There are 6 sections: national income and GNP; cyclical indicators; anticipations and intentions; other key indicators; analytical measures; international comparisons. The BEA also publishes a monthly *Defense Indicators* that contains charts and statistics for about 60 time series on defense activity which influence short-term changes in the national economy.

U.S. Bureau of Labor Statistics. *Monthly Labor Review.* Washington, D.C., U.S. Government Printing Office.
Indispensable for its current statistics covering employment, unemployment, hours, earnings, consumer and wholesale prices, productivity, labor-management data. The articles in this review are indexed in BPI, F&S, PAIS, RGPL.

U.S. Council of Economic Advisers. *Economic Indicators.* Washington, D.C., U.S. Government Printing Office.
Statistical tables and charts for the basic U.S. economic indicators. Includes total output, income and spending; employment, unemployment and wages; production and business activity; prices; money, credit and security markets; federal finance. Statistics in each issue are usually quoted annually for about 6 years and monthly for the past year.

U.S. Department of Commerce. *Survey of Current Business.* Washington, D.C., U.S. Government Printing Office.

This is *the* most important single source for current business statistics. It covers: general business indicators; commodity prices; construction and real estate; domestic trade; labor force, employment and earnings; finance; foreign trade of the U.S.; transportation and communication; chemicals and allied products; electric power and gas; food and kindred products; tobacco; leather and products; lumber and products; metals and manufactures; petroleum, coal and products; pulp, paper and paper products; rubber and products; stone, clay and glass products; textile products; transportation equipment. Besides these regularly quoted statistics there are special statistical reports appearing at intervals, the best known of which is the "National Income Issue" (July). Others include "Aspects of International Investment" (August); "Balance of Payments" (usually quarterly); "Corporate Profits"; "Local Area Personal Income" (April); "Plant and Equipment Expenditures" (in about 3 issues); "State and Regional Income" (twice a year). The articles in the *Survey* are indexed in BPI, F&S, PAIS. An important biennial supplement, *Business Statistics,* provides an historical record of the statistics quoted in each monthly issue. A weekly 4-page supplement to the *Survey,* also titled *Business Statistics,* gives the most recent figures for a few selected statistics.

STATISTICS ON GOVERNMENT FINANCE

In this section are the names of several good sources for statistics on government finance. Although they may not be used as often as the other statistics in this chapter, these are still publications all economic and business researchers should be aware of.

Bond Buyer. *Statistics on State and Local Government Finance.* New York (annual).

A handy compilation of historical tables and a few charts, including state and municipal bonds sold, from 1966; money market indicators since 1950; range of the Bond Buyer's Index, from 1917; tabular study of tax-exempt bond funds; toll road statistics; state and local total expenditures, from 1902; state and local tax burden per capita; major municipal bond issues for the past year; obligations of states and political subdivisions held by the 100 largest banks; tax-exempt pollution control financing for the past year.

Municipal Yearbook. Washington, D.C., International City Management Association.

This is a U.S. and Canadian yearbook and statistical volume covering administrative, legislative and judicial trends (including education); management issues and trends; public manpower (employment and safety); public safety; the environment. Includes also a directory of state municipal leagues, state agencies, municipal officers, mayors, and appointed county administrators.

Tax Foundation. *Facts and Figures on Government Finance.* New York (biennial).

Statistics on fiscal activities of federal, state and local governments; also selected basic economic statistics.

U.S. Bureau of the Census. *Census of Governments* (Series G).

This provides the most detailed statistics on U.S. government finance. The census is taken every 5 years, and the volumes in the 1972 census are: Vol. 1, "Governmental Organization"; Vol. 2, "Taxable Property Values and Assessment-Sales Price

Ratios"; Vol. 3, "Public Employment"; Vol. 4, "Government Finances" (including finances of school districts, special districts, county governments, municipalities and township governments); Vol. 5, "Local Government in Metropolitan Areas"; Vol. 6, "Topical Studies" (5 reports covering various aspects of state and local governments); Vol. 7, "State Reports"; Vol. 8, "Guide to 1972 Census of Governments."

U.S. Office of Management and Budget, Executive Office of the President. *The Budget of the United States Government.* Washington, D.C., U.S. Government Printing Office (annual).

An overview of the president's budget proposals, with summary statistical tables including budget authority and outlays by agency, budget receipts by source, offsetting receipts by type, budget authority and outlays by function and agency; also some historical tables. A large "Appendix" volume contains detailed information on the various appropriations and funds that comprise the budget. This agency also publishes a more concise and less technical overview with summary statistics called *The United States Budget in Brief* (U.S. Government Printing Office, annual).

U.S. Treasury Department. *Treasury Bulletin.* Washington, D.C., U.S. Government Printing Office (monthly).

Up-to-date statistics on federal fiscal operations (including budget receipts and outlays); also federal obligations, account of the U.S. Treasury, federal debt, public debt operations, U.S. savings bonds, market quotations on Treasury securities, average yields of long-term bonds, international financial statistics, capital movements, foreign currencies acquired by the U.S. government, financial operations of government agencies and funds.

GUIDES TO STATISTICS

American Statistics Index: A Comprehensive Guide and Index to the Statistical Publications of the U.S. Government. Washington, D.C., Congressional Information Service (monthly, with annual cumulations).

This is a comprehensive, descriptive index to the statistics published by all government agencies, Congressional committees and statistics-producing programs. The 2 main volumes of the annual are arranged by issuing agency and give a full description of the data in each publication including time period covered, geographical breakdown, relevant technical notes and references to related publications. A separate index volume provides access by detailed subjects and names, by categories (such as breakdowns by age and sex, by commodity or industry, by geographic area), and by titles and report numbers. Microfiche copies of almost every report are available from ASI on a subscription basis.

Andriot, John L. *Guide to U.S. Government Statistics.* 4th ed. McLean, Va., Documents Index, 1973.

An annotated list of government statistical publications, arranged by issuing agency. For a list that covers all government serials and periodicals, regardless of whether they include statistics, refer to Andriot's *Guide to U.S. Government Publications* (1973, 3 volumes).

Encyclopedia of Business Information Sources. Detroit, Mich., Gale Research Co., 1970. 2 volumes. (A revision of Vol. 1 is in progress, with publication planned for 1976.)

A detailed listing of information sources on subjects and countries, including for each the basic statistical sources, directories, almanacs, periodicals, associations, handbooks, bibliographies, dictionaries, general works, etc. Vol. 1 covers about 2,000 very specific topics and industries, running from "Abrasives" to "Zinc." Vol. 2 covers "Geographic Sources" and gives sources of information about foreign countries as well as U.S. states and cities. This reference work is especially useful as a first place to check for persons unfamiliar with specialized publications in any one industry.

The Marketing Information Guide. Garden City, N.Y., The Trade Marketing Information Guide, Inc. (monthly).

A continuing source for studies and statistics of interest to economic and market researchers. It is a selected, annotated list of the publications of government agencies, universities, associations, publishing firms, etc. The section "Industries and Commodities" occasionally includes a few of the very expensive industry studies published by such research firms as Predicasts and Frost & Sullivan, Inc.

Predicasts. Cleveland, Ohio, Predicasts, Inc. (quarterly).

This quarterly service is also a very useful index of current forecasting statistical sources, since it gives the date and page reference of the current journal, government report or special study from which the statistics were taken. Predicasts also publishes a *Source Directory* (annual, with quarterly supplements), which is a list of 5,000 worldwide information sources that appear in journals, government publications, bank letters, directories, etc., arranged alphabetically by title, with a geographic index and an index by SIC industry.

Statistics Sources. 4th ed. Detroit, Mich., Gale Research Co., 1974.

A subject guide to data on industrial, business, social, educational, financial, and other topics. It is arranged alphabetically by very specific subject or product, from "Abaca" to "Zoology," and publications are cited for each where statistics can be found. Although this concentrates primarily on listing U.S. statistical sources it does index key international publications of the United Nations, the Organization for Economic Cooperation and Development (OECD), and the International Monetary Fund (IMF).

U.S. Bureau of the Census. *Catalog.* Washington, D.C., U.S. Government Printing Office (monthly, with quarterly and annual cumulations).

A good, descriptive list of Census publications, arranged by major subject field, with a detailed subject and a geographic index at end. Part 2 in each cumulation covers "Data Files and Special Tabulations."

The bureau also has published a *Bureau of the Census Guide to Programs and Publications: Subjects and Areas* (U.S. Government Printing Office, 1974), which is a descriptive guide to the 12 different censuses, with geographic and subject indexes at end. For a description of earlier Census publications refer to their *Bureau of the Census Catalog of Publications: 1790–1972* (U.S. Government Printing Office, 1974).

U.S. Bureau of the Census. *Statistical Abstract of the United States.* Washington, D.C., U.S. Government Printing Office (annual).

The "Guide to Sources of Statistics" in this annual is a subject listing of the important primary and a few secondary sources of statistical information. There is also a "Guide to State Statistical Abstracts" and a list of the publications of recent censuses.

United States Department of Commerce Publications: A Catalog and Index.
Washington, D.C., U.S. Government Printing Office (annual).

A partially annotated list of Department of Commerce publications arranged by
each office or bureau, e.g., the Bureau of the Census.

U.S. Department of Commerce. *Measuring Markets: A Guide to the Use of
Federal and State Statistical Data.* Washington, D.C., U.S. Government
Printing Office, 1974.

In a tabular format, this describes federal and state sources for statistics on population, income, employment, sales and selected types of taxes collected by states. A
bibliography at end lists not only the major statistical studies of the federal government but also statistical abstracts published for most states.

5

INDUSTRY STATISTICS

Industry Financial and Operating Ratios — Aerospace Industry — Agriculture and Food — Appliance Industry — Automobiles and Trucks — Brewing and Distilling — Chemicals and Plastics — Commodities Futures and Grain Statistics — Construction Industry — Containers and Packaging — Drug Industry — Electric and Gas Utilities — Electronics — Machinery Industry — Metals and Minerals — Paper and Allied Products — Petroleum — Rubber and Shoes — Textiles and Apparel — Tobacco and Cigars — Transportation and Equipment — Commodity and Consumer Prices

This chapter contains a selection of references to illustrate the wide variety of sources for statistical data on specific industries. These include government agencies, trade associations, commercial organizations, publishers and trade journals. No attempt is made here to cover each industry completely; the statistical publications described are, for the most part, a few of those that were easily accessible in Baker Library. Statistical issues in trade journals often vary widely from year to year. The issues examined were usually those published in 1974 or early 1975. There are many other good trade journals not mentioned here only because they did not contain statistics. Industry statistical sources in other chapters include: department stores, food stores and other retail businesses in Chapter 18; and insurance and real estate in Chapter 15. Financial surveys for industries (Chapter 7) usually also include some basic industry statistics.

When undertaking a statistical search on a U.S. industry most people find it best to start with one or more of the comprehensive publications listed in Chapter 3, such as the *Statistical Abstract,* the statistical service of Standard & Poor's, and the Census Bureau volumes. (Note particularly the detailed industry figures in the *Census of Manufactures.*) Use of the bibliographies described at the end of that chapter will also be worthwhile, especially the *Ency-*

clopedia of Business Information Sources, and perhaps also the "Industries and Commodities" section of *The Marketing Information Guide,* if one wants to cover basic sources as well as some of the very expensive industry studies compiled by several organizations. From there one can identify trade associations by using the directories of associations in Chapter 3 to discover which ones may publish factbooks or other statistical industry data. The names of trade journals in any industry can be found by using the directories of periodicals also in Chapter 3.

For persons interested in researching an industry for economic or industry information other than statistics, there are subject guides to books described in Chapter 2, as well as indexes of articles in business and trade journals. The *F & S Index to Corporations & Industries* is especially useful for this purpose, since it lists articles by SIC industries. Looking through current issues of trade journals can also be of value, since these usually include articles of interest, news of the industry and of people, and regular columns on such topics as new equipment, new products, new literature and coming events.

Some worldwide industry statistics are included in this chapter, but the reader should also consult the more general foreign economic and statistical sources described in Chapter 6 along with bibliographies of foreign statistical sources.

INDUSTRY FINANCIAL AND OPERATING RATIOS

This section describes the best known general sources for financial and operating ratios. Many trade associations, especially in the wholesaling and retailing areas, also compile operating ratios. Some trade journals include operating statistics in their annual statistical issues. Several ratio studies for department and food stores are described in Chapter 18. Others can be located by using Robert Morris Associates' *Sources of Composite Financial Data: A Bibliography* (3d ed., Philadelphia, Pa., 1971).

Barometer of Small Business. San Diego, Calif., Accounting Corp. of America (semi-annual).

Operating statistics for 48 small retail and service businesses compiled from the books of ACA clients. The figures are analyzed and summarized by industry type, size category and geographic region.

Dun & Bradstreet. *Key Business Ratios.* New York (annual).

Financial ratios for 125 retailing, wholesaling, manufacturing, construction lines of business. This appears first in the magazine *Dun's Review* (September through December each year), and then the ratios are reprinted as a separate pamphlet.

Dun & Bradstreet of Canada compiles a similar annual based on data from Canadian companies, also called *Key Business Ratios.*

NCR Corp. *Expenses in Retail Businesses.* New York (published irregularly).

Operating ratios for 36 lines of retail business, as taken from trade associations and other sources including many from the *Barometer of Small Business* mentioned above.

Robert Morris Associates. *Annual Statement Studies.* Philadelphia, Pa.

This contains financial and operating ratios for about 300 lines of business — manufacturers, wholesalers, retailers, services and contractors — based on information obtained from member banks of RMA. It is in 6 parts: Parts 1–4 cover balance sheet and profit-and-loss composites, with selected ratios, all by company size groups; Part 5 contains additional profit and loss data; Part 6 is a finance industry supplement for small loan and sales finance ratios.

Troy, Leo. *Almanac of Business and Industrial Financial Ratios.* Englewood Cliffs, N.J., Prentice-Hall (annual).

Financial and operating ratios for about 160 industries including banks and financial industries, as well as the usual manufacturing, wholesaling, retailing industries. Statistics are based on corporate activity during the latest year for which figures from IRS tax returns are published, so they are usually about 3 years old.

U.S. Federal Trade Commission. *Quarterly Financial Report for Manufacturing, Mining and Trade Corporations.* Washington, D.C., U.S. Government Printing Office.

This gives quarterly financial and operating ratios for 22 manufacturing industries and totals only for mining, retail and wholesale trade.

AEROSPACE INDUSTRY

Aerospace Facts and Figures. Compiled by the Aerospace Industries Association of America. New York, Aviation Week and Space Technology (annual).

A useful statistical annual for U.S. aircraft production, foreign trade, manpower, finance, research and development (r&d), federal missile and space programs, air transportation industry. Includes brief explanatory text. The AIAA publishes a slim quarterly bulletin called *Aerospace,* which includes one page of current "Aerospace Economic Indicators."

Air Transport. Washington, D.C., Air Transport Association of America (annual).

Statistics and explanatory text for airline service, safety and employment, unit revenues and costs, traffic service, as well as operating revenues and expenses for an 11-year period.

Air Transport World. Stamford, Conn., Reinhold Publishing Co. (monthly).

Varying operating, traffic and other data appear in issues from time to time. The annual "Market Development Issue" (May) includes world airline statistics by company (giving number of passengers, freight tonnage, number of employees); also short profiles of airlines, a 15-year analysis of passengers on the North Atlantic arranged by airline, tables on U.S. trunk traffic, etc. Current "Facts and Figures" are in each issue; an "Airline Buyers' Guide & Directory of Suppliers" is in January issue.

Aviation Daily. *Airline Statistical Annual.* Washington, D.C.

"Complete data on (year) operations of U.S. scheduled & supplemental air carriers certified by the Civil Aeronautics Board."

Aviation Week & Space Technology. New York, McGraw-Hill.

Their annual "Aerospace Forecast & Inventory" issue is the third March issue each year, and it contains articles, charts and some statistics on growth trends and specifications for missiles and aircraft. *Aviation Week* is indexed in ASTI, BPI, F&S, PAIS, RGPL.

International Air Transport Association. *World Air Transport Statistics.* Montreal, Canada (annual).

Traffic and operating statistics for IATA member firms.

National Business Aircraft Association. *Business Flying.* Washington, D.C. (annual).

This is a short 4-part statistical annual, with explanatory text, covering aircraft utilization, airports, accidents, employment and training, market influences, etc.

U.S. Civil Aeronautics Board. Bureau of Accounts and Statistics. *Handbook of Airline Statistics.* Washington, D.C. (biennial).

Traffic and financial statistics for individual carriers beginning with the year 1964; historical statistics for carrier groups from 1926. For more recent statistics consult their *Air Carrier Financial Statistics* (quarterly) and *Air Carrier Traffic Statistics* (monthly). The CAB publishes other more specialized periodic statistical reports.

U.S. Federal Aviation Administration. *FAA Statistical Handbook of Aviation.* Washington, D.C., U.S. Government Printing Office. (annual).

Provides a convenient source for historical statistics on airports, air carrier operating data, airmen, aircraft, aeronautical production and exports, aircraft accidents.

World Airline Record. 7th ed. Chicago, Roadcap & Associates, 1972. And "Data Supplements."

Data on over 300 world airlines including operating and traffic statistics for 18 years; also brief history of each, current trends, government policy, affiliated companies, equipment, names of officers.

AGRICULTURE AND FOOD

See also in this chapter: "Brewing and Distilling"; "Commodities Futures and Grain Statistics"; "Textiles and Apparel"; and "Tobacco and Cigars."

U.S. Bureau of the Census. *Census of Agriculture.* Washington, D.C., U.S. Government Printing Office. (quinquennial, in years ending with 4 and 9).

An excellent source of detailed statistics on farms and farming. The 1969 census is in 6 volumes. Vol. 1, "Area Reports," consists of separate reports for every state and U.S. territory, with statistics by county for size of farms, tenure and characteristics of farm operators, farm income and sales, farm production and expenses, etc. Vol. 2, "General Report," contains 9 separate parts covering individual topics, such as farm management; equipment, labor, expenditures, chemicals; livestock, poultry, etc.; crops. Vol. 3 covers "Agricultural Services"; Vol. 4, "Irrigation"; Vol. 6, "Drainage of Agricultural Lands." Vol. 5, "Special Reports," contains 16 supplemental surveys on such topics as type of farm operation, horticulture, farm finance.

U.S. Department of Agriculture. *Agricultural Statistics.* Washington, D.C., U.S. Government Printing Office (annual).

A compilation of the most important USDA statistics on agricultural products, supplies, consumption, facilities, costs and returns, with sources for statistics at foot of each table.

The Department of Agriculture compiles and publishes statistics on many topics. Its *Statistical Bulletin* series includes numbers (some published annually) covering such agricultural commodities as fats and oils, livestock and meat, poultry and eggs, tobacco. Their Economic Research Service publishes a series of periodic "Situation" reports that include current statistics. Several examples are: *Dairy Situation*; *Fats and Oils Situation*; *Feed Situation*; *Fruit Situation*; *Marketing and Transportation Situation*; *Wheat Situation*. These vary in frequency, with most published 4 or 5 times each year. There are a number of bibliographies of USDA publications, for example, *List of Available Publications of the United States Department of Agriculture*, and *Economics of Agriculture: Reports and Publications Issued or Sponsored by USDA's Economic Research Services* (annual). A monthly *Bibliography of Agriculture* (Scottsdale, Ariz., Oryx Press) is a detailed subject index to the literature of agriculture and allied sciences, and it is based on the indexing records prepared by the U.S. National Agricultural Library for its CAIN computer system.

The Food and Agriculture Organization of the United Nations publishes many periodic statistical studies covering agricultural commodities in all UN countries. A few of the more general FAO sources are included in Chapter 6.

Canned Foods

Almanac of the Canning, Freezing, Preserving Industries. Westminster, Md., E. E. Judge & Sons (annual).

The crop statistics section gives harvested acreage, production, total value, etc., for specific crops. There are also U.S. pack statistics, data from the census, prices, international trade, and world packs. Other information in this almanac includes names of associations, regulations, labelling and grading, a "Buyer's Guide."

Frozen Foods

American Frozen Food Institute. *Frozen Food Pack Statistics.* Washington, D.C. (annual).

Pack statistics for the various frozen food categories.

Another organization, the National Frozen Food Association, publishes a *Frozen Food Factbook & Directory* (Hershey, Pa., annual), which is primarily a directory but does include some statistics.

Quick Frozen Foods. New York, Harcourt Brace Jovanovich (monthly)

An annual issue of this trade journal published in the fall (e.g., Oct. 1974) contains a section called "Frozen Food Almanac" that includes retail and institutional poundage and dollar volume for types of frozen foods, as well as freezer storage capacity, foreign trade. Also in this issue is an annual discussion of the "State of the Industry." This journal is indexed in BPI, F&S, PAIS.

Specific Food Products

American Meat Institute. *Financial Facts About the Meat Packing Industry.* Washington, D.C. (annual).

Brief financial data on the industry with explanatory text; also statistics on the U.S. feed and livestock situation.

Fehr, Frank, & Co. *Annual Review for (year) of Oilseeds, Oils, Oilcakes and Other Commodities.* London.

Worldwide production, prices, foreign trade for various oils.

International Sugar Organization. *Sugar Year Book.* London.
> Gives sugar production, consumption, foreign trade by country. Some current statistics are in their *Monthly Statistical Bulletin.*

International Tea Committee. *Annual Bulletin of Statistics.* London.
> This contains production, consumption, stocks, foreign trade, and prices of tea — by country; also production of instant tea and tea duties. Some current figures are in their *Monthly Statistical Summary.*

Tea & Coffee Trade Journal. Whitestone, N.Y. (monthly).
> Tea statistics are in each issue. Frequent articles on the coffee and tea industry often contain some statistics.

The Bureau of the Census series of *Current Industrial Reports* includes monthly reports on production, inventories and orders for flour milling products, confectionery, fats and oils, and an annual for salad dressing and related products.

APPLIANCE INDUSTRY

Appliance. New York, Dana Chase Publications (monthly).
> The April issue each year contains a 10-year "Statistical Review" giving manufacturer shipments or factory sales of specific appliances, housewares and plumbing fixtures. There is also one page for current "Statistics" in each issue. The January issue is an "Appliance Industry Purchasing Directory." Indexed in F&S.

Merchandising. New York, Billboard Publications (monthly).
> The annual "Statistical and Marketing Report" is now (1976) in the March issue each year. It contains 10-year tables of sales growth and performance by individual type of appliance; a "Saturation Index"; replacement and trade-in sales survey; foreign trade; retail sales survey for leading utility companies in major trading areas; monthly retail sales patterns by regions; regional market profiles; and major appliances highlights. An "Annual Statistical and Marketing Forecast Report" (May issue) contains recent trends and estimates for the year. This monthly is indexed in BPI, F&S.

The Bureau of the Census series of *Current Industrial Reports* includes separate annual statistical reports giving production of air conditioning and refrigeration equipment, electric housewares and fans, major household appliances, radio/TV/phonographs/record players and related equipment.

AUTOMOBILES AND TRUCKS

American Trucking Associations. *American Trucking Trends.* Washington, D.C. (annual).
> Statistics and charts on truck registration, ton-miles, carrier size, revenue, costs, manpower, etc.

Automotive Industries. Radnor, Pa., Chilton Co. (semi-monthly).
> The annual "Engineering Specifications & Statistical Issue" (April 1, formerly the March 15 issue) includes car production, registrations, engines and technical data on U.S. passenger cars, imported cars, trucks, as well as specifications for internal combustion engines. Indexed in BPI, F&S.

Automotive News. Detroit, Mich. (weekly).

A special "Almanac Issue" appears as Section 2 of the last April issue each year. It contains useful statistics on U.S. car and truck registrations and production; Canadian production; prices; specifications; cars and trucks in operation; dealer statistics; retail prices; also pictures of current models and imported cars, with prices and specifications. There is a directory of companies, listing officers, and pictures of executives and dealers with a few biographical facts.

Motor Vehicle Manufacturers' Association. *Facts and Figures of the Automotive Industry.* Toronto, Canada (annual).

Provides Canadian statistics for production, factory shipments, foreign trade, retail trade, registrations, motor fuel sales, revenue and tax rates.

Motor Vehicle Manufacturers Association of the United States. *Automobile Facts & Figures.* Detroit, Mich. (annual).

Statistics on automobile production and registrations; auto use and owners; economic impact of the automobile. This association also publishes 2 other annuals: *Motor Truck Facts,* which contains U.S. and Canadian production, truck registration by state, world truck and bus registrations, intercity tonnage, travel by motor trucks and buses, employment, exports, taxes, etc.; *World Motor Vehicle Data,* for auto and truck production, foreign trade, registrations by country, with digests of long-range forecasts for countries other than the United States.

National Association of Motor Bus Owners. *Get on to Something Great.* Washington, D.C. (biennial).

This incorporates the former *Bus Facts,* with statistics in an appendix giving income and expenses for selected years from 1939; also traffic, taxes, employees, revenue, etc.

National Automobile Dealers Association. *The Franchised New Car & Truck Dealer Facts.* Washington, D.C. (annual).

Annual car and truck sales, production, registrations; also number of franchise dealers, employment, earnings, advertising, consumer credit.

Society of Motor Manufacturers and Traders. *Motor Industry of Great Britain.* London (annual).

Automobile production and registrations in the United Kingdom and overseas, as well as detailed statistics for overseas trade.

Trinc's Blue Book of the Trucking Industry. Washington, D.C., Trinc Transportation Consultants (annual).

Financial statistics for the largest U.S. trucking firms, taken from annual reports filed with the Interstate Commerce Commission by Class I and Class II motor carriers of property. The data is in a tabular format and includes balance sheet data, revenues, expenses, equipment, ton-miles, intercity statistics. A directory of companies at front includes the names of officers.

Ward's Automotive Yearbook. Detroit, Mich., Ward's Communications, Inc.

Detailed statistics on U.S. automobile industry trends, imported vehicles, recreational vehicles, tires, materials and engines, production, retail sales, registrations; also Canadian statistics. It includes a directory of car, truck, construction and farm equipment manufacturers, with pictures and data about the vehicles. Ward's also publishes a weekly newsletter called *Ward's Automotive Reports* that includes some statistics; and a monthly management magazine, *Ward's Auto World.*

World Automotive Market. New York, Automobile International (annual).
World production of automobiles, motor census, exports of autos and parts, registrations.

BREWING AND DISTILLING

Distilled Spirits Council of the United States. *Distilled Spirits Industry: Annual Statistical Review.* Washington, D.C.
Statistics on production, withdrawals, stocks, bottled output, estimated distilled spirits entering trade channels, foreign trade, apparent consumption, number of retail licenses, bottles used.

Licensed Beverage Industries. *Alcoholic Beverage Industry.* New York (annual).
The short statistical section in this annual contains total consumer expenditures, sales and consumption of distilled spirits, related economics, federal, state and local revenue.

Liquor Handbook. New York, Gavin-Jobson Associates (annual).
This handbook is in 4 parts: the national liquor market (consumption, sales, etc.); distilling operations; the market for major distilled spirits types; advertising and promotion. A companion volume is *Wine Marketing Handbook.*

United States Brewers Association. *The Brewing Industry in the United States: Brewers Almanac.* Washington, D.C. (annual).
Statistics cover production and withdrawals, consumption and sales, foreign trade, taxes.

CHEMICALS AND PLASTICS

Chemical & Engineering News. Washington, D.C., American Chemical Society (weekly).
The annual "Facts and Figures for the Chemical Industry" is in the first June issue each year. It contains the growth rate of the most important chemicals, employment, r&d spending, trade; also chemical company performance and comparative financial data by industry and company. Other annual statistical articles include a ranking of "The Top Fifty" (e.g., May 5, 1975); "Chemists' Salary and Employment Survey" (June 17, 1974); "Employment Outlook" (Oct. 7, 1974); "World Chemical Outlook" (Dec. 23, 1974). Indexed in ASTI, F&S.

Chemical Engineering. New York, McGraw-Hill (biweekly).
"CPI Forecast Report," with background information and a forecast for the chemical process industries, is in the first January issue each year. One page of "Economic Indicators" appears in each issue. Indexed in ASTI, F&S.

Chemical Industries Association. *U.K. Chemical Industry Statistics Handbook.* London (annual).
A good source for U.K. statistics on chemical production, shipments, employment, foreign trade, industry economic data.

Chemical Marketing Reporter. New York, Schnell Publishing Co. (weekly).
This weekly is especially important for its lengthy, continuing list of "Current Prices of Chemicals and Related Materials." It also contains short market reports for

specific chemicals and news of the industry. For many years this was published under the title *Oil, Paint and Drug Reporter.* Indexed in BPI, F&S.

Chemical Week. New York, McGraw-Hill.

The last issue in April each year contains a special section called "Chemical Week 300," which gives financial statistics for the 300 leading chemical processing companies, arranged by industry. There are also quarterly figures for leading companies that, in 1974, appeared in the issues for Feb. 27, May 21, Aug. 21, Nov. 20. The "Forecast" issue is in the second January issue; the "Foreign Forecast," around the Jan. 30 issue; the "Plant Sites" issue, in the third October issue; the "Buyers' Guide Issue, Part 2 of last October issue. Indexed in BPI, F&S.

Manufacturing Chemists Association. *Chemical Statistics Handbook.* 7th ed. Washington, D.C., 1971 (quinquennial, with annual *Statistical Summary* in intervening years).

This is a compilation from many other sources for production and sales of specific synthetic organic and inorganic chemicals, foreign trade and chemical industry economic data. There is a short section for Canadian chemical statistics.

Modern Plastics. New York, McGraw-Hill (13/yr.).

The January issue includes an article on "Materials and Market Statistics" giving data on sales, materials, market. "Modern Plastics Barometer" is in each issue. There is a separate and useful *Modern Plastics Encyclopedia,* which contains information on specific plastics, some specifications, temperature tables, etc.; also a list of companies. The journal is indexed in ASTI, F&S.

Noble, Patricia, ed. *The Kline Guide to the Chemical Industry.* 2d ed. (Kline Industrial Marketing Guide, IMG-13-74.) Fairfield, N.J., C. H. Kline & Co., 1974.

An economic analysis of the chemical industry, including statistics, information sources, estimated sales by product line for the 465 leading chemical companies. A companion volume is *Kline Guide to the Paint Industry* (Kline Industrial Marketing Guide, IMG-1-75, 4th ed., 1975; to be published triennially).

U.S. Bureau of the Census. *Current Industrial Reports. Series M28A: Inorganic Chemicals.* Washington, D.C. (monthly).

This gives production statistics for many inorganic chemicals. The U.S. Tariff Commission publishes an annual for *Synthetic Organic Chemicals: United States Production and Sales.* Several other reports in the Census Bureau's *Current Industrial Reports* series cover inorganic fertilizer materials; paint, varnish and lacquer; selected plastics products.

For persons interested in current literature on worldwide developments for the chemical process and soft goods industries there is an expensive but useful *Chemical Markets Abstracts* (Cleveland, Ohio, Predicasts, Inc., monthly with quarterly and annual cumulations). It indexes and digests articles in key journals and government reports on the chemical industry and also on building products, drugs and cosmetics, food and beverages, packaging, pulp and paper, rubber and products, textiles and fibers. It covers data on companies, new products, acquisitions, capacities, end-uses, markets, technology, production, environment and foreign trade. The data in this service can also be accessed via the *Predicasts Terminal System* described in Chapter 2.

COMMODITIES FUTURES AND GRAIN STATISTICS

Chicago. Board of Trade. *Statistical Annual.* Chicago.

Detailed trade, commerce, futures price statistics for grains and other commodities traded on the CBT.

Similar volumes are published for other exchanges: Kansas City Board of Trade, *Annual Statistical Report;* Minneapolis Grain Exchange, *Annual Report;* New York Mercantile Exchange, *Statistical Yearbook.*

Commodities. Columbia, Md., Investor Publications (monthly).

This is the magazine of futures trading. The January issue each year is a "Directory of Futures Trading," which contains lists of books, advisory services, periodicals, charting services, computer data services, investment management services, organizations, brokerage firms, etc.

Commodities Chart Service. New York, Commodity Research Bureau (weekly).

Weekly and monthly futures price charts for actively traded commodity contracts; includes also daily price-action charts, technical comments, a computer trend analyzer. The Commodity Research Bureau's useful statistical *Commodity Year Book* includes some futures prices in its coverage of about 99 commodities.

Feedstuffs. Minneapolis, Minn., Miller Publishing Co. (weekly, with extra issue in September).

The "Yearbook" issue (extra issue in third week of September) is in 2 sections. The first is a feed markets and management section, with national, regional and state marketing data on the feed, grain and feeding industries; also a feed milling manual. Section 2 is a "Buyer's Guide." Indexed in F&S.

The daily newspaper *Journal of Commerce and Commercial* (New York, Twin Coast Newspapers) has good coverage of current futures prices for important commodities such as grains, cotton, cocoa, silver, copper, gold, corn and soybeans.

CONSTRUCTION INDUSTRY

For housing and real estate statistics see Chapter 15.

Blue Book of Major Homebuilders. Crofton, Md., CMR Associates (annual).

Information about major homebuilders, arranged by region and state. For each firm the data usually includes production by type of housing and, occasionally, financial data; also names of key personnel, performance record, money and land requirements, operating areas, prices and rents.

Construction Review. Washington, D.C., U.S. Bureau of Domestic Commerce, Department of Commerce (monthly). Purchase from U.S. Government Printing Office.

A useful monthly source for current statistics on construction put in place, housing, building permits, contract awards, cost and price indexes, construction materials, employment, etc. The annual issue in December includes monthly statistics for previous 6 years. Indexed in BPI, F&S, PAIS.

Dodge Construction Statistics. New York, F. W. Dodge Division, McGraw-Hill Information Systems Co. (monthly).

This is an expensive but useful service for persons who need statistics on construction contract awards. It is available as 2 separate publications: (1) a 3-section *United States Summary Bulletin* that gives monthly total construction contracts in square feet and in dollar value, by type of building; a graphic "Dodge Index"; a table of construction contracts for manufacturing and processing plants by industry classification; (2) a more detailed "Region Bulletin," available for any or all of 9 regions in the United States, and giving construction contracts by type of building, total residential and nonresidential building for major marketing areas within each region. The Dodge Division publishes other Dodge Building Cost Services that are widely used in the building industry.

Engineering News Records. New York, McGraw-Hill (weekly).

This trade journal publishes a "Quarterly Cost Roundup" (third issues in March, June, September, December) that contains a building cost index for 22 cities, from 1950 to date; also wage indexes, machinery prices, materials prices, highway bid price indexes, etc. The "Annual Report and Forecast" issue is in the third January issue. The second May issue has a ranking of "The 500 Top Design Firms" by billings; the second April issue has a list of "The 400 Largest Construction Contractors." Materials prices and unit prices are in each issue. Indexed in BPI, F&S.

House & Home. New York, McGraw-Hill (monthly).

A marketing and management publication for housing and light construction. The March issue each year contains a list of "The Biggest Builders," which gives, for each, the number of housing units built and the dollar volume. An annual "Building Costs" issue (May) has a breakdown of construction costs by selected basic jobs or components, and it also has a 2-page table of key homebuilding costs in 102 cities across the country. Statistics on housing stocks are in each issue. These include building companies, savings and loan associations, real estate investment trusts, land developers, suppliers. Indexed in BPI, PAIS.

Professional Builder & Apartment Business. Denver, Colo., Cahners Publishing Co. (monthly).

The July issue each year includes an "Annual Report of Housing's Giants," which lists over 500 firms by dollar volume and gives a brief description of operating plan. It also lists data on the top 10 in for-sale housing, in rental housing, in mobile homes, in modular/pre-fab housing. *Professional Builder* publishes a separate *Marketing Man's Guide to the Housing & Light Construction Industry* (3rd ed., 1973–1974), the "Marketing Information" section of which includes pertinent demographic facts and statistical data on major segments of the industry (single family, multi-family housing, nonresidential construction, remodeling and modernization, industrialized building, tool and machinery). There is also a section on "Media Information." This journal is indexed in F&S.

Rock Products. Chicago, Maclean-Hunter (monthly).

The "Forecast" issue (December each year) gives production and outlook for specific products, such as cement, crushed stone, sand and gravel. The January issue is a "Buyer's Guide." Indexed in ASTI, F&S.

U.S. Bureau of the Census. *Census of Construction Industries.* Washington, D.C., U.S. Government Printing Office (quinquennial, in years ending with 2 and 7).

The 1972 *Census* is an enumeration of U.S. construction establishments operating as general contractors and operative builders, special trade contractors, or land sub-dividers. It is in 2 volumes, with one giving data on 27 industries including number of construction establishments, receipts, employment, payrolls, capital expenditures, payments for materials and for renting equipment. The other volume provides the statistics by state.

The Bureau of the Census also publishes a number of series of *Construction Reports,* on such subjects as *Housing Starts* (monthly), *Housing Completions* (monthly), *Housing Authorized by Building Permits and Public Contracts, States, Selected Standard Metropolitan Statistical Areas and Individual Places* (monthly). There is an historical supplement called *Housing Construction Statistics, 1889–1964* (U.S. Government Printing Office, 1966).

CONTAINERS AND PACKAGING

Containers and Packaging. Washington, D.C., U.S. Bureau of Domestic Commerce, Department of Commerce (quarterly). Purchase from U.S. Government Printing Office.

Regular statistics include shipments and/or production for glass containers, metal cans, closures for containers, plastic bottles, paper, steel pails and drums. April is the annual review issue. Indexed in F&S.

The Bureau of the Census publishes separate *Current Industrial Reports* for each of these products, giving production statistics for each.

Glass Container Manufacturers Institute. *Glass Containers.* New York (annual).

Brief factbook with statistics on total shipments, domestic shipments by end-use, closure shipments.

Modern Packaging. New York, Buttenheim Publishing Corp. (monthly).

The December issue each year is an "Encyclopedia and Planning Guide." There is a short "outlook" article in January with a few statistics and charts. Indexed in BPI, F&S.

Paperboard Packaging. Chicago (monthly).

The "Annual Industry Statistical Review" appears in the August issue each year. It contains a review and statistics on paperboard, woodpulp, paperstock, paperboard mill, corrugated/solid fibre, folding carton, composite can/tubes, fibre drum, rigid box, brief data on corrugated box industry in Europe.

Other trade associations publish annual statistics for paper containers including: Fibre Box Association, *Annual Report, Fibre Box Industry* (New York); National Paper Box Association, *Annual Financial Survey of the Rigid Paper Box Industry* (Haddonfield, N.J.); and Paper Bag Institute, *Statistical Review* (New York), which combines the statistics and charts previously published separately for grocers bags, grocers sacks and merchandise bags.

DRUG INDUSTRY

For statistics on drugstores and products sold in drugstores see Chapter 18.

Prescription Drug Industry Factbook. Washington, D.C., Pharmaceutical Manufacturers Association. (quinquennial).

Statistics and explanatory text, including sales, employment, quality control, r&d,

international operations, health care industry. The 1973 edition has a glossary and a "Sources of Tables and Charts."

ELECTRIC AND GAS UTILITIES

American Gas Association. *Gas Facts: A Statistical Record of the Gas Utility Industry.* Arlington, Va. (annual).

A comprehensive statistical record of the gas utility industry, with a glossary at end. Includes reserves, production, distribution, underground storage, customers, sales-quantity, revenues, finance, labor, prices, appliances. The AGA also publishes an annual *Gas Utility Industry Projections to 1990.*

Edison Electric Institute. *Statistical Year Book of the Electrical Utility Industry.* New York.

Gives generating capacity, electric power supply, generation, energy sales, customers, revenues, operating data and ratios, financial statistics, miscellaneous economic data. The EEI also publishes a semi-annual *Electric Power Survey* and a monthly *Bulletin,* the latter of which is indexed in F&S.

Electrical Wholesaling. New York, McGraw-Hill (monthly).

The "Annual Forecast and Review" issue (December) includes economic and business outlook for the coming year, plans for capital spending, price trends, construction, kwhr sales. Each issue has sales trend statistics and price index. Indexed in F&S.

Electrical World. New York, McGraw-Hill (semi-monthly).

This trade journal includes 2 statistical issues. The "Annual Statistical Report" (Mar. 15) gives U.S. electric utility capital spending by area; new expenditures for lines and substations, construction, generating capability, electric plant maintenance, energy sales, finance, data on co-ops; also some statistics for Canada. The "Annual Electrical Industry Forecast" (Sept. 15) gives statistics and forecasts for kwhr sales, generating capabilities, capital expenditures, and a survey of utility transmission and distribution construction plans. A "Steam Station Design Survey" is in Nov. 1 issue. Indexed in ASTI, F&S.

Moody's Public Utilities Manual. New York, Moody's Investors Service (annual, with semi-weekly supplements).

Financial manual for all kinds of American public utility companies; also Canadian and some foreign companies. Center blue pages include Moody's averages, statistics on the electric light and power industry, comparative data for independent electric operating companies, discussion of U.S. governmental activities, statistics on the gas industry, the telephone industry, the telegraph/cable/radiotelegraph industries; a directory of public utilities by state and city, a list of securities offerings during the past year; a 10-year price range of domestic and Canadian stocks and bonds.

National LP-Gas Association. *LP-Gas Industry Market Facts.* Chicago (annual).

This annual factbook gives LP-gas production, transportation, sales, foreign trade, equipment, appliances and utilization.

U.S. Federal Power Commission. *Statistics of Privately Owned Electric Utilities in the United States.* Washington, D.C., U.S. Government Printing Office (annual).

Financial statistics for Class A and Class B electric utilities. A companion volume is

Statistics of Publicly Owned Electric Utilities in the United States (annual). The FPC publishes other statistics including *Statistics of Interstate Natural Gas Pipeline Companies* (annual).

ELECTRONICS

See also "Appliance Industry" in this chapter.

Electronic Industries Association. *Electronic Market Data Book.* Washington, D.C. (annual).

Useful statistics, charts and explanatory text covering consumer electronics, communications and industrial products, government products, electronic components, world trade, and related information. The Consumer Electronics Group of the EIA also publishes a separate short *Consumer Electronics: Annual Review.*

Electronic News. New York, Fairchild Publications (weekly).

A weekly newspaper for current news about consumer and government electronic products, electronic components, communications, measurement and control, materials/packaging/production, finance (including current stock prices on the ASE, NYSE, and OTC). A useful annual "Looking at the Leaders" is issued as Section 2 of an early July issue each year. It lists electronic companies and gives officers, major facilities, a summary and forecast, electronics sales and total sales; there is a ranking of the 50 leaders at the front. Indexed in BPI, F&S.

Electronic News Financial Fact Book & Directory. New York, Fairchild Publications (annual).

This is a good financial manual covering electronic companies, listing for each the officers, divisions, subsidiaries, products, sales and earnings, income account, balance sheet data, number of employees, plant footage, common stock equity.

Electronics. New York, McGraw-Hill (biweekly).

There are statistics in 3 issues of this trade journal. In the first January issue there is an article on "U.S. Markets" for the coming year, with a folded statistical insert that gives total value (at factory level) of goods shipped by U.S. electronic manufacturers, by specific product, with estimates for the most recent 3 years and forecasts for 3 years in advance. The last December issue contains a special report on the "European Market" with a folded insert giving estimates of factory sales for the components and equipment markets, by country, for 2 years. The last November issue covers "Japan Electronics Markets" with several pages of statistics on components and equipment. This journal is indexed in ASTI, F&S.

The Bureau of the Census publishes an annual *Current Industrial Report* (Series MA-36N), which gives production statistics on "Selected Electronic and Associated Products."

For persons interested in current literature on the electronic and equipment industries there is an expensive but useful *Equipment Market Abstracts* (Cleveland, Ohio, Predicasts, Inc., monthly with quarterly and annual cumulations). This indexes and digests articles and other reports on such industries as machinery, electronics components, consumer equipment, instrumentation and transportation equipment. It covers articles on companies, new products, acquisitions, markets, production, foreign developments, and has indexes by company, country and type of information. The data in this service can also be accessed via the *Predicasts Terminal System* described in Chapter 2.

MACHINERY INDUSTRY

American Machinist. New York, McGraw-Hill (semi-monthly).

The "Outlook" issue (second January issue) is in 2 parts: the economic outlook contains text with charts and statistics for world machine tool production, metalworking shipments, new machinery orders, wages and prices, as well as an "AM Index of Metalworking Production and Prices"; the second part is a discussion of the technical outlook. A continuing feature is a page of AM trends and brief statistics. Every 5 years this trade journal publishes a detailed "American Machinist Inventory of Metalworking Equipment," which is an expensive 4-volume inventory of plants by geographic area, including statistics on type of machinery in 3 age classes. A summary of the latest survey is in the issue for Oct. 29, 1973. *American Machinist* is indexed in ASTI, F&S.

National Machine Tool Builders' Association. *Economic Handbook of the Machine Tool Industry.* McLean, Va. (annual).

Useful statistics on the machine tool industry in general and on shipments and orders, foreign trade, employment and earnings, finance, machine tools in use. Explanation of terms is at end.

The *Current Industrial Reports* series of the Bureau of the Census includes a number of separate reports giving production for specific kinds of machines such as farm, office, mining, metalworking, and vending machines.

For a description of *Equipment Market Abstracts* see note at end of "Electronics" in this chapter.

METALS AND MINERALS

Aluminum Association. *Aluminum Statistical Review.* New York (annual).

Contains U.S. shipments, markets, supply, U.S. foreign trade statistics, also world statistics.

American Bureau of Metal Statistics. *Non-Ferrous Metal Data.* New York (annual).

Worldwide statistics for copper, lead, aluminum, gold and silver and other nonferrous metals.

American Iron and Steel Institute. *Annual Statistical Report.* Washington, D.C.

Financial and economic statistics, employment and wages, shipments of steel products, foreign trade, raw steel products, pig iron and ferroalloys, basic materials (coal, scrap, etc.), Canadian statistics and a few world statistics.

American Iron Ore Association. *Iron Ore.* Cleveland, Ohio (annual).

Production, shipments, consumption, foreign trade for iron ore in the United States and Canada; also grade names and analyses and a directory of companies.

American Metal Market. New York (5/wk.).

An important newspaper for news and current prices of specific metals, including prices for scrap iron and steel and for nonferrous scrap. Indexed in F&S.

British Steel Corp. *Iron and Steel Industry: Annual Statistics for the United Kingdom.* Croydon, England.

This annual is compiled jointly by the British Steel Corporation and the British Independent Steel Producers' Association on behalf of the Iron and Steel Statistics Bureau. Statistics include U.K. production and consumption for iron and steel; also statistics for blast furnaces, iron and steel scrap, crude steel, finished steel, labor, prices, foreign trade.

Canadian Minerals Yearbook. Ottawa, Information Canada.

Chapters for each of 53 minerals and metals important to the Canadian economy, giving information somewhat similar to that in the U.S. *Minerals Yearbook* noted below, including the publication of preprints for each chapter.

Copper. Washington, D.C., U.S. Bureau of Domestic Commerce, Department of Commerce (quarterly). Order from U.S. Government Printing Office.

Each issue gives production, consumption, shipments, inventories, foundry data, employment, prices; some foreign country data. Indexed in F&S.

Dun & Bradstreet. *Metalworking Directory.* National ed. New York (annual).

Section 4 of this directory is a "statistical summary," which gives total number of plants and total employees for each SIC by county, and also statistics broken down into 3 employee size categories. The rest of this directory is described in Chapter 3.

E/MJ: Engineering and Mining Journal. New York, McGraw-Hill (monthly).

The "Annual Survey and Outlook for Mineral Commodities" (March) contains from 1 to 3 pages of text and some statistics on each of 43 minerals, discussing demand, supply, new developments, market outlook, consumption. Separate tables give specific metal and mineral prices. The January issue contains a "Survey of Mine & Plant Expansion"; the June issue is a "Buying Directory." A "Markets" section in each issue has average prices of metals, and also Metals Week Quotations, and London Metal Exchange Quotations. Indexed in ASTI, F&S.

Financial Post. *Survey of Mines.* Montreal, Quebec, Canada (annual).

A Canadian financial manual with the company reviews in 3 parts: major producing and exploration companies; active companies of lesser stature; other companies whose status is in doubt. Contains statistics of mineral production at front; also a 7-year price range of mining stocks.

Foundry Management & Technology. Cleveland, Ohio, Penton Publishing Co. (monthly).

The January issue contains an annual "Outlook" that includes some metal casting statistics. This journal also publishes a separate *Metal Casting Industry Census Guide: Summary Report* (biennial), which gives total foundries in each state and Canadian province and has a breakdown of metals cast (7 kinds of metals), departments operated (for 6 types of departments) and 7 casting methods. One table analyzes 48 foundry market areas. The full Foundry Census gives more statistics on a detailed market area and state basis. Indexed in ASTI, F&S.

International Tin Council. *Tin Statistics.* London (annual).

Annual worldwide data for 11 years on tin and tin plate production, consumption, trade and tin prices. Current figures in their *Monthly Statistical Bulletin.*

Iron Age. Radnor, Pa., Chilton Co. (weekly).

The "Annual Statistical Review" is in the first January issue. It gives metal production and prices and has articles on the metalworking outlook and future resources. There is also a list of trade associations. Each issue contains steel production and prices and nonferrous metals prices. Indexed in ASTI, BPI, F&S.

Metal Bulletin Handbook. London, Metal Bulletin Ltd. (annual).

Comprehensive worldwide coverage of prices and statistics on production, consumption and trade of nonferrous metals, iron and steel and scrap. Includes lists of ferrous and nonferrous associations by country; also brands, tariffs and other miscellaneous information at end.

Metallgesellschaft. *Metal Statistics.* Frankfurt am Main, West Germany (annual).

Worldwide statistics for nonferrous metals for an 11-year period.

Metal Statistics. New York, American Metal Market, Fairchild Publications (annual).

A very useful statistical annual. For each metal this usually gives U.S. consumption, production, shipments, foreign trade, prices, world production; also industry highlights or profiles for each metal and a short directory section at end.

Metals Week. New York, McGraw-Hill.

Useful principally for its current, weekly nonferrous metals prices on an international basis and also some daily prices. There is an annual compilation of prices called *Metals Week Price Handbook*. These daily and weekly price data and monthly averages of over 70 metals prices are also available through a computer time-sharing service.

Mining International Year Book. London.

Financial data for the world's principal mining and kindred companies, including property, capital, production, reserves.

National Coal Association. *Bituminous Coal Data.* Washington, D.C. (annual).

This gives bituminous coal production, coal markets/stocks/distribution, machines and efficiency, value and prices, reserves, manpower and safety, energy production and fuel use, etc. The NCA also publishes a biennial *Coal Facts* that gives brief facts about the coal industry with a statistical section covering some of the same basic areas as their annual but not in as much detail.

U.S. Bureau of Mines. *Minerals Yearbook.* Washington, D.C., U.S. Government Printing Office. 3 volumes.

Vol. 1, "Metals, Minerals and Fuels," contains chapters on all the metallic, nonmetallic and mineral fuel commodities important to the U.S. economy. The discussion and statistics for each include production, consumption, stocks, prices, foreign trade, technology, world review. Vol. 2, "Area Reports: Domestic," consists of chapters on the mineral industries of each state and U.S. possession and includes a list of principal producers in each state. Vol. 3, "Area Reports: International," gives the latest mineral data for over 130 foreign countries. Preprints are issued as each chapter is completed, and these are eventually superseded by the 3 bound volumes.

The Bureau of Mines issues several other useful statistical compilations. Their *Mineral Industry Surveys* are periodic (weekly, monthly, quarterly or annual) statistical releases giving production, consumption, stocks, etc., for over 80 individual metals, nonmetals and fuels. Their annual *Commodity Data Summaries* consists of 2-page summaries on 95 individual commodities discussing production, events/trends/world resources, salient statistics, government programs, tariff.

U.S. Bureau of the Census. *Census of Mineral Industries.* Washington, D.C., U.S. Government Printing Office (quinquennial, in years ending with 2 and 7).

Statistics on establishments engaged in extracting minerals for 42 4-digit SIC industries. The 1972 *Census* is in 2 volumes, with Vol. 1 containing the summary and the industry statistics and Vol. 2 the area data. Includes number of establishments, employment, payroll, man-hours, cost of materials, value of shipments, and capital expenditures; also quantity and value of materials consumed and products shipped.

There are other short statistical factbooks for more specialized metals industries, such as the Lead Industries Association's *Annual Review: U.S. Lead Industry* and the Zinc Institute's *Annual Review: U.S. Zinc Industry.*

PAPER AND ALLIED PRODUCTS

American Paper Institute. *Statistics of Paper and Paperboard.* 8th ed. New York, 1964. And annual supplements from 1967 to date.

Production and shipments for paper, paperboard, etc.; also financial data on the paper industry, labor statistics, statistics from the Census Bureau, statistics on the paper and allied products industry from GNP accounts.

American Paper Institute. Pulp, Fiber & Raw Materials Group. *Wood Pulp and Fiber Statistics.* New York (annual).

This gives capacity, production, consumption, foreign trade, with Section 1 covering the United States; Section 2, foreign countries; Section 3, other fibers; Section 4, world summaries.

National Paper Trade Association. *Paper Merchant Performance.* New York (annual).

Operating statistics for printing paper, industrial paper and dual paper merchants; also charts and brief text.

Noble, Patricia, ed. *Marketing Guide to the Paper and Pulp Industry.* 2d ed. (Kline Industrial Marketing Guide, IMG-10-73.) Fairfield, N.J., C. H. Kline & Co., 1973.

Economic analysis of the industry, including statistics, information sources, estimated sales by product line for the 400 leading U.S. paper companies.

Paper Trade Journal. New York, Vance Publishing Corp. (semi-monthly).

This is a leading trade journal, with one-page statistical "Trends" in each issue. Indexed in BPI, F&S.

Printing and Publishing. Washington, D.C., U.S. Bureau of Domestic Commerce, Department of Commerce (quarterly). Order from U.S. Government Printing Office.

Each issue gives production, employment, wages, foreign trade for the printing and publishing industry. There is also usually a feature article or two with statistics. Indexed in F&S.

Pulp & Paper. San Francisco, Calif., Miller Freeman Publications (monthly except semi-monthly in June).

The last June issue is a special "Profile of the North American Pulp and Paper Industry." It has sections for the United States and for Canada that discuss capacity and production trends and include some statistics. There are also company profiles, a few financial and production statistics for the 73 leading pulp and paper producers in the United States and Canada, world statistical trends, pulp trade (including a directory of world market pulp producers).

Pulp, Paper and Board. Washington, D.C., U.S. Bureau of Domestic Commerce, Department of Commerce (quarterly). Order from U.S. Government Printing Office.

Statistics for raw materials, production/consumption/shipments of pulp, board and paper products, employment, prices, foreign trade; also several varying statistical articles. Indexed in F&S.

The Bureau of the Census publishes a monthly *Current Industrial Report* that gives current production statistics for *Pulp, Paper and Board* (Series M26A).

PETROLEUM

For statistics on the gas utility industry see "Electric and Gas Utilities" in this chapter.

American Petroleum Institute. *Petroleum Facts and Figures.* Washington, D.C., 1971. Kept up to date by an *Annual Statistical Review.*

This contains over 500 pages of historical statistics on the U.S. petroleum industry, including production, refining, transportation, marketing and utilization, prices and taxation. Includes some worldwide statistics at end. The most important statistics are kept up to date by their *Annual Statistical Review: Petroleum Industry Statistics,* which each year includes an "Index of Industry Related Reference Material." The API also publishes a *Weekly Statistical Bulletin* and an annual *Gasoline Consumption in the United States.*

British Petroleum Co., Ltd. *BP Statistical Review of the World Oil Industry.* London (annual).

A short annual giving brief worldwide statistics and charts on petroleum reserves, production, consumption, trade, refining, tankers, energy.

Canadian Petroleum Association. *Statistical Year Book.* Calgary, Alberta, Canada.

Canadian statistics on consumption, crude oil, drilling, expenditures, natural gas, pipelines, prices, products, etc.

Chase Manhattan Bank. *Financial Analysis of a Group of Petroleum Companies.* New York (annual).

This short, annual financial study of 30 companies consists of brief text with charts. Chase Manhattan also publishes another annual pamphlet, *Capital Investments of the World Petroleum Industry.*

DeGolyer and MacNaughton. *Twentieth Century Petroleum Statistics.* Dallas, Tex. (annual).

Worldwide statistics and charts, arranged by country and covering oil production, reserves, demand, refining capacity, well completions, tank ships.

Financial Post. *Survey of Oils.* Montreal, Quebec, Canada (annual).

A Canadian financial manual reviewing vital data on crude oil and natural gas exploration, producing, refining and pipeline companies, both active and inactive.

Some statistics at front; also data on oil and gas fields by province, a 7-year price range of oil and gas stocks, maps of oil and gas areas.

Herold, John S., Inc. *Oil Industry Comparative Appraisals.* Greenwich, Conn. (loose-leaf monthly).

An international financial service for petroleum companies. Industry statistics are included with each issue. Their *Petroleum Outlook* is a monthly investment service and includes statistics, company analyses, price charts.

Independent Petroleum Association of America. *The Oil Producing Industry in Your State.* Washington, D.C. (annual).

A compilation of statistics taken from a variety of sources and arranged by state. Includes production and reserves, exploration and development. The IPA also publishes a bimonthly, *Petroleum Independent.*

National Petroleum News. New York, McGraw-Hill (monthly, and an extra mid-May issue).

A special "Factbook Issue" (mid-May) containing useful annual statistics on advertising, capital spending, distribution, the gasoline market, international data, LP-gas sales, operations, retail market, tires/batteries/accessories market, financial data for leading companies, share of market statistics. There is also a list of brand names, a directory of marketing management personnel, associations, U.S. refineries with capacity. Indexed in BPI, F&S.

Oil & Gas Journal. Tulsa, Okla., Petroleum Publishing Co. (weekly).

The "Forecast/Review" issue (last January each year) includes statistics on U.S. production, reserves, forecast of supply and demand, well forecast by state, rotary-rig activity by state; also a section on technology. Current API statistics are in each issue and also gasoline prices, worldwide crude-oil and gas production. This journal includes many other annual issues, e.g., "Annual Refining Issue," first April issue; "Offshore Report," first May; "Midyear Report/Worldwide Finance," last July; "Pipeline Economics and Progress," mid-August; "Annual Drilling Issue," mid-September; "Annual Production Number," last September; "Annual Pipeline Number," last October; "Worldwide Issue," last December. The dates of these issues may vary from year to year. The journal is indexed in BPI, F&S.

Oil & Petroleum International Year Book. London.

Financial details for leading oil companies of the world.

Platt's Oil Price Handbook and Oilmanac. New York, McGraw-Hill (annual).

A complete record of monthly prices for specific kinds of oil and gas at various locations. There is also a daily *Platt's Oilgram Price Service.*

U.S. Bureau of Mines. *Mineral Industry Surveys.* Washington, D.C.

Several numbers in this statistical series cover petroleum: *Petroleum Refineries in the United States* (annual); *Petroleum Products Survey* (irregular); *Petroleum Statement* (monthly).

World Oil. Houston, Tex. (monthly, with extra issues in February and August).

The 2 extra issues: "Annual Forecast-Review Issue" (Feb. 15) gives statistics and short range forecasts for supply and demand, drilling, well completions; also drilling costs, production, number of wells, U.S. reserves, world crude output; "International Outlook Issue" (Aug. 15) discusses trends in exploration, drilling and production by region and country. Indexed in BPI, F&S.

RUBBER AND SHOES

American Footwear Industries Association. *Footwear Manual.* Arlington, Va. (annual, with monthly statistical releases).
Sections cover manufacturing, labor, foreign trade, marketing, financial, ratios, raw materials. Includes some data for OECD countries.

Footwear News. New York, Fairchild Publications (weekly).
The weekly newspaper for the shoe trade. Each issue includes an "FN Stock Index" and current statistics on shoe stocks. An annual *Fact Book* is issued separately each year and includes consumer buying habits, U.S. footwear production and shipments, foreign trade; also independent shoe store operating and merchandising results. Indexed in F&S.

International Rubber Study Group. Secretariat. *Rubber Statistical Bulletin.* London (monthly).
Worldwide statistics on natural rubber, natural latex, synthetic rubber, reclaimed rubber, major sectors and end products, production, consumption, foreign trade. This organization also publishes a quarterly statistical release called *Rubber Statistical News Sheet.*

Rubber Age. New York, Palmerton Publishing Co. (monthly).
The "Review/Preview" issue (January) is a general assessment of the industry, with charts and statements on the outlook by a few executives. Indexed in ASTI, F&S.

Rubber Manufacturers Association. *Rubber Industry Facts.* New York (annual).
World and U.S. rubber statistics, U.S. vehicle and tire statistics, U.S. inner tube statistics, U.S. operating and financial ratios, expenditures for plant and equipment and for r&d. This association also publishes *RMA Rubber Report Statistical Highlights* (monthly) and *RMA Tire Report Statistical Highlights* (monthly).

Rubber World. New York, Rubber/Automotive Division of Hartman Communications, Inc. (monthly).
A list of prices of rubber ingredients appears semi-annually, usually in the March and September issues. A forecast article is often in the January issue.

The Bureau of the Census publishes a monthly *Current Industrial Report* giving production statistics for specific kinds of *Shoes and Slippers* (M31A).

TEXTILES AND APPAREL

Cotton-World Statistics. Washington, D.C., International Cotton Advisory Committee (quarterly).
Consists of world and country tables for supply and distribution, foreign trade, cotton yarn, cotton piece goods, man-made fibers, etc. This is received with *Cotton: Monthly Review of the World Situation,* which discusses recent trends and prospects.

Kayser-Roth Corp. *Financial Survey of Selected Companies.* New York (annual).
Selected key facts and figures on 112 leading apparel and related companies including textile companies, textile and apparel machinery, cosmetic companies, home furnishings, jewelry, etc. Much of the data is from company annual reports, including the president's letter and "Sources and Use of Funds Statement."

National Association of Hosiery Manufacturers. *Hosiery Statistics.* Charlotte, N.C. (annual).

Charts and annual tables for production and shipments by specific kind of hosiery; also foreign trade, plants, employment and other data.

Textile Hi-Lights. Washington, D.C., American Textile Manufacturers Institute (quarterly, with monthly supplements).

This gives statistics and charts for U.S. production and related data; also prices, consumption, labor, international trade.

Textile Organon. New York, Textile Economics Bureau (monthly).

The basic source for current statistics on U.S. man-made fibers. The January/February issue is an annual statistical summary for the previous year. The June issue, "World Man-Made Fiber Survey" gives world production of textile fibers, non-cellulosic fibers, rayon-acetate; also foreign trade and a directory of producers by country. There is a June supplement that has data in metric tons. Indexed in F&S, PAIS.

Textile World. New York, McGraw-Hill (monthly).

The January issue usually includes several articles on the textile outlook. The July issue is a "Buyer's Guide/Fact File" that includes varying U.S. and foreign statistics; also employment data and costs for plant site selections, financial statistics for 15 U.S. textile companies, names of trade associations; directory of suppliers, by products and services; lists of non-U.S. manufacturers with U.S. representatives, and U.S. representatives and their non-U.S. affiliates. Each issue contains "Textile Activity Indicators" and a pricing outlook. Indexed in BPI, F&S.

The Department of Agriculture publishes two "Situation" reports on textiles: *Cotton Situation* (5/yr.) and *Wool Situation* (semi-annual). The Bureau of the Census issues a number of separate reports in its *Current Industrial Reports* series for production of apparel and specific kinds of textile mill products.

TOBACCO AND CIGARS

Cigar Association of America. *Statistical Record Bulletin.* New York (loose-leaf, with periodic supplements).

A comprehensive statistical volume covering U.S. cigar production and consumption, cigar leaf tobacco production and prices, U.S. international trade, taxation of large cigars in the United States, general tobacco industry statistics.

U.S. Department of Agriculture. *Annual Report on Tobacco Statistics.* Washington, D.C.

This annual report is published as a number in the department's *Statistical Bulletin* series, and it covers leaf production, stocks, auction markets, manufactured products, tax rate, consumption, foreign trade. The Economic Research Service also publishes a quarterly *Tobacco Situation* for current data on tobacco products, foreign trade, the situation and outlook.

TRANSPORTATION AND EQUIPMENT

See also "Aerospace" and "Automobiles and Trucks" in this chapter. Books, bibliographies, financial manuals and periodicals on traffic and transportation are decribed in Chapter 20.

British Road Federation. *Basic Road Statistics.* London (annual).

British statistics on motor vehicles, road traffic, accidents, road transport, road mileage.

British Shipping Statistics. London, Chamber of Shipping of the United Kingdom (annual).

Statistics on the world merchant fleet; merchant ships owned and registered in the United Kingdom; shipbuilding; overseas earnings; world and U.K. seaborne trade; freights and costs.

International Union of Railways. *International Railway Statistics.* Paris (annual).

Statistical data for specific railroads of the world, including lines and tracks, rolling stock, technical operating results, financial results.

Railway Age. Bristol, Conn., Simmons-Boardman (semi-monthly).

The "Review of (year) Railroad Operations" (second January issue) includes financial and operating statistics, capital expenditures, inventory, labor, etc.; also car and locomotive orders and signaling statistics, outlook for the coming year. Carloading statistics are in each issue. Indexed in BPI, F&S, PAIS.

Transportation Association of America. *Transportation Facts & Trends.* Washington, D.C. (annual).

A statistical analysis to illustrate the importance of transportation to the United States and to point out trends in the field. Detailed source data information is at end.

U.S. Bureau of the Census. *Census of Transportation.* Washington, D.C., U.S. Government Printing Office. (quinquennial, in years ending with 2 and 7).

The 1972 census consists of 3 independent surveys. The *Truck Inventory and Use Survey* collected data on the physical characteristics and operational use of the nation's private and commercial trucks based on a sample of 114,000 registered trucks. It includes number of vehicles, major use, vehicle miles, model and body type, type of fuel, range of operation, etc. The *National Travel Survey* provides profiles of the volume and characteristics of nonlocal travel based on a sample of 24,000 civilian households in the United States. Information includes means of transport, purpose of trip, number of persons taking trips, characteristics of traveler. The *Commodity Transportation Survey* reports on a sample that provides statistics on the volume and characteristics of intercity commodity shipments originated by manufacturers. It covers ton-miles, means of transport, length of haul, commodity, weight of shipment, origin and destination areas.

U.S. Federal Highway Administration. *Highway Statistics.* Washington, D.C., U.S. Government Printing Office (annual).

Brings together statistics in 3 major areas of highway transportation: highway use (ownership and operating of motor vehicles, motor fuel, federal taxes); highway finance (receipts and expenditures for highways by public agencies); the highway plant (changing characteristics of the mileage of highways, roads and streets).

U.S. Interstate Commerce Commission. Bureau of Accounts. *Transport Statistics in the United States.* Washington, D.C., U.S. Government Printing Office. 9 parts in 6 sections (annual).

Financial and operating data for each mode of transportation. Part 1 covers railroads and includes REA Express, Inc., and electric railways: Part 5, carriers by water; Part 6, pipelines; Part 7, motor carriers; Part 8, freight forwarders; Part 9, private car lines. The ICC publishes many other financial statistical publications including *Financial and Operating Statistics of Class 1 Railroads in the United States* (semi-annual); *Freight Commodity Statistics . . . Class 1 Railroads in the United States* (annual).

Yearbook of Railroad Facts. Washington, D.C., Association of American Railroads, Economics and Finance Department.

This annual includes statistics on financial results, traffic, train and car miles, operating averages, plant and equipment, capital expenditures, employment and wages, price and wage index, Amtrak and auto-train statistics. The AAR publishes other statistics: *Operating and Traffic Statistics* (annual); *Railroad Revenues, Expenses and Income, Class 1 Railroads in the United States* (quarterly); *Statistics of Railroads of Class 1 in the United States* (annual).

COMMODITY AND CONSUMER PRICES

Commodity Prices

Commodity prices can be found in many of the statistical volumes mentioned in this chapter. Several of the trade journals quote current prices in each issue for commodities of principal interest to their industry. See, for example, *Chemical Marketing Reporter* for prices of many chemicals, oils, drugs, and related products; *Journal of Commerce and Commercial,* a daily newspaper that quotes current prices for important food, grain, textile, metal, and other commodities; *Metals Week,* for weekly prices of many nonferrous metals. In addition, some journals include prices less frequently, such as those for building materials in the "Quarterly Cost Roundup" issues of *Engineering News Record,* or the semi-annual prices of rubber ingredients in *Rubber World.* Price data is also given in statistical publications of several government agencies, for example, U.S. Bureau of Labor Statistics, *Wholesale Prices and Price Indexes* (monthly), and the U.S. Crop Reporting Board, *Agricultural Prices* (monthly).

Bibliographies

Wasserman, Paul and Diane Kemmerling. *Commodity Prices.* Detroit, Mich., Gale Research Co., 1974.

This is "a source book and index providing reference to wholesale and retail quotations for more than 5,000 agricultural, commercial, industrial, and consumer products." It is arranged alphabetically by commodity and covers prices quoted currently in many U.S. and Canadian publications.

Consumer Prices

Although consumer prices are an important economic indicator rather than an industrial indicator it seems logical to discuss a few of the sources for statistics here in this section on pricing. The Consumer Price Index is a monthly measure of changes in the prices of a fixed list of goods and services purchased by urban families and individuals. Although it is often called the "cost of living index" there is a difference, since the CPI measures only one of several important factors affecting living costs (price change). The principal source for the CPI is:

U.S. Bureau of Labor Statistics. *CPI Detailed Report.* Washington, D.C. (monthly).

This gives the "consumer price index U.S. and city averages" for specific food items, for housing (including rent, fuel and utilities), specific apparel and upkeep, transportation (including new and used automobiles), health and recreation (including medical care, personal care, reading), tobacco products, alcoholic beverages, financial services. These figures are also quoted in other BLS publications, such as the *Monthly Labor Review* and the historical *Handbook of Labor Statistics*. Although the CPI does include figures for 23 U.S. cities, these indexes do not measure differences in the level of prices among these several cities, they only measure the average change in prices for each area as compared with the base period of the index.

Several sources for living costs are: two quarterly *Cost of Living Indicators* published by the American Chamber of Commerce Researchers Association (Nashville, Tenn.): one is a *Price Report,* which gives the dollar and cents values of 25 food items and 18 nonfood items in 169 cities; the other is an *Inter-City Index Report,* which is a comparative index (with the U.S. average equaling 100) for 6 broad categories of products and services in these 169 cities (It should be noted that not all large cities in the United States are included); and an annual statistical release of the Bureau of Labor Statistics on *Urban Family Budgets and Comparative Indexes for Selected Urban Areas,* which gives annual costs of a hypothetical 4-person family with a lower, intermediate and higher budget for the broad categories in the consumer price index (food, housing, transportation, clothing, personal care, medical care, and other family consumption) in 39 cities, as well as an index of comparative costs. The index tables also appear annually in the BLS *Monthly Labor Review* as "Family Budgets" (see June 1975 issue, formerly August).

Foreign consumer price indexes are included in the several foreign labor sources mentioned in Chapter 19. Worldwide comparative cost of living figures are in the following:

Monthly Bulletin of Statistics. New York, United Nations.

The February and August issues each year contain a special table for "Retail Price Indexes Relating to Living Expenditures of United Nation Officials." This consists of a living-cost index by country, with New York City being the base city equaling 100. It also gives exchange rates.

Schweizerische Bankgesellschaft. *Prices and Earnings Around the Globe.* Zurich (annual).

This informative little brochure discusses and compares purchasing power in 37 cities of the world and includes tables giving comparative prices for food and beverages, clothing, apartment rents, restaurants and hotels, newspaper subscriptions, automobile prices, transportation. An appendix gives comparative earnings and working hours for 6 categories of workers.

U.S. Department of State. *Indexes of Living Costs Abroad and Living Quarters Allowances.* Washington, D.C. (quarterly).

An index similar to the one published by the UN above, but using Washington, D.C., as the base city equaling 100.

Business International offers a series of *Survey of Living Costs* for 47 cities. These are usually 6-page statistical tables of costs for specific items such as household supplies, personal care, clothing, transportation and education. It is kept up to date but is quite expensive to purchase.

Purchasing Power of the Dollar

Purchasing power of the dollar is a reciprocal of the price index and can be computed from either the wholesale or consumer price indexes depending upon whether one wants prices at the primary market level or the consumer level (divide the price index number for the base period by the price index number for the date to be compared and express the result in dollars and cents). This has already been computed and tables can be found in several of the basic statistical compilations in Chapter 4, for example, *Statistical Abstract of the United States; Standard & Poor's Trade and Securities: Statistics;* the biennial *Business Statistics* published by the U.S. Department of Commerce for historical statistics, with current figures in their *Survey of Current Business.*

6

FOREIGN STATISTICS AND ECONOMIC TRENDS

Foreign Economics Conditions — Basic International Statistics — Financial Statistics and Balance of Payments — Foreign Trade Statistics — National Income Statistics — Production Statistics — Social Statistics — Regional Economic and Financial Data — Bibliographies and Indexes

This chapter concentrates on basic publications covering foreign economic statistics and foreign economic trends. The various foreign tax and trade guides and reference data for exporters can be found in Chapter 16 with books and other material on international management. These trade guides contain useful summaries of the various factors affecting trade and investment in each country, including information on the government, laws dealing with finance, labor, licensing, taxation. A few sources for foreign labor statistics are in Chapter 19. Financial manuals covering foreign companies are in Chapter 7, and directories of foreign companies are in Chapter 3.

FOREIGN ECONOMIC CONDITIONS

Economist Intelligence Unit. *Quarterly Economic Reviews.* London.

The EIU publishes 77 separate concise, quarterly reviews covering economic and business conditions and prospects for over 150 countries. They discuss the political scene, the economy, trade and finance, government, economic plans and policies, major investment projects, etc. In each issue there are indicators of economic activity, foreign trade statistics and a few graphs.

EIU also publishes a number of more specialized publications: (1) *European Trends* (quarterly) for reports and current news about policies and issues concerning the European economy; (2) *Marketing in Europe* (monthly), which studies markets for specific consumer products in Europe, including statistics for food/drink/tobacco, clothing/furniture/leisure goods, domestic appliances/household and chemical goods; (3) *Multinational Business* (quarterly), consisting of several articles and news on international management; (4) *Retail Business* (monthly), which is concerned with consumer goods markets, marketing, management and distribution in the United Kingdom and often includes reviews of specific kinds of retail businesses, special reports of industries, with statistics included; (5) *World Commodity Outlook* for current worldwide trends in 36 metals, fibers, cereals, oilseeds and oils, beverages, and miscellaneous commodities; (6) *International Tourism Quarterly* and quarterlies for *Paper & Packaging Bulletin; Motor Business; Rubber Trends.*

Europa Year Book. London, Europa Publications. 2 volumes (annual).

This is an international reference work rather than an economic review, but it is packed so full of useful data that it deserves mention here as well as in Chapter 16. It is an international encyclopedia, with Vol. 1 covering international organizations and Europe and Vol. 2 covering Africa, the Americas, Asia and Australasia. For each country the data includes recent history, basic economic statistics, constitution, government, political parties, religion. There are also lists of the various media, financial institutions, trade and industrial organizations, transportation companies and universities. Europa publishes 3 regional yearbooks: *Africa South of the Sahara; The Far East and Australasia; The Middle East and North Africa.* These give much the same information for each country and also contain a "who's who" section on prominent people in each country covered by these yearbooks.

Organization for Economic Cooperation and Development. *OECD Economic Surveys.* Paris (annual).

Separate annual reviews for each of the 24 OECD member countries provide a discussion of recent trends, economic policy, prospects for the coming year. A "statistical annex" usually contains statistics for basic economic indicators, such as national product and expenditures, employment and the labor market, foreign trade, balance of payments, money and credit — usually for a 10-year period — plus a folded table of international comparisons. The OECD publishes an *OECD Economic Outlook* (semi-annual), which surveys latest developments and assesses future prospects. This is supplemented by "Occasional Studies." The various important OECD statistical volumes are described in the following sections of this chapter. The OECD has also published studies on many industries of interest to member countries, including annuals for cement, chemical, iron and steel, nonferrous metals, pulp and paper, and textile industries.

United Nations. Department of Economic and Social Affairs. *World Economic Survey.* New York (annual).

This annual survey reviews current trends in the world economy and in the developed market economies, in the centrally planned economies, in developing countries. Some statistics on production and trade are included.

The UN is organized into separate "Economic and Social Commissions" for the various geographic regions (Africa, Asia and the Pacific, Europe, Latin America), and they each publish various economic bulletins or surveys reviewing and analyzing developments in countries of the region. Some of the most important UN statistical publications are described later in this chapter. For citations to all UN publications consult the descriptions of UN publications listed at the end of this chapter.

U.S. Bureau of International Commerce, Department of Commerce. *Foreign Economic Trends and Their Implications for the United States.* Washington, D.C., U.S. Government Printing Office. (semi-annual or annual series of reports).

This is a continuing series of brief reports for over 100 countries covering the current economic situation, trends, and their implications for the United States. These are compiled by the various U.S. embassies abroad, and each includes a table of "Key

Economic Indicators." These reports are indexed in *Index to International Business Publications,* described at the end of this chapter.

U.S. Domestic and International Business Administration, Department of Commerce. *Overseas Business Reports.* Washington, D.C., U.S. Government Printing Office.

A useful series of reports on about 100 countries. Many are "Market Profiles" of the country that include industry trends, data on the tariff system, trade regulations, taxes, transportation, credit, direct foreign investment, business etiquette, and a bibliography of sources of economic and commercial information.

Several other DIBA series are: (1) *Global Market Surveys,* which are separate one-time studies on each of about 10 industries such as "Electronic Components," "Metalworking and Finishing Equipment"; (2) *Market Share Reports,* a series of 74 country reports and 1,109 commodity reports (by standard international trade classification [SITC] number) providing basic data to help exporters evaluate trends in the market, changes in import demand, etc. The Department of Commerce bi-weekly, *Commerce America,* is of interest for both its domestic and international news, and it is described in Chapter 16. Most of the reports listed above are indexed by country in *Index to International Business Publications,* described at the end of this chapter.

There are two other types of information source about countries that are described elsewhere: (1) yearbooks, some covering all countries such as the *Statesman's Year-Book,* and others on individual countries (see Chapter 1 for several examples); and (2) various country-by-country tax and trade guides, providing brief but useful facts about each country and meant for companies considering doing business in that country (see Chapter 16).

BASIC INTERNATIONAL STATISTICS

Business International Corporation. *BI/DATA.* New York.

This is a new (1974) on-line international statistical data base made available on General Electric's Worldwide Mark III Network. It analyzes economic trends and risk factors in 70 key countries, providing instant access to more than 130 time series, from 1960 to the present, with annual data on national accounts (including gross domestic product, personal consumption components), demographic and labor statistics, interest and exchange rates, wholesale and consumer prices indexes, foreign trade, industrial production. It also includes short-term forecasts covering key indicators of economic activity for the leading 30 markets of the world.

Demographic Yearbook. New York, United Nations.

Statistics on population, natality, mortality, life expectancy, marriages, divorces for almost 250 geographical entities; with special topic tables giving country-by-country population by age, sex, religion, literacy, educational attainment, etc.

International Marketing Data and Statistics. London, Euromonitor Publications, Ltd. (annual).

The first edition of this companion volume to *European Marketing Data and Statistics* is scheduled for publication in January 1976. It will contain statistics similar to that publication (see descriptive note in "Europe" section below) for 43 key countries outside Europe.

United Nations. *Statistical Yearbook.* New York.

This is a basic reference work for statistics on all UN countries. The sections cover: population, manpower, agriculture, production, mining, manufacturing, construction, energy, foreign trade, transport, communications, consumption, balance of payments, wages and prices, national accounts, finance, public finance, development assistance, health, housing, education, science and technology, culture. Current figures are in their *Monthly Bulletin of Statistics.*

Worldcasts. Cleveland, Ohio, Predicasts, Inc. 8 volumes (quarterly).

This detailed and expensive service gives both short- and long-range forecast statistics for basic economic indicators of specific countries and also for industries outside the United States. Its 8 volumes are in 2 parts: *World Region Casts* (4 volumes covering: the Common Market; other Europe; Americas exclusive of United States.; Africa, Asia and Oceania); *World Product Casts* (4 volumes for: General Economics; Utilities and Services; Extractive, Food, Textiles, Wood and Paper; Chemicals, Polymers, Drugs, Oil, Rubber and Glass; Metals, Equipment and Electronics). Any of these 8 volumes can be subscribed to separately. Like its companion series covering the United States (*Predicasts*), this includes the date and page reference of the current journal, government report or special study from which each statistic is taken, so it is a useful index as well as a statistical source. By the end of 1975 *Worldcasts* will also be available via the *Predicasts Terminal System* (described in Chapter 2).

There are a number of sources for brief summary statistics on a worldwide basis. One is the *World Business Outlook* (New York, McGraw-Hill, annual), which gives country-by-country totals from 1964 for GNP, index of industrial production, wholesale price index and cement/electricity/crude steel production. Another is a two-part folded table of *Indicators of Market Size for 131 Countries* (New York, Business International Corp. annual), which is a handy compilation of totals by country for one year (with a 5-year percentage increase), Part 1 covering population, national accounts, and international trade and Part 2 focusing on private expenditures, passenger cars, trucks and buses in use, and other pertinent indicators, such as steel, cement, energy, telephones, motor vehicles and the broadcast media. These BI tables are first printed each year in the four December issues of *Business International,* and then they are reprinted as a separate table.

Asia

United Nations. Economic and Social Commission for Asia and the Pacific. *Statistical Yearbook for Asia and the Pacific.* Bangkok, Thailand. Order from the UN.

Statistics are by country, often for an 11-year period, and cover population, manpower, national accounts, agriculture, forestry and fishing, industry, consumption, transport and communication, foreign trade, wages, prices and household expenditures, finance and social statistics. A list of principal sources is at end.

Europe

European Marketing Data and Statistics. London, Euromonitor Publications, Ltd. (annual).

Includes statistics for population, manpower, employment, natural resources, production, foreign trade, standard of living (including prices and expenditures), the consumer (consumption of specific products), for European countries; also statistics on factors in European society such as housing, health, education, media, politics, leisure.

Federal Reserve Bank of St. Louis. *Rates of Change in Economic Data for Ten Industrial Countries.* St. Louis, Mo. (quarterly and annual).

Statistical tables cover rate of change during about 15 years for money supply, price indexes, employment, measures of output and international trade. European countries included are Belgium, France, Germany, Italy, Netherlands, Switzerland, the United Kingdom. Other countries are Canada, Japan and the United States.

Organization for Economic Cooperation and Development. *Main Economic Indicators.* Paris (monthly).

A current guide to recent basic economic and financial statistics for the 24 OECD countries. A separate section contains foreign trade indicators. Includes a quarterly supplement for *Industrial Production.* There is a separate biennial that covers statistics for the past 11 years called *Main Economic Indicators: Historical Statistics.* Computer tapes are also available for this economic time series, beginning with 1955.

Statistical Office of the European Communities. (Eurostat). *Almen Statistik (General Statistics).* Brussels (monthly).

Current economic statistics both for the original 6 European Communities countries and also for the present 9 countries (adding Denmark, Ireland, and the United Kingdom). Includes population and labor, national accounts, industrial production, foreign trade, prices/wages, finances, balance of payments. The titles of all EUROSTAT publications are in 6 languages, and the text is usually in 2 languages.

United Nations. Economic Commission for Europe. *Statistical Indicators of Short Term Economic Changes in ECE Countries.* New York (monthly).

Country-by-country economic and financial indicators for the 32 ECE countries, to show current monthly trends.

U.S. Domestic and International Business Administration, Department of Commerce. *International Economic Indicators and Competitive Trends.* Washington, D.C., U.S. Government Printing Office (quarterly).

A new quarterly (1974) that contains charts and statistical tables for economic indicators and trends in the United States and in its 7 principal industrial competitors (France, Federal Republic of Germany, Italy, Netherlands, United Kingdom, Japan and Canada). In 4 parts: general indicators, trade indicators, price indicators, finance indicators. Sources for statistics are at end.

Latin America

Organizacion de los Estados Americanos. *America en Cifras.* Washington, D.C. (biennial).

This is a multi-volume statistical work, with the Latin American economic situation covered in 5 volumes: agriculture, hunting and fishing; industry; trade, services, transport, communication and tourism; balance of payments, national product, national income and finance; prices, wages, consumption and other economic statistics. Still other volumes contain demographic, social and cultural statistics.

University of California, Los Angeles. Latin American Center. *Statistical Abstract of Latin America.* Los Angeles (annual).

A useful compilation of over 500 pages containing statistics relating to demography, manpower/wages/prices, health and welfare, education, agriculture, mining and industry, transportation and communicatiqns, national accounts, foreign trade and finance. A bibliography of sources is at end. There are also 5 numbers in a supplementary series to cover special topics, such as political statistics, urbanization, land reform.

FINANCIAL STATISTICS AND BALANCE OF PAYMENTS

International Financial Statistics. Washington, D.C., International Monetary Fund (monthly, with annual supplements).

For each country this gives statistics on exchange rate, international liquidity, money and bank statistics, interest, prices, production, international transactions, government finance. Daily exchange rates, exchange transactions, international reserves, changes in money, etc., are in comparative tables at front. This monthly is published in English, French and Spanish editions, and it is also available on computer tapes.

International Monetary Fund. *Balance of Payments Yearbook.* Washington, D.C. (loose-leaf, with monthly supplements).

Five-year detailed balance of payments statistics for about 100 countries, including statistics for goods, services and unrequited transfers; capital; allocation of special drawing rights (SDRs); reserves and related items — with notes to the tables accompanying each country. This data is also available on computer tapes.

International Monetary Market Year Book. Chicago, The Staff of IMM.

Daily futures prices during one year for the currencies of 10 countries traded on the IMM; also silver and gold prices and bank interest tables.

Organization for Economic Cooperation and Development. *OECD Financial Statistics.* Paris (semi-annual, with bimonthly supplements).

Part 1 is the major section and consists of country tables for each OECD country giving lending and borrowing rates; supply and demand for capital on the security market; value of outstanding securities; security issues; central government finance. Part 2 covers the international market, and Part 3 has comparative tables.

Pick's Currency Yearbook. New York, Pick Publishing Corp.

For each country, this gives complete descriptions of over 100 currencies, including history, currency varieties, transferability, currency administration, statistics on currency in circulation outside banks, official exchange rates. Includes also a section on the Eurodollar market, on gold — its prices and movements in 38 international trading centers.

Statistical Office of the European Communities (EUROSTAT). *Zahlungsbilanzen (Balances of Payments).* Brussels (annual).

Section 1 contains comparative tables; Section 2, country tables; Section 3, tables for selected items; Section 4, statistical tables.

U.S. Board of Governors of the Federal Reserve System. *Federal Reserve Bulletin.* Washington, D.C., U.S. Government Printing Office (monthly).

There is a short section for "International Statistics" in each issue of this important financial bulletin, and it contains balance of payments, foreign trade, U.S. reserve assets, gold reserves of central banks and governments, international capital transactions, open market rates, foreign exchange rates.

U.S. Department of Commerce. *Survey of Current Business.* Washington, D.C., U.S. Government Printing Office (monthly).

Besides being very useful for current domestic statistics this important monthly contains feature articles with statistics on topics of interest to international business. These are: (1) "Aspects of International Investment" (Part 2 of August 1974 issue), contains articles with statistics on the international investment position of the United States, foreign direct investment in the United States, U.S. direct investment abroad, and sales of majority-owned foreign affiliates of U.S. companies (In 1975 these articles appear in issues for August and October); (2) "Balance of Payments Developments" (usually quarterly in March, June, September, December); (3) "International Travel and Passenger Fares in the U.S. Balance of Payments" (annual, e.g., May 1974); (4) "Property, Plant and Equipment Expenditures by Majority-Owned Foreign Affiliates of U.S. Companies" (semi-annual, e.g., March and September 1974).

World Currency Charts. San Francisco, Calif., American International Investment Corp. (annual).

Folded graphs and statistics by country for currencies of 65 countries, often covering from 1929 to date. Gives par value, annual average official exchange rate.

World Financial Markets. New York, Morgan Guaranty Trust Co. (monthly).

An excellent bank letter on international financial and monetary developments, with a "Statistical Appendix" containing tables and some charts on Eurodollar deposit rates, money market rates, bond yields by country, commercial bank deposits and lending rates, etc.; also a list of new international bond issues.

Individual foreign governments and foreign banks also publish useful financial statistics. Several examples are given with "Regional Economic and Financial Data," later in this chapter.

FOREIGN TRADE STATISTICS

United Nations trade statistics are arranged by an SITC commodity number, which provides internationally comparable categories for the economic analysis of trade. This scheme is explained in United Nations Statistical Office, *Statistical Paper, Series M, No. 38: Commodity Indexes for the Standard International Trade Classification, Revised* (New York, 1963, 2 volumes). Vol. 1 is a list by revised SITC number and describes the commodities included under each number; Vol. 2 is an alphabetical index. The original SITC system was begun in 1950 and the revised scheme replaced it in 1960. *Statistical Paper Series M,* No. 34 (United Nations, 1961) describes the revised scheme and gives related headings of the original SITC.

Direction of Trade. Washington, D.C., International Monetary Fund and International Bank for Reconstruction and Development (monthly and annual).

Gives monthly and annual statistics for value of exports and imports in U.S. dollars and arranged by country. This data is also available on computer tapes.

Food and Agriculture Organization of the United Nations. *Trade Yearbook.* Rome.

Export and import statistics of food and agricultural commodities arranged by SITC number, and covering each country for a 12-year period.

Organization for Economic Cooperation and Development. *Foreign Trade Statistics Bulletins.* Paris.

These consist of 3 separate series: Series A, *Statistics of Foreign Trade* (monthly) gives total trade by country and area of origin and destination; Series B, *Trade by Commodities, Country Summaries* (quarterly) gives trade for member countries by main SITC categories; Series C, *Trade by Commodities, Market Summaries* (annual) gives imports (in 2 volumes) and exports (in 3 volumes) by main SITC commodities and partner countries. This data is also available on computer tapes.

Statistical Office of the European Communities (EUROSTAT). *Aussenhandel, Monatsstatistik (Foreign Trade, Monthly Statistics).* Brussels.

Statistics are on intra-EC trade, extra-EC trade, trade by commodity groups; also EC trade in agricultural products.

United Nations. Statistical Office. *Yearbook of International Trade Statistics.* New York.

Annual export and import statistics for 139 countries, with figures for each country given by SITC commodity number and covering about 4 years. Current quarterly statistics are in its *Commodity Trade Statistics* (published irregularly as the UN's *Statistical Papers, Series D*).

World Trade Annual. Prepared by the Statistical Office of the United Nations. New York, Walker & Co. 5 volumes.

Detailed foreign trade statistics for one year, by SITC number and then by country. Gives both quantity and dollar value.

NATIONAL INCOME STATISTICS

Organization for Economic Cooperation and Development. *National Account Statistics.* Paris (annual).

This gives 10-year statistics for national account aggregates by country, with separate tables covering rates of change for selected aggregates. Beginning with the volume for 1973 this annual is issued in several volumes as data for groups of countries become available. Hopefully this will eliminate previous long delays in publishing. A new *Quarterly National Accounts* is scheduled for publication beginning in late 1975.

Statistical Office of the European Communities. (EUROSTAT). *Volkswirtschaftliche Gesamtrechnungen (National Accounts).* Brussels (annual).

Comparative national income figures usually for a 30-year period, for EC member countries and also Japan and the United States.

United Nations. Statistical Office. *Yearbook of National Accounts Statistics.* New York. 3 volumes.

Volumes 1-2 contain detailed national account statistics for 121 countries and areas and include gross domestic product and expenditures, national income and national disposable income, capital transactions of the nation, etc., for a 12-year period. Vol. 3 covers "International Tables."

Some individual foreign countries also publish national income studies, for example, Statistics Canada's *System of National Accounts: National Income and*

Expenditure Accounts (quarterly and annual); and Great Britain, Central Statistical Office, *National Income and Expenditure of the United Kingdom* (annual).

PRODUCTION STATISTICS

Food and Agriculture Organization of the United Nations. *Production Yearbook.* Rome.

Annual data on population, index of agricultural production, crops, livestock, means of production, food supplies, prices and wages. Statistics cover the most recent 3 years and a 5-year average prior to that. The FAO's *Monthly Bulletin of Agricultural Economics and Statistics* gives current production, trade and prices. The *FAO Commodity Review and Outlook* (annual) summarizes production and trade developments of major agricultural commodities and includes some statistics.

Organization for Economic Cooperation and Development. *Industrial Production: Historical Statistics.* Paris (biennial).

Historical production statistics by OECD country by product for a 17-year period, with 1971 the latest year covered as of spring 1975. Current statistics are in a quarterly "Industrial Production" supplement to the OECD's *Main Economic Indicators.* This data is also available on computer tapes.

Statistical Office of the European Communities (EUROSTAT). *Industriestatistik, Jahrbuch (Industrial Statistics, Yearbook).* Brussels.

Production statistics on about 500 products for each EC country, covering several years. This is brought up to date by a quarterly called *Industrial Statistics.*

United Nations. Statistical Office. *The Growth of World Industry.* New York. 2 volumes (annual).

Vol. 1, "General Industrial Statistics" gives 10-year industry data for each country, including basic indicators of industrial activitiy, number of establishments, number of employees, wages and hours, cost of goods and materials, value added. Vol. 2 contains detailed "Commodity Production Data" also for a 10-year period and arranged by an ISIC code (International Standard Industrial Classification; for more information about this classification scheme refer to UN Statistical Office, *Statistical Paper, Series M, No. 4, Revised*).

SOCIAL STATISTICS

Great Britain. Central Statistical Office. *Social Trends.* London, H. M. Stationery Office (annual).

U.K. statistics, charts and explanatory text on population, employment, leisure, personal income and wealth, personal expenditure, health, education, housing, environment, justice and law, resources. Includes an international section at end.

Statistical Office of the Economic Communities (EUROSTAT). *Jahrbuch der Sozialstatistik (Social Statistics, Annual).* Brussels.

For EC countries this covers population, employment and unemployment, hours worked and industrial disputes, wages, standard of living, education, social accounts, industrial accidents. EUROSTAT also publishes *Sozialstatistik (Social Statistics)* (6/yr.), which gives current statistics.

United Nations Educational, Scientific and Cultural Organization. *Statistical Yearbook (Annuaire Statistique).* Louvain, Belgium.
Detailed statistical tables for education; also statistics on population, science and technology, culture and communication (including libraries and museums, book production, newspapers and other periodicals, paper consumption, film and cinema, radio broadcasting, TV).

REGIONAL ECONOMIC AND FINANCIAL DATA

It is impossible to cover all of the important sources for economic and financial data on every country. This section only mentions several kinds of information that will be useful and includes a few titles primarily as examples. To find other information the bibliographies at the end of this chapter will be helpful. Use of a large public or university library may be of value in searching for books on countries, as well as lists of foreign government publications, lists of publications of the various regional organizations such as the UN, names of foreign trade associations (several directories are listed in Chapter 3), names of foreign trade journals, indexes to foreign journal articles, etc. Consulting with a reference librarian may also be beneficial in tracing specific data.

Statistical Yearbooks of Foreign Governments

Many countries publish excellent statistical annuals, similar to the one published in this country, which abstract the more important statistics and sometimes include bibliographical sources at the foot of each table. Several examples from different parts of the world are:

Brazil. Departmento de Divulgação Estatística. *Anuário Estatística do Brasil.* Rio de Janeiro.
Germany (Democratic Republic). *Statistisches Jahrbuch.* Berlin, Staatsverlag der Deutschen Demokratischen Republik.
Great Britain. Central Statistical Office. *Annual Abstract of Statistics.* London, H. M. Stationery Office. (Includes index of sources by subject.)
Japan. Bureau of Statistics. *Japan Statistical Yearbook.* Tokyo.
United Arab Republic. Central Agency for Public Mobilization and Statistics. *Statistical Handbook.* Cairo (annual).

Yearbooks published for individual countries are useful for their reviews of the economic, social and political developments in that country. Several examples are given in Chapter 2.

Monthly and Quarterly Statistical Publications

The governments of many countries also publish good periodic reviews that provide current monthly or quarterly statistics. Several examples are:

Belgium. Institut National de Statistique. *Statistiques Industrielle.* Brussels (bimonthly).
Canadian Statistical Review. Ottawa, Information Canada (monthly, with a weekly supplement).

France. Institut National de la Statistique et des Études Économiques. *Bulletin Mensuel de Statistique.* Paris (monthly).

Great Britain. Central Statistical Office. *Monthly Digest of Statistics.* London, H. M. Stationery Office. The Central Statistical Office publishes other useful current statistical publications including *Economic Trends* (monthly) and *Financial Statistics* (monthly).

India. Central Statistical Organisation. *Monthly Abstract of Statistics.* New Delhi.

Statistical Publications of Banks

Many banks publish bulletins or bank letters that are either partially or entirely statistical reviews. Several examples are:

Bank of Canada Review. Ottawa (monthly). Entirely statistical.
Bank of England. *Quarterly Bulletin.* London.
Banque Nationale de Belgique. *Bulletin.* Brussels (monthly). Entirely statistical.
Deutsche Bundesbank. *Monthly Report.* Frankfurt am Main.
South African Reserve Bank. *Quarterly Bulletin.* Cape Town.

Bank Letters

These are examples of short bank letters, which analyze current financial and economic trends. A bibliography of American and foreign bank letters is in the final stages of production by a group of U.S. bank librarians, with publication planned by Special Libraries Association in 1976.

Banco Nacional de México, S.A. *Review of the Economic Situation of Mexico.* Mexico City (monthly).
Bank Leumi Le-Israel B.M. *Economic Review.* Tel-Aviv (irregular).
Bank of Japan. *Monthly Economic Review.* Tokyo.
Bank of Montreal. *Business Review.* Montreal (monthly).
Barclays Bank. *Barclays Review.* London (quarterly).
Creditanstalt-Bankverein. *Economic Letter.* Vienna (monthly).
Kansallic-Osake-Pankki. *Economic Review.* Helsinki (quarterly).
Skandinaviska Enskilda Banken. *Quarterly Review.* Stockholm.

Data on Foreign Companies

Foreign financial manuals are described in Chapter 7. Directories of foreign companies are included in Chapter 3.

BIBLIOGRAPHIES AND INDEXES

Edwards, Bernard. *Sources of Economic and Business Statistics.* London, Heinemann, 1972.

This is a bibliographical guide to the effective use of British official statistical publications, with chapters covering each area, e.g., manpower and wage statistics, production and industrial statistics, national income and expenditure, family expenditure survey.

The monthly catalog of British *Government Publications* published by H. M. Stationery Office includes the titles of many U.K. statistical sources.

Encyclopedia of Business Information Sources. Vol. 2: Geographic Sources. Detroit, Mich., Gale Research Co., 1970.

For specific foreign countries (and also U.S. states and cities) this lists basic information sources such as statistical publications, directories, almanacs, periodicals (including bank letters), guides for doing business, bibliographies.

F & S International. Cleveland, Ohio, Predicasts, Inc. (monthly, with quarterly and annual cumulations).

A useful index for locating articles on foreign companies and industries that have appeared in many foreign and domestic periodicals. It is arranged in 3 parts: (1) by SIC number or product; (2) by region and country; (3) by company. Since many of the entries refer to very brief citations it is important to note that major articles are designated by a black dot, which precedes the name of the journal.

Harvey, Joan M. *Statistics — Europe: Sources for Market Research.* 2d ed. Beckenham, Kent, England, CBD Research Ltd., 1972 (Distributed in the U.S. by Gale Research Co., Detroit, Mich.). The 3d ed. is scheduled for publication late in 1975.

This and 3 companion volumes — for Africa (1970), for America (1973), for Asia and Australasia (1974) — are lists arranged by country for the principal statistical organizations and publications. These include the names of the central statistical offices, principal libraries, bibliographies of statistics and descriptive lists of major statistical publications in the following standard groups: general, production, external trade, internal distribution, population, standard of living.

International Bibliography, Information, Documentation. New York, R. R. Bowker/Unipub (quarterly).

A continuing annotated list of current publications of the UN System, arranged by broad subject.

International Executive. Hastings-on-Hudson, N.Y., Foundation for the Advancement of International Business Administration (3/yr.).

The second half of this useful abstracting journal is an annotated "Reference Guide," which describes books, pamphlets and articles of interest to the international businessman. It is arranged by broad management function, with the last section listing background sources on specific regions and countries. The other sections also contain some regional references.

Joint Library of the International Monetary Fund and International Bank for Reconstruction and Development. *List of Recent Additions.* Washington, D.C. (monthly).

Each issue lists, by country, the books on the country added to this joint library, including annual statistical abstracts and bank annual reports. A companion publication is *List of Recent Periodical Articles* (monthly).

Public Affairs Information Service: Foreign Language Index. New York (quarterly, with annual cumulations).

This companion index to PAIS is a selective subject index of periodicals and a few books, pamphlets, government publications, reports of public and private agencies, covering economics and public affairs materials in French, German, Italian, Portuguese and Spanish sources. It includes an author index in each issue and a list of periodicals covered at front.

Sources of European Economic Information. Epping, Essex, England, Gower Press/Bowker Publishing Co., 1974.

A good source for descriptions of foreign statistical data, economic surveys, bank letters, etc. It is arranged by country, and the short descriptions are written in 3 languages (English, French, German). An international section is at end.

United Nations. *UNDEX: United Nations Documents Index.* Series A, B and C. New York, 1974 (10/yr.).

Series C is the periodic "List of Documents Issued," which gives bibliographical descriptions of all documents and publications of the UN System received by the Dag Hammarskjold Library at UN headquarters in New York, except for restricted material. Series A is a "Subject Index" and Series B, a "Country Index."

United Nations. Industrial Development Organization. *UNIDO Guides to Information Sources.* New York.

To date (1975) UNIDO has published 15 separate bibliographies in this series to promote the use of industry information in developing countries. Each is on a different industry (cement, furniture, agricultural implements, pesticides, pulp and paper, etc.), and each is a selected, annotated list of directories, associations, handbooks, periodicals, abstracts, statistics, proceedings, dictionaries, bibliographies, etc., on each topic. UNIDO also publishes a bimonthly, *Industrial Development Abstracts.*

U.S. Domestic and International Business Administration, Department of Commerce. *Index to International Business Publications.* Washington, D.C. (annual?).

This indexes, by country, the DIBA publications in the following series: *Export Market Reports; Foreign Economic Trends; Global Market Surveys; Overseas Business Reports.* A separate monthly, *Index to Foreign Market Reports,* indexes the last three of these titles by country and by SIC, but is more difficult to use. The latest reports in these series are listed in *Commerce America.*

Winton, Harry N. M., comp. and ed. *Publications of the United Nations System: A Reference Guide.* New York, R. R. Bowker, 1972.

This is a useful guide to the basic publications of the UN System. Part 1 gives an overview of the organizations and their publications; Part 2 describes a number of valuable reference works in 29 subject areas; Part 3 describes periodicals.

Worldcasts. Cleveland, Ohio, Predicasts, Inc. 8 volumes (quarterly).

This service is also a useful index of current forecasting statistical sources both for foreign countries and for industries because it gives the date and page reference of the current journal, government report or special study from which the statistics were taken. Its 8 quarterly volumes are in 2 parts: *World Region Casts* and *World Product Casts.* For the titles of each volume consult the description that appears in the "International Statistics" section of this chapter.

7

INVESTMENT SOURCES

U.S. INVESTMENT INFORMATION SOURCES — Comprehensive Investment Services — Industry Surveys — Concise Statistical Data and Stock Prices — Charting Services — Dividends — Stock Price Indexes — Weekly Investment Advisory Services — Corporate Reports — Brokerage House Reports — Computerized Financial Data — Securities and Exchange Commission Publications — Capital Changes Services — New Security Offerings — Stock Exchange Publications — Lists of Largest U.S. Companies — Credit Rating Services — Investment Companies — Governments and Municipals — Guides to Financial Services and Statistics — Indexes to Financial Publications — Investment Newspapers and Periodicals — **FOREIGN INVESTMENT INFORMATION SOURCES** — International Investment Services — European Sources — U.K. Sources — Guides to Foreign Stock Exchanges — Lists of Largest Foreign Companies — Bibliographies and Indexes on Foreign Companies and Industries — **INVESTMENT MANAGEMENT BOOKS** — General Books on Investments — Security Analysis and Portfolio Management — The Stock Market and Investment Management Guides — Commodity Futures Trading — Bibliographies of Investment Books — Investment Dictionaries — Securities Regulation — Directories of the Securities Industry — Securities Industry Associations

Of equal importance with statistical data are the various investment sources, both for their current evaluations of industries and for their detailed analyses of companies. Probably no business activity is as well supplied with advisory and statistical publications as is the investment field. And in no other area is the presence of a good business/financial library more imperative, since most investment services are far too expensive for the individual pocketbook.

The serious investor is without exception a regular and frequent library user. Although he almost always heads for the same few services he has learned to trust, he will be the first to warn would-be investors that no *one* service is infallible — that it is important to become thoroughly familiar with several services as well as with corporate records, articles in leading journals, etc., before making an investment decision.

This chapter describes a selection of published investment information — financial manuals, advisory services, statistical data, corporate reports, indexes and journals. It concentrates primarily on data about U.S. companies, although there is a short section describing several basic foreign investment sources. This is followed by descriptions of a few good books on investment management.

U.S. INVESTMENT INFORMATION SOURCES

COMPREHENSIVE INVESTMENT SERVICES

The first two of these services are the most comprehensive and best known sources for financial information on American companies.

Moody's Investors Service. *Moody's Manuals.* New York. 6 volumes (annual, with semi-weekly supplements).

The titles of these 6 separate financial manuals are:
Moody's Bank and Finance Manual
Moody's Industrial Manual (2 volumes)
Moody's Municipal & Government Manual (2 volumes)
Moody's OTC Industrial Manual (weekly supplements)
Moody's Public Utilities Manual
Moody's Transportation Manual
Each of these important manuals covers U.S., Canadian and other foreign companies listed on U.S. exchanges. The information about each company usually includes a brief corporate history; a list of subsidiaries, principal plants and properties; business and products; officers and directors; comparative income statements, balance sheet statistics, selected financial ratios; description of outstanding securities. The center blue sections in each manual provide useful statistics, including a "Ten Year Price Range of Stocks and Bonds," Moody's averages, lists of largest companies.

Standard & Poor's Corp. *Standard Corporation Records.* New York. 6 volumes (loose-leaf, with bimonthly supplements).

This is an excellent financial service comparable to Moody's above, covering companies having both listed and unlisted securities. Its scope and subject matter are similar, but it is arranged differently and has a well-indexed *Daily News Section.* S & P also publishes a more specialized loose-leaf service for convertibles called *Convertible Bond Reports.*

Standard & Poor's Corp. *Stock Reports.* New York (loose-leaf, with semi-weekly supplements).

These stock reports are really 3 separate services with the following titles:
Over-the-Counter and Regional Exchange Stock Reports (4 volumes)
Standard A.S.E. Stock Reports (4 volumes)
Standard NYSE Stock Reports (4 volumes)

Each 2-page company report gives fundamental position, recent developments, earnings and balance sheet data, capitalization, prospects, etc.

Value Line Investment Survey. New York, A. Bernhard & Co. (loose-leaf, with weekly additions).

This popular investment service continuously analyzes and reports on about 1,500 stocks in 76 industries. The statistics, charts and brief explanatory text are reviewed and updated, industry-by-industry, on a rotating basis so that the information on each company in every industry is revised quarterly. Data includes a 10-year statistical history on 23 key investment factors plus future estimates for the next 3 to 5 years; also quarterly sales, earnings and dividends, Value Line ratings, review of latest developments and future prospects. Received with this service is a weekly letter called "Selection & Opinion," which gives views on business and the economic outlook, advice on investment policy, data on one "especially recommended stock," Value Line's stock price averages, etc. A new (1976) *Value Line Data Base* now makes easy access possible to detailed annual (some for about 20 years) and quarterly (from 1963) financial data and projections for these many companies, either via computer timesharing or magnetic tape. This publisher also issues 2 other services: the *Value Line OTC Special Situations Service,* a semi-monthly report; and *Value Line Convertible Survey,* a weekly statistical evaluation of convertibles and warrants.

Walker's Manual of Western Corporations & Securities. San Francisco, Calif. 3 volumes (annual).

A financial manual for corporations headquartered in the 16 western and southwestern states and in western Canada. Vol. 1 gives information on over 360 financial institutions; Vols. 2-3 cover about 1,140 industrial corporations. Each volume contains a geographic and a subject index.

INDUSTRY SURVEYS

Standard & Poor's Corp. *Analysts Handbook.* New York (annual, with monthly supplements).

Composite corporate per share data, from 1946 to date, for over 90 industries. Statistics and percentages cover 13 components, including sales, operating profits, depreciation, earnings, dividends, etc.

Standard & Poor's Corp. *Industry Surveys.* New York (separate pamphlets for 36 industries, updated quarterly and annually).

This is a valuable source for basic data on 36 important industries, with financial comparisons of the leading companies in each industry. The "Basic Analysis" for each is a pamphlet of about 40 pages, revised annually. A short "Current Analysis" of about 8 pages is published quarterly for each industry. Received with this is a 4-page monthly on "Trends & Projections," which includes tables of economic and industry indicators.

Forbes. "Annual Report on American Industry" (appears as the first January issue each year).

While this cannot be compared with the preceding surveys, it is still a useful issue that contains short sections on 17 industries. Its "Yardsticks of Management Performance" for each, rank leading companies in profitability (return on equity, return on total capital) and in growth (sales and earnings per share).

A number of the largest brokerage houses publish services or reports that give industry and comparative company data. Articles in financial journals such as *Barron's* also often discuss the outlook for an industry. Several financial manuals reporting on companies in just one industry are described with other information on that industry, for example, the *Electronic News Financial Fact Book & Directory* is described with other sources on the electronics industry in Chapter 5.

CONCISE STATISTICAL DATA AND STOCK PRICES

The most up-to-date stock and bond price information will be found in daily newspapers such as the *Wall Street Journal* and the *New York Times*. The weekly *Barron's* also has a convenient tabulation of security prices. Several other useful, concise sources are listed below.

Bank & Quotation Record. New York, National News Service (monthly).

This is a companion publication to the *Commercial and Financial Chronicle*. It gives a monthly summary of price ranges for stocks and bonds listed on the American, New York, and 4 other U.S. stock exchanges; also prices for OTC securities and government bonds, money rates, daily foreign exchange rates.

Commercial and Financial Chronicle. New York, National News Service (weekly).

The *Chronicle* has been in existence for over 100 years and is an important source for daily stock prices. It has recently changed in both format and frequency, currently including a lengthy "Statistical Section," which gives daily stock prices on the NYSE, the AMEX, and on the Midwest, Pacific and Toronto exchanges. It also quotes weekly bond prices; weekly price range for the National Stock Exchange, the OTC, and mutual funds; dividends declared and payable; stock price indexes; foreign exchange rates. The "Markets Section" includes notices about letter stock, notices of insider trading, and market letters digest. There is a section that lists securities now in registration, prospective offerings, new issue calendar. Several short articles are in each issue, also news and a "Financial News Digest."

M/G Financial Weekly. New York.

This weekly newspaper provides detailed tabulations and charts for over 3,450 stocks, including statistics on price, volume, trend to market, earnings per share, dividends, shareholdings, financial position; also commodity prices, stock options, general news and Media General's stock price indexes.

Moody's Bond Record: Municipals, Corporates, Governments, Convertibles and Preferred Stock Ratings. New York, Moody's Investors Service (monthly).

Includes call price, price range, yield to maturity, assets to liabilities, times charges earned, etc., for over 19,000 bond issues.

Moody's Handbook of Common Stocks. New York, Moody's Investors Service (quarterly).

Each issue contains price charts and concise financial statistics for over 1,000 common stocks, with data covering a 10-year period.

National Quotation Bureau. *National Monthly Bond Summary* and *National Monthly Stock Summary*. New York.

Summaries of bid and offering prices for over-the-counter and inactive listed securities, cumulating for a 6-month period and including dealer's name and date.

Over-the-Counter NASDAQ Securities Handbook. Jenkintown, Pa., Review Publishing Co. (annual).

One-paragraph descriptive and statistical summaries of leading OTC industrial, utility and financial companies quoted by NASDAQ (National Association of Securities Dealers Automated Quotation System).

Standard & Poor's Corp. *Bond Guide.* New York (monthly).

Financial data in tabular format on a broad list of American and some Canadian corporate bonds, including convertibles.

Standard & Poor's Corp. *Daily Stock Price Record: American Stock Exchange; Daily Stock Price Record: New York Stock Exchange;* and *Daily Stock Price Record: Over the Counter.* New York (quarterlies).

Each of these 3 sets of quarterly volumes gives a daily and weekly record of the volume, high/low and closing prices of stocks. Daily market indicators, such as the Dow Jones averages, are at front of each volume.

Standard & Poor's Corp. *Earnings Forecaster.* New York (weekly).

A continuously updated list of current corporate earnings estimates made by leading investment organizations. Covers 1,600 companies and, for each, gives the source and date of estimate, per-share earnings for past full year, estimate for current year and, where possible, an estimate for the next year.

Standard & Poor's Corp. *Security Owner's Stock Guide.* New York (monthly).

Concise data in tabular format for about 5,000 common and preferred stocks, giving for each the S & P rating, stock price range, capitalization, annual and interim earnings, dividends, and institutional holdings. Includes also many mutual fund issues.

Business Week includes a useful quarterly table called "Survey of Corporate Performance," which gives financial statistics such as sales and profits for over 880 top companies in 35 industry categories. In 1974 these appeared in the second issues in March, May, August and November. They publish a similar "Annual Survey of Bank Performance" in a September issue, e.g., September 21, 1974. Their annual "Investment Outlook" issue (last issue each year) contains statistical tables that give earnings, stock prices, etc., for 890 large corporations.

CHARTING SERVICES

Securities Research Corp. *3-Trend Cycli-Graphs* (quarterly) and *3-Trend Security Charts* (monthly). Boston.

The first of these 2 services provides a 12-year graphic presentation of prices, earnings and dividends for over 1,000 leading stocks, on a quarterly basis; the second covers a 2-year period on a weekly basis, and also includes quarterly and annual figures.

Standard & Poor's Corp. *Trendline Stock Chart Services.* New York.

Three separate publications comprise this comprehensive service: *Daily Basis Stock Charts* (published weekly), which shows daily trends for the past 9 months on over 700 popular and active NYSE and some AMEX stocks; *Current Market Perspectives* (monthly), giving weekly graphic data on 1,000 stocks arranged by industry and covering a 3- or 4-year period; *OTC Chart Manual* (bimonthly), with charts on over 800 actively traded unlisted issues for a 2-year period.

There are other well-known charting services, and most are described in advertisements in such publications as *Barron's* and the *Wall Street Journal*. Useful price charts can also be found in several financial services mentioned elsewhere in this chapter, such as, *M/G Financial Weekly*; *Moody's Handbook of Common Stocks*; and *Value Line Investment Survey*.

DIVIDENDS

Both Moody's and Standard & Poor's have separate publications covering declarations and payments of cash and stock dividends, stock splits, and right offerings. These are *Moody's Dividend Record* (semi-weekly, with 9 cumulated issues and an annual) and Standard & Poor's *Dividend Record* (weekly, with quarterly and annual cumulations). Recent dividend statistics can also be found in a number of financial sources, for example, Standard & Poor's monthly *Security Owner's Stock Guide*.

STOCK PRICE INDEXES

The two best known stock price indexes are the Dow Jones averages and the Standard & Poor's averages, and they are quoted in the following publications:

Dow Jones & Co. *Dow Jones Investor's Handbook*. Chicopee, Mass., Dow Jones Books (annual).

Dow Jones compiles the most widely quoted averages, and they cover not only industrial stocks but also transportation and public utility stocks. This annual *Handbook* gives daily closing DJ averages for the most recent year; monthly closing averages, quarterly earnings, dividend yield, price-earnings ratios for over 10 years; also the record for one current year (sales, high/low/last price) of NYSE and AMEX stocks and bonds, OTC and mutual funds.

The most recent DJ averages are quoted in many financial journals and newspapers, especially in *Barron's* and the *Wall Street Journal*. Retrospective statistics can be found in *The Dow Jones Averages, 1885–1970*, edited by M. L. Farrell (Dow Jones Books, 1972).

Standard & Poor's Corp. *Security Price Index Record*. New York (published annually as a section of *Standard & Poor's Trade and Securities Statistics*, and also available separately).

Standard & Poor's averages include: weekly indexes on over 90 industries for a 10-year period and monthly averages prior to that; daily indexes for industrials, railroads, public utilities, and the composite 500 stocks, from 1928 to date; daily NYSE sales, from 1918; corporate bond indexes and high-grade bond yields, from 1900; weekly bond indexes by rating; municipal and government bond price and yield indexes; also Dow Jones averages from 1899. The most recent monthly issue of *Standard & Poor's Trade and Securities Statistics* includes recent stock price averages up to within the past month, and the most current figures are in their weekly advisory service, *The Outlook*.

There are other lesser-known but still useful stock price indexes: the American Stock Exchange "Market Value Index" and the New York Stock Exchange "Common Stock Index," both quoted in *Barron's, Commercial & Financial Chronicle,* and the *Wall Street Journal,* with historical figures in the annual fact-books published by each exchange; Moody's "Common Stock Averages," quoted in *Moody's Manuals* and also in several of their other publications; "Value Line Averages," quoted in *Value Line Investment Survey;* "NASDAQ OTC Stock Price Indexes," in the periodical *Market Chronicle* and also in the *Commercial & Financial Chronicle* and the *Wall Street Journal.*

Short but helpful discussions of these indexes can be found in several books. See, for example, under the subject "Market Averages" in *Glenn G. Munn's Encyclopedia of Banking and Finance,* or in the chapter on "Sources of Investment Information" in the Cohen et al. text on *Investment Analysis and Portfolio Management* (1973) described under "General Books on Investments" in this chapter.

WEEKLY INVESTMENT ADVISORY SERVICES

Babson's Reports: Investment & Barometer Letter. Wellesley Hills, Mass.
A 6-page investment letter with comments on the market and on buy, hold or sell opinions.

Moody's Bond Survey. New York, Moody's Investors Service.
Gives trends and prospects for the market and for individual bonds, with recommendations for purchase or sale. Convertible bond coverage is included in the third issue each month.

Standard & Poor's Corp. *The Outlook.* New York.
Analyses and forecasts for business and for stock market trends. Includes brief data on individual securities, with purchase recommendations; also current S & P stock market indexes.

United Business Service. Boston.
Commentary on the current situation, including forecasts of business, financial and economic conditions, with recommended stocks. Each month there is a tabular summary of "Current Views of Economic Authorities Briefly Interpreted," representing the thinking of 9 economic and financial publishers on general economic conditions, the stock market, etc.

CORPORATE REPORTS

With all these important investment sources one must not overlook the fact that corporate financial reports and other disclosure documents are excellent sources for current financial statistics and for other detailed information about the operations of publicly traded companies. These documents include not only annual reports to stockholders but also 8 reports that companies are required to file with the Securities and Exchange Commission: Annual Report to the SEC (10-K); Quarterly Financial Report (10-Q); Report of Unscheduled Material Events or Corporate Changes (8-K); Proxy Statement; Registration Statement; Prospectus; and 2 reports required of registered management investment companies: Annual Report (N-1R) and Quarterly Report (N-1Q). *Listing Applications* statements, required by the NYSE and AMEX before listing a security on one of those exchanges, also contains useful information.

Today many more libraries keep relatively complete collections of these disclosure documents due primarily to the availability of this data on microfiche. Disclosure, Inc., a commercial firm located in Silver Spring, Maryland, is a distributor for these reports, and they offer a variety of tailor-made "package" subscriptions to reports for all NYSE, AMEX, OTC, and investment companies. Although this service is very expensive, many libraries now maintain full or partial subscriptions not only because of the importance of this material but also because microfiche files are significant space savers over original paper copies and they save much library staff time that would otherwise be required for requesting and processing reports on each company separately. Consequently, the libraries in most banks, accounting and investment firms and many large public and university libraries have files of corporate reports. These reports can also be consulted on microfiche in the SEC office in Washington, D.C., and in their New York, Chicago and Los Angeles regional offices. Other regional SEC offices usually have the paper copies of recent reports for those companies headquartered in their particular region. An individual can order a copy of any report from the SEC or can subscribe to a series of reports through Disclosure, Inc. Another commercial firm, the National Investment Library (located in New York), offers a quick copying service for 10-Ks, 8Ks, 10-Qs and other company documents.

Readers unfamiliar with the use of microfiche may want to refer to the short, general note on microforms in Chapter 2 of this book.

BROKERAGE HOUSE REPORTS

There exists in the investment world a large number of reports and analyses on a wide variety of companies and industries, prepared by research departments of leading investment houses and usually available free of charge primarily to customers. Most public and university libraries do not attempt to collect these reports. However, many libraries do have the following compilation:

Wall Street Transcript. New York (weekly).

This reproduces the text of selected brokerage house reports on companies and industries, and also speeches of company officials to financial analysts groups, interviews with leading investment managers, excerpts from corporate annual and interim reports. Other useful weekly features include news about companies, recent mergers, executive promotions, summaries of new issue prospectuses, and even a "Connoisseur's Corner," for weekly articles on valuation of artworks or antiques. A cumulated index is in each issue.

COMPUTERIZED FINANCIAL DATA

The recent development of computer-based financial data is of major importance to the investment community. Not only has it relieved the professional investment man from time-consuming calculations while speeding up the retrieval of data and increasing its accuracy, it has also made possible a much more complex manipulation of masses of statistical information. To date the cost of these computer services is still so high that their use is limited primarily to investment managers and financial researchers. These costs should decrease somewhat in the near future as their potential becomes better known and better understood and as they are used with more frequency. In the meanwhile, the businessman is already benefiting from these exciting new developments through published computer-developed tabulations, reports and research articles.

By far the best known of these computerized services is *Compustat,* magnetic tapes that provide annual and quarterly financial information for over 3,000 U.S. industrial companies, banks and utilities and 500 Canadian companies, all of which offers wide possibilities for statistical analysis over a 20-year period. These figures are prepared and updated weekly by Investors Management Sciences, Inc., in Denver, Colorado, a subsidiary of Standard & Poor's Corp. Five published statistical services have been generated from the Compustat tapes to date. One of these is the very expensive but very comprehensive *Financial Dynamics,* 14 loose-leaf volumes containing annual statistics on 111 important financial ratios for top companies in over 100 industries, quarter-to-quarter comparisons for a lesser number of ratios, annual and moving 12-month comparisons and annual industry comparisons. All of these data are continuously revised to give the latest information.

A brief, general note about computer services, including the names of several directories describing computerized data bases and information storage and retrieval systems, is in Chapter 2.

SECURITIES AND EXCHANGE COMMISSION PUBLICATIONS

U.S. Securities and Exchange Commission. *Statistical Bulletin.* Washington, D.C., U.S. Government Printing Office (monthly).

Presents statistical data on new securities offerings, registrations, volume and value of trading on exchanges, round-lot and odd-lot trading on the NYSE and AMEX, OTC volume in listed stocks, block distribution and other financial series, current reports of material corporate developments (8-Ks), and sales of restricted securities and securities held by persons in a controlled relationship with an issuer (Form 144s). Quarterly or semi-annually there are also statistics on working capital (current assets and liabilities of nonfinancial corporations); assets of noninsured pension funds; foreign securities sold in the United States.

Other publications of the SEC include: *Official Summary of Security Transactions and Holdings,* a monthly summary of security transactions and holdings reported by officers, directors, and other "insiders"; *Annual Report,* which notes important changes in the securities law and includes statistics on the securities industry, broker-dealers, etc.; *SEC News Digest,* a daily report of SEC decisions, orders, rules, etc. The SEC also publishes an annual *Directory of Companies Filing Annual Reports with the Securities and Exchange Commission Under the Securities Exchange Act of 1934.*

CAPITAL CHANGES SERVICES

Commerce Clearing House. *Capital Changes Reports.* Chicago. 5 volumes.

This gives the capital histories of companies. It is arranged alphabetically by company, and the information for each, given chronologically, includes date of incorporation, stock rights, stock splits, stock dividends; exchanges of securities in recapitalization, reorganizing, mergers and consolidations, etc. Vol. 5 contains historical tables on taxability of dividends, list of worthless securities, investors' tax guide.

Prentice-Hall, Inc. *Capital Adjustments.* Englewood Cliffs, N.J. 3 volumes.

A service similar to the one above, but with a different arrangement. Vols. 1 and 2 are loose-leaf and contain current capital adjustments since 1970. In the back of the second volume are supplementary data on the taxable status of dividends, amortized convertible bond premiums, list of worthless securities, etc. Vol. 3 is a permanent volume for the historical record of capital changes prior to 1970.

F & S Index of Corporate Change. Cleveland, Ohio, Predicasts, Inc. (quarterly, with annual cumulations).

This is a continuing guide to information in newspapers and periodicals on mergers, acquisitions and other organizational changes that affect corporate identity. It is in 3 sections, the principal one of which lists companies by SIC, briefly citing the corporate change involved and giving the date of the newspaper or periodical article. Section 1 is an alphabetical company index; Section 3 contains special tabulations of name changes, new companies, reorganizations, bankruptcies, liquidations, subsidiary changes, foreign operations, joint ventures. An index of sources is at end.

Persons researching obsolete companies may want to use the *Directory of Obsolete Securities* (Jersey City, N.J., Financial Stock Guide Services). This is a biennial list of companies whose identity has been lost as a result of name change, merger, acquisition, dissolution, liquidation, reorganization, bankruptcy, charter cancellation and related capital changes.

NEW SECURITY OFFERINGS

Finance. "Investors Issue." New York (annual, July issue).

This annual directory issue of the magazine *Finance* lists the leading underwriting firms, giving for each: names of key personnel; capital position and fails to deliver (during the year); underwriting and syndication of corporate issues by number, type and dollar volume. It also contains a capital position ranking of the top 400 firms. A ranking of the top 100 firms is in the March issue each year.

Institutional Investor. "Annual Corporate Financing Directory." New York.

Profiles of investment banking firms, with details of managed underwritings during the year. Also lists top underwriters by category of corporate underwriting.

Investment Dealers' Digest. "Corporate Financing Directory" issue. New York (semi-annual; usually published as Section 2 of the last March and first October issues).

Recent corporate security offerings arranged alphabetically by issuer, with details as to offering date, amount and character of the issue, name of underwriter. Includes also offerings arranged by name of underwriter; lists of secondary and special offerings, rights and exchange offerings, corporate issues placed privately, Canadian financing. Each issue of *Investment Dealers' Digest* includes a continuing list in a "New Issues Digest" section.

The *Commercial and Financial Chronicle* has a "Securities Now in Registration" section, listing companies in registration, recent issues filed with SEC, effective registrations, prospective offerings and a new issue calendar.

STOCK EXCHANGE PUBLICATIONS

American Stock Exchange. *AMEX Databook.* New York (annual).
   Short statistical profile of AMEX, including membership, listed companies, stock trading volume, monthly AMEX "Price Change Index" for about 8 years. Their *Weekly Bulletin* contains changes in AMEX membership, new listings, dividends, stockholders meetings, etc. Their *American Investor* (10/yr.) gives current news and statistics on AMEX companies.

New York Stock Exchange. *Fact Book.* New York (annual).
   Statistics on market activity, listed companies, stock price trends, securities market credit, shareholders, etc. Includes an historical section, which gives the annual "NYSE Common Stock Index" for about 30 years. Their *Monthly Review* has current figures on their stock price indexes and on credit and market activity; their *Weekly Bulletin* contains changes in NYSE membership, new listings, dividends, stockholders meetings, etc.

Commerce Clearing House. *New York Stock Exchange Guide.* Chicago. 3 volumes.
   This is the official guide prepared by CCH for the NYSE and covering constitution and rules, laws and regulations and a directory of members.
   CCH has also published similar guides for the AMEX, the Boston, Midwest, Pacific, PBW exchanges, and for the Chicago Board Options Exchange.

LISTS OF LARGEST U.S. COMPANIES

Lists of the largest U.S. companies rank firms either by sales or by asset size and usually include other financial data in a concise tabular format. The first two of the following annuals are the most comprehensive and best known lists. Many more specialized lists appear annually in periodicals, and a few of these are mentioned elsewhere in this book. Several lists of largest foreign companies are described in the "Foreign Investment Information Sources" section of this chapter.

The Fortune Double 500 Directory. Chicago (annual).
   This is an annual reprint of the lists that appear in 3 issues of *Fortune* magazine each year — the first 500 industrial corporations (May), the second 500 (June), the 50 largest commercial banking, life insurance, diversified financial, retailing, transportation and utility companies (July). A fourth part lists the 300 largest foreign industrial corporations, 50 largest foreign banks, 50 largest industrial companies of the world (August), and the reprint for that is called *Fortune World Business Directory*. These companies are ranked by sales, assets, net income, stockholders' equity, employees, net income as a percentage of stockholders' equity, earnings per share, total return to investors. Fortune maintains a data bank containing 20 years of the surveys for the 500 largest U.S. industrial companies.

News Front. *30,000 Leading U.S. Corporations.* New York, Year, Inc. (annual).
   A computerized list of the largest corporations in 21 manufacturing and 37 non-

manufacturing SIC industries. The largest public companies are ranked by sales and include also other financial data such as net income, total assets, long-term debt, depreciation, P/E ratio, stockholders' equity. Lesser information for private companies. Tables at front list top performing U.S. corporations by sales size categories; indexes (geographic and by company) are at end. This data is also available on magnetic tapes.

Forbes. "Annual Directory Issue." (May 15th issue, each year).

This annual issue ranks the 500 largest corporations by assets, sales, net profits, stock market value, and assets growth. There is also a roster of over 800 chief executives ranked by salary. Includes an alphabetical list of companies giving ranking numbers in first 4 categories and in executive's salary.

CREDIT RATING SERVICES

Dun & Bradstreet. *Business Information Reports.* New York.

Since the mid-nineteenth century D & B has offered a confidential service for information about companies as a basis for credit, insurance, marketing and other business decisions. The reports prepared on each company include information on personnel, finance, how the companies pay their bills, whether they have a court record, their operations and history. D & B publishes with this service a 4-volume *Reference Book* (bimonthly), which is a detailed geographic list of U.S. and Canadian business firms of all types, giving for each the SIC number, an abbreviation for line of business, a code for estimated financial strength and for composite credit appraisal. A companion credit rating service for foreign companies is *International Report.* For further information prospective subscribers should contact Dun & Bradstreet.

INVESTMENT COMPANIES

Several guides to foreign investment companies are described in the "International Investment Services" section of this chapter.

American Institute for Economic Research. *Investment Trusts and Funds from the Investor's Point of View.* Great Barrington, Mass. (annual).

An annual reference guide for background and development, basic information on different types of investment companies, regulations, characteristics, performance records.

Fundscope. Los Angeles (monthly). Ceased publication in 1976.

This investment company magazine contains several articles but is of interest primarily for the statistics, tables and charts in each issue on performance and prices of many mutual funds. Their annual "Mutual Fund Guide" (April each year) is a useful reference guide in 4 sections: Section 2 is a directory of mutual funds and closed-end companies that also has a glossary and a ranking of funds by size; Section 4 gives detailed performance data for specific funds (by year for 10 years); Section 3 provides vital data on funds other than performance.

Investment Company Institute. *Mutual Fund Fact Book.* Washington, D.C. (annual).

Basic statistics for the industry, with explanatory text, including assets, total sales, redemption, etc., and a glossary.

Investment Dealers' Digest. *Mutual Fund Directory.* New York (semi-annual).

Background information and statistics about each mutual fund. This directory was formerly published as Section 2 of the *Digest* but is now issued separately. The "Fall" issue gives information revised as of June 30 each year; the "Year-End Edition" covers the whole year. A list of "Mutual Funds in Registration" is in each issue of *Investment Dealers' Digest.*

Mutual Funds Almanac. Old Tappan, N.J., The Hirsch Organization (annual).

The last half of every volume is a directory of over 600 funds, giving 7-year performance data, total assets, etc. The first half is an introduction for persons interested in mutual fund investing. Includes a glossary. Their quarterly *Mutual Funds Scoreboard* updates the statistics on performance and ranking for about 550 funds.

United Mutual Fund Selector. Boston, United Business Service Co. (semi-monthly).

A short newsletter, giving performance comparisons and other information, including data on specific recommended funds.

Wiesenberger Services, Inc. *Investment Companies.* New York (annual, with quarterly supplements).

This is the most important single source for basic information on mutual funds and investment companies. It gives background, management policy, and financial record for all leading U.S. and Canadian investment companies. General data and statistics are at front; there is also a glossary and a short, annotated bibliography. Wiesenberger Services, Inc., are specialists in mutual funds, and they publish several other annuals and monthlies, including *Mutual Funds Charts & Statistics* (annual), which contains statistical data on withdrawal and accumulation plans for each fund.

Several financial periodicals include statistics or special issues: *Barron's* "Quarterly Mutual Fund Record" (in issues at beginning of February, May, August and November); *Financial World's* quarterly "Independent Appraisals of Listed Stocks" (in first issues for March, June, September, December); and *Forbes'* "Annual Mutual Fund Survey" (Aug. 15 issue).

GOVERNMENTS AND MUNICIPALS

Blue List of Current Municipal Offerings. New York, Blue List Publishing Co. (5/wk.).

This is a daily list, by state, of municipal bond offerings, giving price, maturity date, underwriting firm.

First Boston Corp. *Handbook of Securities of the United States Government and Federal Agencies and Related Money Market Instruments.* New York (biennial).

A handy reference volume for information about government securities, meant for students and market participants. Gives simple explanations of the budget, public debt, federal agencies, money market instruments, the government securities market, federal taxation of income from government securities.

Moody's Municipal & Government Manual. New York, Moody's Investors Service. 2 volumes (annual, with semi-weekly supplements).

This is the basic financial manual for details on federal, state and municipal finances and obligations, usually including assessed value, tax rates, tax collections, schedule of bonded debt, bond rating, etc. A foreign section at back of Vol. 2 gives details on foreign government obligations. The center blue pages in each volume contain statistics on government and municipal bond yield averages; analysis of state highway fund operations; 7-year price range for Canadian and foreign government bonds; personal income by state; per-capita personal income for selected years, 1929 to date.

Salomon Brothers. *An Analytical Record of Yields and Yield Spreads.* New York (loose-leaf).

Gives historical yield and yield spread tables from 1945 for U.S. government securities; corporates and mortgages; municipals; short-term market rates (yield on Treasury bills, bankers' acceptances, finance paper and commercial paper, certificates of deposit, Eurodollar deposits). Current statistics and information are in their *Quarterly Bond Market Review; Bond Market Roundup* (weekly); *Comments on Credits* (monthly); *Comments on Values* (monthly); *High Grade Corporate Bond Performance Index* (monthly).

Securities Industry Association. *Municipal Marketing Developments.* New York (monthly).

The figures in this monthly formerly appeared in their *SIA Municipal Statistical Bulletin.* Each issue includes bond sales by type of issue and use of proceeds, sales by rating and by state, new issue reoffering yields; also a list of leading 25 managing underwriters of new municipal issues.

Weekly Bond Buyer. New York.

Current news about the state and local bond market. Includes data on municipal sealed bids invited (by state), official municipal bond notices; also new issue delivery dates, current statistics on state and local government bonds, etc. Monthly pink sheets contain all municipal bond and note sales reported during that month. The Bond Buyer also publishes a handy annual compilation of *Statistics on State and Local Government Finance.*

Two weekly newsletters are *Reporting on Governments* (New York) and *Weekly Government Bond Letter* (New York, Aubrey G. Lanston & Co.).

GUIDES TO FINANCIAL SERVICES AND STATISTICS

Grant, Mary M. and Norma Cote, eds. *Directory of Business and Financial Services.* 7th ed. New York, Special Libraries Association, 1976.

This is the latest edition of an indispensable directory that describes business, economic and financial services that are published periodically or with regular supplements. It is arranged by title, with indexes by subject and by name of publisher.

Select Information Exchange. *Investment Sources & Ideas.* New York (semi-annual?).

A descriptive list of those business and investment services and periodicals that are available through this subscription agency. Includes many small, specialized services and is arranged by topic, e.g., chart services, growth stock investments, real estate investments. The title of this list varies.

Woy, James B. *Investment Information: A Detailed Guide to Selected Sources* (Management Information Guide, 19). Detroit, Mich., Gale Research Co., 1970.

A detailed subject index to regularly recurring financial statistics that appear in 16 financial journals, newspapers and services. Now quite old but still of value.

Several of the general books on investment management include short chapters discussing basic sources of investment information. These usually describe sources both for industries and for companies, as well as those for current economic conditions. One of the best is in Cohen et al., *Investment Analysis and Portfolio Management* (rev. ed., Irwin, 1973). Others are in the texts by Bowyer, Christy and Clendenin, Latané and Tuttle, Smith and Eiteman (all listed elsewhere in this chapter).

INDEXES TO FINANCIAL PUBLICATIONS

F & S Index of Corporations & Industries. Cleveland, Ohio, Predicasts, Inc. (weekly, cumulated monthly and annually).

This is the best periodical index to use when searching for current information on companies or industries in a wide selection of business, industrial and financial publications and also in a few brokerage house reports. The yellow pages in the weeklies and the green pages in cumulated issues list articles (or data in articles) on SIC industries; the white pages list articles on companies. Since many of the entries refer to very brief citations it is important to note that major articles are designated by a black dot, which precedes the abbreviated title of the journal. A companion index for articles on foreign industries and companies is described elsewhere in this chapter.

INVESTMENT NEWSPAPERS AND PERIODICALS

The general periodicals on finance, corporate finance and banking are in Chapter 15. This section describes those financial newspapers and periodicals that are of most interest in investment management.

Barron's. New York, Dow Jones & Co. (weekly).

This is an indispensable "national business and financial weekly" with excellent articles on prospects for industries and individual companies, on investment companies, new regulations, and other business and financial topics of interest to investors. Includes weekly stock and bond prices for the NYSE, AMEX, OTC, and CBOE (Chicago Board Options Exchange), and for mutual funds. It also quotes current Dow Jones averages and other market indicators, basic economic and financial indicators, foreign exchange rates. Indexed in BPI, F&S.

Commercial and Financial Chronicle. New York, National News Service (weekly).

An important journal especially for its "Statistical Section," which is described under "Concise Statistical Data and Stock Prices" in this chapter.

Financial Analysts Journal. New York, Financial Analysts Federation (bimonthly).

Authoritative articles covering both theory and practical problems in relation to new developments in investment management, security analysis, corporate finance, industry studies, etc. Includes news about securities laws and regulations and also book reviews. Indexed in BPI, F&S.

Financial World. New York, Butler Publishing Corp. (weekly).

A weekly analysis of general investment situations, prospects for industries and for individual companies. Statistics in each issue cover corporate earnings, dividends declared; also NYSE, AMEX and OTC statistics, money indicators and basic business indicators. Their quarterly "Independent Appraisals of Listed Stocks" appears in first issues for March, June, September, December. A "Directory of Top Growth Companies" is in last August issue each year. Indexed in BPI, F&S.

Forbes. New York (semi-monthly).

Short, readable articles of interest to business and financial executives, including prospects for industries and individual companies and brief sketches of individuals. Includes special issues for banking (July 1), mutual funds (Aug. 15), and insurance (Sept. 1). Their "Annual Report on American Industry" (first issue each year) and their "Annual Directory Issue" (May 15) are both described elsewhere in this chapter. Indexed in BPI, F&S, RGPL.

Institutional Investor. New York, Institutional Investor Systems (monthly).

See descriptive note in Chapter 14 section for "Finance Periodicals."

Investment Dealers' Digest. New York (weekly).

A weekly news magazine of finance, with 3 to 4 articles on companies in each issue and also useful regular features that include current information on stocks and bonds, municipals, regional news, new securities. Their special "Corporate Financing Directory" and "Mutual Fund Directory" are described elsewhere in this chapter. Indexed in F&S, PAIS.

Journal of Portfolio Management. New York, Institutional Investor Systems (quarterly).

A new journal (1974) for articles by professionals on problems of risk adjustment, security selection, and timing, of interest to portfolio managers and academicians. Includes book reviews.

Market Chronicle. New York, W. G. Dana Co. (weekly).

This weekly newspaper, until July 1975, was called *O-T-C Market Chronicle* and was devoted exclusively to news about companies and other financial matters of interest to the OTC market. It still gives OTC stock price quotations and the NASDAQ OTC stock price indexes, but it is now expanded to cover news also about AMEX and NYSE companies. Indexed in F&S.

Over-the-Counter Securities Review. Jenkintown, Pa., Review Publishing Co. (monthly).

Business and financial news about over-the-counter companies; also a monthly review of the market, statistics on annual earnings reported by OTC companies.

Wall Street Journal. New York, Dow Jones & Co. (5/wk.).

This is the leading U.S. daily financial newspaper, indispensable for all businessmen. It includes business and financial news, several interesting articles, company news and digest of earnings, commodity prices, stock market price quotations, P/E ratios, and sales for the NYSE, AMEX, OTC, CBOE, etc.: also Dow Jones and other averages, foreign exchange rates. Indexed in F&S, PAIS.

There is a very detailed *Wall Street Journal Index,* published monthly, with annual cumulations. Each issue is in 2 parts: corporate news; general news. Since there are several editions of the *Journal,* it is important to note that the indexing is based on the Final New York Edition.

Back files of the *Wall Street Journal* are available on microfilm for easy storage, and there is also a relatively new Wall Street Journal Microfiche Service for persons interested in maintaining subject files of *Journal* articles and statistics in a handy compact format. This service is available in 3 parts; microfiche of the general news articles; microfiche on corporate news; complete files of the stock, bond and commodity quotations.

FOREIGN INVESTMENT INFORMATION SOURCES

This section does not attempt to cover foreign investment sources completely; it does mention a few of the best known international and European services and several covering British companies. G. P. Henderson's *European Companies: A Guide to Sources of Information* (listed below in "Bibliographies") includes descriptions of financial services for each European country.

INTERNATIONAL INVESTMENT SERVICES

Capital International Perspective. Geneva, Capital International S.A. (monthly and quarterly).
  This is a charting service. The quarterly issues consist of 15-year graphic data for 1,100 of the largest companies outside North America, arranged by broad industry. International stock market trends, by industry, are at front. The monthly issues focus on recent stock market performance and comparisons of market valuation factors within countries and international industry groups.

Financial Times. *International Business Year Book.* London.
  The main portion of this yearbook is a financial manual, which lists industrial, financial, retailing, transportation, utility, oil and mining companies and, for each, gives officers, subsidiaries, capital and some financial statistics. A list of companies by country is at front, with very brief key data on each country. Important facts on international financial markets and international statistical comparisons are at end.

Informations Internationales. Paris, Hoppenstedt & Co., and DAFSA-Documentation et Analyses Financières S.A. 8 volumes (loose-leaf).
  A basic financial manual for the principal international companies, arranged by industry and within each industry first by country and then by company. Text is in French, German and English and data usually include corporate history, names of officers, list of subsidiaries, balance sheet and operating statistics, stock price range, number of employees.

International Fund Year Book. London, Throgmorton Publications.
  A guide to off-shore investment companies, giving for each the objective, directors, purchase procedures and charges, redemption procedures and charges, management fees, etc., as well as percentage breakdown of investments, financial record (shares/units in issue, net assets, net sales, redemptions, stock price quotations).

Standard & Poor's Corp. *International Stock Report.* New York (monthly).
  Analyzes some of the top foreign securities, giving fundamental position, earnings/dividends record, recent developments, balance sheet data.

Business Week publishes an "Annual Survey of International Corporate Performance," which is a tabular list of 500 companies arranged by 37 countries and gives for each sales, profits, earnings per share, book value per share. This usually appears in the first or second July issue, for example, July 14, 1975.

EUROPEAN SOURCES

Extel European Company Service. London, Extel Statistical Services, Ltd.

This is a card service similar to their service for British companies that is described in the following section for U.K. sources. It covers a selection of about 400 large companies whose shares are quoted on the Continental exchanges.

Jane's Major Companies of Europe. New York, F. Watts (annual).

Financial information on 1,000 Western European companies, arranged by industry, with indexes both by company and by country at end. Summary data for these and for 400 additional companies is in tabular form at front, also classified by industry.

Key Figures of European Securities. Brussels, Belgium, Investment Research Group of European Banks' International (3/yr.).

Basic information on important European shares presented in a concise tabular format similar to that in the monthly *Standard & Poor's Security Owner's Stock Guide*. Each issue is arranged by country and gives equity per share, balance sheet data, earnings and prices for individual stocks. Includes also data on convertible bonds.

Noyes Data Corp. *European Mutual Funds.* Park Ridge, N.J., 1973.

This guide to mutual funds is arranged by country, and for each firm it gives background information, officers, breakdown of investments, etc.

U.K. SOURCES

Extel British Company Service. London, Extel Statistical Services, Ltd.

This is a comprehensive financial service for about 5,000 companies quoted on British stock exchanges. It consists of 2 sets of what are called "cards" but are in fact sheets of paper, one being a white "Annual Card" that gives the basic facts and statistics usually found in financial manuals; the other is a buff-colored "News Card" issued daily as there is significant news to report, with this news cumulative. Extel also offers a supplementary card service for European companies and one called *Extel Unquoted Companies Service,* which provides data on about 1,500 large private companies in the United Kingdom.

Moodies Digest of Company Records. London, Moodies Services, Ltd. (annual).

Profiles on over 650 major British companies, giving balance sheet statistics for 10 years and also graphs of stock prices. (It is similar in format to *Moody's Handbook of Common Stocks.*) A quarterly that contains comparative statistical information on about 1,000 leading British companies is *Moodies Investment Handbook.* Part 1 contains industrial companies, and Part 2, other companies grouped by subject category. Their weekly investment advisory service is *Moodies Review of Investment.*

Stock Exchange Official Year-Book. London, T. Skinner & Co.

A basic financial manual for officially listed British securities. The industrial section is arranged by company; nonmanufacturing companies are grouped by subject category. There is an alphabetical index and a list of parent companies and their subsidiaries. This same publisher issues a *Register of Defunct and Other Companies Removed from the Stock Exchange Official Year-Book* (annual). The London Stock

Exchange publishes a quarterly *Stock Exchange Fact Book,* which contains statistics on total listed securities classified by industry; also lists of 100 largest U.K. companies, 50 largest overseas companies, 25 largest Irish companies.

Newspapers and Periodicals

Financial Times. London (daily).

An important British newspaper that provides worldwide coverage for business, financial and economic news, including news of companies, quotations on the London Stock Exchange, selected overseas share information, U.S. and foreign stock price indexes, etc.; also news of general interest.

Investment Analyst. London, Society of Investment Analysts (3/yr.).

Professional journal for articles on financial analysis and investment management.

Investors Chronicle. London (weekly).

A financial weekly covering news about British companies, the London markets, company analyses, international investment; also London stock prices, stock yields and stock market information. Many issues include detailed "Surveys" of a country, region, industry, or financial topic. There are also occasional supplements. Indexed in F&S, PAIS.

Canada

Financial Post. *Survey of Industrials.* Toronto, Ontario, Maclean-Hunter. 2 volumes.

This is the basic financial manual for Canadian companies, with Vol. 1 covering manufacturing companies and Vol. 2, "Sales and Services," covering banking and finance, communications, data processing, management and holding, merchandising, publishing, utilities, real estate, recreation, transport and storage and general services. A separate tabulation for private companies is at end of Vol. 1; both volumes contain a 7-year price range for Canadian industrial stocks. The Financial Post also publishes the following specialized manuals: *Survey of Funds* (data on leading investment companies); *Survey of Oils; Survey of Mines.*

The weekly *Financial Post* itself is the most important current source for news about Canadian business, investments and public affairs, and each issue includes stock price quotations.

GUIDES TO FOREIGN STOCK EXCHANGES

European Stock Exchange Handbook. Park Ridge, N.J., Noyes Data Corp., 1973.

Factual data on the stock exchanges of 18 European countries, with more details given for each than is in the source listed below. Includes listing requirements and trading procedures; also sources for further information, newspapers and periodicals, indices and statistics, lists of stockbrokers.

International Stock & Commodity Exchange Directory. 1974–1975 ed. Ed. by Peter Wyckoff et al. Canaan, N.H., Phoenix Publishing, 1974.

A useful guide to all the important exchanges, arranged by country. Brief data for each exchange includes names of officers, total members, commissions or fees, trading hours, total issues traded and volume. A glossary of commodity market terms is at end.

LISTS OF LARGEST FOREIGN COMPANIES

Entreprise. "Les Dossiers d'Entreprise." Paris (annual, e.g., Nov. 1974).

This special issue includes a list of the 500 largest French companies, with financial statistics for each; also lists the 5,000 largest French companies by industry and the 1,000 largest European companies.

Europe's 5,000 Largest Companies. London, Gower Press; New York, Bowker (annual).

A ranking of Europe's 4,000 largest industrials and 750 trading companies by sales and number of employees. It is patterned after the *Fortune* list of U.S. companies, including assets, equity capital, profit, exports, and several percentage figures for each company. There is also a ranking of the 400 largest industrials by profit, the 200 most profitable industrials (profit as percentage of sales), the largest industrials both by industry and by country, the 50 money losers.

Fortune World Business Directory. Chicago (annual).

This is the annual reprint of the list of the 300 largest foreign industrial corporations, the 50 largest foreign banks, the 50 largest industrial companies of the world, that originally appears in the August issue of *Fortune* each year.

The President Directory. Tokyo, President Magazine (annual).

A good example of the various lists of largest companies published for one specific country. It gives financial statistics and a ranking of the 500 leading Japanese mining/manufacturing corporations, the 260 leading nonmanufacturing corporations, the 200 leading export corporations. There is also a ranking of the 500 leading Japanese corporations in terms of growth and one for the 100 leading foreign capital-affiliated corporations in Japan.

The Times 1000. London, The Times (annual).

This ranks and gives financial statistics for the 1,000 largest U.K. industrial companies, with separate rankings for various kinds of financial companies and for discount houses. There are also lists of the 500 leading European companies and the 100 leading American companies.

BIBLIOGRAPHIES AND INDEXES ON FOREIGN COMPANIES AND INDUSTRIES

Business International Corp. *Master Key Index.* New York.

The blue section indexes information on specific companies that appears in BI publications. This is more fully described in Chapter 16.

F & S International. Cleveland, Ohio, Predicasts, Inc. (monthly, with annual cumulations).

Indexes articles on foreign companies and industries that have appeared in over 1,000 foreign and domestic periodicals and other documents. It is arranged in 3 parts: (1) by SIC industry or product number; (2) by region and country; (3) by company.

Henderson, G. P., comp. and ed. *European Companies: A Guide to Sources of Information.* 3d ed. Beckenham, Kent, England, CBD Research Ltd., 1972.

This is a useful descriptive list, by country, of sources for information about European companies, including official records, financial and commercial services, directories, newspapers and journals.

Research Index. Wallington, Surrey, England, Business Surveys, Ltd. (fortnightly).

> This is an index to articles on British industries and companies, covering over 100 British business, trade and economics journals as well as several newspapers. Each issue is in 2 parts: an index to articles by subject; an index to articles on companies, arranged alphabetically. This is rather similar to the abbreviated type of entry used by *F & S International,* but unfortunately *Research Index* does not include periodic cumulations.

INVESTMENT MANAGEMENT BOOKS

Recent investment management texts no longer are strictly descriptive as they were some 10 years ago. Now they are much more analytical, which perhaps makes them of more interest to students and theorists than to potential investors. The several investment guides and books on the stock market will be of more practical interest to investors, but there is no attempt here to include any of the many "how-to-get-rich" books that are often well publicized but are of little real value. Books and reference sources on corporate finance and banking (including books on the mathematics of finance) are covered in Chapter 14.

GENERAL BOOKS ON INVESTMENTS

Handbooks
Levine, Sumner N., ed. *Financial Analyst's Handbook.* Homewood, Ill., Dow Jones-Irwin, 1975.

> An excellent, comprehensive guide to the principles and procedures necessary for successful investment management. Vol. 1 covers "Methods, Theory and Portfolio Management" in 47 chapters, each by a recognized authority. The 7 major sections are: introduction; investment vehicles (stocks, bonds, etc.); special investment vehicles (warrants and options, venture capital investments, tax shelter concept, etc.); analysis of financial reports; economic analysis and timing; mathematical aids; portfolio management and theories. Vol. 2 contains an "Analysis by Industry" for 27 industries. These studies are meant to provide examples of the factors that each of 33 leading industry specialists feels are important in analyzing a particular industry. Two chapters at end, written by expert librarians, discuss key business reference sources; another chapter has a useful "Guide to Industry Publications" compiled by the New York Society of Security Analysts.

Books
Amling, Frederick. *Investments: An Introduction to Analysis and Management.* 3d ed. Englewood Cliffs, N.J., Prentice-Hall, 1974.

> Revision of a detailed text on the investment decision-making process that retains much of the description necessary for an introductory study but also includes the theoretical framework for making analytical decisions, particularly in investment analysis and portfolio management. There are 8 basic sections and bibliographies at end of each of its 24 chapters.

Christy, George A. and John C. Clendenin. *Introduction to Investments.* 6th ed. New York, McGraw-Hill, 1974.

This latest revision of a good, popular beginning textbook on the theory and practices of investments stresses personal investment plans along with policies and
problems of the professional investor. It is in 6 parts: introduction; corporate
securities; the securities market; investment analysis (chapters for each type); other
investments (investment companies, social security, life insurance, real estate, etc.);
investment administration. Chapter 11 has a useful discussion of "Investment Information and Advice." Includes bibliographies at end of chapters, and a glossary at
end.

Cohen, Jerome B., Edward D. Zinbarg and Arthur Zeikel. *Investment Analysis
and Portfolio Management.* Rev. ed. Homewood, Ill., Irwin, 1973.
Another good introduction to investments, in 4 parts: the setting; security evaluation; investment timing; ultimate decisions. This last section, which is completely
revised to reflect current trends, has chapters on personal portfolio management, institutional investment trends, institutional investors, the quantitative revolution,
applying capital market theory to practice, the role of the computer. The first section
contains an especially useful chapter discussing "Sources of Investment Information." Bibliographies are at end of chapters.

Dougall, Herbert E. *Investments.* 9th ed. Englewood Cliffs, N.J., Prentice-Hall,
1973.
This major revision of a popular text was undertaken to include the recent "dramatic
changes" in the whole investment scene. It is in 5 parts: the economics of investment;
investment media; investment mechanics (includes mathematics, a chapter on
sources of investment information and advice, buying and selling securities, taxation); the investment program; analysis of corporate securities. Bibliographies are at
end of chapters.

Frederikson, E. Bruce, ed. *Frontiers of Investment Analysis.* Rev. ed. Scranton,
Pa., Intext Educational Publishers, 1971.
A selection of 42 readings to stimulate thinking, discussion and research on the
nature of investment values. Arranged in 5 parts: risk and investment analysis; investment return; investment environment; equity valuation; studies in stock market
behavior.

Sauvain, Harry C. *Investment Management.* 4th ed. Englewood Cliffs, N.J.,
Prentice-Hall, 1973.
Thorough revision of a standard text on the management of investments in securities.
It is in 5 major sections: the problem and the setting; investment risk and return;
financial analysis; investment constraints; investment policies. Includes a bibli-
ography.

Smith, Keith V. and David K. Eiteman. *Essentials of Investing.* Homewood, Ill.,
Irwin, 1974.
This introduction to investing is arranged in the following 5 parts: introduction;
valuation of investments; security analysis (financial statement analysis, accounting
adjustments, forecasting future benefits); nonindustrial securities (chapters on public
utilities, transportation companies, financial institutions, investment companies, service organizations); investor activities (includes chapter on sources of investment information, procedures, timing, performance evaluation). Bibliographies are at end of
chapters; "Time Value of Money Tables" and exercises are at end. This same book
was also published without the exercises and with a different title, *Modern Strategy*

for Successful Investing: A Guide to Preserving Your Capital and Making it Grow (Dow Jones-Irwin, 1974).

Williamson, J. Peter. *Investments: New Analytic Techniques.* New York, Praeger, 1970.

This is a good book for the nonmathematically inclined investment person. It discusses various new techniques of investment analysis available because of recent developments in computer technology, including those connected with performance measurement, portfolio selection, security analysis. There are 2 chapters reviewing the basic investment mathematics and statistical techniques needed. Annotated bibliographies are at end of chapters.

Two other standard texts are *Investments: Principles/Practices/Analyses* by Douglas Bellemore and John C. Ritchie, Jr. (4th ed., Cincinnati, Ohio, South-Western, 1974); and *Investment Analysis and Management* by John W. Bowyer (4th ed., Homewood, Ill., Irwin, 1972).

SECURITY ANALYSIS AND PORTFOLIO MANAGEMENT

Ellis, Charles D. *Institutional Investing.* Homewood, Ill., Dow Jones-Irwin, 1971.

A good, readable book that "seeks to organize and integrate into coherent form the most useful concepts, programs, and techniques developed by professional investment managers in recent years." It is oriented toward decision-making, and the emphasis is on management of portfolios.

Fischer, Donald E. and Ronald J. Jordan. *Security Analysis and Portfolio Management.* Englewood Cliffs, N.J., Prentice-Hall, 1975.

An introductory text that attempts to blend descriptive with quantitative analysis; requires use only of simple algebra and elementary statistics. It is divided into 6 sections: the investment environment; framework of risk-return analysis; common-stock analysis; bond analysis; technical analysis and the efficient markets theory; portfolio analysis selection and management. Bibliographies are with each chapter.

Friend, Irwin, Marshall Blume and Jean Crockett. *Mutual Funds and Other Institutional Investors: A New Perspective.* New York, McGraw-Hill, 1970.

"This study analyzes the implications for the economy as a whole of the increasing importance of institutional investors in the stock market, with particular emphasis on mutual funds." It was undertaken by 3 University of Pennsylvania professors for the Twentieth Century Fund, and much of the material is an updating of the Wharton School, *Study of Mutual Funds* (Washington, D.C., U.S. Government Printing Office, 1962), which was the first comprehensive study of the mutual fund industry.

Graham, Benjamin, David L. Dodd and Sidney Cottle. *Security Analysis: Principles and Technique.* 4th ed. New York, McGraw-Hill, 1962.

Ever since its first edition (1934) this has been the "bible" for security analysts, and it is still required reading today. There are 6 parts: survey and approach; analysis of financial statements; fixed-income securities; the valuation of common stocks; senior securities with speculative feature; other aspects of security analysis.

Homer, Sidney and Martin L. Leibowitz. *Inside the Yield Book: New Tools for Bond Market Strategy.* Englewood Cliffs, N.J., published jointly by Prentice-Hall and the New York Institute of Finance, 1972.

This is a useful and well-written book that explores "some of the basic but less obvious relationships between coupon, maturity, price and yield with the aim of aiding the investor in judging and comparing bond values." It is in 2 parts, with Part 1 studying the tools for bond portfolio management (bond yields, bond prices, bond investment) and Part 2 covering the mathematics of bond yields, for the investor who wants to explore further the mathematics of bond yields and prices on which the authors' conclusions are based. An appendix lists and explains the general formulas.

Latané, Henry, Donald L. Tuttle and Charles P. Jones. *Security Analysis and Portfolio Management.* 2d ed. New York, Ronald, 1975.

A good quantitative approach to the title subjects, for students, analysts and portfolio managers. There are 5 main parts: characteristics of financial assets; security analysis — the basic approach; security analysis — underlying factors; portfolio management and performance; reference material. Part 2 includes chapters on both internal and external sources of financial information; Part 5 includes discussions of financial mathematics, decision-making and analytical techniques for persons who need additional background.

Loll, Leo M. and Julian G. Buckley. *The Over-the-Counter Securities Market.* 3d ed. Englewood Cliffs, N.J., Prentice-Hall, 1973.

Designed to help potential security salesmen pass the NASD qualifying exam, but it can also be of use to private investors interested in learning about the OTC market. Covers the basic principles of finance, stock and bond transactions, and regulations concerning mutual funds and OTC securities.

Lorie, James H. and Richard Brealey, eds. *Modern Developments in Investment Management: A Book of Readings.* New York, Praeger, 1972.

An excellent selection of 37 important articles on the development of a modern theory of portfolio management. They are arranged in 3 parts: behavior of the stock market; portfolio management; valuation of securities. Introductory comments at beginning of each subsection mention which articles require some knowledge of algebra and statistics.

An equally good selection of 31 readings, 8 of which are in both of these books, is *Security Evaluation and Portfolio Analysis,* edited by Edwin J. Elton and Martin J. Gruber (Englewood Cliffs, N.J., Prentice-Hall, 1972).

Rosen, Lawrence R. *Go Where the Money Is: A Guide to Understanding and Entering the Securities Business.* Rev. ed. Homewood, Ill., Dow Jones-Irwin, 1974.

Basic information on the securities business meant to help persons prepare for NASD and SEC exams. It includes chapters on the securities acts, SEC policies, investment banking, exchanges. Review questions conclude chapters and a bibliography is at end.

Smith, Keith V. *Portfolio Management: Theoretical and Empirical Studies of Portfolio Decision-Making.* New York, Holt, Rinehart and Winston, 1971.

Focuses on the decision-making process of institutional portfolio management. Part 1 explores the institutional setting; Part 2 presents theory; Part 3 sets forth the results of empirical studies, particularly with respect to the mutual fund industry; Part 4 reviews potential applications of computers and indicates how portfolio theory can be applied to decision problems other than the management of securities. Bibliographies and exercises are at end of each chapter. This book requires some prior exposure to calculus, probability and statistics, as well as finance and microeconomics.

THE STOCK MARKET AND INVESTMENT MANAGEMENT GUIDES

Handbooks

1971 — Encyclopedia of Stock Market Techniques. Larchmont, N.Y., Investors Intelligence, 1970.

This is the third edition of a survey of many stock market techniques, with chapters written by 43 experts to cover charting and fundamental, technical and specialized approaches.

Zarb, Frank G. and Gabriel T. Kerekes, eds. *The Stock Market Handbook: Reference Manual for the Securities Industry.* Homewood, Ill., Dow Jones-Irwin, 1970.

A comprehensive handbook covering all important aspects of the securities industry in 65 chapters, each written by one of 74 specialists. The 5 main sections cover: the scope of the securities industry (including chapters on the principal exchanges); securities (chapters on mutual funds, options, margin trading, arbitrage, etc.); the integrated securities firm (30 chapters on such topics as organization, personnel, sales management, research, accounting and control); the specialty securities houses; elements of investment decision-making. Includes a glossary.

Books

Brealey, Richard A. *An Introduction to Risk and Return from Common Stocks.* Cambridge, Mass., MIT Press, 1969.

This is a short book for investors and students that aims "to provide in three largely self-contained sections a description of the stock market as seen through the eyes of the statistician." The sections are: stock prices; earnings; the portfolio. References are at end of the book.

Darst, David M. *The Complete Bond Book: A Guide to all Types of Fixed-Income Securities.* New York, McGraw-Hill, 1975.

Aims to be a clear and concise guidebook "on how to analyze, purchase, and sell U.S. government and Federal Agency securities, corporate bonds and preferred stocks, tax-exempt securities, short-term money market securities, and international securities." Includes examples, simplified formulas and a useful chapter discussing sources of further information.

Engel, Louis. *How to Buy Stocks.* 5th ed., rev. Boston, Little, Brown, 1971.

One of the best, simple books on fundamentals of investing in stocks and bonds for the beginning investor.

Esslen, Rainer. *How to Buy Foreign Securities: The Complete Book of International Investing.* Frenchtown, N.J., Columbia Publishing Co., 1974.

This guide contains chapters on investing in 20 countries, and for each it includes "partial lists" of banks, brokerage houses, actively traded stocks, investment funds, sources of investment information, newspapers, financial and business journals.

Graham, Benjamin. *The Intelligent Investor: A Book of Practical Counsel.* 4th rev. ed. New York, Harper & Row, 1973.

Latest edition of a classic guide on the principles of sound investing, with the main objective "to guide the reader against areas of possible substantial error and to develop policies with which he will be comfortable."

Gross, LeRoy. *The Stockbroker's Guide to Put and Call Option Strategies.* New York, New York Institute of Finance, 1974.
A concise guide to the OTC option market and the CBOE market. Includes a glossary.

Hagen, Robert and Chris Mader. *What Today's Investor Should Know About the New Science of Investing.* Homewood, Ill., Dow Jones-Irwin, 1973.
This book offers practical advice based on factual information gleaned from many scientific research studies, which are referred to throughout the text. After an introductory section, the first part explains what one needs to know to understand the new science; the last part applies the new science to personal investing. Includes a bibliography.

Hardy, C. Colburn. *Dun & Bradstreet's Guide to Your Investments.* New York, T. Y. Crowell (biennial).
A handy guide for the beginning investor arranged in 4 parts: how to make your basic investment decisions; common stocks for profits; profits in other securities; how to set up your portfolio. Includes a bibliography.

Jessup, Paul F. *Competing for Stock Market Profits.* New York, Wiley, 1974.
An introductory nontechnical book for actual and potential investors to tell them what they need to know about the stock market, how to evaluate stocks, basic investment strategies, how to decide when to buy or sell stocks.

Knowlton, Winthrop and John L. Furth. *Shaking the Money Tree: How to Find New Growth in Common Stocks.* New York, Harper & Row, 1972.
One of the best books written on how to make a fair return on investments in the stock market. The authors consider the 4 basic problems of objectives, philosophy, selection, and implementation, with the most importance given to the problem of selection. This book is based to a certain extent on Knowlton's earlier study of *Growth Opportunities in Common Stocks* (Harper & Row, 1965).

Lorie, James H. and Mary T. Hamilton. *The Stock Market: Theories and Evidence.* Homewood, Ill., Irwin, 1973.
"This book attempts to organize, summarize, translate into simple language, and interpret the voluminous and scientific literature" on the stock market. It is in 3 sections: the behavior of the market (behavior of stock prices and rates of return on stocks); the valuation of securities; portfolio management. Includes a glossary and a bibliography.

Roalman, Arthur R. *Investor Relations Handbook.* New York, AMACOM, American Management Associations, 1974.
Short essays by 14 experts dealing with investor relations — what it is, how it is budgeted, the annual meeting, financial press relations. Includes 2 case histories and an appendix listing laws, court decisions, reference aids, etc.

Shade, Philip A. *Common Stocks: A Plan for Intelligent Investing.* Homewood, Ill., Irwin, 1971.
"Designed to bridge the gap between theory and practice by presenting the important fundamental concepts of security evaluation at a level that can be understood by

the intelligent layman." Includes a glossary; also a bibliography for readers who want to delve more deeply into the concepts presented.

COMMODITY FUTURES TRADING

Sources for statistics on commodities and commodity futures are included in Chapter 5.

Arthur, Henry B. *Commodity Futures as a Business Management Tool.* Boston, Division of Research, Harvard University Graduate School of Business Administration, 1971. (Now distributed by Harvard University Press.)

This study focuses on how commodity futures fit into the business management picture. The first 2 parts consider the total industry position and futures as a management instrument; the policies functions, and risk management problems of the individual firm. Part 3 reviews actual applications practices in 5 important agribusiness industries; Part 4 summarizes the significant findings and suggests important policy applications. Appendixes include a note on hedging, contract and trading information. A glossary and bibliography are at end.

Gould, Bruce G. *Dow Jones-Irwin Guide to Commodity Trading.* Homewood, Ill., Dow Jones-Irwin, 1973.

A practical guide written for the novice trader by a professional commodities speculator. It is in 3 parts: Part 1 is a "general overview of the market — why it exists, who uses it, how they use it, and the position of the speculator in all this." Part 2 considers the important pricing factors; Part 3 discusses a trading program. Reference data and a glossary are in appendixes.

Hieronymus, Thomas A. *Economics of Futures Trading for Commercial and Personal Profit.* New York, Commodity Research Bureau, 1971.

Designed either as a text or as a "how to" book for the serious student rather than for the speculator. It is in 4 parts: description of exchanges, commodities and the mechanics; the economics of futures trading (including risk shifting, equity financing, speculative pricing); use of futures markets; market operations. It is well written by an experienced practitioner.

Another book by the same publisher is *Modern Commodity Futures Trading* by Gerald Gold (7th rev. ed., 1975).

Teweles, Richard J., Charles V. Harlow and Herbert L. Stone. *The Commodity Futures Game: Who Wins? Who Loses? Why?* New York, McGraw-Hill, 1974.

This book was based on a search of the literature and the many years experience of its authors, and it attempts to give the intelligent layman an understanding of commodity futures in a readable form. There are 5 sections: basics of the game; playing the game (trading); losers and winners; the broker in the game; choosing the game (markets). This last section consists of 15 chapters covering facts and figures on 29 commodity markets (soybeans, wheat, cotton, metals, etc.), including sources of published information for each. A bibliography arranged by topic is at end.

Bibliographies and Periodicals

Chicago. Board of Trade. *Commodity Futures Trading: A Bibliography, 1967–1973.* Chicago, 1973.

A list (not annotated) of books and articles arranged by author. Annual supplements are planned.

Commodities. Columbia, Md., Investor Publications (monthly).

This magazine of futures trading usually has about 4 or 5 articles in each issue as well as regular columns and current news. The January issue each year is a "Directory of Futures Trading," which contains lists of books, advisory services, periodicals, charting services, computer data services, investment management services, consultants, research services, brokerage firms, exchanges.

BIBLIOGRAPHIES OF INVESTMENT BOOKS

Guides to financial services and indexes of financial articles are listed earlier in this chapter.

Brealey, Richard A. and Connie Pyle, comps. *A Bibliography of Finance and Investment.* London, Elek Books; Cambridge, Mass., MIT Press, 1973.

A comprehensive (but not annotated) list of over 3,600 books, articles and dissertations arranged in 150 subject areas. Those in the investment area include: the securities markets; investment institutions and the ownership of securities; market indexes and the return on equities; portfolio selection and capital asset pricing theory; random walk hypothesis; technical analysis; performance measurement; options and convertible securities; bonds and preferred stocks.

Wall Street Review of Books. Pleasantville, N.Y., Docent Corp. (quarterly).

Lengthy, signed reviews of selected books covering a wide range of financial and business topics.

Woy, James B. *Investment Methods: A Bibliographic Guide.* New York, R. R. Bowker, 1973.

The major portion of this combined dictionary/bibliography is a listing of 150 popular investment strategies or factors (such as "dollar averaging," "trend following"), with a definition for each and a descriptive note about books where information about each term can be located. The rest of the guide contains a subject listing of periodical articles, a short list of books and periodicals. The emphasis is on investment writing that is easy to understand.

Zerden, Sheldon. *Best Books on the Stock Market: An Analytical Bibliography.* New York, R. R. Bowker, 1972.

A classified bibliography of 150 books about the stock market, with analytical reviews for each. The section for methods of investing covers technical analysis, fundamental analysis, mutual funds, options, psychology, speculation. The other main headings are for: history, biography, books for the beginner, how to beat the market, general books. There is also a list (without reviews) of textbooks and reference works, as well as a supplementary list of a few classics that the author feels should be on any list of great books.

INVESTMENT DICTIONARIES

Garcia, F. L., ed. *Glenn G. Munn's Encyclopedia of Banking and Finance.* 7th ed., rev. and enl. Boston, Bankers Publishing Co., 1973.

The latest edition of an excellent one-volume encyclopedia covering the whole area of banking and finance, with entries varying in length from one paragraph to several pages. Well-written definitions, often with discussion of uses and examples; also occasional statistics and bibliographies for persons who wish to read about any topic in more depth. Includes investment terms as well as data on the major stock and commodity exchanges, and lists of AMEX and NYSE abbreviations.

Schultz, Harry D. *Financial Tactics and Terms for the Sophisticated International Investor.* New York, Harper & Row, 1974.

A dictionary that defines many new terms and techniques in international money management.

Securities Industry Association. Purchase & Sales Data Processing Division. *A Primer on Brokerage Operations.* New York, New York Institute of Finance, 1973.

This little primer briefly explains brokerage terms and procedures relating to customers, securities, brokers and traders.

Wyckoff, Peter. *The Language of Wall Street.* New York, Hopkinson and Blake, 1973.

A glossary of standard financial and investment terms, compiled by a financial writer.

SECURITIES REGULATION

Loss, Louis. *Securities Regulation.* 2d ed. Boston, Little, Brown, 1961–1969. 6 volumes.

The first 3 volumes (published in 1961) are a detailed study of government regulation of securities, primarily in the United States but with some comparative reference to treatment in England, Canada and other parts of the Western world. Vols. 4-6 (published in 1969) are supplements, which cover the many developments and changes that took place in intervening years.

Udell, Gilman G., comp. *Laws Relating to Securities Commission Exchanges and Holding Companies (With Indices).* Washington, D.C., U.S. Government Printing Office, 1973.

For persons who do not have access to one of the services noted below, this is a handy compilation of the texts of securities laws.

Washington Analysis Corp. *Securities Markets Regulation: A Chronology of Events and Selected Documents.* Prepared by Jerome H. Gross and Susan H. Glendon. Washington, D.C., 1975. 3 volumes.

A compilation of documents, running from Oct. 4, 1941, to March 13, 1975, and covering commission rates, institutional membership, reciprocity, floor trading, Central Market System, Composite Quote System, etc.

Legal Services

Commerce Clearing House. *Federal Securities Law Reports.* Chicago. 5 volumes (with weekly supplements).

A comprehensive loose-leaf service covering federal regulations of securities — laws, regulations, forms, rulings and court decisions. Vol. 1 covers the Securities Act of 1933; Vols. 2-3, the Securities Exchange Act of 1934; Vol. 3 also covers the Public Utility Holding Company Act of 1935; Vol. 4, the Investment Company Act of 1940; Vol. 5, accounting releases, finding lists, a case table, a descriptive list of securities law articles. A last unnumbered volume contains current cases, rulings, court decisions.

CCH publishes a separate one-volume service for *SEC Accounting Rules,* which provides detailed information on the latest accounting regulations (especially Regulation S-X) and releases of the SEC. There is also a separate 3-volume *Blue Sky Law Reports* covering state securities laws, regulations and decisions; a *Commodity Futures Law Reporter* (1 volume); a *Mutual Funds Guide* (2 volumes).

Prentice-Hall, Inc. *Securities Regulation.* Englewood Cliffs, N.J. 3 volumes (loose-leaf).

Provides complete coverage on all laws administered by the SEC, as well as a *Blue Sky Laws Guide* for operating under state securities laws.

DIRECTORIES OF THE SECURITIES INDUSTRY

Commerce Clearing House. *NASD Manual.* Chicago (monthly).

The official manual of the National Association of Securities Dealers, giving bylaws, rules, codes, etc., and a list of member firms.

Financial Analysts Federation. *Membership Directory.* New York (annual).

Arranged alphabetically by the U.S. and Canadian cities that have local affiliated organizations, with the list not only by individual name but also by firm affiliation.

Investment Managers of America. Washington, D.C., Boston Research Associates, 1974.

A list of investment management firms, giving for each, background data, performance, key investment personnel, prominent clients.

Securities Dealers of North America. New York, Standard & Poor's Corp. (semi-annual).

The most complete list of brokers, dealers, underwriters, distributors of securities in the United States and Canada. It is arranged geographically with an alphabetical index, and includes top officers, location of branches, nature of business.

Who's Who in the Securities Industry. Chicago, Economist Publishing Co. (annual).

This is published each year for the annual Securities Industry Association Convention, and it gives biographical information on leaders in the securities industry, including a picture of each.

Two annual directories of underwriting firms that give details of managed underwriting during the year are included in the "New Security Offerings" section of this chapter.

SECURITIES INDUSTRY ASSOCIATIONS

Investment Company Institute, Suffridge Building, 1775 K Street, N.W., Washington, D.C. 20006.

National Association of Securities Dealers, 1735 K Street, N.W., Washington, D.C. 20006.

National Security Traders Association, 55 Broad Street, 27th Floor, New York, N.Y. 10004.

Securities Industry Association, 20 Broad Street, New York, N.Y. 10005 (formerly Investment Bankers Association of America).

8

U.S. BUSINESS AND ECONOMIC TRENDS

Newspapers and News Weeklies — Business and Economic Periodicals — Current Economic Trends and Forecasts — Bank Letters — Regional Statistics — *ECONOMICS LITERATURE* — Introductory Economics Texts — Managerial Economics — Economics Bibliographies and Indexes — Economics Dictionaries — Directories of Economists and Associations — Business Cycles and Forecasting Methods — Technological Forecasting

Urgent social, economic and financial problems within the United States and throughout the world make it important to keep well informed in areas beyond the day-to-day operations of a business. This chapter concentrates on publications that provide daily and weekly news of national and world events, current analyses of business and the economy, regional trends and economic forecasts. For persons who want a refresher in basic economics, there are several introductory economics texts, economics reference works, and books on managerial economics. These are followed by a few recent books on forecasting methods and techniques.

NEWSPAPERS AND NEWS WEEKLIES

To keep abreast of current domestic and international events the businessman will want to read or skim several daily newspapers. Besides the indispensable *Wall Street Journal* this may include the *New York Times* with its excellent business and finance section, and perhaps *The Times* of London if he is interested in foreign opinion. (All three of these newspapers publish detailed periodic indexes.) He will also want to have access to a good metropolitan daily in his area, such as the *Chicago Tribune,* the *Los Angeles Times,* the *Washington Post,* and of course a local paper as well. The *Journal of Commerce and Commercial* (New York, Twin Coast Newspapers) is another important daily that contains general business and industrial news but is especially important for its coverage of commodities, commerce and shipping.

Depending upon one's personal preference, regular reading of either *Newsweek* or *Time* magazine is essential for a quick, weekly summary of national and international news and also for news about business, science, medicine, religion, sports, the arts and other current topics. Both of these news magazines are published in New York. *U.S. News & World Report* (Washington, D.C.), concentrates on popular, short articles about current economic, social and political topics.

Several weekly "confidential" advisory letters are available for persons who like a concise analysis and appraisal of political, economic and financial trends, with possible implications for business and for the economy. These are usually quite expensive but have strong followings. Probably the most popular is *Kiplinger Washington Letter* published in Washington, D.C. There is also a companion weekly covering the foreign scene called *Kiplinger European Letter.*

BUSINESS AND ECONOMIC PERIODICALS

This is a list of the most important general business and economic periodicals. For those that are oriented more toward management, such as the *California Management Review* or the *Harvard Business Review*, refer to Chapter 10. Those covering finance, marketing, personnel and other management functions are included in chapters covering each subject. A selection of trade journals is in Chapter 5.

Business Economics. Washington, D.C., National Association of Business Economists (quarterly).
Contains papers presented at NABE meetings, contributed articles and news of association activities. One issue each year is a directory of members. Indexed in F&S, PAIS.

Business Week. New York, McGraw-Hill.
This is the most useful and widely read business news magazine, with short, readable articles on new business trends and developments in management, markets, industries, companies, international business, regions, the environment, government, etc. There is usually a longer feature article in each issue and often one book review. A page of "Figures of the Week" includes important business indicators. A quarterly statistical "Survey of Corporate Performance" (usually in second issues for March, May, August and November) gives sales, profits, etc., for over 880 top companies in 35 industry categories. An "Annual Survey of International Corporate Performance" (first or second issue in July, e.g., July 14, 1975) contains financial statistics for 500 companies in 37 countries and is arranged by country. There is also an "Annual Survey of Bank Performance" (mid-September, e.g. Sept. 21, 1974) giving statistics for the top 200 banks; and "Survey of Capital Requirement of Nonfinancial Corporations" (annual, e.g. Sept. 22, 1975) which gives key debt and equity data for 550 companies. The last issue each year is an "Investment Outlook" issue and it includes a statistical table giving earnings, stock prices, etc., for 890 large corporations. This important weekly is indexed in BPI, F&S, PAIS, RGPL.

Conference Board Record. New York, The Conference Board (monthly).
Short articles, reporting on research conducted by staff members of this well-known nonprofit research organization; also speeches and other comments on a wide range of economic, business, personnel and public affairs subjects. Some articles include

highlights of surveys of company practices; a continuing feature article studies various aspects of consumer markets. Indexed in BPI, F&S, PAIS.

Dun's Review. New York, Dun & Bradstreet (monthly).

Short, practical and highly readable articles on topics of interest to executives. D & B's very useful annual financial ratios for about 125 lines of business appear first in 3 issues of this journal each year, and then are published separately — retailers ratios are in September, wholesalers in October, manufacturers in November. This journal is indexed in BPI, F&S, RGPL.

The Economist. London (weekly).

This long-time highly respected weekly contains feature articles and news on economic and political trends, focusing primarily on the U.K. but also covering Europe, the international scene and the U.S. There are book reviews and occasional, excellent, in-depth surveys on topics of interest, e.g., "Freight Transport Survey" (Nov. 16, 1974), "World Financial Survey" (Dec. 14, 1974), "A Survey of Gold and South Africa" (Mar. 22, 1975). Indexed in BPI, F&S, PAIS, SSI.

Entreprise. Paris (weekly).

The most popular French weekly, with many practical articles (written in French) of special interest to European executives. Includes an annual list of largest companies, "Les Dossiers d'Entreprise" (for example, Nov. 1974).

Fortune. New York (monthly).

This prestigious business and management monthly contains thoroughly researched and interestingly written articles. A typical issue might include one or two articles on a U.S. or foreign company, one on a prominent U.S. or international executive, an economic or financial problem, an industry or a city, a new product or technological development, a government agency; also usually one book review and several regular features. *Fortune*'s famous list of largest companies appears first in the following issues each year before being reprinted and sold as 2 separate pamphlets: 500 largest U.S. industrial corporations (May); second largest 500 corporations (June); largest U.S. nonindustrial corporations (July); top foreign corporations (August). *Fortune* is indexed in BPI, F&S, PAIS, RGPL.

Industry Week. Cleveland, Ohio, Penton Publishing Co. (weekly).

A popular trade journal formerly published just for metalworking executives but now covering about 5 short feature articles in each issue on current business and management topics of practical and general interest; also a "Trends & Forecasts" section that contains metals prices, news about emerging technologies, etc. The third March issue each year contains a "Financial Analysis of Industry," brief profiles of 17 manufacturing industries with earnings of the leading companies in each. Indexed in BPI, F&S.

Journal of Business. Chicago, University of Chicago Press (quarterly).

This excellent academic journal, edited by the Faculty of the Graduate School of Business at the University of Chicago, is "devoted to professional and academic thinking and research in business." Its articles consist of original research on business and economic theory and methodology, with many of the studies using quantitative techniques. Each issue includes book reviews and a topical list of new books received. The January issue usually includes several articles on the year's business outlook as well as a subject list of doctoral dissertations accepted at American universities during the past year. This journal is indexed in BPI, F&S, PAIS.

Management Today. London, Management Publications, Ltd. (monthly).

This is meant to serve as the British counterpart to *Fortune,* and it is similar in type of articles and coverage. It contains 2 annual lists of large companies: "British Business Growth League" (June) and "British Business Profitability League" (October). Indexed in F&S, F&SI, PAIS.

MSU Business Topics. East Lansing, Graduate School of Business Administration, Michigan State University (quarterly).

A good selection of articles primarily by academic persons and covering a wide range of business topics. Indexed in BPI, PAIS.

Nation's Business. Washington, D.C., Chamber of Commerce of the United States (monthly).

Popular articles representing the business viewpoint on business, economic and political topics, government activity and other areas of interest to businessmen. Includes interviews with top executives called "Lessons of Leadership" and continuing departments such as "Business: A Look Ahead." Indexed in BPI, F&S, RGPL.

Quarterly Review of Economics & Business. Urbana, Bureau of Economic and Business Research, University of Illinois.

An academic journal reporting on empirical research in economics and business. Includes book reviews. Indexed in BPI, PAIS, SSI.

Review of Economics and Statistics. Cambridge, Mass., Harvard University Press (quarterly).

Another academic periodical containing empirical studies on economics, finance and statistical methods, edited by Harvard's Department of Economics. Indexed in BPI, PAIS, SSI.

University of Michigan Business Review. Ann Arbor, Graduate School of Business Administration, University of Michigan (bimonthly).

Concise articles covering all aspects of business and economics, including relations of business with society and with the government. Indexed in BPI, F&S, PAIS.

CURRENT ECONOMIC TRENDS AND FORECASTS

Basic sources of current business and economic statistics — including the important economic and financial indicators — are described in Chapter 4. Various business barometers and indicators (such as GNP, prices, employment, production, construction) are described and discussed in books on forecasting methods (mentioned later in this chapter) and occasionally in textbooks on business and economic statistics (see Chapter 17).

Of the three publications noted below, by far the most useful for economic forecasts is the quarterly *Predicasts,* because it not only provides actual forecast figures, but it also serves as a comprehensive index to the many articles being written on short- and long-range forecasts. If this service or the NPA series is too expensive for a library there are alternatives. The Department of Commerce's *U.S. Industrial Outlook* below is a handy source and is reasonably priced. Also many business and trade journals publish special outlook issues or articles either at the end of one year or at the beginning of the next. Some of these can be identified by using a periodical index such as *Business Periodicals*

Index or *Public Affairs Information Service.* To cover forecast articles in those journals not indexed it may be necessary to look at files of the most likely issues.

National Planning Association. *National Economic Projections Series* (NEPS) and *Regional Economic Projections Series* (REPS). Washington, D.C. (issued irregularly).

These are two expensive but useful long-range forecasting series. NEPS focuses primarily on the development of detailed 10-year forecasts of GNP and its components, including consumption expenditures by specific item; also population, labor force, consumer and wholesale price indexes and implicit price deflators. REPS gives projections of key indicators for states and SMSAs including employment, personal income, personal consumption expenditures for over 80 product items. Subscribers also receive copies of *Projection Highlights,* which are usually 4-page summaries of research with a few statistics, published irregularly.

Predicasts. Cleveland, Ohio, Predicasts, Inc. (quarterly).

As mentioned above, this is the most useful continuing source for short- and long-range forecast statistics both for business and economic indicators and for individual products (by SIC number). Accompanying each forecast is the date and page reference of the current journal, government report or special study from which the statistics were taken. A companion service, *Worldcasts,* covers foreign countries and industries and is described in Chapter 6.

U.S. Department of Commerce. *U.S. Industrial Outlook.* Washington, D.C., U.S. Government Printing Office (annual).

A handy volume for concise information on recent trends and outlook (for about 5 years) in over 200 individual industries. The short narrative with the statistics usually contains discussions of changes in supply and demand for each industry, developments of domestic and overseas markets, price changes, employment trends, capital investment.

The Conference Board (New York) publishes a monthly *Statistical Bulletin* consisting of short-range forecasts for leading economic and business indicators. The Survey Research Center at the University of Michigan publishes a quarterly *Economic Outlook USA,* which contains short articles on the economic outlook, cyclical trends and statistics and charts.

Several universities, banks and other organizations publish brief, annual outlooks for the coming year. A few examples are:

Conference Board. *Business Outlook.* New York.
Harris Trust and Savings Bank. *Business and Money: Review and Outlook.* Chicago.
United California Bank. *Forecast.* Los Angeles.
University of California, Los Angeles. *The UCLA Business Forecast for the Nation and California.*
University of Michigan. Department of Economics. *The Economic Outlook for (year): Papers Presented at a Conference on the Economic Outlook.* Ann Arbor.

Very expensive studies are often published on individual industries or products by several research and consulting firms such as Frost & Sullivan, Inc. (New York). These are carefully researched studies on the industry and on the leading companies in the industry, and they usually include an analysis of prospects for the future. It is unfortunate that these are priced too high ($400 to $600) to be found in most public or university libraries, but it may be possible to find one in a library specializing in any of the topics covered. These publications are occasionally listed in the "Marketing Abstracts" section of the *Journal of Marketing* or in *The Marketing Information Guide*. Lists can also be obtained from each publisher.

BANK LETTERS

The research departments of many large banks prepare excellent brief letters or bulletins analyzing current financial and economic trends. A comprehensive bibliography of these bank letters and also the various bank statistical monthlies is in the final stage of production by a group of bank librarians, with publication planned by Special Libraries Association for 1976. This list will include full bibliographical data about each publication and a note as to whether the data is regional or national. Following are the names of four of the most widely read bank letters.

Chase Manhattan Bank. *Business in Brief.* New York (bimonthly).
> Each issue highlights one or two financial or economic trends of interest to business. The first page always contains general comments on the outlook for the economy.

Cleveland Trust Co. *Business Bulletin.* Cleveland, Ohio (monthly).
> A 4-page sheet of charts and interpretative text covering business activity and economic indicators. Indexed in F&S.

Citibank. *Monthly Economic Letter.* New York.
> This is the best known bank letter, highly respected for its current summary of economic and financial conditions and trends. Includes quarterly total net income figures of leading corporations, by industry groups. Indexed in BPI, PAIS.

Morgan Guaranty Survey. New York, Morgan Guaranty Trust Co. of New York (monthly).
> Brief analyses of business and financial conditions in each issue, with charts for several economic and monetary indicators. One or two varying economic or financial topics are also highlighted.

Each of the 12 district banks of the Federal Reserve System publish monthly reviews devoted to banking, economic and financial topics, often with statistics relating to the district. These are good sources for current regional data. There is a useful quarterly cumulative index to the subjects covered in these monthly reviews called *The Fed in Print,* published by the Federal Reserve Bank of Philadelphia. That bank has also prepared a retrospective index, *Federal Reserve Bank Reviews: Selected Subjects, 1950-1972* (Philadelphia, Pa., 1973).

REGIONAL STATISTICS

The Census Bureau statistics described in Chapter 4 include excellent figures for regions, states, counties, SMSAs and cities. Several rather old bibliographical guides to these regional census data are listed at the end of this section. Marketing guides mentioned in Chapter 18 are good sources for regional estimates of such important market indicators as population, effective buying income, households, and retail sales. Following are several other types of publication that provide useful regional information:

State Statistical Abstracts

Every state in the United States publishes statistical abstracts, almanacs or economic data books covering statistics for the state, its counties and its cities, as compiled from a variety of sources. These are usually published either by a state agency or a business school bureau of business research. They are often patterned after the *Statistical Abstract of the United States,* are quite comprehensive, and give the source for the statistics at the foot of each table. A complete list of these abstracts is in the back of each volume of the *Statistical Abstract,* and also in several of the bibliographic guides noted in the section below. Several examples are:

Florida Statistical Abstract. Gainesville, published for the Bureau of Economic and Business Research, College of Business Administration, University of Florida (annual).

Michigan Statistical Abstract. East Lansing, Division of Research, Graduate School of Business Administration, Michigan State University (biennial).

Nebraska Statistical Handbook. Lincoln, Nebraska Department of Economic Development (biennial).

Regional Periodicals

The 12 Federal Reserve District banks not only publish monthly bulletins (often with useful economic and financial data about each district), but a few banks also publish reviews of the economy, economic factbooks, etc. For example, the Federal Reserve Bank of Richmond publishes a *Fifth District Figures* (12th ed., 1974), which contains statistics compiled from various government sources.

The bureaus of business research at a number of business schools publish bulletins that are especially good for regional data. Several of these are:

Bulletin of Business Research. Columbus, Center for Business and Economic Research, Ohio State University (monthly).

Business & Economic Dimensions. Gainesville, Bureau of Economic & Business Research, University of Florida (bimonthly).

Colorado Business Review. Boulder, Business Research Division, Graduate School of Business Administration, University of Colorado (monthly).

Georgia Business. Athens, Division of Research, University of Georgia (bimonthly).

Indiana Business Review. Bloomington, Division of Research, Indiana University (bimonthly).

Pittsburgh Business Review. Graduate School of Business, University of Pittsburgh (bimonthly).

Texas Business Review. Austin, Bureau of Business Research, University of Texas (monthly).

Other possible sources for information about states and cities are state agencies such as a Department of Commerce and Development, a Department of Labor and Industry, and local organizations such as chambers of commerce.

Bibliographical Guides for Regional Data

Encyclopedia of Business Information Sources. Vol. 2: Geographic Sources. Detroit, Mich., Gale Research Co., 1970.

For each U.S. state and for the biggest cities, this lists almanacs and yearbooks, bibliographies, directories, gazetteers and guides, periodicals, statistical sources (including the various state statistical abstracts), university bureaus of business research periodicals, bank letters, and Chamber of Commerce magazines.

Hernon, Peter. "State Publications: A Bibliographic Guide for Reference Collections." In *Library Journal,* Nov. 1, 1974, pp. 2810–2819.

This is a list, by state, of the bluebooks or manuals, checklists, state statistical abstracts, industrial or manufacturing directories, and other relevant publications issued for each state.

Public Affairs Information Service Bulletin. New York (weekly, with periodic cumulations).

Includes occasional reference to articles and books indexed under the name of a state or city. For a complete description of this index see Chapter 2.

U.S. Bureau of the Census. *Directory of Federal Statistics for States: A Guide to Sources.* Washington, D.C., 1967. Also their *Directory of Federal Statistics for Local Areas: A Guide to Sources.* 1966.

These are two guides to sources of federal statistics on social, political and economic subjects, arranged by topic, for example, population, health, education, banking and finance. They are both very old and probably available only for use in a library, but they continue to have some use since many of the same statistics are still being published by the Census. A companion guide is their *Directory of Non-Federal Statistics for State and Local Areas: A Guide to Sources* (1970), which covers statistics from private organizations and has an appendix containing the names of state statistical abstracts.

U.S. Department of Commerce. *Measuring Markets: A Guide to the Use of Federal and State Statistical Data.* Washington, D.C., U.S. Government Printing Office, 1974.

In a tabular format, this describes state as well as federal sources for statistics on population, income, employment, sales and selected types of taxes collected by states. A bibliography at end lists state statistical abstracts and factbooks.

ECONOMICS LITERATURE

The large body of materials being written in the area of economics has already been well documented in several full-length bibliographies. Here we will mention only three standard introductory texts, several books on managerial economics, the important bibliographies, indexes, dictionaries and associations. This is followed by short sections on business and technological forecasting methods. A few books on international economics are described in Chapter 16.

INTRODUCTORY ECONOMICS TEXTS

Bach, George L. *Economics: An Introduction to Analysis and Policy.* 8th ed. Englewood Cliffs, N.J., Prentice-Hall, 1974.

Professor Bach has focused his popular introductory text toward kindling an interest in economics by emphasizing only the essential concepts, principles and models and by showing the student how he can "apply these analytical tools to big and little, real-world 'relevant' problems." Its 46 chapters are in 8 parts: some foundations; national income, employment and prices; markets, the price system, and the allocation of resources; incomes, economic power, and public policy; public goods, externalities, and the public sector; the international economy; economic growth; the changing economic world. Case problems are with chapters.

Peterson, Willis L. *Principles of Economics: Micro.* Rev. ed. Homewood, Ill., Irwin, 1974.

An introductory text in paperback, which aims to strike a balance between principles and their application to current economic problems and decisions. It begins by discussing consumer choice and product demand, then studies producer choice and product supply, demand and supply in the product market, competition, the labor and capital markets. The last 2 chapters consider the economics of education and of science and technology. A companion volume is *Principles of Economics: Macro* (Rev. ed., Irwin, 1974).

Samuelson, Paul A. *Economics.* 9th ed. New York, McGraw-Hill, 1973.

The latest revision of one of the best known and most popular texts, covering the fundamentals of economics in 6 parts: basic economic concepts and national income; determination of national income and its fluctuations; the composition of pricing and national output; distribution of income — the pricing of the productive factors; international trade and finance; current economic problems.

MANAGERIAL ECONOMICS

Brigham, Eugene F. and James L. Pappas. *Managerial Economics.* Hinsdale, Ill., Dryden, 1972.

A study of the application of economic theory and methodology to business practices. Includes the standard microeconomic topics (cost theory, market structure, pricing practices, business investment decisions, etc.) as well as a consideration of optimization and risk analysis. Includes selected references; appendixes discuss compound interest and forecasting techniques.

Grossack, Irvin M. and David D. Martin. *Managerial Economics: Microtheory and the Firm's Decisions.* Boston, Little, Brown, 1973.

This text builds "the theory of the firm on a programming (both linear and non-linear) foundation, in contrast to the more traditional approach of focusing on the cost and revenue functions, and their marginal derivatives, as the basis for the firm's decisions." The authors have tried to keep the mathematics simple.

Haynes, W. Warren and William R. Henry. *Managerial Economics: Analysis and Cases.* 3d ed. Dallas, Tex., Business Publications, 1974.

An introductory textbook on those theoretical and analytical tools of economics that are useful in managerial decision-making, including also illustrations of applications and cases in each of its 6 parts: introduction; demand and forecast; production and cost; pricing and output; strategy and capital budgeting; managerial economics in nonprofit organizations. Assumes mathematical and statistical knowledge at the sophomore level.

Mantell, Leroy H. and Francis P. Sing. *Economics for Business Decisions.* New York, McGraw-Hill, 1972.

"This is a book in descriptive and normative applied microeconomics to which has been added some material in econometrics, finance, location theory, and, in a broad sense, behavioral theory of management." It is organized around the kinds of problems and decisions that must be made when introducing a new product. The 5 major sections are: demand analysis (including business forecasting); cost analysis; pricing; financial management and control (includes capital budgeting, capital expenditure decisions); expansion and other decisions. Mathematical material has been held to a minimum; suggested reading lists are at end of chapters.

Palda, Kristian S., ed. *Readings in Managerial Economics.* Englewood Cliffs, N.J., Prentice-Hall, 1973.

A selection of 29 readings arranged in 6 parts and designed to supplement an upper-level or graduate course in managerial or business economics.

Sharpe, William F. *Introduction to Managerial Economics.* New York, Columbia University Press, 1973.

A concise introduction in paperback, designed for business school students and concentrating "on matters such as price discrimination, peak-load pricing, costs, and output patterns over time." A familiarity with college algebra and beginning calculus is assumed.

A new edition of *Managerial Economics: Text, Problems and Short Cases* by Milton H. Spencer, K. K. Seo and Mark G. Simkin (4th ed., Homewood, Ill., Irwin) will be published in late 1975.

ECONOMICS BIBLIOGRAPHIES AND INDEXES

Economic Books: Current Selections. Pittsburgh, Pa., Department of Economics and University Libraries of the University of Pittsburgh (quarterly).

A useful, annotated list of economic books classified by subject and coded by budget size of college or university library for which each book is recommended. Includes sections for: international economics; administration (business finance, marketing, accounting); industrial organization; reference works.

Fletcher, John, ed. *The Use of Economics Literature.* London, Butterworth & Co.; Hamden, Conn., Archon Books (Shoe String Press), 1971.

Bibliographical essays by a group of British librarians on the literature of economics, with 7 chapters on various kinds of material (bibliographies, periodicals, government publications, economic statistics, etc.) and 14 chapters covering different subject areas, such as labor economics, industrial economics, monetary economics. Includes international sources as well as those published in the U.K. and U.S. This is still useful although quite out of date.

Index of Economic Articles in Journals and Collective Volumes. Sponsored by the American Economic Association. Homewood, Ill., Irwin (annual).

This is a classified list, with author index, for English-language articles in major professional economic journals and in collective volumes. Vols. 1–7 are for the years 1886–1965; since then each volume covers just one year, with Vol. 10, 1968, the latest published as of summer 1975.

International Bibliography of Economics. Prepared by the International Committee for Social Science Information and Documentation. London, Tavistock; Chicago, Aldine (annual).

An international, classified bibliography of articles, pamphlets and books, with author and subject indexes.

Journal of Economic Literature. Nashville, Tenn., American Economic Association (quarterly).

This is a very useful, bibliographical quarterly. Each issue includes: an annotated list of new books, classified by subject; a subject index of articles in current periodicals; selected abstracts of the more significant articles, by subject; tables of contents for current economics journals. Critical book reviews are at the beginning of each issue.

Melnyk, Peter. *Economics: Bibliographic Guide to Reference Books and Information Resources.* Littleton, Colo., Libraries Unlimited, 1971.

A selection of bibliographies, dictionaries and encyclopedias, directories, handbooks, surveys and statistics, monographic treatises (published prior to 1971) in 9 areas of economic theory and its applications. Descriptive annotations are with most items listed.

White, Carl and Associates. *Sources of Information in the Social Sciences: A Guide to the Literature.* 2d ed. Chicago, American Library Association, 1973.

An excellent compilation of basic books and reference sources in the 8 fields that comprise the social sciences: history, geography, economics and business administration, sociology, anthropology, psychology, education, political science. Fourteen subject specialists have assisted in this monumental work. The lists of books on each topic are preceded by useful short introductions; the reference guides are usually annotated and cover the important bibliographies, indexes, directories, dictionaries, encyclopedias, handbooks, almanacs, yearbooks, statistical sources, services, journals, organizations.

ECONOMICS DICTIONARIES

Hanson, J. L. *A Dictionary of Economics and Commerce.* 4th ed. London, Macdonald & Evans, 1974.

Definitions and explanations of approximately 5,000 pure and applied economics terms and concepts, with a British orientation.

McGraw-Hill Dictionary of Modern Economics: A Handbook of Terms and Organizations. 2d ed. New York, McGraw-Hill, 1973.

This is a particularly useful dictionary because, not only are the definitions usually longer than just one sentence, but each also includes at least one bibliographic citation to which the user can turn for a more detailed explanation. Descriptions of over 200 organizations and associations are at end.

Nemmers, Erwin E. *Dictionary of Economics and Business.* 3d ed. Totowa, N.J., Adams & Co. 1974.

A handy paperback giving short definitions for terms commonly used in college courses in accounting, economics, finance, investments, management science, marketing, statistics, etc.

Sloan, Harold S. and Arnold J. Zurcher. *Dictionary of Economics.* 5th ed. New York, Barnes & Noble, 1970.

Covers the entire field of economics and includes some sketches of agencies and associations, a few Supreme Court decisions. A descriptive classification of defined terms is at end.

U.S. Social and Economic Statistics Administration, Department of Commerce. *Dictionary of Economic and Statistical Terms.* 2d ed. Washington, D.C., U.S. Government Printing Office, 1972.

Definitions of terms for persons who use the statistics in *Business Conditions Digest* and the *Survey of Current Business.* There are 5 parts covering: national income; balance of payments; economic indicators; demography; technical economic and statistical terms.

DIRECTORIES OF ECONOMISTS AND ASSOCIATIONS

American Economic Association (1313 21st Avenue South, Nashville, Tenn. 37212). *Directory of Members.*

This directory is revised periodically and usually appears as an issue of the *American Economic Review* (e.g., October 1974). It includes biographical information about each member.

American Men and Women of Science: Economics. New York, R. R. Bowker, 1974.

Contains full-length biographical information about the leading American economists.

Association for University Business and Economic Research. *Membership Directory.* Tempe, Bureau of Business and Economic Research, Arizona State University (annual).

A directory of bureaus of business and economic research and divisions of research at American universities, giving names of directors and professor in charge, number of staff, names of periodical publications. The headquarters address for AUBER is: Business Research Division, University of Colorado, Boulder, Colo. 80302.

National Association of Business Economists (888 17th Street, N.W., Washington, D.C. 20006). *Membership Directory.*

Published each year as an issue of *Business Economics* (for example, March 1974).

BUSINESS CYCLES AND FORECASTING METHODS

Books on long-range corporate planning are described in Chapter 10.

Butler, William F., Robert A. Kavesh and Robert B. Platt, eds. *Methods and Techniques of Business Forecasting.* Englewood Cliffs, N.J., Prentice-Hall, 1974.

A collection of essays by 30 experts who have focused their talents on discussing the tools, techniques and problems of business forecasting. The editors divided these into

6 parts: the forecasters' kit of tools; major approaches to business forecasting; aggregate forecasting in practice (chapters on forecasting defense expenditures, plant and equipment outlay, construction, inventories, employment, etc.); industrial and sales forecasting (chapters for automobile market, steel industry, national advertising); financial forecasting; the accuracy of forecasts and their uses by business and government. Bibliographies are with many chapters. Of special interest to researchers is the chapter on "Sources of Data" by J. F. Rodriguez (pp. 124–158), which describes statistical sources including such basic indicators as output and income, components of demand (government expenditures, residential construction, inventories, etc.).

Chambers, John C., Satinder K. Mullick and Donald D. Smith. *An Executive's Guide to Forecasting.* New York, Wiley, 1974.

An overview of the principles and commonly used techniques of forecasting and how the various techniques can be applied to the typical decisions made during different phases of the product life cycle. It was written for the manager and for others who have had little exposure to forecasting. An annotated bibliography covering forecasting and market research techniques is at end. A tabular summary of the various techniques is on pp. 63–70 and includes the authors' estimations of accuracy, time required and cost.

Chisholm, Roger K. and Gilbert R. Whitaker, Jr. *Forecasting Methods.* Homewood, Ill., Irwin, 1971.

This is a concise paperback on business forecasting, with chapters covering important quantitative techniques (naive models, polls or survey methods, barometric and opportunistic forecasts, forecasting with input-output analysis, models by means of regression analysis).

Dauten, Carl A. and Lloyd M. Valentine. *Business Cycles and Forecasting.* 4th ed. Cincinnati, Ohio, South-Western, 1974.

An upper level or graduate text on fluctuations in economic activity that covers: causal factors in the cyclical process; national income analysis; the record of business fluctuations; forecasting economic activity; forecasting sales; proposals for achieving economic growth and stability. Suggested reading lists are at end of chapters.

Silk, Leonard S. and M. Louise Curley. *A Primer on Business Forecasting, With a Guide to Sources of Business Data.* New York, Random House, 1970.

This is a slim guide but is handy for its inclusion of concise data on important business indicators, such as income accounts, production, prices, construction. It cites the most important sources for published statistics and has a separate descriptive index of source materials. The first 60 pages briefly explain the principal techniques of business forecasting, and it includes a bibliography.

Wheelwright, Steven C. and Spyros Makridakis. *Forecasting Methods for Management.* New York, Wiley, 1973.

The authors' aim in writing this book is to provide the manager with an easy-to-understand discussion on a wide range of forecasting methods which management can use and to give guidelines relating to performance of the forecasting function within the organization. Six chapters describe quantitative forecasting techniques and one chapter covers the qualitative approaches. Other chapters deal with organizing the forecasting function and data acquisitions and handling. Suggested references are at end of chapters.

TECHNOLOGICAL FORECASTING

Bright, James R. *A Brief Introduction to Technology Forecasting: Concepts and Exercises.* 2d ed. Austin, Tex., Pemaquid Press, 1972.

A paperback workbook meant for students and others who want a brief introduction to TF concepts, with an emphasis on exercises to illustrate applications to industrial and governmental problems. Mr. Bright has also edited (with Milton E. F. Schoeman) a collection of papers by experts prepared for use at a series of Industrial Management Center seminars, 1968–1971. These are in a big, expensive volume with the title *A Guide to Practical Technological Forecasting* (Englewood Cliffs, N.J., Prentice-Hall, 1973).

Cetron, Marvin J. and Christine A. Ralph. *Industrial Applications of Technological Forecasting: Its Utilization in R&D Management.* New York, Wiley-Interscience, 1971.

In writing this book the authors said it was their "intention to look at various types of industry, and at companies of different size, in order to discover, if technological forecasting was being used, the methods being applied and the reasons for forecasting and for choosing particular techniques; or, if forecasting was not being used appreciably, the reason for its lack of popularity." The book is in 2 parts: the first contains reports of survey questionnaires and short case studies based on interviews with companies to examine applications in 7 industries; the second consists of essays on various aspects of forecasting by expert contributors. Cetron has had wide experience especially in the military services, and he has written other books and papers on TF.

Jantsch, Erich. *Technological Planning and Social Futures.* New York, Wiley, 1972.

An informative book consisting mainly of a series of articles, which this well-known authority has written since 1967 on the many aspects of forecasting, planning, decision-making and action. They are grouped under 6 thematic headings. A short list of suggested books is at end.

Martino, Joseph P. *Technological Forecasting for Decisionmaking.* New York, American Elsevier, 1972.

This is a comprehensive and serious "state of the art" book emphasizing TF as an important element in the decision-making process. It is in 3 parts: discussion of forecasting methods (Delphi, analogy, growth curves, trend extrapolation, analytical models, etc.); applications to various types of decisions (including R&D planning, product development and TF use in government and social decisions as well as in business); guidance for the preparation and use of specific forecasts. Includes many useful examples; references are at the end of chapters. Presupposes some knowledge of calculus, and an appendix is included for readers with no knowledge of statistics. Martino has also edited a collection called *An Introduction to Technological Forecasting* (London and New York, Gordon and Breach, 1972), which is a small volume of "papers by well known researchers intended for the serious reader who wants to know about technological forecasting, but not necessarily to do it himself."

Periodicals

Futures. Haywards Heath, Sussex, England, IPC Science and Technology Press in cooperation with the Institute for the Future (6/yr.).

An international journal of forecasting and planning with authoritative articles on methodology and practices; also news of conferences, meetings, book reviews. Indexed in SSI.

Technological Forecasting and Social Change. New York, American Elsevier (quarterly).

This is also an international journal and is "devoted to the methodology of normative forecasting to encourage applications to dynamic integrative planning." Includes book reviews.

9

BUSINESS IN AMERICAN SOCIETY

Introductory Business Texts — Business, Society and the Environment — Business and Government — Business Law — Public Relations and Communications — Business History

The first part of this book has been concerned with types of information — bibliographies, indexes, directories, statistical, financial and other reference sources. Beginning with this chapter the emphasis shifts to the enterprise itself, and here we cover published information on the place of business in American society. It need hardly be mentioned that recent revolutionary social and economic changes are having a profound effect on the way business is conducted. No longer is the businessman concerned solely with operating his company effectively. He is now earnestly trying to adjust to changing ideas and values and to respond to the public's insistence that his company take a more active role in solving problems of society and the environment.

Books may help give the manager a better understanding of these changes and alert him to possible implications for future company planning and policy-making. This chapter describes a few recent books, bibliographies and journals on social responsibilities and on several other important aspects of the external environment of business.

INTRODUCTORY BUSINESS TEXTS

The following three texts are written not for the practicing manager but for the beginning college student, to give him a simple yet comprehensive overview of the nature of the business enterprise — its organization and management, its traditional functions, its relation to society and the environment and its regulation. Each is a standard text, recently revised to cover new developments in matters of social and environmental concern, new data processing and statistical techniques, etc. Each includes either a bibliography or suggested readings for further study.

Glos, Raymond E., Richard D. Steade and James R. Lowry. *Business: Its Nature and Environment.* 8th ed. Cincinnati, Ohio, South-Western, 1976.

Keith, Lyman A. and Carlo E. Gubellini. *Introduction to Business Enterprise.* 4th ed. New York, McGraw-Hill, 1975.

Musselman, Vernon A. and Eugene H. Hughes. *Introduction to Modern Business: Analysis and Introduction.* 6th ed. Englewood Cliffs, N.J., Prentice-Hall, 1973.

BUSINESS, SOCIETY AND THE ENVIRONMENT

When most of us talk about business in society we are thinking primarily of the social responsibilities of business. This is a topic that businessmen and journalists have been writing about for many years; they used to call it "business ethics" or "business morality." Today, as society and business become larger and more complex, social and economic problems also become more difficult and more urgent. With all this one finds an explosion of writings on every imaginable issue, problem, and possible solution. Several recent, general texts, two books of readings and a classic collection of essays are cited below. No attempt has been made to include the many books in any one particular pressing problem area, such as pollution control, minority employment, or consumer protection, but these can easily be located in bibliographies or in libraries. For discussions about socioeconomic problems as they relate to specific management functions refer to recent books in each area. For example, several of the marketing books in Chapter 18 include pertinent chapters on environmental forces that are influencing marketing.

Articles abound, not only in the two journals listed in this section, but in all types of periodicals, whether they are business, technical, or general interest magazines. For easy identification of these many articles, consult the periodical indexes mentioned in Chapter 2.

Ackerman, Robert W. *The Social Challenge to Business.* Cambridge, Mass., Harvard University Press, 1975.

In this new study Ackerman takes a different approach from that of other books by addressing himself to the ways managements of large corporations have responded to changing social demands and the effects these efforts have had on the administration of the firm. His research was conducted from 1972 to 1974 and includes data from interviews with executives and specialists in over 40 corporations and extensive field research in 2 corporations, focusing in one on problems relating to the environment and in the other on equality in employment.

Anshen, Melvin, ed. *Managing the Socially Responsible Corporation.* New York, Macmillan, 1974.

Thirteen thought-provoking lectures given by a group of distinguished business and professional leaders at Columbia University's Graduate School of Business, 1972–1973, in a series of Garrett Lectures on Managing the Socially Responsible Corporation.

Chamberlain, Neil W., ed. *Business and the Cities: A Book of Relevant Readings.* New York, Basic Books, 1970.

A well-chosen anthology, covering material from government reports, research papers, company statements, as well as journal articles, on this important topic. The

78 selections are divided into 8 sections: the nature of business interests in the city; demographic data; business and racial relations; business and the poverty sector; business and manpower development; business and education; business and urban economic development; business and the future of the cities. Chamberlain has also written a thoughtful study on *The Place of Business in America's Future: A Study in Social Values* (Basic Books, 1973).

Davis, Keith and Robert L. Blomstrom. *Business and Society: Environment and Responsibility.* 3d ed. New York, McGraw-Hill, 1975.

An excellent text both for students and for managers, focusing on business as it relates to the whole social system. There are 26 chapters with section headings for: the interface of business and society; business ideology; business and its publics; business and the community; business in an international world. This book is made more interesting by the inclusion of illustrative examples and quotations from other authorities; several short case incidents are with each chapter and 9 cases are at end.

Eels, Richard and Clarence Walton. *Conceptual Foundations of Business.* 3d ed. Homewood, Ill., Irwin, 1974.

Aims to stimulate a broadened view by considering "the meaning of today's business in the light of those ideas and concepts that are the foundations upon which our society is constructed: freedom, ownership, governance and constitutionalism, technology and value, and the idea of progress with stability." The authors feel the very survival of business depends on the values that businessmen see in the concepts discussed in this thoughtful book. Both "Recommended Readings" and "Further Readings" are at end of most chapters.

Jacoby, Neil H. *Corporate Power and Social Responsibility: A Blueprint for the Future.* New York, Macmillan, 1973.

A good, objective "social assessment" of corporations written by a well-qualified economist. It is policy oriented, examining recent changes and proposing reforms of corporate and public policies. Its 5 parts give one a good idea of its approach: criticism and reality; postwar developments in organization and operations; leading economic and political issues; critical social roles; the future. This book was issued as one of several useful "Studies of the Modern Corporation" by Columbia University's Graduate School of Business.

Linowes, David F. *The Corporate Conscience.* New York, Hawthorn Books, 1974.

In this interesting book on corporate social responsibility the author presents a suggested social audit and reporting program, which he calls the Socio-Economic Operating Statement (SEOS). This company statement makes it possible to isolate both the company's socially beneficial and harmful actions so that management and the public can see how it is meeting its social responsibilities to people, to products, to the environment.

Mason, Edward S., ed. *The Corporation in Modern Society.* Cambridge, Mass., Harvard University Press, 1960.

This is a classic selection of 13 significant essays on various legal, economic, political and social aspects of the American corporate system, each written by a well-known authority. Although now quite old it is still widely read.

Monsen, R. Joseph. *Business and the Changing Environment.* New York, McGraw-Hill, 1973.

An objective and readable analysis of problems, issues and values of the business firm written for use as a textbook but also of interest to businessmen. Part 1 covers contemporary issues (pollution, minorities, consumers); Part 2 considers capitalism as a business system; and Part 3 discusses tradition and change of values in American society.

Steiner, George A. *Business and Society.* 2d ed. New York, Random House, 1975.

Probably the most widely used text but also of interest to businessmen for its broad view of the interrelationships and issues between business and society. There are 7 sections: the road to today's complex interrelationships; today's business setting — an overview; business and changing values; business and community problems (7 chapters covering business and the environment, consumers, minorities, education, the arts, technology, etc.); business and government (6 chapters); business and its employees; the future. A bibliography is on pp. 569–598. Steiner has also compiled a book of readings called *Issues in Business and Society* (Random House, 1972), and a book of *Cases in Business and Society* (Random House, 1975).

Bibliographies and Abstracts

Bank of America NT & SA. *Bibliography: Corporate Responsibility for Social Problems.* San Francisco, Calif. (annual).

A continuing, annotated list on the impact of current social problems in business, and corporate responses to them. The emphasis is on budgets, costs and expenditures, and the bibliography lists not only books but also articles, pertinent corporate and organization reports, speeches, annual reports and other materials. It is arranged by topic, for example, employment, energy, environment, pollution, recycling, urban affairs.

Newsweek. *Corporate Social Responsibility: A Bibliography.* 2d ed. New York, 1972.

A short list of books, pamphlets and articles.

Two bibliographies of older material are: *Ethics in Business Conduct: A Guide to Information Sources,* compiled by Portia Christian and Richard Hicks (Detroit, Mich., Gale Research Co., 1970, issued as Gale's Management Information Guide, 21); and *A Selected Bibliography of Applied Ethics in the Professions, 1950–1970: A Working Sourcebook with Annotations and Indexes,* by Daniel L. Gothie (Charlottesville, University Press of Virginia, 1973).

Environment Abstracts. New York, Environment Information Center (monthly).

Abstracts of articles from a wide range of journals, arranged in 21 broad areas, with subject, industry and author indexes. Also includes critical reviews of a few environmental books and descriptions of films. An annual *Environment Index* lists key literature published during the year. The EIC also issues an annual *Energy Index,* which is a comprehensive guide to energy literature and to a few statistics. Since these indexes are all stored in a computerized data bank it is possible to use EIR's on-call research services for bibliographic searches and document retrieval.

Human Resources Abstracts. Beverly Hills, Calif., Sage Publications (quarterly).

Short abstracts of selected studies and current articles on the human, social and manpower problems and solutions facing cities and nations. Published in cooperation with the Institute of Labor and Industrial Relations, University of Michigan and Wayne State University, and arranged in 11 general subject sections, such as education, health and medical care, urban and regional planning, labor force and market. Author and subject indexes at end.

Loose-leaf Services

A number of loose-leaf legal services and guides are now being published to help the many businessmen and other specialists who must keep informed on the latest laws, regulations, rulings, and new developments in environmental protection, pollution control and product safety. Several of these are:

Bureau of National Affairs. *Energy Users Reports* (3 volumes); *Environment Reports* (10 volumes); *Product Safety & Liability Reports* (3 volumes).

Commerce Clearing House. *Consumer Product Safety Guide* (2 volumes); *Energy Management and Federal Energy Guidelines* (2 volumes); *Food, Drug, Cosmetic Law Reports* (5 volumes); *Pollution Control Guide* (4 volumes); *Products Liability Reports* (2 volumes).

Prentice-Hall, Inc. *Energy Controls.*

Periodicals

Business and Society Review/Innovation. Boston, Warren, Gorham & Lamont (quarterly).

An attractively presented and informative journal with articles covering a wide range of topics on the role of business in a free society. "Company Performance Roundup" in each issue briefly reviews notable achievements or failures of specific companies in areas of public concern. Includes book reviews. Indexed in F&S, F&SI, PAIS, SSI.

Journal of Environmental Economics and Management. New York, Academic Press (quarterly).

A new international journal for scholarly articles both on quantitative and qualitative economic/management aspects of all human problems involving both the natural environment and social interdependence.

BUSINESS AND GOVERNMENT

Several books on public policy and marketing are included in Chapter 18.

Corson, John J. *Business in the Humane Society.* New York, McGraw-Hill, 1971.

A thoughtful and readable attempt "to enlist businessmen and government officials in more effective, continuing consideration of how a free people shape and adapt the politico-economic system to satisfy a broadening variety of individual and of social wants, as underlying forces change the kind of world we live in." Corson considers the growth of a "grants economy" (subsidies, contracts, grants), why regulations are necessary, consequences of changes and the new role of business in society.

Mund, Vernon A. and Ronald H. Wolf. *Industrial Organization and Public Policy.* New York, Appleton-Century-Crofts, 1971.

A text aimed at giving "a broad understanding of market structure and conduct and of the role which public policy plays in shaping and directing the business economy to achieve economic welfare." Special attention is given to the structure of industry, its conduct and performance, and the laws made to maintain or modify business structure and conduct. Includes suggested readings.

Wilcox, Clair and William G. Shepherd. *Public Policies Toward Business.* 5th ed. Homewood, Ill., Irwin, 1975.

The latest revision of a basic university text intended to instill an ability to analyze the design, effects and fitness of the 3 major types of public policies toward business: antitrust, regulation, public enterprise. There are 6 sections: the setting for policies; policies to promote competition (chapters on antitrust, restrictive practices, mergers, etc.); the financial sector; regulation; public enterprise; special cases (including policies toward health care, arts and sports, and weapons buying). Mr. Shepherd has edited a volume called *Public Policies Toward Business: Readings and Cases* (Irwin, 1975), which is meant to complement this text.

BUSINESS LAW

Anderson, Ronald A. and Walter A. Kumpf. *Business Law.* 10th ed., UCC Comprehensive Volume. Cincinnati, Ohio, South-Western, 1976.

This textbook for a basic course in business law has been revised to include chapters on consumer protection, environmental law, franchises, and expanded sections on contracts, sales, commercial paper. Case problems are with each chapter; a glossary and text of the Uniform Commercial Code are at end. A shorter version (859 pages instead of 1,103 pages) was published in 1973 as the "9th edition, UCC Standard Volume." These authors have also written a book that is equally divided between textual material and cases, called *Business Law Principles and Cases* (5th ed., South-Western, 1971).

Corley, Robert N. and William J. Robert. *Principles of Business Law.* 10th ed. Englewood Cliffs, N.J., Prentice-Hall, 1975.

The latest edition of Dillavou and Howard's classic text for businessmen and lawyers retains the use of text plus cases but is revised to feature an environmental approach and to stress those aspects of law that are essential to the decision-making process. Its length is awesome (1,110 pages), and it is in 7 basic sections: law, its sources and procedures; contracts; the Uniform Commercial Code; creditors and debtors; agency; business organizations; property. A glossary and the text of the Uniform Commercial Code are at end. Professor Corley has also written a separate text (with Robert L. Black) on *The Legal Environment of Business* (3d ed., New York, McGraw-Hill, 1973), which is designed specifically for businessmen and covers what the law is and how it works, how business is regulated and taxed, legal aspects of mergers, labor-management relations, property rights, torts, etc.

Lusk, Harold F. et al. *Business Law: Principles & Cases.* 3d UCC ed. Homewood, Ill., Irwin, 1974.

This third edition based on the UCC is actually the 10th edition of this standard text. It provides expanded treatment of torts and added chapters dealing with some of the constitutional issues underlying government regulation of business, a chapter on regulation of business through the security laws, and on law dealing with environmental problems. Case problems are at end of each chapter; an appendix includes text of the UCC and a glossary of legal terms.

Bibliographies and Indexes

Marke, Julius J. and Edward J. Bander. *Commercial Law Information Sources* (Management Information Guide, 17). Detroit, Mich., Gale Research Co., 1970.

An annotated list of general texts and books by specific topics, such as contracts, franchise, product liability. Includes also names of dictionaries, directories, bibliographies, periodicals. Now rather old but still of some use.

Index to Legal Periodicals. New York, H. W. Wilson in cooperation with the American Association of Law Libraries (monthly except September; cumulates quarterly).

Subject and author index to legal periodicals in the U.S., Canada, Great Britain, Australia and New Zealand. Table of cases and a book review index are at end.

Dictionaries

Black, Henry C. *Black's Law Dictionary.* Rev. 4th ed. St. Paul, Minn., West Publishing Co., 1968.

"Definitions of the terms and phrases of American and English jurisprudence, ancient and modern."

Corporate Legal Services

Legal services covering specific aspects of business are described elsewhere in this book: securities regulations in Chapter 7; tax regulations, Chapters 12 and 16; banking regulations, Chapter 14; insurance and real estate law, Chapter 15; antitrust and trade regulation, Chapter 18; labor laws, Chapter 19.

Commerce Clearing House. *Corporation Law Guide.* Chicago. 2 volumes (loose-leaf).

Reports on current federal/state corporation law and practice and on the major controls affecting modern business operations.

Prentice-Hall, Inc. *Corporation Guide* and *Corporation Service.* Englewood Cliffs, N.J. (2 loose-leaf services).

The *Guide* is a handy one-volume service designed to give business executives quick and accurate answers to questions of corporate practices, procedures and laws. Includes such topics as organization, responsibilities of officers, financing, state taxes. It is also published, with the title "Explanations," as the first of their 6-volume *Corporation Service.* Four volumes of this service give state statutes, court decisions and rulings affecting the operations of business corporations; the last volume contains *Corporation Forms* for every important situation from pre-incorporation agreements to dissolution.

The Corporation Manual. New York, United States Corporation Co. 2 volumes (annual).

"Statutory provisions relating to the organization, regulation and taxation of domestic business corporations, to the admission, regulation and taxation of foreign business corporations, and arranged under a uniform classification."

Periodicals

American Business Law Journal. Austin, Tex., American Business Law Association (3/yr.).

A professional journal with 3 to 6 lengthy, scholarly articles in each issue, with notes of interest to ABLA members, and book reviews.

Business Lawyer. Chicago, Section of Corporation, Banking and Business Law, American Bar Association (quarterly).

Articles on a wide range of business, financial and legal subjects, written by practicing lawyers and of interest to both lawyers and managers. List of "Recent Literature," by subject, included in each issue. Indexed in PAIS.

PUBLIC RELATIONS AND COMMUNICATIONS

Handbooks

Darrow, Richard W. and Dan J. Forrestal. *Dartnell Public Relations Handbook.* (A second edition is scheduled for publication by Dartnell Corp. in early 1976.)

This promises to be just as comprehensive and practical a handbook as was the 1967 edition, but with revisions and changes to reflect new trends and techniques, and with many helpful examples of campaigns and ideas taken from actual company practice. Supplementary data in appendix of 1967 edition includes a bibliography, lists of special-interest journals, postal rates, zip codes, rules for writing and punctuation.

Lesly's Public Relations Handbook. Ed. by Philip Lesly. Englewood Cliffs, N.J., Prentice-Hall, 1971.

A comprehensive introduction to public relations, with 53 chapters written by 41 professionals. It covers: what public relations is; what PR includes (such as its role in public affairs, financial public relations, employee and consumer relations); how an organization utilizes PR; the techniques of communication; the organization and function of corporate public relations departments. A bibliography and glossary are at end.

Stephenson, Howard, ed. *Handbook of Public Relations: The Standard Guide to Public Affairs and Communications.* 2d ed. New York, McGraw-Hill, 1970.

Another comprehensive guide, with contributions by 31 experts who treat the principles of public relations in 5 chapters; PR, as it relates to various areas of public affairs and to private enterprise, in 17 chapters; specific communication methods and media, in 9 chapters.

Texts

Adelstein, Michael E. *Contemporary Business Writing.* New York, Random House, 1971.

This useful text focuses on writing processes and covers correctness, brevity, vigor, clarity, style, as well as the "what and why of business writing," forms and formats. It is written for students but can also be of benefit to anyone in any kind of organization where writing to inform and to persuade is important.

Canfield, Bertrand R. and H. Frazier Moore. *Public Relations: Principles, Cases, and Problems.* 6th ed. Homewood, Ill., Irwin, 1973.

A good, basic text, with 26 chapters grouped into sections on: the field; the function; the tools; the various corporate publics; specific applications (welfare agencies, associations, armed forces, international public relations); social responsibility. Includes a bibliography.

Cutlip, Scott M. and Allen H. Center. *Effective Public Relations.* 4th ed. Englewood Cliffs, N.J., Prentice-Hall, 1971.

This is probably the most widely used text on public relations. Its main focus is on the role of the practitioner, and it covers essentially the same material as the book above: principles, processes, tools, the various publics, the practice as it relates to business, urban affairs, government, associations, education and related topics. This edition is thoroughly revised to include recent developments in areas of social responsibility. Includes suggested readings.

Hayakawa, S. I. *Language in Thought and Action.* 3d ed. New York, Harcourt Brace Jovanovich, 1972.

Knowing about the role of language in human life and its different uses is basic to an understanding of people and how to communicate with them. In this excellent volume a well-known authority discusses the principles of semantics and their applications. Hayakawa's imaginative and sometimes amusing examples add much to the interest of his book and may encourage readers to test the principles presented. Includes bibliography.

Bibliographies

Blum, Eleanor. *Basic Books in the Mass Media.* Urbana, University of Illinois Press, 1972.

An "annotated, selected booklist covering general communications, book publishing, broadcasting, film, magazines, newspapers, advertising, indexes, and scholarly and professional periodicals."

Carter, Robert M. *Communication in Organizations: An Annotated Bibliography and Sourcebook* (Management Information Guide, 25). Detroit, Mich., Gale Research Co. 1972.

Lists books and selected articles on the many aspects of organizational communications, arranged within 8 major sections: theories and systems; barriers; vertical communication; horizontal communication; media; informal communication channels; organizational change; evaluation of effectiveness.

Norton, Alice. *Public Relations Information Sources* (Management Information Guide, 22). Detroit, Mich., Gale Research Co., 1970.

An annotated bibliography of: general sources; books and pamphlets in special fields or for special publics (corporate, financial, government agencies, political campaigns, etc.); public relations tools (publicity, mass media, etc.); international public relations. Also lists periodicals and reference sources. This is now quite old but is the most recent list published.

Periodicals

Communication Research. Beverly Hills, Calif., Sage Publications (quarterly).

A new journal reporting the results of research, both theoretical and methodological, on communication processes at all levels.

Public Relations Journal. New York, Public Relations Society of America (monthly).

Short articles on a wide variety of PR-related subjects; also notes of interest to PRSA members, and book reviews. Indexed in BPI, PAIS.

Directories

PR Blue Book International. 4th ed. Meriden, N.H., PR Publishing Co., 1973.

Profiles of PR firms arranged alphabetically on a worldwide basis, giving names of officers, areas of specialization, number of employees and names of typical clients. Includes 2 indexes: a geographic index; an index to the typical clients, arranged alphabetically in 20 groups by the nature of the services rendered, e.g., corporate, environmental, financial.

Public Relations Society of America. *Public Relations Register.* New York (annual).

Lists individual members, with index by geographic location and by name of firm.

BUSINESS HISTORY

Beard, Miriam. *A History of Business.* Ann Arbor, University of Michigan Press, 1963. 2 volumes.

The first attempt to write a complete history of the businessman. Starting with the heritage of antiquity in Vol. 1, Professor Beard discusses development from the patrician city ruler up through the monopolist of the eighteenth century. In Vol. 2 she continues with the period of the individualist, on up to the organization makers of the twentieth century. This book was originally published in 1938 with title *A History of the Business Man.*

Chandler, Alfred D., Jr. *Strategy and Structure: Chapters in the History of Industrial Enterprise.* Cambridge, Mass., MIT Press, Massachusetts Institute of Technology, 1972. (Anchor Books Edition, 1966).

This highly significant volume is the first scholarly study of the administrative history of American industry. It is based on a survey of almost 100 large industrial companies, with an exhaustive analysis of the 4 companies that first developed a decentralized, multidivisional structure — du Pont, General Motors, Standard Oil (New Jersey), and Sears. Extensive bibliographical notes are at end. Professor Chandler has a work in progress, "The History of Modern Managerial Business Enterprise," which will concentrate on U.S. firms in the 70 years between 1840 and the First World War. This will be published in 1976.

For a study of the evolution of the strategy and structure of the 100 largest British industrial enterprises, 1950–1970, in a book inspired by Chandler's classic work, see Derek F. Channon, *The Strategy and Structure of British Enterprise* (Boston, Harvard Business School, 1973. Now distributed by Harvard University Press).

Cochran, Thomas C. *Business in American Life, A History.* New York, McGraw-Hill, 1972.

Professor Cochran is one of our most outstanding business historians, and in this excellent volume he studies the history of business in relation to its social and physical environment. Among his other publications is an interesting study of *American Business in the Twentieth Century* (Harvard University Press, 1972).

Krooss, Herman E. and Charles Gilbert. *American Business History.* Englewood Cliffs, N.J., Prentice-Hall, 1972.

An excellent history of American business by 2 experienced economic historians. Written, not from a theoretical point of view, but from a concern "with the problems that businessmen have faced and their attempts at solutions, with their successes and reasons for success, and with their contribution to American life." Cites names of companies and businessmen throughout, and concludes with a chapter discussing relations of business with society. Includes a bibliography. Professor Krooss has also recently revised his standard text on *American Economic Development: The Progress of a Business Civilization* (3d ed., Prentice-Hall, 1974).

Bibliographies

Larson, Henrietta M. *Guide to Business History* (Harvard Studies in Business History, No. 12). Cambridge, Mass., Harvard University Press, 1948. Reprinted in Boston by J. S. Canner Co., 1964.
An old but indispensable guide to materials for the study of American business, including annotated lists of business histories, biographies of businessmen, histories of industries, and research and reference sources.

Lovett, Robert W. *American Economic and Business History Information Sources* (Management Information Guide, 23). Detroit, Mich., Gale Research Co., 1971.
An excellent selected, annotated bibliography of recent U.S. and some Canadian works on economic and business history, as well as on agricultural and labor history and on the history of science and technology. Includes histories of industries, corporate histories and biographies.

An earlier bibliography of American and Canadian company histories and biographies of businessmen (not annotated) is *Studies in Enterprise,* compiled by Lorna M. Daniells (Boston, Baker Library, Harvard University Graduate School of Business Administration, 1957). This is now out of print but available from Xerox University Microfilms.

Institute of Chartered Secretaries and Administrators. *Company Histories.* London, 1972.
A complete list of the British company histories in the library of this institute.

Some British and Irish company histories are also included in the annual "List of Publications on the Economic and Social History of Great Britain and Ireland," by N. B. Harte and D. J. Tierney, which appears in the May issue, each year, of the *Economic History Review.*

Periodicals

Business History Review. Boston, Harvard University, Graduate School of Business Administration (quarterly).
An excellent selection of articles on companies, industries and other topics of interest to business and economic historians. Includes book reviews. Indexed in BPI, PAIS, SSI.

Journal of Economic History. New York, published for the Economic History Association by the Graduate School of Business Administration, New York University (quarterly).

Good professional articles on economic history and related aspects of the history of economics. Includes book reviews. Indexed in PAIS, SSI.

The two comparable British publications are:

Business History. London, F. Cass (semi-annual).

Four or five good, scholarly articles in each issue on histories of British industries, companies, and related subjects. Includes book reviews.

Economic History Review. Welwyn Garden City, Hertfordshire, England, Broadwater Press for Economic History Society (quarterly).

Lengthy, professional articles covering all aspects of economic and social history, with special interest for British and European economic historians. Includes book reviews. Indexed in PAIS, SSI. The May issue each year includes a "List of Publications on the Economic and Social History of Great Britain and Ireland" published during the previous year.

10

MANAGEMENT

Management Handbooks — Books on Management Principles and Practices — Organization Theory — Management Bibliographies — Management Abstracts — Dictionaries and Encyclopedias — Management Periodicals — Associations — Corporate Planning — Human Factors in Organizations — History of Management Thinking — Functions of Directors — Management of New and Small Businesses

The managing of any organization in today's fast-paced and changing world is very complex. Computer technology, the development of quantitative techniques, the new social consciousness, the expansion into foreign markets — all these have had a revolutionary impact on management. Businessmen are finding it imperative to keep themselves informed about all new techniques and methods, and this requires not only taking traditional courses, and attending seminars but also planning a continuous independent reading program of both books and journals.

This chapter is intended to help the manager by suggesting basic management sources: bibliographies, indexes, abstracts, handbooks, periodicals, and a sampling of useful, general books, most of them quite recent. One will also find here a selection of books and periodicals on corporate planning, on human factors in organizations and on small business management. Books on decision-making, on the other hand, are described in Chapter 17, because most of them stress quantitative and statistical techniques.

The previous chapter covered material on the social and environmental aspects of business. The remainder of this book will concentrate on management sources, with separate chapters for each of its principal functions as well as a chapter on international management.

MANAGEMENT HANDBOOKS

Bull, George, ed. *The Director's Handbook.* London and New York, McGraw-Hill, 1969.

A basic guide to current British management practices, with each chapter written by an authority. Discussions are concise and clear. Includes short reading lists and names of associations with each chapter.

Glover, John D. and Gerald A. Simon, eds. *Chief Executive's Handbook.* Homewood, Ill., Dow Jones-Irwin, 1976.

An excellent compilation of the views and practical insights of 91 experienced business leaders whose contributions were sought "to bring together in one volume, to the extent this is possible, the essence of what the chief executive of the modern corporation most needs to know to be effective in that job." It is arranged in 6 parts: overview; organization, motivation, accomplishment; corporate strategy; directing the functions of the business (development engineering and research, production, marketing, finance, management information and control, international business, other functions of the business); managing the company's external relationships; the personal side of the chief executive.

Horton, F. W., Jr. *Reference Guide to Advanced Management Methods.* New York, American Management Association, 1972.

A good, simple guide that defines and explains 61 of the most important new management concepts, techniques and methods, such as decision trees, learning curves, management by exception. Good for the beginner who needs a starting point for brief explanations but limited in topics covered. References to works of other authors are included with each discussion.

Maynard, Harold B., ed. *Handbook of Business Administration.* New York, McGraw-Hill, 1967.

Probably the most ambitious attempt to cover the many aspects of management function and practices. Each of the 166 chapters within 17 broad subject areas is written by an expert. Although it does not cover current developments in new management concepts and methods, it is still good for the older, "tried-and-true" practices. Bibliographies at end of most chapters list some older works. Maynard is a management engineer who has edited several other useful handbooks, notably his *Handbook of Modern Manufacturing Management* and *Industrial Engineering Handbook,* both described in Chapter 20.

Moore, Russell F., ed. *AMA Management Handbook.* New York, American Management Association, 1970.

An excellent guide to management policies and procedures, both for general managers and for students; compiled with the collaboration of many authorities. Within each of 11 broad subject areas (finance, manufacturing, personnel, R&D, etc.) the arrangement is outlined at the beginning of each section. A detailed index is also useful for locating information on specific topics.

Morrison, Robert S. *Handbook for Manufacturing Entrepreneurs.* Cleveland, Ohio, Western Reserve Press, 1973.

Morrison has had wide experience as a successful owner/manager of manufacturing firms, and he has written this comprehensive handbook for the would-be entrepreneur and for students and other businessmen. He covers it all "from the decision to go into business to maintaining the operation after the owner-manager retires." It is a good, practical book.

BOOKS ON MANAGEMENT PRINCIPLES AND PRACTICES

Connor, Patrick E., Theo Haimann and William G. Scott, comps. *Dimensions in Modern Management.* Boston, Houghton Mifflin, 1974.

Readings are often a good means of obtaining a broad view of the complexities and many varied factors of management, and they can be used either to supplement a text or as a completely independent work. This is an excellent anthology, arranged in 5 basic functional areas: planning, organizing, staffing, influencing, controlling. It contains many significant articles or short parts of books. Professors Haimann and Scott have also revised their introductory text on *Management in the Modern Organization* (Houghton Mifflin, 1974), which covers these same 5 areas and also includes some brief case problems.

Dale, Ernest. *Management: Theory and Practice.* 3d ed. New York, McGraw-Hill 1973.

An outstanding general treatise by a well-known professor, consultant and writer. It contains 4 chapters on management and its environment, 3 on management beginnings, 13 on management functions (planning, staffing, control, innovation, etc.), 3 on management of foreign operations, and 4 on current trends and the future. The author says his "approach has been to assume no previous knowledge on the part of the reader but to lead gradually from the simpler concepts to the more difficult ideas and techniques." Short annotated lists of selected readings enhance the usefulness of this well-written book. A new edition of Dale's *Readings in Management: Landmarks and New Frontiers* (3d ed., McGraw-Hill, 1975) follows the same plan and chapter headings as his text.

Drucker, Peter F. *Management: Tasks, Responsibilities, Practices.* New York, Harper & Row, 1974.

The latest of many widely read books by this management authority is a lengthy book (839 pages), with 61 chapters. Its purpose is to give managers all the information they need in order to prepare for effective performance. It is based on Drucker's many years of experience as a management consultant, and thus it draws to a certain extent on some of his earlier works. He considers first "the tasks" (business performance, performance in the service institution, productive work and achieving worker, social impacts and social responsibilities); in the second section he covers "the manager" (work; job, skills, organization); and third he discusses "top management" (tasks, organization, strategies). Because of its length this book may well be treated more as a handbook — to be kept near at hand for frequent reference rather than to be read from cover to cover in one sitting. All managers and students will find it a practical, informative and important book both to read and to consult.

Drucker, Peter F. *The Practice of Management.* New York, Harper, 1954.

This management classic was written both to help managers evaluate and improve their performance and also to explain to younger men just what management is and what qualifications one needs to be a good manager. It is still "must" reading for all managers.

Holden, Paul E., Carlton A. Pederson and Gayton E. Germane. *Top Management.* New York, McGraw-Hill, 1968.

This is a research study of the current management policies and practices of 15 leading manufacturing companies, with an evaluation of changes between the findings in this study and those of an earlier, similar project also conducted under the auspices of Stanford's Graduate School of Business. Conclusions are presented in 11 areas, including long-range planning, organization structure, product line direction and control, international operations, management information systems, selection and training of executive personnel. It provides interesting and informative reading.

Koontz, Harold and Cyril O. O'Donnell. *Management: A Systems and Contingency Analysis of Managerial Functions.* 6th ed. New York, McGraw-Hill, 1976.

A substantial revision of one of the best known texts on the operational theory and science of management that emphasizes the essentials of management pertinent to practicing managers. Five of its six sections cover the basic functional areas of planning, organizing, staffing, directing and leading, controlling. Includes a glossary and a few bibliographical footnotes. Koontz and O'Donnell have also written two related books: one is a concise (482 pages) version of this text written to meet the demand for a much shorter book dealing only with the *Essentials of Management* (McGraw-Hill, 1974); the other is a new edition of their *Management: A Book of Readings* (4th ed., McGraw-Hill, 1976). This latter book is arranged in the same broad sections as is their *Management* and so it can be used either to amplify the text or as a completely separate selection of excellent management readings.

McCarthy, Daniel J., Robert J. Minichiello and Joseph R. Curran. *Business Policy and Strategy: Concepts and Readings.* Homewood, Ill., Irwin, 1975.

This book utilizes both text and readings in "developing a framework for the formulation and implementation of strategy for business and other organizations." It studies the job of general managers or top executives and examines the skills required to perform well. Meant for an undergraduate or graduate course or for practicing managers.

McGregor, Douglas. *The Human Side of Enterprise.* New York, McGraw-Hill, 1960.

Professor McGregor's current classic has had more influence on managers than any other book of its kind in a continuing search for better ways of managing, motivating and developing personnel. In it he presents his Theory Y, a strategy to integrate the individual's goals with those of the organization, and a large portion of the book discusses practical implications of Theory Y. Also covers the development of managerial talent.

McGuire, Joseph W., ed. *Contemporary Management: Issues and Viewpoints.* Englewood Cliffs, N.J., Prentice-Hall, 1974.

Twenty-two well-known management experts have contributed chapters on their major area of interest, with two additional experts commenting on each essay. Covers: the disciplinary foundations of management; the environment of management (internal and external); the management "core" (planning, leadership, control, motivation, etc.).

Newman, William H., Charles E. Summer and E. Kirby Warren. *The Process of Management: Concepts, Behavior and Practice.* Englewood Cliffs, N.J., Prentice-Hall, 1972.

An excellent introductory text emphasizing use of new developments from behavioral science and decision-making research and theories. The authors examine four basic elements in the process of management that are present in every kind of enterprise: organizing, planning, leading and controlling. Includes readings. Harold Lazarus, with Professor Warren and Jerome E. Schnee, has compiled a book of related readings, *The Process of Management: Process and Behavior in a Changing Environment* (2d ed., Prentice-Hall, 1972).

Raia, Anthony P. *Managing by Objectives.* Glenview, Ill., Scott, Foresman, 1974.

This is the most recent of a number of books on a technique for improving management performance, which have received wide interest and use. It is a concise discussion of the fundamental concepts and tools necessary for an effective MbO system, included here particularly for its useful, annotated bibliography (pp. 173–199), which will refer the reader to other recent, good books, including one by the best known proponent of MbO (*Management by Objectives,* by George S. Odiorne. Rev. ed., London, Pitman, 1970).

For persons interested in keeping up to date on MbO and related methods there is a useful journal, *Management by Objectives,* published quarterly in Weybridge, Surrey, England, by Classified Media, Ltd.

Sloan, Alfred P. *My Years with General Motors.* Ed. by John McDonald, with Catharine Stevens. Garden City, N.Y., Doubleday, 1964.

The story of the management of General Motors over the 23 years (1923–1946) when Mr. Sloan served as its chief executive. This is a very informative, readable book and provides valuable insight into the kinds of decisions and problems faced by this outstanding administrator.

Terry, George R. *Principles of Management.* 6th ed. Homewood, Ill., Irwin, 1972. (The 7th edition is scheduled for publication in 1976).

Another good, standard text written both for students and for active managers and brought up to date to include new social and environmental concerns. Like the Koontz and O'Donnell book it considers the four basic management functions of planning, organizing, actuating, controlling, and it includes a very useful annotated bibliography (pp. 659–673).

There are many other good, standard introductory texts, two of which are *Principles of Management: A Modern Approach* by Henry H. Albers (4th ed., New York, Wiley, 1974); and *Management: Principles and Practices,* by Dalton E. McFarland (4th ed., New York, Macmillan, 1974).

ORGANIZATION THEORY

Barnard, Chester I. *The Functions of the Executive.* Cambridge, Mass., Harvard University Press, 1968.

In the introduction of this thirtieth-anniversary edition of Barnard's contemporary classic (1938), Professor K. R. Andrews says that this book "remains today, as it has been since its publication, the most thought-provoking book on organization and management ever written by a practicing executive." Barnard, who was a president of New Jersey Bell Telephone Company, divides his study into 2 parts: (1) consideration of cooperative systems and the theory and structure of formal organizations; (2) a study of the elements of formal organizations and the functions of executives in cooperative systems. Although well worth the effort, this book is difficult to read and to understand. Such being the case, readers will benefit greatly by using with it a newly published summary and interpretation by William B. Wolf called *The Basic Bar-*

nard: An Introduction to Chester I. Barnard and His Theories of Organization and Management (Ithaca, New York State School of Industrial and Labor Relations, Cornell University, 1974).

Kast, Fremont E. and James E. Rosenzweig. *Organization and Management: A Systems Approach.* 2d ed. New York, McGraw-Hill, 1974.

In this new approach to organization theory and management the authors "view the organization as a sub-system of its environmental suprasystem." They concentrate on its 5 primary subsystems: goals and values; technology; structure; psychosocial; managerial. Includes a bibliography. Professors Kast and Rosenzweig published a related book of readings containing a selection of 17 articles and sections from books reflecting the development of *Contingency Views of Organization and Management* (Chicago, Science Research Associates, 1973). Another text they recently revised, with Richard A. Johnson as first author, is *The Theory and Management of Systems* (3d ed., McGraw-Hill, 1973). It focuses on systems concepts, techniques and examples of managerial applications. For books on management information systems see Chapter 13.

Litterer, Joseph A. *The Analysis of Organizations.* 2d ed. New York, Wiley, 1973.

An introduction to the theory of organizations, bringing together material from such varied disciplines as social psychology and management science. It is written for both the student and manager and includes references at the end of chapters.

Scott, William G. and Terence R. Mitchell. *Organization Theory: A Structural and Behavioral Analysis.* Rev. ed. Homewood, Ill., Irwin, 1972.

This major revision was undertaken both to incorporate a widening interest of behavioral scientists in organization research and to include consideration of contemporary issues and problems. It is another good, thorough text that considers historical aspects, a general analysis of organizational theory, the various organization processes, organizational change, research and methodology, and concludes with a discussion of organizational issues.

Shrode, William A. and Dan Voich, Jr. *Organization and Management: Basic Systems Concepts.* Homewood, Ill., Irwin, 1974.

A good text on the new systems approach for handling complex problems of managing organizations today. Covers the systems philosophy and its relationships to management assumptions, principles and theory. Includes suggested readings.

Another good book on this increasingly important topic, *Management: A Systems Approach* by David I. Cleland and W. R. King (New York, McGraw-Hill, 1972), focuses on the application of systems concepts to the management process in general.

MANAGEMENT BIBLIOGRAPHIES

Bibliographies in the broad area of business are covered in Chapter 2. Following are several general management bibliographies — a comprehensive guide by a British management bibliographer, a short, basic list compiled by the British Institute of Management, an example of a reading list prepared for use by executives in a corporation, and a list of publications of the American Management Associations. In addition to these, many basic management books also include useful bibliographies, such as those by Dale and Terry in the section above on "Management Principles and Practices."

American Management Associations. *AMACOM Resources for Professional Management.* New York (annual, with monthly supplements).

An annotated listing of all AMA publications including recordings and programmed instruction courses. The monthly four-page supplement highlights recent publications and is called "Management Bookshelf." AMA books cover a wide range of important management topics in all functional areas. They vary greatly in quality, but some are good, concise and practical treatises, which may suit the manager's needs better than a lengthy classroom text. It is worth checking these descriptive listings occasionally to keep informed on what this association is publishing.

Bakewell, K. G. B. *Management Principles and Practices.* Detroit, Mich., Gale Research Co., 1976.

This promises to be a very useful, annotated "guide to literature, organizations and other information sources concerned with all aspects of management," scheduled for publication in Gale's *Management Information Guide* (No. 32) series late in 1976. There are 21 sections covering management, planning, and the behavioral sciences, and also specific management functions, such as marketing, production, personnel, It includes a good representation of British and European sources, as well as those published in the United States, since its author is an experienced British bibliographer and lecturer. His earlier book, somewhat similar in coverage but written as a bibliographical essay, was *How to Find Out: Management and Productivity* (2d ed., Oxford, England, and New York, Pergamon, 1970).

British Institute of Management. *A Basic Library of Management.* London, 1974.

The second edition of a useful, short list arranged by topic within 12 functional areas, such as production, marketing, personnel. Selection is based on usage in the BIM library, so it includes more British than American texts. The BIM library has also produced a series of short reading lists on 170 very specific business and management topics. These are revised periodically and can be purchased either separately or as a set.

Deere & Co. *Staying Ahead: Reading for Self-Development.* Moline, Ill., 1974.

This is a good, short, annotated list of management books, especially useful for the busy businessman who prefers to choose from a small selection of the many books being written in the 20 broad subject areas covered. Also includes programmed instruction, recordings, videotapes. It is revised occasionally by the librarian at Deere for use in their Management Development Training Programs. Not widely distributed outside the company, but it can be found in many libraries with large business collections.

Two annotated bibliographies described in Chapter 11 include some important books on management and administration of interest to business managers as well as to public administrators. These are *Public Administration: A Bibliography* by Howard E. McCurdy (Washington, D.C., College of Public Affairs, American University, 1973) and *Administration and Management: A Selected and Annotated Bibliography* by William G. Hills and others (Norman, University of Oklahoma Press, 1975). See also K. D. C. Vernon's useful bibliographical guide on the *Use of Management and Business Literature* (London and Boston, Butterworths, 1975) described in Chapter 2; also Agnes O. Hanson's source book on *Executive and Management Development for Business and Government,* in Chapter 19.

MANAGEMENT ABSTRACTS

Although the United States is far ahead of other countries in the publication of good periodic subject indexes to business articles (see Chapter 2), the British have done more in publishing basic management bibliographies and abstracting services, as evidenced by several lists noted above and two of the publications below.

Anbar Management Services. Wembley, England, Anbar Publications. (5 sections, 8/yr.).

Each of the 5 sections specializes in describing articles in a specific management area, and each is co-sponsored by an allied British professional association:

Top Management Abstracts (British Institute of Management)
Accounting + Data Processing Abstracts (Institute of Chartered Accountants in England and Wales)
Marketing + Distribution Abstracts (Institute of Marketing)
Personnel + Training Abstracts (Institute of Personnel Management)
Work Study + O and M Abstracts (Institute of Work Study Practitioners)

This service is meant primarily for the busy businessman who wants to monitor a selection of some of the better articles and then order copies of those he wishes to read in full. It is not as satisfactory a service for the researcher, who is usually looking for material on a very specific topic, because the listing is arranged alphabetically by name of journal rather than by topic, and a classified index is published only twice a year. Particularly good for its selective coverage of British as well as some American management journals. Received with this service is a separate *Anbar Management Services: Bibliography,* which is an annual listing of books, pamphlets and films reviewed in the journals covered by the Anbar service. It is arranged in the same 5 categories as the service itself. The publisher also offers an annual abstracting service called *The Compleat Anbar.*

Management Review & Digest. London, British Institute of Management (quarterly).

Each issue includes a section of "Management Abstracts," briefly describing a selection of U.S. and U.K. articles in 8 broad management areas, and it also reviews a few new management books. Other sections describe new management research, new management information in sound and visual form, new books in the BIM library.

Personnel Management Abstracts. Ann Arbor, Division of Management Education, Graduate School of Business Administration, University of Michigan (quarterly).

Since this descriptive listing of recent articles for personnel managers includes material on management functions, decision-making, planning, motivation, etc., it is of value to include in this management section. Contains an annotated subject listing of articles, with an index by author and title, followed by more detail about the more important articles that are starred in the first section. It also covers a few books.

DICTIONARIES AND ENCYCLOPEDIAS

Encyclopedia of Management. Ed. by Carl Heyel. 2d ed. New York, Van Nostrand Reinhold, 1973.

An excellent encyclopedic dictionary, completely revised and updated with the help of over 200 expert contributing editors. The definitions run from "accounting" to "zero defects," and the entries vary in length from about a half page to more detailed articles of over 10 pages. References to texts or organizations included with many definitions.

French, Derek and Heather Saward. *Dictionary of Management.* New York, International Publications Service, 1975.

Contains definitions of nearly 4,000 management and economic terms and techniques chosen for inclusion because of their use by managers and writers about management. It is meant to be equally useful to American and British readers and so distinguishes varying usage in the 2 countries. Includes abbreviations and short descriptions of important associations and organizations.

Horton, F. W., Jr. *Reference Guide to Advanced Management Methods.* New York, American Management Association, 1972.

A good, simple guide that defines and explains 61 important new management concepts, techniques and methods, such as decision trees, learning curves, management by exception. Good for the beginner who needs a starting point for brief explanations, but limited in topics covered. Reference to works of other authors is included.

Johannsen, Hano and G. Terry Page. *International Dictionary of Management: A Practical Guide.* Boston, Houghton Mifflin, 1975.

This is an up-to-date dictionary covering the whole area of business and management. Its 5,000 entries define terms, concepts, initials and acronyms in international usage and also give concise data on institutions such as government and nongovernment agencies, associations, trade unions, stock exchanges. Includes many cross-references.

MANAGEMENT PERIODICALS

Articles on management appear in all varieties of business publications. Even magazines discussing business in general (for instance, *Business Week* and *Fortune*) frequently run articles on important management subjects or touch on them in articles dealing with other topics. Trade journals published for a particular industry or trade also carry management articles. The best commercial indexes for finding articles on any specific business or management topic are described in Chapter 2.

This is a selection of the most important academic, professional and trade journals dealing directly with management subjects. Business periodicals are listed in Chapter 8.

Academy of Management Journal. Tampa, Fla. (quarterly).

Scholarly articles on management theory and practice, organizational behavior, management education and so forth, many of them based on research studies undertaken at various universities. Includes occasional literature review articles that are useful. Indexed in BPI.

Administrative Science Quarterly. Ithaca, N.Y., Graduate School of Business and Public Administration, Cornell University.

The science of management in all kinds of organizations is discussed in excellent, authoritative articles that are based both on empirical investigation and on theoretical analysis. Includes book reviews. Indexed in BPI, PAIS.

Business Horizons. Bloomington, Graduate School of Business, Indiana University (bimonthly).

One of the best academic journals, with useful, well-written articles on all aspects of management and business planning. Includes a short book review section and brief data about ongoing research. Indexed in BPI, F&S, F&SI, PAIS.

Business Quarterly. London, Canada, School of Business Administration, University of Western Ontario.

The best Canadian academic journal, with scholarly articles aimed particularly at the Canadian executive. Indexed in PAIS.

California Management Review. Berkeley, Graduate School of Business Administration, University of California (quarterly).

Another excellent academic journal. Articles are on all aspects of enterprises — both public and private — with priority given to those reporting results of original research and analysis. Indexed in BPI, F&S, F&SI, PAIS.

The Director. London, Institute of Directors (monthly).

An informative journal, with short articles on a wide range of business and management topics of special interest to British managers. Includes book reviews. Indexed in BPI.

European Business. Paris, Société Europeenne d'Edition et de Diffusion (quarterly).

Well-written articles (in English) devoted to "stretching the thinking" of top European executives by studying and analyzing new trends and innovations in management. Indexed in PAIS.

Harvard Business Review. Boston, Graduate School of Business Administration, Harvard University (bimonthly).

One of the most outstanding professional management journals, with practical articles by recognized authorities on all aspects of general management and policy. Indexed in BPI, F&S, F&SI, PAIS, RGPL. Their "Reprint Series" of recent past articles provides excellent collections of thoughtful writings on related topics of special interest, such as business policy, executive compensation, forecasting, human relations, planning. There are over 50 of these currently available (1975), and titles of the newest in the series are usually described in each issue of the *Review.*

Journal of General Management. London, Mercury House Business Publications in Association with the Administrative Staff Colleges (quarterly).

A relatively new journal whose aim is to help keep executives up to date on new developments in the theory and practice of top management. Authoritative articles of special interest to the European manager. Indexed in PAIS.

Journal of Management Studies. Oxford, England, B. Blackwell (3/yr.).

Scholarly articles on management theory and research, written primarily by British educators and researchers. Includes book reviews.

Management International Review. Wiesbaden, Germany, T. Gabler (6/yr.).

This international review covers management practice, managerial sciences and management education, with each article written either in French, German or English and summary translations in the other languages. An annotated booklist is in each issue. It is published under the auspices of the European Foundation for Management Development with the cooperation of three other management associations.

Management Review. New York, AMACOM, American Management Associations (monthly).

This little review consists of digests of about 7 good articles from other journals, about 4 short feature articles of practical interest, book notes and summaries of other timely articles. Indexed in BPI.

S.A.M. Advanced Management Journal. New York, Society for Advancement of Management (quarterly).

Short, readable articles on current management theory and practice by businessmen and educators. Annotated booklists in most issues. Indexed in BPI.

Sloan Management Review. Cambridge, Alfred P. Sloan School of Management, Massachusetts Institute of Technology (3/yr.).

One of the best academic journals, designed to inform the practicing manager of ongoing research in management. Articles are selected to provide an analytical, application-oriented approach to management problems. The Winter Issue each year lists the Sloan School of Management Working Papers. Includes book reviews. Indexed in BPI, F&S, PAIS.

ASSOCIATIONS

Academy of Management (address varies; check a current issue of their *Journal*).

American Management Associations, 135 West 50th Street, New York, N.Y. 10020.

British Institute of Management, Management House, Parker Street, London WC2B 5PT, England.

Society for Advancement of Management, 135 West 50th Street, New York, N.Y. 10020.

CORPORATE PLANNING

The success or failure of a firm and its executives is often directly related to the presence or absence of effective planning. Fortunately there is a good body of literature to help give executives the background necessary for learning about the principles and objectives of planning, the strategies and steps to follow, and the various techniques. There are also many articles being written, some of which briefly relate the experience of a specific company in one or more of the planning areas. Following are a few recent books; articles can be located by using the periodical indexes in Chapter 2.

Ackoff, Russell L. *A Concept of Corporate Planning.* New York, Wiley-Interscience, 1970.

A concise treatment of the philosophy of planning — its nature and content, objectives, design and control. A selected, annotated bibliography is included.

Argenti, John. *Systematic Corporate Planning.* London and New York, Wiley, 1974.

This book, by a British consultant and planning authority, is in 2 parts: Part 1 considers principles and objectives of corporate planning; Part 2 covers the technology (target-setting, strategies, techniques of forecasting, evaluation).

Ewing, David W., ed. *Long-Range Planning for Management.* 3d ed. New York, Harper & Row, 1972.

An excellent selection of current articles and sections from books, written both by businessmen and by academic specialists and meant to cover a broad spectrum of long-range planning practices and policies. Ewing has also written several related books, among which is his concise analysis of *The Practice of Planning* (Harper & Row, 1968).

Hussey, David. *Corporate Planning: Theory and Practice.* Oxford, England, and New York, Pergamon, 1974.

A comprehensive yet concise assessment of current thinking and practice on the whole corporate planning process, with a British focus. Includes examples from actual companies and many quotations from other authorities. References are at end of each chapter, and Kettlewell's comprehensive "European Bibliography of Corporate Planning," prepared for the journal *Long Range Planning,* is reproduced on pp. 333–390.

Jones, Harry. *Preparing Company Plans: A Workbook for Effective Corporate Planning.* Epping, Essex, England, Gower Press; New York, Wiley, 1974.

This guidebook for top executives and corporate planners is written by an experienced planner. Its purpose is not to "sell" corporate planning but rather "to provide a guide to the adoption of corporate planning and its practice as a systematic working procedure." It includes chapters on corporate planning systems and organization, practical phases of planning, format and presentation of plans, monitoring and control. Standard forms and a short bibliography are at end.

Another practical book, now out of print but available for use in libraries, is J. R. Collier's *Effective Long-Range Business Planning* (Englewood Cliffs, N.J., Prentice-Hall, 1968).

Mockler, Robert J. *Business Planning and Policy Formulation.* New York, Appleton-Century-Crofts, 1972.

A good basic text summarizing what both business planning and corporate policy development are and how they are used in business enterprises. It covers all important aspects in the various steps of the planning process, including information systems for planning and some quantitative and graphic techniques, as well as planning for the small company. A list of books cited is on pp. 415–421, and the more important studies are briefly summarized on pp. 324–335. Mockler discusses 30 of the leading studies on the "Theory and Practice of Planning" in an article in the *Harvard Business Review,* March/April 1970, pp. 148–159.

Steiner, George A. *Top Management Planning.* New York, Macmillan, 1969.

The best and most complete volume, covering all aspects of comprehensive business planning: nature and concept; process of developing plans; tools for planning; planning in selected major functional areas. It was issued as one of a number of excellent "Studies of the Modern Corporation" at Columbia's Graduate School of Business. This is a long book (795 pages) — preferably not to be read at one sitting — but it is an indispensable guide that should be in every planner's library. A detailed bibliography of related books and articles published prior to 1969 is on pp. 733–770.

Other books usually mentioned in any basic list are: H. I. Ansoff, *Corporate Strategy: An Analytic Approach to Business Policy for Growth and Expansion* (New York, McGraw-Hill, 1965); and J. T. Cannon, *Business Strategy and*

Policy (New York, Harcourt, Brace & World, 1968). For descriptions of these and other books refer to the two bibliographies noted below. See also the lists in Steiner and in Mockler. A few books on business forecasting and business cycles are described in Chapter 8.

Bibliographies and Periodicals

Kettlewell, P. J. *A European Bibliography of Corporate Planning, 1961–1971.* London, Pergamon, 1972. Issued as a supplement to the June 1972 issue of *Long Range Planning.*

A good, annotated bibliography of English-language books and articles published in the United Kingdom and in Europe and compiled by the librarian at Sandoz Products & Wander Ltd. For a short supplement see the February 1974 issue of *Long Range Planning* (pp. 72–78). This bibliography, with supplement incorporated, appears also in David Hussey's *Corporate Planning,* listed above.

Lightwood, Martha B. *Public and Business Planning in the United States: A Bibliography* (Management Information Guide, 26). Detroit, Mich., Gale Research Co., 1972.

The business planning sections of this useful annotated bibliography of planning materials published primarily in the United States are: strategic planning and planning theory; managerial and organizational planning; planning business decisions; planning for specific functions; business forecasting. Also included are the following reference sources: general reference works; indexes and abstracts; bibliographies; statistical sources; names of periodicals and planning associations.

Long Range Planning. Journal of the Society for Long Range Planning. London, Pergamon (bimonthly).

Excellent selection of articles on various aspects of company strategy and planning by British and a few American authorities. Includes book reviews and "A Current Awareness Service for Long Range Planning," which is a selected, annotated list of articles. Indexed in PAIS.

Managerial Planning. Oxford, Ohio, Planning Executives Institute (bimonthly).

A professional journal with short practical articles on budgeting, profit planning and corporate planning. Indexed in PAIS.

HUMAN FACTORS IN ORGANIZATIONS

The study of the interaction of people within organizations spans the fields of psychology and sociology as well as business. The literature is legion, not only for general books on human behavior but also for those on its several aspects, such as motivation, morale, communication, leadership, group behavior, conflict and change. The titles of many excellent books on these topics are missing from this very short list, as are the names of important and influential behavioral theorists, such as Chris Argyris, Frederick Herzberg, Rensis Likert, Douglas McGregor (listed elsewhere in this chapter), and the teams of Blake/Mouton and Lawrence/Lorsch. The contributions of these and other important theorists are usually discussed in basic books on organizational behavior and, occasionally, in recent texts on personnel administration (Chapter 19). Persons who wish to investigate the writings of any individual can start by reading pertinent chapters in the books following (Whyte, for example), checking the bibliographies and bibliographical footnotes to identify specific titles. The separate bibliographies below and many general management lists also cite these important works.

The entire area of human relations is also an important part of the literature on personnel administration, and so many of the sources listed in Chapter 19 will also be of special interest.

Bennis, Warren G. *Organization Development: Its Nature, Origins, and Prospects.* Reading, Mass., Addison-Wesley, 1969.
This is one of a series of six concise paperback volumes in the widely acclaimed "Addison-Wesley Series on Organization Development," each written by important theorist-practitioners to explain their views of OD and their own style of working with client systems. The other volumes in the series (all published in 1969) are: *Organization Development: Strategies and Models* by Richard Beckhard; *Developing Organizations: Diagnosis and Action* by Paul R. Lawrence and Jay W. Lorsch; *Building a Dynamic Corporation Through Grid Organization Development* by Robert R. Blake and Jane S. Mouton; *Process Consultation: Its Role in Organization Development* by Edgar H. Schein; *Interpersonal Peacemaking: Confrontations and Third-Party Consultation* by Richard E. Walton.

Davis, Keith. *Human Behavior at Work: Human Relations and Organizational Behavior.* 4th ed. New York, McGraw-Hill, 1972.
A good introductory text covering fundamentals (motivation, morale, climate), leadership and its development, organizational environment, social environment, communication and group processes. Professor Davis has also published a book of readings, which can be used with this, called *Organizational Behavior* (4th ed., McGraw-Hill, 1974).

Dubin, Robert. *Human Relations in Administration: With Readings.* 4th ed. Englewood Cliffs, N.J., Prentice-Hall, 1974.
A good selection of readings by well-known persons, with brief introductory text at beginning of each chapter. Arranged in 6 parts: administrative perspectives; organizations; administrative personnel; administrative relationships (power, authority, status); administrative action (communication, decision-making, leadership, etc.); internal and external environment.

DuBrin, Andrew J. *The Fundamentals of Organizational Behavior: An Applied Perspective.* New York, Pergamon, 1974.
Focuses on human behavior in organizations as it concerns managerial and professional personnel and attempts to include topics and case illustrations that are current and will be of real interest to the reader. His 3 main sections consider organizational behavior from the point of view of the individual, then behavior in small groups, and in the total organization. Bibliographical notes are at end of chapters. Professor DuBrin has also written *The Practice of Managerial Psychology: Concepts and Methods for Manager and Organization Development* (Pergamon, 1972). This is intended for persons who want "to learn how psychological techniques are applied to improve managerial and organizational effectiveness." It includes chapters on managerial development, motivation, obsolescence, etc., and has a bibliography.

French, Wendell L. and Cecil H. Bell, Jr. *Organization Development: Behavioral Science Interventions for Organization Improvement.* Englewood Cliffs, N.J., Prentice-Hall, 1973.

These authors define OD as "a long-range effort to improve an organization's problem-solving and renewal processes, particularly through a more effective and collaborative management of organization culture — with special emphasis on the culture of formal work teams — with the assistance of a change agent, or catalyst, and the use of the theory and technology of applied behavioral science, including action research." This book tells the story of OD — what it is, where it came from, both its theory and practice, some key considerations and issues. Includes bibliographical notes.

Hampton, David R., Charles E. Summer and Ross A. Webber. *Organizational Behavior and the Practice of Management.* Rev. ed. Glenview, Ill., Scott, Foresman, 1973.

Another introductory text, this one in three parts: individual and group behavior; tasks, technology and structure; management of conflict and change.

Kolb, David A., Irwin M. Rubin and James M. McIntyre. *Organizational Psychology: A Book of Readings.* 2d ed. Englewood Cliffs, N.J., Prentice-Hall, 1974.

An excellent selection of readings meant to "represent the frontiers of thinking and research about the human side of organizational life." The authors include such important names as Lawrence, Likert, McClelland, Roethlisberger, Schein, and Blake/Mouton. The authors have also written a companion text, *Organizational Psychology: An Experiential Approach* (2d ed., Prentice-Hall, 1974).

Lawler, Edward E., III. *Motivation in Work Organizations.* Monterey, Calif., Brooks/Cole, 1973.

Professor Lawler presents a summation of his research and thinking in this book about the motivational determinants of behavior in organizations. Chapters 2-4 deal with motivation theory; Chapters 5-9 "emphasize research and practice and translate theory into action by discussing topics such as how job design, leadership style, and pay systems affect motivation." Includes a bibliography.

Leavitt, Harold J. *Managerial Psychology.* 3d ed. Chicago, University of Chicago Press, 1972.

This is a revision of an excellent and not too difficult book on the concepts of human behavior relevant to management problems, as seen by a well-known social psychologist. Professor Leavitt considers people as individuals (the units of management), people in pairs (problems of influence and authority), people in groups (efficiency and influence), and people in large organizations (problems of organizational design). Useful "Notes and Suggested Readings" included at end. Leavitt also edited, with L. R. Pondy, a good selection of *Readings in Managerial Psychology* (University of Chicago Press, 1973), which can be used with his text.

Luthans, Fred. *Organizational Behavior: A Modern Behavioral Approach to Management.* New York, McGraw-Hill, 1973.

Luthans' elementary text studies the formal organization system (structure, processes and technology) and the human being (examination of the perceptual, learning and motivational processes). He also covers the historical and conceptual foundations, as well as group dynamics, applications and new dimensions for the management of organizational behavior. Includes bibliographies. His *Contemporary Readings in Organizational Behavior* (McGraw-Hill, 1972) is designed to accompany the text.

McCormick, Ernest J. and Joseph Tiffin. *Industrial Psychology.* 6th ed. Englewood Cliffs, N.J., Prentice-Hall, 1974.

This is a widely used text that the authors have revised for a sixth time to include the newer methods, techniques and procedures relating to industrial psychology. It emphasizes practical applications and so is of special interest to personnel administrators, but it is also excellent for students and managers. Twenty chapters provide good coverage, especially for consideration of the various aspects of personnel selection and evaluation, as well as the organizational and social context of human work. Includes frequent bibliographical footnotes rather than a separate bibliography.

Two other standard and practical texts are: *Psychology in Industrial Organizations* by Norman R. F. Maier (4th ed., Boston, Houghton, Mifflin, 1973); *Psychology of Industrial Behavior,* by Henry C. Smith and John H. Wakeley (3d ed., New York, McGraw-Hill, 1972).

Porter, Lyman W., Edward E. Lawler III and J. Richard Hackman. *Behavior in Organizations.* New York, McGraw-Hill, 1975.

An introductory study on behavior of people in work situations, focusing on the individual and on the organization and especially on their interaction. The 5 main section headings cover: individuals, organizations and their interaction; the development of individual-organizational relationships; influences on work behavior — structural factors; influences on work behavior — organizational practices and social processes; improving organizational effectiveness. Includes a bibliography.

Schein, Edgar H. *Organizational Psychology.* 2d ed. Englewood Cliffs, N.J., Prentice-Hall, 1972.

An excellent, concise and readable study of the behavioral aspects of an organization, meant to stimulate thinking rather than to present a complete picture. Includes a bibliography.

Steers, Richard M. and Lyman W. Porter. *Motivation and Work Behavior.* New York, McGraw-Hill, 1975.

Attempts "to bring together in one volume the major contemporary theories, research, and applications in the area of motivation and work behavior." There are 4 principal parts: initial considerations (the role of motivation in organizations); contemporary theories and research; central issues in motivation at work; motivation theory in perspective. Bibliographies are at end of chapters.

Whyte, William F. *Organizational Behavior: Theory and Application.* Homewood, Ill., Irwin, 1969.

Professor Whyte's significant and well-written study is an expansion of his earlier *Men at Work* (1961). It is based to a great extent on his own research and experience as well as the research of others, and he includes many useful quotations and examples throughout the volume. Its 33 chapters are in 9 parts: historical and theoretical framework; framework for analysis; groups and intergroup relations; individual and group in the organization context; vertical relations; lateral and diagonal relations; union-management relations (5 chapters); introducing change (7 chapters); progress report. The short, annotated bibliographies with each chapter include important books of individual behaviorists.

Bibliographies

American Behavioral Scientist. *The ABS Guide to Recent Publications in the Social and Behavioral Sciences.* New York, 1965. And annual supplements to date.

A selective, annotated, interdisciplinary bibliography of books and articles, arranged by author, with subject and author indexes. It is kept up to date not only by annual supplements but also by a special section in each issue of *American Behavioral Scientist* called "New Studies."

Franklin, Jerome L. *Organization Development: An Annotated Bibliography.* Ann Arbor, Center for Research on Utilization of Scientific Knowledge, Institute for Social Research, University of Michigan, 1973.

This annotated list of books and articles on organization development emphasizes the social aspects of organizational functions. It is arranged alphabetically by author and includes some of the most influential books by organizational theorists such as Bennis, Likert, Lawrence/Lorsch.

Murrell, Kenneth L. and Peter B. Vaill. *Organization Development: Sources and Applications.* Washington, D.C., American Society for Training and Development, Organization Development Division, 1975.

Provides a guide to the most useful OD sources, selected to assist practitioners actively engaged in conducting organization development programs. The list is divided into the following sections: basic books and articles (this section is annotated), new directions and critiques, OD methods, the consulting process, OD case studies, books of readings, bibliographies.

Neuhauser, Duncan. *Organizational Behavior Literature in Health Administration Education.* Washington, D.C., Association of University Programs in Hospital Administration, 1972.

This is an annotated list of books in use by graduate programs in hospital and health administration. Part I covers books on organizational behavior in general (pp. 5–31), and Part II (pp. 32–36) lists health-related books.

U.S. Civil Service Commission. Library. *Improving Employee Performance* (Personnel Bibliography Series, No. 45). Washington, D.C., U.S. Government Printing Office, 1972.

An annotated list of books, theses and selected articles, published 1969–1971, on organizational relationships, organizational change and development, morale and job satisfaction, attitude surveys, motivation and productivity, etc. For references to similar material published 1965–1969 see their *Managing Human Behavior* (Personnel Bibliography Series, No. 35).

Abstracting Services

Psychological Abstracts. Washington, D.C., American Psychological Association (monthly, with semi-annual indexes).

Abstracts of worldwide journal articles, technical reports and books in psychology and related disciplines. It is arranged by 48 topics within 17 major subject areas, including: social behavior and interpersonal processes; communication and language; personality; applied psychology (management and leadership, organizational structure and climate, job performance, etc.). Each issue has an index by specific subject, and there is also a separately published and very detailed semi-annual index. This abstracting service is also available on machine readable tapes, which make automated search and retrieval services possible.

Sociological Abstracts. Brooklyn, N.Y. (5/yr.).

Abstracts of international journal articles classified by 58 topics within 12 basic sections, including: social psychology; group interactions; complex organizations (management); social change and economic development; environmental interactions.

Each issue includes a subject and author index, and there is a separately published annual cumulated index. In 1976 these abstracts will also be available for on-line searches.

Periodicals

American Behavioral Scientist. Beverly Hills, Calif., Sage Publications (bimonthly).

Each issue of this journal is usually devoted to a special topic and includes a bibliographic section called "New Studies," which supplements their separately published bibliography listed above. Indexed in PAIS, SSI.

Human Relations. London, Plenum Press (9/yr.).

"A journal of studies towards the integration of the social sciences," with most of the papers written by American and British academicians in the areas of organizational behavior, sociology and psychology. This journal is sponsored by Tavistock Institute of Human Relations. Indexed in SSI.

Journal of Applied Behavioral Science. Arlington, Va., NTL Institute for Applied Behavioral Science (monthly).

An excellent selection of empirical studies on the theory and practice of planned change. Indexed in SSI.

Journal of Applied Psychology. Washington, D.C., American Psychological Association (bimonthly).

Short articles reporting on original investigations in many areas of applied psychology that are of interest and concern to businessmen. Indexed in SSI.

The American Psychological Association publishes a number of other journals, including the *Journal of Personality and Social Psychology,* a monthly that contains original research in the areas of social psychology and personality dynamics.

Organizational Behavior and Human Performance. New York, Academic Press (bimonthly).

"A journal of fundamental research and theory in applied psychology," with many of the articles based on the use of quantitative research.

Organizational Dynamics. New York, AMACOM, American Management Associations, (quarterly).

This is a new and excellent journal for professional managers, with each issue usually containing 4 or 5 good articles by recognized authorities. Covers both the behavioral and management sciences, both the public and private sector, some articles practical and others theoretical.

HISTORY OF MANAGEMENT THINKING

With the exception of only a few recent management classics cited elsewhere in this chapter (see Barnard, Drucker, McGregor), no attempt is made in this work to include the important pioneer books on management. The four historical compilations listed below will be useful for studying the history of management and its writers. The bibliographies in each are important for those persons interested in identifying and reading further in the works of any individual pioneer. A few of these early books are still in print, such as Henry

Fayol, *General and Industrial Management* (London, Pitman, 1949); Mary Parker Follett, *Dynamic Administration* (London, Pitman, 1965); Herbert A. Simon, *Administrative Behavior* (3d ed., New York, Free Press, 1976); and Frederick W. Taylor, *Principles of Scientific Management* (New York, Norton, 1967). The important books that are now out of print can usually be found and borrowed from a large library that has a good business collection.

George, Claude S., Jr. *The History of Management Thought.* 2d ed. Englewood Cliffs, N.J., Prentice-Hall, 1972.

A history of management thinking as it evolved from ancient civilizations up through the classical economists of the 19th-century; then on to scientific management and early 20th-century concepts; the contributions of various minor writers and critics; managerial philosophers such as Follett and Barnard; and concluding with the emerging schools of management thought such as the behavioral school and the quantitative school. Includes a good "Selected Bibliography of Management Literature" (pp. 189–216), arranged in chronological time periods so that it is convenient to find sources in any particular era.

Merrill, Harwood F., ed. *Classics in Management.* Rev. ed. New York, American Management Association, 1970.

Selections from the writings of 18 of the great names in the history of management thought and practice: Owen, Babbage, Metcalfe, Towne, Taylor, Gantt, Robb, Emerson, Church, Alford, Fayol, Gilbreth, Sheldon, Follett, Hopf, Mayo, Barnard, McGregor. A "Selected Bibliography" (pp. 485–495) lists the most important books and papers of each.

Pollard, Harold R. *Developments in Management Thought.* New York, Crane, Russak, 1974.

A British college lecturer and former businessman summarizes the contributions of 19 writers who have played an important part in the development of management thought as it relates to people. Besides considering 8 of the pioneers in the preceding book, Pollard also covers Argyris, J. A. C. Brown, W. Brown, Cartwright, Drucker, Herzberg, Likert, Mooney, Rowntree and Zander. Includes short lists of books.

Wren, Daniel A. *The Evolution of Management Thought.* New York, Ronald, 1972.

As the preface states, "this book traces the evolution of management thought from its earliest, informal days to the present by examining the backgrounds, ideas, and influence of the major contributors." In the process it also describes the various stages in this development and the interaction of management thinking with existing economic, social and political values and institutions. Arranged chronologically, it includes a selected bibliography (pp. 527–536), which is divided into the same 4 sections as is the book itself: early management thought; the scientific management era; the social man era; the modern era.

FUNCTIONS OF DIRECTORS

Koontz, Harold. *The Board of Directors and Effective Management.* New York, McGraw-Hill, 1967.

A good discussion of "the role of boards of directors in top management," with a short bibliography and typical position descriptions at end.

Louden, J. Keith. *The Effective Director in Action.* New York, AMACOM, American Management Associations, 1975.

A short guide for directors of corporations, with a supplement, covering public agency boards, written by Jack Zusman.

Mace, Myles L. *Directors: Myth and Reality.* Boston, Division of Research, Graduate School of Business Administration, Harvard University, 1971. (Now distributed by Harvard University Press.)

This study, based on many years of research by Professor Mace, reports on a survey undertaken to measure what he felt was the "considerable gap between what directors in fact do and what the business literature said they should do." His book is written for the businessman and includes quotes from the many interviews he conducted with executives and with board members of both public and family corporations.

For a British guide to the role and functions of directors see Walter Puckey, *The Board-Room* (London, Hutchinson, 1969). The law as it relates to U.S. officers and directors is discussed in Mortimer Feuer, *Personal Liabilities of Corporate Officers and Directors* (2d ed., rev. by J. F. Johnston, Jr., Englewood Cliffs, N.J., Prentice-Hall, 1974).

MANAGEMENT OF NEW AND SMALL BUSINESSES

An increasing number of future businessmen are expressing interest in learning about the management of small firms, and many business schools now offer courses to meet this demand. Hence it is important to know about books, guides and bibliographies that may be of some help to entrepreneurs and to small businessmen. Several directories of venture capital companies are listed in Chapter 14.

Baumback, Clifford M., Kenneth Lawyer and Pearce C. Kelley. *How to Organize and Operate a Small Business.* 5th ed. Englewood Cliffs, N.J., Prentice-Hall, 1973.

This is the latest edition of Kelley's standard text covering the role of small business in the economy, how to get started, important factors in operating a business, and new directions for the future. Useful features include short, annotated lists of readings at end of chapters, a list of "Sources of Information on Organizing and Operating Specific Types of Small Business" (this indexes by specific business some of the series published by the Small Business Administration noted below in the bibliographies section), index of recent SBA management and marketing reading aids. Baumback has also compiled (with Joseph R. Mancuso) a selection of 35 articles on *Entrepreneurship and Venture Management* (Prentice-Hall, 1975), which can be used as a companion to a text on small business management or in a course on entrepreneurship. It has a bibliography at end.

Broom, H. N. and Justin G. Longenecker. *Small Business Management.* 4th ed. Cincinnati, Ohio, South-Western, 1975.

Another newly revised text, with expanded treatment of business strategy and the process of strategic planning for small firms and reflecting current environmental concerns. Section headings are: the environment for small business entrepreneurs; managerial functions, relations and practices; initial problems in starting a small business; selling and marketing research; financial and administrative controls; legal and governmental controls; operating certain types of small business. Cases are at end of each section.

Cohn, Theodore and Roy A. Lindberg. *Survival & Growth: Management Strategies for the Small Firm.* New York, AMACOM, American Management Associations, 1974.

Meant for managers of small firms ($1 million to $25 million sales) who do not need a study of the functional approach to small business management, but instead would benefit by a book to stimulate thinking about ways to improve performance and use of managerial time.

Dible, Donald M. *Up Your Own Organization!* Santa Clara, Calif., Entrepreneur Press, 1971.

A readable, practical handbook on how to start and finance a new business. Chapters cover characteristics and motivations of the entrepreneur, sources of assistance in getting started, the various aspects of the business plan, where to get financial resources. Useful data in appendix includes an annotated list of directories and guides to venture capital sources, a list of SBICs, several business start-up checklists.

Greene, Gardiner G. *How to Start and Manage Your Own Business.* New York, McGraw-Hill, 1975.

This is not meant as a textbook but rather as a practical, readable book of facts, tips and strategies, written by a small businessman to help other small businessmen. There are 5 parts: financial strategies; selecting professional services; management tips; constructive thinking; cautionary thinking.

Klatt, Lawrence A., ed. *Managing the Dynamic Small Firm: Readings.* Belmont, Calif., Wadsworth, 1971.

A collection of interesting articles, many of which discuss a particular topic in more detail than is usually possible in a general text. Includes bibliographies.

Lasser (J. K.) Tax Institute. *How to Run a Small Business.* 4th ed., rev. and enl. New York, McGraw-Hill, 1974.

Another standard work, which gives a broad background of information both for persons planning a new enterprise and also those operating an existing business

Mancuso, Joseph. *The Entrepreneur's Handbook.* [Dedham, Mass.] Artech House, 1974. 2 volumes.

A selection of readings intended "to provide a convenient single source of solutions for starting, financing, and managing a technical firm." It is arranged chronologically in 8 chapters, starting with the idea stage, on to the start-up problem, venture financing; Vol. 2 continues with growth crises, the maturity crisis, the impossible transition, the entrepreneur's philosophy.

Guides to Specific Small Businesses

These series of short brochures contain data on important factors, such as location of the business, finance and personnel, for the successful operation of specific kinds of small business. Baumback, listed above, includes an index to most of these pamphlets as of 1973, arranged by type of business.

Bank of America NT & SA. *Small Business Reporter.* San Francisco. Calif.
Twenty-eight profiles have been published to date (1975) covering such small businesses as bookstores, health food stores, sporting goods stores. Sources for further information are at end of each profile.

How to Start Your Own Small Business. New York, Drake, 1973–1975. 4 volumes.
Vol. 1 contains brief information on 15 businesses that originally appeared as an *Urban Business Profile* series published in 1972 by the U.S. Office of Minority Business Enterprise. Vols. 2 through 4 each cover 4 to 6 other businesses in more detail, and some include bibliographies.

U.S. Small Business Administration. *Starting and Managing Series.* Washington, D.C.
Twenty booklets published to date (1975) covering such businesses as a carwash, flower shop, service station. Bibliographies included for each.

Bibliographies and Periodicals

The Small Business Administration in Washington, D.C., is the first place to contact for information on small business. It is organized to help small firms not only by giving management, procurement and financial assistance but also by conducting workshops and preparing useful booklets, aids and bibliographies. Following is a general description of some of their series, two other bibliographies on small business, and a journal.

Center for Venture Management. *The Entrepreneur and New Enterprise Formation: A Resource Guide.* Comp. by J. W. Schreir and J. L. Komives. Milwaukee, Wisc., 1973.
A partially annotated list of books, pamphlets, articles and tape cassettes arranged in sections covering such topics as the entrepreneur, small business, finance and venture capital, innovations, titles of SBA publications.

Spier, S. L. "The Many Aspects of Small Business." In *Business Literature,* Public Library of Newark, N.J., Vol. 44, No. 3/5 (Dec. 1971/Jan. 1972) pp. 5–10.
A short, annotated list.

U.S. Small Business Administration. *For-Sale Booklets* (SBA-115B) and *Free Management Assistance Publications* (SBA-115A).
These two annual lists describe the many booklets, aids and bibliographies that are available from the SBA. Copies of SBA publications can be obtained either from the SBA's main office in Washington, D.C., or from any of its field offices located in about 90 large U.S. cities. Most large libraries also have files of SBA publications that anyone can use.
   The series of booklets for sale are:
      Small Business Management Series
      Small Business Research Series
      Starting and Managing Series
   Free publications include:
      Management Aids (for small manufacturing plants)

Small Business Bibliographies — a series of useful, annotated bibliographies on specific types of business, such as drugstores, hobby shops, motels, suburban shopping centers.

Small Marketers Aids

Technical Aids

Journal of Small Business Management. Morgantown, National Council for Small Business Management Development and the Bureau of Business Research, West Virginia University (quarterly).

Each issue is devoted to a specific topic. Indexed in PAIS.

11

MANAGEMENT OF PUBLIC
AND NONPROFIT ORGANIZATIONS

Arts Administration — Educational Administration — Health Care Administration — Public Administration — Urban Administration

$\mathbf{O}$rganizations of all kinds have been facing new and more complex problems and uncertainties during the past few years due to many of the same factors that make living more complicated today. This has been true particularly for organizations in the nonprofit sector. For instance, the health care industry has been growing by leaps and bounds. Educational, welfare, arts, government and urban agencies — all these and many other organizations are trying to cope with almost insurmountable problems that only the most highly qualified managers and policy makers can hope to deal with successfully. Most business schools have responded to this need for better trained managers by introducing courses and programs to give students the skills necessary in these specialized areas. Some schools have even changed their names from "School of Business Administration" to "School of Management" or "College of Business and Administration," to describe more accurately the scope of the programs offered.

The literature has kept pace with this new concern. Many recent texts on organization and management are now being written to include a discussion of factors important for the management of both business and nonbusiness enterprises. See, for example, those by Koontz, Litterer and Newman in Chapter 10. The number of books devoted entirely to such subjects as health care administration, urban administration is increasing rapidly and will continue to do so. There are also books on specific functions such as accounting that are devoted to nonprofit organizations (see Gross, *Financial and Accounting Guide for Nonprofit Organizations,* in Chapter 12). It is not possible to cover all of these topics in a book about business information sources, but because these new areas of management are so important, this short chapter is included to call attention to a few pertinent reference sources. These references are admittedly spotty and incomplete and are meant merely to identify a few bibliographies, indexes, abstracts and periodicals that the reader can use as a basis for pursuing his search in a library that collects material in these and other areas of managing public and nonprofit organizations.

ARTS ADMINISTRATION

Bibliographies arᵈ Periodicals

Georgi, Charlotte. *The Arts and the World of Business: A Selected Bibliography.* Metuchen, N.J., Scarecrow Press, 1973. And Supplement No. 1, 1974.

A useful bibliography of books and articles on the performing and visual arts, with 15 sections covering such topics as business and economic aspects; relations to government, law, labor unions; fund-raising; various aspects such as museum, music, theater management. Sections 16 through 20 list journals, indexes to journal articles, directories and handbooks, names of organizations and other bibliographies. It is based on several earlier lists prepared for use in UCLA's Master's Degree Program in Arts Management. Supplement No. 1 (64 pages) was issued in September 1974 as UCLA, Graduate School of Management, *Research Paper* No. 23, and future supplements are planned.

Prieve, E. Arthur and Ira W. Allen. *Administration in the Arts: An Annotated Bibliography of Selected References.* 3d ed. Madison, Center for Arts Administration, Graduate School of Business, University of Wisconsin, 1973.

An excellent, annotated list of books and articles, often citing references from the field of business, since many of the activities are similar. It is in 3 sections: the arts organization (management, planning, financing, etc.); marketing the arts organization; the environment and the arts organization (relations to business, law, unions, etc.). A short list of business and arts journals is at end.

Two pertinent arts journals are: *Arts Management* (New York, Radius Group, 5/yr.) and a monthly 2-page newsletter, *Arts Business* (New York, Business Committee for the Arts).

EDUCATIONAL ADMINISTRATION

Unlike the relatively new interest in arts management, the problems of administering educational institutions are so varied and have been with us for so long that there are whole libraries devoted exclusively to collecting and making available the overwhelming amount of writings on all aspects and levels of education. In an effort to collect, index and make available for retrieval the large volume of hard-to-find research reports and documents of potential interest to educators, the U.S. Office of Education in 1960 established its very active Educational Resources Information Center (widely known as ERIC). Besides this national computerized information system, ERIC also maintains a network of clearinghouses, each specializing in a particular aspect of education. The Clearinghouse for Educational Management (ERIC/CEM) is located at the University of Oregon, in Eugene, and its specialized staff can provide information on all aspects of the theory and practice of educational administration.

Two useful abstracts of journal articles are:

Current Index to Journals in Education. New York, Macmillan Information (monthly, with annual cumulations).
This is a descriptive index of articles in over 700 professional educational journals and a few business/management journals as well. It is based on information submitted by ERIC Clearinghouses and is arranged by the Clearinghouse accession number, with subject and author indexes.

Educational Administration Abstracts. Columbus, Ohio, University Council for Educational Administration with Ontario Institute for Studies in Education (3/yr.).
An excellent source for abstracts of articles not only in educational journals but also in basic management, behavorial science and personnel journals. It covers all aspects of the organization and administration of educational institutions.

For a simple, good author/subject index to educational periodicals, proceedings and yearbooks in the English language see *Education Index* (New York, H. W. Wilson, published monthly except July and August, with annual cumulations).

Two trade journals are *College Management* and *School Management,* both published 9 times a year by Macmillan Professional Magazines in Greenwich, Connecticut. The *Educational Administration Quarterly* is a professional journal of the University Council for Educational Administration, in Columbus, Ohio.

Since the total volume of publishing on educational topics is so vast and so varied there is no one good, recent bibliographic source covering books on the overall topic of educational administration. As a result, one must search under specific kinds of education, such as school administration or higher education, to find current bibliographies, or recent books with bibliographies, that may be pertinent. For instance, the December issue each year of *American School Board Journal* (Evanston, Ill, National School Boards Association) includes a good list of "The Books You Should Have Read This Year — And Still Can." This reviews and gives capsule summaries for important books of value to professional and lay administrators in the management of public schools. The following book is another useful source:

National Association of College and University Business Officers. *College & University Business Administration.* 3d ed. Washington, D.C., 1974.
An authoritative reference manual of value to all college and university administrators and representing the work of many members of this association. Its selected bibliography of books, pamphlets, periodicals and NACUBO publications (pp. 229–245) will be especially useful for locating more detailed information on each topic. The major part of this guide is in 4 of its 6 sections: administrative management; business management; financial accounting; reporting.

HEALTH CARE ADMINISTRATION

Bibliographies

American Health Congress. *Administrator's Collection.* Chicago, 1972.

A collection of significant books, periodicals and audio-visual sources on the organization, financing and delivering of health care services, as selected by a panel of expert administrators for this congress in 1972. Includes basic management books as well as those devoted specifically to health care.

Levey, Samuel and N. Paul Loomba. *Health Care Administration: A Selected Bibliography.* Philadelphia, Pa., Lippincott, 1973.

This list of books and many articles was prepared as a companion volume to the authors' *Health Care Administration: A Managerial Perspective* (Lippincott, 1973). It is organized in the same 14 parts as is the book, and it covers: the framework of health care systems; decision making; planning; evaluation and control; management science models. The authors hope to update this bibliography every two years.

Neuhauser's annotated bibliography of *Organizational Behavior Literature in Health Administration Education* is listed in the section for "Human Factors in Organizations," Chapter 10. A series of *Exchange Bibliographies* published by the Council of Planning Librarians may also be of interest, since it occasionally includes bibliographies on health care planning. Examples are: "Health Systems and Health Planning in International Perspective," "Comprehensive Health Planning Bibliography," (Exchange Bibliography, Nos. 265 and 392), 1972 and 1973.

Abstracts and Indexes

Abstracts of Hospital Management Studies. Ann Arbor, Cooperative Information Center for Hospital Management Studies, School of Public Health, University of Michigan (3 quarterly issues, with a 4th annual cumulation).

An international journal, which abstracts current studies and research on management, planning and public policy as it relates to health care. It is in 41 sections of which several are: administrator and board; accounting and business office; management science and operations research; personnel administration.

Excerpta Medica. Section 36: Health Economics and Hospital Management. Amsterdam, The Netherlands (10 issues published in 1972).

This is an international medical abstracting service, classified in 9 broad headings, including health care organizations, hospital management and organization.

Hospital Abstracts. London, H.M. Stationery Office (monthly).

"A monthly survey of world literature prepared by the Department of Health and Security." It covers the whole field of hospitals and administration except for strictly medical and related professional matters and is classified by topics such as organization and administration (with 9 subdivisions), finance and accounting.

Hospital Literature Index. Chicago, American Hospital Association (quarterly, with annual and quinquennial cumulations).

This is "an author-subject index of literature about administration, planning, and financing of hospitals and related medical care institutions, and the administrative aspects of the medical, paramedical, and prepayment fields."

Medical Care Review. Ann Arbor, Bureau of Public Health Economics, School of Public Health, University of Michigan (monthly, except September).

Part of each issue contains abstracts of selected books and articles arranged by broad topic. The rest includes summaries of news about legislation, government programs, etc., and lists of recent publications.

Medical Socioeconomic Research Sources. Chicago, American Medical Association (monthly, with annual cumulations).

A subject "guide to information on the social and economic aspects of medicine and health," covering all significant publications in the English language.

Periodicals

Professional and trade journals include: *Hospital Administration* (Chicago, American College of Hospital Administrators, quarterly); *Hospital Financial Management* (Chicago, Hospital Financial Management Association, monthly); *International Journal of Health Services* (Farmingdale, N.Y., Baywood, quarterly); *Medical Care* (Philadelphia, Pa., J. B. Lippincott for the Medical Care Section, American Public Health Association, monthly); and *Medical Marketing & Media* (Stamford, Conn., Navillus Publishing Co., monthly).

PUBLIC ADMINISTRATION

Texts

Bartholomew, Paul C. *Public Administration.* 3d ed. Totawa, N.J., Littlefield, Adams & Co., 1972.

This little book gives a bird's-eye view of public administration. It is simple and concise, with chapter headings paralleling topics treated in management texts, e.g., administrative organization; personnel management; budget formulation and adoption; procurement; public relations. Suggested readings at end of chapters.

Caiden, Gerald E. *The Dynamics of Public Administration: Guidelines to Current Transformations in Theory and Practice.* New York, Holt, Rinehart and Winston, 1971.

Caiden's book is not meant to be a basic text but rather a guide to the literature, to research and to highlights of both the theory and practice. As such it should be used with established texts such as *Public Administration* by John M. Pfiffner and Robert V. Presthus (5th ed., New York, Ronald, 1967). Its annotated "Bibliographic Guide" (pp. 298–333) provides an excellent listing of general and specialized texts, bibliographies and professional journals.

Bibliographies and Abstracts

ABC Pol Sci. (Advance Bibliography of Contents: Political Science and Government). Santa Barbara, Calif., American Bibliographical Center-Clio Press (9/yr.).

Contents pages for about 300 domestic and foreign journals not only in political science and government but also in law, sociology and cultural anthropology. Subject, author and law indexes in each issue. The publisher also offers subscribers an "article copying service" for single copies of articles in those selected journals that have granted copying privileges.

Hills, William G., et al. *Administration and Management: A Selected and Annotated Bibliography.* Norman, University of Oklahoma Press, 1975.

The books that were selected for inclusion in this annotated list are those that the compilers felt would be most relevant for public administrators, but many will also be of interest to business managers. It is in 6 sections: development, scope, and emphasis; the organization; the administrative process; personnel; the administrative environment; comparative administration. An appendix lists journals and a few handbooks.

International Review of Administrative Science. Brussels, Belgium, International Institute of Administrative Science (quarterly). (Published also in French and Spanish editions.)

Each issue includes an annotated list of books on organization and management in a section called "Bibliography — A Selection."·

Joint Reference Library. *Recent Publications on Governmental Problems.* Chicago (semi-monthly).

This is a useful checklist of books, pamphlets and a few articles, arranged alphabetically by subject. Among many other topics it occasionally lists books on administrative management, city planning, municipal government, and educational, environmental, hospital, policy and public administration. It is sponsored by 7 professional associations among which are the American Society of Planning Officials, the International Personnel Management Association, the Municipal Finance Officers Association, the Public Administration Service.

McCurdy, Howard E. *Public Administration: A Bibliography.* Washington, D.C., College of Public Affairs, American University, 1973.

Part 2 lists 1,000 books cited by scholars, in 33 categories, and includes many of the more important works in management, organization theory, behavioral science, management science as well as those on public administration, bureaucracy, etc. Part 1 is an annotated list of those 187 books cited most often.

Public Administration Review. Washington, D.C., American Society for Public Administration (bimonthly).

The "Book Notes" section provides a good, annotated list of recent books, and the excellent book reviews will also be of interest. This is an outstanding professional journal, and its authoritative articles cover the entire field of public administration. Indexed in SSI.

Sage Public Administration Abstracts. Beverly Hills, Calif., Sage Productions (quarterly).

Each issue includes about 250 abstracts of important recent literature — books, articles, pamphlets, speeches, research studies — on public administration in six sections (administration; organization and structure; personnel; policy and decision-making; operations planning; government and politics).

Periodicals

Four good professional journals and one trade journal are: *Administration & Society* (formerly the *Journal of Comparative Administration;* Beverly Hills, Calif., Sage Publications, quarterly); *Government Executive* (Washington, D.C., Executive Publications, monthly); *Policy Sciences* (an international journal published quarterly in New York by American Elsevier Publishing Co.); *Public*

Administration Review (Washington, D.C., American Society for Public Administration, bimonthly); *Public Policy* (Cambridge, Mass., Harvard University Press for the John Fitzgerald Kennedy School of Government, Harvard University, quarterly).

URBAN ADMINISTRATION

Abstracts and Periodicals

Sage Urban Studies Abstracts. Beverly Hills, Calif., Sage Publications (quarterly).

Abstracts of significant books, articles, pamphlets, government publications on all aspects of urban studies. Each issue is arranged in 10 broad areas, e.g., planning, environment and energy, social conditions.

Urban Affairs Abstracts. Washington, D.C., National League of Cities and the United States Conference of Mayors (weekly, with 3 quarterly and an annual cumulation).

The annual cumulation of this weekly is especially good for its longer selection of abstracts of articles relating to urban information. Subject headings used include: business and industry; community development; environment; finances; health; municipal administration; organization management; public administration.

Three journals of urban policy and planning are: *Journal of the American Institute of Planners* (Montpelier, Vt., bimonthly); *Journal of Urban Analysis* (London and New York, Gordon and Breach Science Publishers, semi-annual); and *Urban Affairs Quarterly* (Beverly Hills Calif., Sage Publications).

12

ACCOUNTING/CONTROL AND TAXATION

Accounting Handbooks — Introductory Accounting Books — Advanced Financial Accounting — Budgeting and Advanced Management Accounting — Cost Accounting — Auditing — Financial Statements and Analysis — Governmental and Non-business Accounting — Surveys of Accounting Practices — Accounting Services — Accounting Bibliographies — Accounting Indexes and Abstracts — Accounting Dictionaries — Accounting Periodicals — Directories of Accountants — Accounting Associations — *TAXATION* — Books on Tax Management — Tax Services — Tax Bibliographies and Indexes — Taxation Periodicals

Probably no function of business has such a prolific literature, written over as long a span of history, as does the field of accounting. Its roots go back to the year 2000 B.C. with early records of Babylonian and Egyptian businessmen found preserved on clay tablets and on papyrus rolls. There is an interesting and well-documented account of this development in *A History of Accounting Thought* by Michael Chatfield (Hinsdale, Ill., Dryden Press, 1974).

Today accounting continues to be one of the best documented fields of business. A few recent books, important reference works, the best professional journals and a few trade journals are listed in this chapter. The broad topic of management information systems is treated separately in Chapter 13 along with books on computers and data processing. Books on mathematical techniques are in Chapter 17.

ACCOUNTING HANDBOOKS

The businessman seeking information on accepted practices in accounting and knowledge of forms and procedures will often find that handbooks provide the maximum of facts with a minimum of effort. Both Davidson and Wixon give good, concise coverage on all phases of accounting. Cashin's *Handbook for Auditors* and Dickey's *Accountants' Cost Handbook* are listed elsewhere in this chapter.

Davidson, Sidney, ed. *Handbook of Modern Accounting.* New York, McGraw-Hill, 1970.

Provides comprehensive and well-organized information both on theory and practice of accounting and on new developments and techniques. Written with the assistance of 49 experts, it includes short bibliographies at end of most chapters.

Lipkin, Lawrence, Irwin K. Feinstein and Lucile Derrick. *Accountant's Handbook of Formulas and Tables.* 2d ed. Englewood Cliffs, N.J., Prentice-Hall, 1972.

Compilation of formulas and tables often used by accountants, including interest, inventory, depreciation, cost and production, ratio analysis, present value.

Wixon, Rufus, Walter G. Kell and Norton M. Bedford, eds. *Accountants' Handbook.* 5th ed. New York, Ronald, 1970.

The latest edition of a standard work that is the cooperative effort of 47 expert contributors or consultants, this handbook "presents in compact form the full range of essential principles, rules, and procedures of commercial and financial accounting." Its usefulness is enhanced by frequent references to and excerpts from the literature of accounting and allied fields.

A more specialized handbook is *Professional Accounting in 30 Countries* (New York, International Practice Executive Committee, American Institute of Certified Public Accountants, 1975), which contains descriptions of the accounting profession, auditing and reporting standards and accounting principles in 30 foreign countries. It also gives brief descriptions of forms of business organization, requirements for stock exchange listing and security offerings.

INTRODUCTORY ACCOUNTING BOOKS

Most standard one-volume texts cover the principles of both basic branches of accounting — financial accounting (concerned with providing financial statements, reports, etc., of interest to bankers, investors and other outsiders who must make a financial assessment of the company) and management accounting (which emphasizes the use of accounting data for internal purposes, to help management in the planning and controlling functions of the company). Following are just a few of the many books that offer good introductions to the principles of accounting. It is possible to find a more detailed treatment of the accounting requirements for individual industries by checking under the name of the industry in the *Accountants' Index,* listed in the index section of this chapter.

Anthony, Robert N. and James S. Reece. *Management Accounting Principles.* 3d ed. Homewood, Ill., Irwin, 1975.

The title of this high-level introductory text refers back to the time in 1956 when the term "management accounting" meant any accounting of interest to managers. The book itself covers both financial accounting and management accounting (in the newer sense of the term) in about equal parts, and this edition brings the material up to date to include rapid developments of the past 5 years. Bibliographies are at ends of chapters, and present value tables are at end of book. The authors have also revised *Management Accounting: Text and Cases* (5th ed., Irwin, 1975), which contains the same text material but has cases with each chapter for use in case-study courses.

Professor Anthony has written (with Glenn A. Welsch) two separate lower-level introductory texts, one the *Fundamentals of Management Accounting* (Irwin, 1974), using the newer meaning of the term, and the other (with Welsch as primary author), *Fundamentals of Financial Accounting* (Irwin, 1974).

Dixon, Robert L. *The Executive's Accounting Primer.* New York, McGraw-Hill, 1971.

As the title implies, this book is designed for executives with little or no recent experience in accounting as well as for lawyers and others who would benefit from an understanding of accounting principles and practices. It starts with the balance sheet and income statement and proceeds to other accounting reports, then to the application of accounting methods in such areas as inventories, assets, taxes, and ends with a chapter on the "Recognition of Effects of Inflation."

Gentry, James A. and Glenn L. Johnson. *Finney and Miller's Principles of Accounting: Introductory.* 7th ed. Englewood Cliffs, N.J., Prentice-Hall, 1970. The 8th edition is scheduled for publication in 1976.

This latest edition of a highly successful introductory text, originally written by Harry A. Finney, is a blend of financial accounting with managerial accounting. The authors' two companion volumes are listed in the following section.

Horngren, Charles T. *Accounting for Management Control: An Introduction.* 3d ed. Englewood Cliffs, N.J., Prentice-Hall, 1974.

A general introductory text on the role of accounting in management, with an emphasis on accounting for planning and control in all kinds of business. Includes suggested readings, a glossary and present value tables.

Another well-written text, similar in coverage, is *Managerial Accounting* by Carl L. Moore and Robert K. Jaedicke (4th ed., Cincinnati, Ohio, South-Western, 1976).

Meigs, Walter B., A. N. Mosich and Charles E. Johnson. *Accounting: The Basis for Business Decisions.* 3d ed. New York, McGraw-Hill, 1972.

Another popular text for a first college-level course in accounting. It presents a balanced coverage from both the financial and managerial viewpoints, and it is brought up to date to include a discussion of data processing systems. This is one of three volumes in a series covering the whole field of accounting; the other two are listed in the following section. The authors have also written an introductory text on *Financial Accounting* (2d ed., McGraw-Hill, 1975).

Nickerson, Clarence B. *Accounting Handbook for Nonaccountants.* Boston, Cahners Books, 1975.

This book for the nonfinancial manager approaches the subject through income and funds flow statements rather than through the balance sheet. It aims to minimize bookkeeping aspects while stressing the importance of transaction analysis and to consider in greater depth such critical accounting areas as depreciation, inventory valuation, cost accounting and budgeting. Present value tables are at end.

Pyle, William W. and John A. White. *Fundamental Accounting Principles.* 7th ed. Homewood, Ill., Irwin, 1975.

A standard, elementary text that "describes how accounting data are accumulated and gives an understanding of the concepts necessary to use such data effectively." Balanced treatment of financial and managerial material.

Two other popular introductory texts are *Accounting: A Management Approach* by Myron J. Gordon and Gordon Shillinglaw (5th ed., Homewood, Ill., Irwin, 1974) and *Accounting Principles* by C. Rollin Niswonger and Philip E. Fess (11th ed., Cincinnati, Ohio, South-Western, 1973).

ADVANCED FINANCIAL ACCOUNTING

Gentry, James A. and Glenn L. Johnson. *Finney and Miller's Principles of Accounting: Intermediate.* 7th ed. Englewood Cliffs, N.J., Prentice-Hall, 1974; and *Finney and Miller's Principles of Accounting: Advanced.* 6th ed. Prentice-Hall, 1971.

The intermediate text (with Johnson's name appearing first) concentrates on financial accounting, with chapters on valuation and on specific parts of the balance sheet. Their advanced text is concerned with accounting techniques involved in partnerships, branches, consolidated statements, foreign operations, installment and consignment sales, compounding and present value concepts, fiduciaries and fund accounting.

Griffin, Charles H., Thomas H. Williams and Kermit D. Larson. *Advanced Accounting.* Rev. ed. Homewood, Ill., Irwin, 1971. (The 3d edition is scheduled for publication in 1976.)

This revision covers: accounting for partnerships; accounting for combined corporate entities (mergers and acquisitions, consolidated financial reports); consolidated statements — an expanded analysis (includes accounting for branches and for international operations); institutional and social accounting (governmental and national income accounting); special sales contracts (consignments and installment sales).

Hawkins, David F. *Financial Reporting Practices of Corporations.* Homewood, Ill., Dow Jones-Irwin, 1972.

Designed to give both management policy makers and users of financial statements (bankers, investors, etc.) an understanding of company financial reporting practices. Includes readings and also present value tables. Professor Hawkins has also written a casebook patterned after this called *Corporate Financial Reporting: Text and Cases* (Irwin, 1971).

Hendriksen, Eldon S. *Accounting Theory.* Rev. ed. Homewood, Ill., Irwin, 1970.

"Designed to provide a frame of reference for . . . courses in financial accounting, accounting theory, and seminars in theory of income, asset valuation, and the history of accounting thought." Suggested readings at end of chapters.

Meigs, Walter B., A. N. Mosich, Charles E. Johnson and Thomas F. Keller. *Intermediate Accounting.* 3d ed. New York, McGraw-Hill, 1973; and *Modern Advanced Accounting* by Meigs, Mosich and E. John Larsen. McGraw-Hill, 1975.

In their *Intermediate Accounting* text "emphasis throughout is on accounting theory and concepts and an analysis of the special problems that arise in applying these underlying concepts to financial accounting." Deals with problems of controlling cash, receivables, liabilities; problems of investment in inventory, plant and equipment, intangible assets; problems peculiar to corporate organizations (stockholders' equity and long-term debt); financial statements. The authors' advanced text focuses on relevant new problems of significance to future accountants concerning partnerships, branches, consolidated financial statements, segment reporting, financial reporting by multinational companies, present value, government entities, etc.

Welsch, Glenn A., Charles T. Zlatkovich and John A. White. *Intermediate Accounting.* 3d ed. Homewood, Ill., Irwin, 1972.

Emphasizes accounting theory, and covers: the accounting cycle, mathematical principles and applications; inventories; assets; liabilities; retained earnings; special problems of income determination; changes in accounting methods; funds flow; ratio analysis; variation analysis; consignments; installment sales.

BUDGETING AND ADVANCED MANAGEMENT ACCOUNTING

With the growing complexity of business and the resulting increased emphasis on management systems and quantitative methods, more attention is being paid to writings on that branch of accounting concerned with data for managerial decisions. Several books and readings are included in this section, but attention is called also to the following chapter, which covers the whole area of management information systems and information processing.

Anderson, David R., Leo A. Schmidt and Andrew M. McCosh. *Practical Controllership.* 3d ed. Homewood, Ill., Irwin, 1973.

Designed to give a broad view of the controllership function. Its 5 basic sections cover: the controllership concept (functions and organization); basic techniques (manufacturing and operating costs, inventory, depreciation); operational planning and control (budget, profit planning, financial reports); long-range planning; advanced techniques (computers, operations research, simulation in financial planning).

Anthony, Robert N., John Dearden and Richard F. Vancil. *Management Control Systems: Text, Cases, and Readings.* Rev. ed. Homewood, Ill., Irwin, 1972.

This text focuses on some of the newer management control topics and is in 3 sections: an overview; the management control structure (discretionary expense centers, profit centers and transfer pricing, investment centers); the management control process (planning/programming/budgeting, project planning and control). Professor Anthony has also written (with Regina E. Herzlinger) a text on *Management Control in Nonprofit Organizations* (Irwin, 1975).

Jones, Reginald L. and H. George Trentin. *Budgeting: Key to Planning and Control.* Rev. ed. New York, American Management Association, 1971.

A practical and nontechnical guide on budgeting as a vital part of business management, written for managers, and including many useful explanations, diagrams and exhibits.

Lemke, B. C. and James D. Edwards, eds. *Administrative Control and Executive Action.* 2d ed. Columbus, Ohio, C. E. Merrill, 1972.

A good selection of 39 articles meant "to provide a balanced, concise and varied source for the study of the many aspects of control," each by recognized authorities, such as Anthony, Davidson, Dean.

Skousen, K. Fred and Belverd E. Needles, Jr. *Contemporary Thought in Accounting and Organizational Control.* Encino, Calif., Dickenson Publishing Co., 1973.

A selection of short articles "to provide insights into some modern concepts and techniques applicable to accounting and organizational control." Additional references are at end of each of the 6 sections.

Welsch, Glenn A. *Budgeting: Profit Planning and Control.* 4th ed. Englewood Cliffs, N.J., Prentice-Hall, 1976.

Designed as a practical text on profit planning and control within the management process. Covers the conceptual foundations and their practical application in decision making, planning and controlling. Includes some case examples but others are found in his *Cases in Profit Planning and Control* (Prentice-Hall, 1970).

COST ACCOUNTING

Handbooks

Dickey, Robert I., ed. *Accountants' Cost Handbook.* 2d ed. New York, Ronald, 1967.

A comprehensive yet concise handbook dealing with the important principles, procedures and facts on accounting for manufacturing costs. It is based not only on the experience of its expert contributors but also on a review of the literature, occasionally including examples and illustrations of applications quoted from other sources.

Books

Anton, Hector R. and Peter A. Firmin, eds. *Contemporary Issues in Cost Accounting: A Discipline in Transition.* 2d ed. Boston, Houghton Mifflin, 1972.

A selection of articles on cost planning, decision and control, and on motivation, performance and evaluation. Readings and bibliographies at end of each of 5 sections.

Horngren, Charles T. *Cost Accounting: A Managerial Emphasis.* 3d ed. Englewood Cliffs, N.J., Prentice-Hall, 1972.

A very good, comprehensive text on cost accounting, with emphasis on costs for planning and control. Includes a list of NAA Research Publications, a glossary and present value tables.

Another excellent, readable analysis of cost accounting, similar in coverage, is *Cost Accounting: Analysis and Control* by Gordon Shillinglaw (3d ed., Homewood, Ill., Irwin, 1972).

Neuner, John J. W. *Cost Accounting: Principles and Practices.* 8th ed. Homewood, Ill., Irwin, 1973.

A popular text in 4 parts: cost determination and analysis; planning and control of costs; profit planning by making special cost analyses; applied cost determination procedures.

Another good, standard text is *Cost Accounting: Planning and Control* by Adolph Matz and Milton F. Usry (6th ed., Cincinnati, Ohio, South-Western, 1976).

AUDITING

Handbooks

Arkin, Herbert. *Handbook of Sampling for Auditing and Accounting.* 2d ed. New York, McGraw-Hill, 1974.

A working manual intended "to meet the practical need of accounting practitioners to understand and use efficiently statistical sampling techniques." More than half of this book contains tables of random numbers, tables for estimating sample size, tables for sample precision for relative frequency, etc.

Cashin, James A., ed. *Handbook for Auditors.* New York, McGraw-Hill, 1971.

An excellent, comprehensive handbook covering all phases of auditing. Includes good discussions of new techniques and procedures, such as computerized systems, quantitative analysis, fraud, auditing international operations, to name just a few. The many expert contributors frequently cite other works in their discussions, and most of the 52 chapters have a bibliography.

Books

Brink, Victor Z., James A. Cashin and Herbert Witt. *Modern Internal Auditing: An Operational Approach.* 3d ed. New York, Ronald, 1973.

The largest part of this book discusses major operational activities with which the internal auditor is concerned, and there is also a section on problems of administering the internal auditing department.

Defliese, Philip L., Kenneth P. Johnson and Roderick K. Macleod. *Montgomery's Auditing.* 9th ed. New York, Ronald, 1975.

Just published is a complete revision of Robert H. Montgomery's comprehensive text on auditing principles which has been a standard work since 1912. Based on an examination of its 8th edition it "emphasizes auditing objectives, the coordination of the examination of related accounts, and the influence of the interdependence of the balance sheet and income statement upon accounting principles and auditing procedures."

Holmes, Arthur W. and Wayne S. Overmyer. *Auditing: Standards and Procedure.* 8th ed. Homewood, Ill., Irwin, 1975.

A thorough revision of a standard text on auditing standards and procedures, written for both the student and the practitioner. It covers auditing practices applicable to all types of business organizations. The authors' shorter *Basic Auditing Principles* (4th ed., Irwin, 1972) covers "objectives of an audit and the reasons for the examination of each area of an audit." It is not meant as an abridgement of the text.

Meigs, Walter B., E. John Larsen and Robert F. Meigs. *Principles of Auditing.* 5th ed. Homewood, Ill., Irwin, 1973.

This newest edition continues the emphasis on internal control but reflects new developments, with expanded chapters on professional ethics, the use of electronic data processing systems and of sampling.

Several other standard texts are: *Auditing Principles* by Howard F. Stettler (3d ed., Englewood Cliffs, N.J., Prentice-Hall, 1970); Stettler's more specialized *Systems Based Independent Audits* (2d ed., Prentice-Hall, 1974); and *Auditing Concepts and Methods* by John J. Willingham and D. R. Carmichael (2d ed., New York, McGraw-Hill, 1975). Carmichael and Willingham have also revised their collection of recent readings, *Perspective in Auditing* (2d ed., McGraw-Hill, 1975).

FINANCIAL STATEMENTS AND ANALYSIS

Bernstein, Leopold A. *Understanding Corporate Reports: A Guide to Financial Statement Analysis.* Homewood, Ill., Dow Jones-Irwin, 1974.

Aims to give a comprehensive understanding of financial statements and of the tools and methods employed in their analysis, and it is written for all persons who must make decisions based on financial data.

Graham, Benjamin and Charles McGolrick. *The Interpretation of Financial Statements.* 3d rev. ed. New York, Harper & Row, 1975.

The latest revision of a short, simple manual dealing with the elements that enter into the typical balance sheet and income account. Definitions of financial terms and phrases are on pp. 87–120.

Kennedy, Ralph D. and Stewart Y. McMullen. *Financial Statements: Form, Analysis, and Interpretation.* 6th ed. Homewood, Ill., Irwin, 1973.

Explains the techniques for analyzing and interpreting the financial statements of business enterprises, both for managers and for investors and creditors. Section 4 considers special problems for air carriers, public utilities and banks.

GOVERNMENTAL AND NONBUSINESS ACCOUNTING

It is not possible to list the many books written on specialized accounting. However, an exception is made for the following two books as examples of topics of growing importance. For a list of accounting books in 52 subject categories see Rosemary Demarest's *Accounting Information Sources.* For books and articles on accounting in any industry, consult *Accountants' Index.*

Gross, Malvern J., Jr. *Financial and Accounting Guide for Nonprofit Organizations.* New York, Ronald, 1972.

Intended "to help the nonprofit organization better communicate its financial activities and financial condition to its members and to the public." In 6 parts: key financial concepts; financial statement presentation; accounting and reporting guidelines (for health and welfare organizations, educational institutions, hospitals); controlling the nonprofit organization; tax and compliance reporting requirements; setting up and keeping the books. Includes "Tables of Accounting and Reporting Alternatives" and a bibliography.

Hay, Leon E. and R. M. Mikesell. *Governmental Accounting.* 5th ed. Homewood, Ill., Irwin, 1974.

A standard text on accounting for governmental and nonprofit entities, with 9 of its 21 chapters covering techniques of fund accounting. Chapters also on accounting for hospitals, public schools, colleges and universities. Has a glossary, mathematical tables, and bibliographies at end of chapters.

SURVEYS OF ACCOUNTING PRACTICES

Each of these useful, annual surveys is arranged by subject, which makes it possible to compare company accounting practices on many specific topics.

American Institute of Certified Public Accountants. *Accounting Trends and Techniques.* New York (annual).

A useful survey of accounting practices, based on a study of stockholders' reports for 600 industrial and commercial corporations.

Haskins & Sells. *Accounting Practices.* New York. 2 volumes (annual).

Contains "illustrative items of current interest from published annual reports" of over 300 companies.

Peat, Marwick, Mitchell & Co. *Principles of Presentation.* New York (annual).

Studies the financial statements of the 100 largest U.S. commercial banks.

Surveys similar to the first two listed above are published in the United Kingdom and in Canada: *Survey of Published Accounts* (London, Institute of Chartered Accountants in England and Wales), which annually covers 300 major British industrial companies, also major property companies and investment trusts; and *Financial Reporting in Canada* (Toronto, Canadian Institute of Chartered Accountants), a biennial survey of 325 Canadian public companies.

ACCOUNTING SERVICES

Commerce Clearing House publishes several loose-leaf services, which are important sources for current information on accounting laws, regulations, court decisions, rules and standards. Loose-leaf services in general are discussed in Chapter 2. Tax services are listed elsewhere in this chapter. The CCH accounting services are:

Accountancy Law Reports. 2 volumes.

State laws regulating the right to practice accounting. This service is published in cooperation with the American Institute of Certified Public Accountants.

AICPA Professional Standards. 3 volumes.

Standards and by-laws of the American Institute of Certified Public Accountants. Vol. 3 contains the AICPA's Accounting Research Bulletins, Opinions and Statements of the Accounting Principles Board, Accounting Interpretations and Statements on Financial Accounting Standards issued by the Financial Accounting Standards Board (successor to APB).

SEC Accounting Rules.

Securities and Exchange Commission rules on accounting practices and procedures for financial statements.

For a text that systematically analyzes all Securities and Exchange Commission requirements relating to accounting principles and practices, auditing standards and procedures, financial statements, etc., see *Accounting Practice and Procedure* by Louis H. Rappaport (3d ed., New York, Ronald, 1972).

ACCOUNTING BIBLIOGRAPHIES

Demarest, Rosemary R. *Accounting Information Sources* (Management Information Guide, 18). Detroit, Mich., Gale Research Co., 1970.

An excellent, annotated bibliography of accounting books, periodicals, services and associations, still of value although much new material has been published since 1969. The major part describes books in 52 specific subject categories relating to accounting, and specialized materials on accounting in 54 particular industries. A useful feature is its short "Basic Accounting Library," which was updated and issued separately by Price, Waterhouse & Co. in 1973 and again in 1975.

"How Does Your Library Grow? — Updated." In *Journal of Accountancy*, November 1974, pp. 102–106.

A good list of basic accounting books compiled by the AICPA library committee. It updates one they prepared for a 1971 issue of the *Journal*, and it is especially useful because it enables one to select from a short list arranged by subject.

Institute of Chartered Accountants in England and Wales. *Current Accounting Literature.* Ed. by M. G. J. Harvey. London, Mansell, 1971.

A catalog of books, pamphlets and periodicals in the library of the institute, listed both by author and by topic. A supplement was published in 1972 and future periodic supplements are planned. Of particular interest to British accountants.

ACCOUNTING INDEXES AND ABSTRACTS

Accountants' Index. New York, American Institute of Certified Public Accountants (biennial through 1970; now quarterly, with last issue an annual cumulation).

An indispensable, comprehensive index to English-language books, pamphlets, government documents and articles on accounting and related fields of auditing, data processing, financial management, investments, management and taxation. Includes references for both business and nonbusiness organizations and on accounting in many specific industries. Listing is by author and title as well as by subject.

Accounting Articles. Chicago, Commerce Clearing House (monthly).

A cumulated, annotated loose-leaf service, abstracting articles in English-language accounting and business journals, as well as a few books and pamphlets. It is arranged topically within 8 major subject sections and has 2 cumulated indexes — by author and by subject.

Accountants' Digest. Syracuse, N.Y., Germain Publishing Co. (quarterly).

Digests some of the most important articles selected from leading English-language accounting journals.

The British *Anbar Management Services* publishes a section for "Accounting + Data Processing Abstracts," described in Chapter 10.

ACCOUNTING DICTIONARIES

Kohler, Eric L. *A Dictionary for Accountants.* 5th ed. Englewood Cliffs, N.J., Prentice-Hall, 1975.

A good, complete dictionary, listing terms and phrases both for accounting and for related fields. The length of definitions vary from one sentence to several paragraphs and even occasionally to a page or two.

ACCOUNTING PERIODICALS

Accounting Review. Sarasota, Fla., American Accounting Association (quarterly).

A professional journal reporting scholarly research on all aspects of accounting and finance. Includes an excellent book review section. Indexed in BPI.

Federal Accountant. Washington, D.C., Federal Government Accountants Association (quarterly).

Practical articles on governmental accounting and control. Indexed in PAIS.

Financial Executive. New York, Financial Executives Institute (monthly).

Authoritative and readable articles for the financial manager. Covers the whole area of corporate finance but concentrates especially on accounting and control. Occasional book reviews. Indexed in BPI, F&S, PAIS.

Internal Auditor. Orlando, Fla., Institute of Internal Auditors (bimonthly).

Short articles of interest to auditors and controllers.

Journal of Accountancy. New York, American Institute of Certified Public Accountants (monthly).

Articles on new trends and topics of current interest on all aspects of accounting theory and practice. Includes "Current Reading" section. Indexed in BPI, PAIS.

Journal of Accounting Research. Baltimore, Md., joint publication of the Institute of Professional Accounting, Graduate School of Business, University of Chicago, and the London School of Economics and Political Science, University of London (semi-annual).

Scholarly articles written primarily by academic persons, with an emphasis on accounting theory. Subscribers receive with this an annual supplement, *Empirical Research in Accounting*.

Management Accounting. New York, National Association of Accountants (monthly).

Well-written, short and practical articles on cost accounting and related topics of interest to management, written both by practicing accountants and by educators. Annotated lists of books in each issue. Indexed in BPI.

National Public Accountant. Washington, D.C., National Society of Public Accountants (monthly).

Short articles on a wide range of accounting topics of interest to the public accountant, banker, small businessman, etc.

There are probably more professional journals published on accounting than on any other business area. A more complete list is in the Demarest bibliography. These include not only official journals of U.S. professional societies but also those of other countries, publications of U.S. state societies, and a few journals published by the larger U.S. accounting firms.

Probably the best example of a journal issued by a state CPA society is the New York State Society of Certified Public Accountants' monthly *CPA Journal*. Several examples of journals published by accounting firms are: *Arthur Andersen Chronicle* (quarterly); *Arthur Young Journal* (quarterly); Peat, Marwick, Mitchell's *Management Controls* (monthly); *Price Waterhouse Review* (quarterly); and *Touche Ross Tempo* (quarterly). These are usually written both by and for members of the firm, but they are often available for use in a large business library or directly from the firm.

Several good Canadian and British accounting journals are:

Accountancy. London, Institute of Chartered Accountants in England and Wales (monthly). This institute also published a quarterly on *Accounting and Business Research.*

The Accountant. London, Gee & Co. (weekly). The best general trade journal.

CA Magazine. Toronto, Canadian Institute of Chartered Accountants (monthly).

Certified Accountant. London, Association of Certified Accountants (monthly).

Cost and Management. Hamilton, Ontario, Society of Industrial Accountants of Canada (bimonthly).

Management Accounting. London, Institute of Cost and Management Accountants (monthly).

DIRECTORIES OF ACCOUNTANTS

American Accounting Association. *Membership Roster.* Columbus, Ohio. Irregularly published list of teachers and practitioners.

American Institute of Certified Public Accountants. *Accounting Firms & Practitioners.* New York (biennial). A geographic listing of firms. The AICPA also publishes an alphabetical *List of Members.*

Two British associations each publish an annual *List of Members:* the Institute of Chartered Accountants in England and Wales and the Association of Certified Accountants. There is also an annual *Directory of Canadian Chartered Accountants* published by the Canadian Institute of Chartered Accountants.

ACCOUNTING ASSOCIATIONS

American Accounting Association, 653 South Orange Avenue, Sarasota, Fla. 33577.

American Institute of Certified Public Accountants, 666 Fifth Avenue, New York, N.Y. 10019.

Federal Government Accountants Association, 727 South 23d Street, Arlington, Va. 22202.

Financial Executives Institute, 633 Third Avenue, New York, N.Y. 10017.

Institute of Internal Auditors, 5500 Diplomat Circle, Orlando, Fla. 32810.

National Association of Accountants, 919 Third Avenue, New York, N.Y. 10022.

TAXATION

This section concentrates on tax reference sources of interest to business managers. Only two books are included, both of which are on tax management rather than on taxation in general.

BOOKS ON TAX MANAGEMENT

Holtzman, Robert S. *Dun & Bradstreet's Handbook of Executive Tax Management.* New York, T. Y. Crowell, 1974.

A practical guide to give managers the know-how for understanding the limits and benefits available under tax laws and their importance for business decisions.

Raby, William L. *The Income Tax and Business Decisions.* 2d ed. Englewood Cliffs, N.J., Prentice-Hall, 1972.

For the nonspecialist accountant and for the manager, this book focuses on basic tax planning, with special emphasis on provisions of income tax laws and their effect on business investment decisions. After first considering income tax, it then takes a closer look at 10 specific areas such as capital gains and depreciation, concluding with a section on practical problems of tax practice such as fraud, tax audit.

TAX SERVICES

Federal and state tax regulations have multiplied so rapidly and have become so complex that it is essential for the businessman, accountant, banker and lawyer to have ready access to the very latest in tax laws, regulations and rulings, in order to ensure compliance with the law and to minimize the amount of tax paid. Both of the best known loose-leaf service publishers offer complete federal and state tax services, kept right up to date with supplementary pages inserted weekly. They also publish several condensed but still useful guides and services. A few U.S. tax services are listed below. Foreign tax services are noted in Chapter 16. Loose-leaf services as a basic source of information are discussed in Chapter 2.

Comprehensive Federal Tax Services

Commerce Clearing House. *Standard Federal Tax Reports.* Chicago. 13 volumes (annual, with weekly supplements).

Prentice-Hall, Inc. *Federal Taxes.* Englewood Cliffs, N.J. 10 volumes (annual, with weekly supplements).

These two services are very similar in coverage, and so it is primarily a matter of personal preference as to which one an individual uses. They both give complete information about all federal tax laws, regulations, court decisions, administrative rulings, etc. Each is arranged by topic or Internal Revenue Code section; they have good instructions on how to use the service; they have complete indexes, charts, finding lists, tax planning information, supplementary brochures. They differ somewhat in arrangement of volumes:

Of the 13-volume CCH set, 7 volumes cover income tax, and one each are for the following: Internal Revenue Code; Procedures, Administration, Provisions; New Matters, Legal Periodicals and Symposia; Citator volume; U.S. Tax Cases; Index. The *Federal Excise Tax Reports* and *Inheritance, Estate and Gift Tax Reports* (both federal and state) are published separately, as is the semi-annual *U.S. Tax Cases,* which publishes the text of all federal court decisions on federal income, excise, estate and gift taxes.

Prentice-Hall's 10-volume service consists of: 5 volumes for the index plus data on income tax arranged by code section, and one volume each for: Internal Revenue Code; New Matters; American Federal Tax Reports Advance Shees; Excise tax; Estate and Gift Taes. Their 3-volume *Cumulative Changes* an 5-volume *Federal Tax*

Citator are published separately, as is the semi-annual *American Federal Tax Reports,* which reprints all federal tax decisions.

Both CCH and P-H also publish complete services that contain the text of all Reported Decisions and Memorandum Decisions of the Tax Court of the United States and the Board of Tax Appeals.

Condensed Services and Guides

Although complete tax services are essential, it is often possible to find the tax information needed by using one of the shorter guides or handbooks, which are easier to keep nearby for answering simple tax questions that arise daily. Several of these are:

Commerce Clearing House. *Federal Tax Guide.* 4 volumes.

Prentice-Hall, Inc. *Federal Tax Guide.* 5 volumes.

>These are condensed versions of their complete services, and they are geared to answer many of the everyday corporate and individual tax questions with clearly written, short explanations. Kept up to date for new laws, regulations, rulings, by weekly loose-leaf supplements.

Commerce Clearing House. *Federal Tax Course* (annual).

Prentice-Hall, Inc. *Federal Tax Course* (annual).

>Each is a handy one-volume "course" enabling beginners and others to learn about federal income tax principles and current changes in laws, regulations, decisions and procedures. Simple examples are used throughout to make explanations easier to understand. Prentice-Hall offers its volume to students and also to tax and business men for self-study and brush-up. CCH makes their *Course* available only for use in university or college teaching, but they publish a separate *Federal Tax Return Manual* for businessmen.

Commerce Clearing House. *U.S. Master Tax Guide* (annual).

Prentice-Hall, Inc. *Federal Tax Handbook* (annual).

>These are very simple, shortcut guides providing basic information on how to prepare income tax returns for individuals, corporations and small businesses.

State and Local Services

Comprehensive loose-leaf services are published to cover state and local taxes:

Commerce Clearing House. *State Tax Reports.*

Prentice-Hall, Inc. *State and Local Taxes.*

>These are similar services, with the choice as to which is used dependent on personal preference. Each publishes a separate volume for every state, providing complete up-to-date coverage on state and local taxes. Each also has an "All States" volume, with charts, tables and data to show which taxes are imposed by which states.
>
>   CCH publishes two other state tax services: *State Tax Cases Reports* and *All-State Sales Tax Reports.* Prentice-Hall's related services are: *State Income Taxes* and *Sales Taxes.*

Commerce Clearing House. *State Tax Guide.*

Prentice-Hall, Inc. *State Tax Guide.*

>Handy, condensed, one-volume tax guides that are easy-to-use sources for finding basic state tax laws.

TAX BIBLIOGRAPIES AND INDEXES

Commerce Clearing House. *Federal Tax Articles.* Chicago (monthly).

This loose-leaf service describes tax articles (covering income, estate, gift, excise and employment taxes) that have appeared in legal, accounting, tax and other related journals. It is arranged by Internal Revenue Code sections, with indexes by subject and by author.

Monthly Digest of Tax Articles. Albany, N.Y., NewkirkProducts, Inc.

As the title indicates, each issue digests a selection of about 7 current tax articles, many from law journals. Includes a section for cases and rulings.

National Tax Association and Tax Institute of America. *NTA-TIA Bookshef.* Columbus, Ohio (frequency varies).

A classified guide to articles and to some books on public finance and taxation. Each issue contains 7 basic sections 2 of which list material on specific kinds of taxes and on foreign public finance arranged by country. Other sections cover expenditures, public debt, fiscal policy, fiscal administration.

Prentice-Hall includes an "Index to Tax Articles" in Volume 1 of its *Federal Taxes* service noted in the previous section.

TAXATION PERIODICALS

Journal of Taxation. Tampa, Fla., Tax Research Group, Ltd. (monthly).

"A national journal of current news & comment for professional tax men." Includes annotated list of books. Indexed in BPI, PAIS. The staff of this journal also publishes a monthly *Taxation for Accountants.*

National Tax Journal. Columbus, Ohio, National Tax Association/Tax Institute of America and Fund for Public Policy Research (quarterly).

Professional journal reporting on research at all levels of taxation. Indexed in BPI, PAIS.

Tax Executive. Washington, D.C., Tax Executives Institute (quarterly).

Articles by practicing lawyers and accountants covering tax practices and problems in other countries as well as the United States. Includes book reviews. Indexed in PAIS.

13

COMPUTERS AND MANAGEMENT INFORMATION SYSTEMS

Computers and Data Processing — Management Information Systems — Computer Bibliographies — Indexes and Abstracts — Computer Dictionaries — Periodicals — Computer Directories — Associations — Office Management

Businessmen have had ways of getting information and keeping records since ancient times. It has only been with recent rapid developments in computer capabilities that revolutionary changes have occurred in the kinds of data available and in the whole flow of information throughout an organization. Managers of the 1970s are finding it essential both to understand and to use these new systems in their continuing effort to make faster, more accurate decisions and forecasts.

This chapter aims to help managers by listing current sources on computers, on data processing, and on management information systems (MIS) in general. Chapter 17 will cover the important topics of mathematical techniques and decision-making. Chapter 2 includes a short discussion on the use of computerized data bases as a relatively new, fast way of doing literature searches and of retrieving statistical data. Books on all of these subjects are so quickly dated that continuing use of various indexes, abstracts and journals is particularly important for keeping informed on latest trends and techniques.

COMPUTERS AND DATA PROCESSING

Davis, Gordon B. *Introduction to Electronic Computers.* 2d ed. New York, McGraw-Hill, 1971.

This is a good "general introduction to the concepts and basic features of electronic computers (hardware, software, and systems). The basic elements of machine-oriented programming are explained, as are the 3 popular machine-independent languages (BASIC, FORTRAN, and COBOL)." Includes many illustrations and diagrams; also selected references, a list of computer organizations and selected periodicals. Professor Davis has written a similar text, *Computer Data Processing* (2d ed., McGraw-Hill, 1973), which concentrates more on computers and has less on the languages. It includes bibliographies and a glossary.

Diebold, John, ed. *The World of the Computer.* New York, Random House, 1973.

An anthology selected by a well-known computer technology expert to survey the development of the computer, its uses and its impact on society.

Kanter, Jerome. *Management Guide to Computer System Selection and Use.* Englewood Cliffs, N.J., Prentice-Hall, 1970.

"This is a useful guide that focuses on the role management must play throughout the entire computer selection cycle — beginning with the feasibility study, proceeding through the selection of the computer task force, the analysis of business problems, the study of a company's information flow, and the detailed systems study, and ending with the computer implementation plan." Includes bibliographies.

Kenney, Donald P. *Minicomputers: Low-Cost Computer Power for Management.* New York, AMACOM, American Management Associations, 1973.

This guide for managers describes the possibilities for using a low-cost minicomputer system within the organization.

Lundell, E. Drake, Jr., and Edward J. Bride. *Computer Use: An Executive's Guide.* Boston, Allyn and Bacon, 1973.

A clearly written guide on "the hows and whys of selecting, procuring and installing computer systems." It is designed both for executives and for DP professionals to give each a better understanding of the other's needs, problems and role within the organization.

Another book that aims to bridge this gap is *Computers and Management: The Executive Viewpoint* by Victor Z. Brink (Englewood Cliffs, N.J., Prentice-Hall, 1971). Brink's book is based in large part on research involving over 100 large industrial corporations.

Martin, James. *Introduction to Teleprocessing.* Englewood Cliffs, N.J., Prentice-Hall, 1972.

The essential facts about data transmission, for nontechnical persons. Much of this book consists of the rewriting of previous works so as to form an introduction. Includes a bibliography. Among several other books, Martin has also written (with Adrian R. D. Norman) an appraisal of the impact of computers on society over the coming years called *The Computerized Society* (Prentice-Hall, 1970).

National Academy of Sciences, Washington, D.C., Project on Computer Databanks. *Databanks in a Free Society: Computers, Record-Keeping and Privacy.* Alan F. Westin, Project Director. New York, Quadrangle Books, 1972.

A factual study of computerized databanks in American society and their effect on personal privacy and on confidentiality. It presents detailed profiles of 14 of the 50 site visits made during the course of the study. These visits represented governmental, commercial and private organizations that were leaders in their fields in the use of computers for record-keeping. The study ends with consideration of future directions in computer technology and of implications for public policy.

Sanders, Donald H. *Computers in Business, An Introduction.* 3d ed. New York, McGraw-Hill, 1975.

A newly revised edition of an excellent, beginning college text that aims to provide: (1) an introduction to the development of information processing; (2) a general orientation to the computer — what it is, how it operates, what it can and cannot do; (3) an insight into the implications for management and for society. No mathematics or data processing background is needed. Many illustrations and diagrams are included throughout; bibliographies are at end of chapters, and a glossary is at end of book. Professor Sanders has also written a separate introductory text on *Computers and Management in a Changing Society* (2d ed., McGraw-Hill, 1974).

Withington, Frederic G. *The Use of Computers in Business Organizations.* 2d ed. Reading, Mass., Addison-Wesley, 1971.

A well-written, concise introduction to give the nonspecialist essential knowledge and understanding for making decisions about the acquisition and use of computers. Includes a glossary and a bibliography.

Wooldridge, Susan and Keith London. *The Computer Survival Handbook: How to Talk Back to Your Computer.* Boston, Gambit, 1973.

A concise, sometimes humorous but still practical, "working brief" on what to do when a computer system is planned.

MANAGEMENT INFORMATION SYSTEMS

Handbooks

McFarlan, F. Warren and Richard L. Nolan, eds. *Information Systems Manager's Handbook.* Homewood, Ill., Dow Jones-Irwin, 1975.

This comprehensive handbook covers the field of information systems management in 40 chapters, each written by an expert. There are 6 basic parts: the information systems manager as a member of the top management team; the information systems manager as the administrator of a major corporate function; information systems manpower administration; financial and economic analysis of acquisition (includes performance measurement, computer options, purchase/lease, etc.); applications development management (the longest section, with 13 chapters on such subjects as computer-based system life cycle, project management, business systems analysis, managing the operating system environment, data base administrator and design); computer room administration.

Books

Albrecht, Leon K. *Organization and Management of Information Processing Systems.* New York, Macmillan, 1973.

Especially useful for its practical in-depth treatment of the basic processes and techniques involved in managing and operating an effective information systems organization within a business.

Benjamin, Robert I. *Control of the Information System Development Cycle.* New York, Wiley-Interscience, 1971.

A concise treatise that develops a conceptual methodology for controlling the development of information systems applicable to the needs of many types of organizations. This paperback is less than 100 pages and belongs to a "Wiley Communigraph Series on Business Data Processing," which aims to offer the busy manager a succinct treatment of specialized topics on business/management applications of the computer.

Blumenthal, Sherman C. *Management Information Systems: A Framework for Planning and Development.* Englewood Cliffs, N.J., Prentice-Hall, 1969.

This is a classic in its field, which "attempts to bridge the gap between theory and practice by detailing the specific technical and organizational steps which must be taken to synthesize a comprehensive, integrated systems plan for the corporate enterprise, in its parts and as a whole." It is addressed to systems professionals, to managers and to advanced students and presumes some knowledge of computer systems, management science and control.

Bocchino, William A. *Management Information Systems: Tools and Techniques.* Englewood Cliffs, N.J., Prentice-Hall, 1972.

"A nontechnical explanation of the tools and techniques for the planning, analysis, design and implementation of management information systems." Includes many diagrams, a glossary and annotated bibliographies.

Couger, J. Daniel and Robert W. Knapp, eds. *Systems Analysis Techniques.* New York, Wiley, 1974.

A wide selection of readings describing specific techniques that use the computer as an aid in systems analysis.

Davis, Gordon B. *Management Information Systems: Conceptual Foundations, Structure, and Development.* New York, McGraw-Hill, 1974.

A first attempt to define the contents and coverage of an introductory text in this new field of study, written by a well-qualified academic authority. Professor Davis concentrates on the 3 areas of the subtitle: conceptual foundations; structure of a management information system (hardware, software, data base, procedures and operating personnel); MIS development and management. Includes bibliographics.

Head, Robert V. *Manager's Guide to Management Information Systems.* Englewood Cliffs, N.J., Prentice-Hall, 1972.

Concise explanation of the concepts and principles of MIS for the management person with no computer background. Includes a glossary and an annotated bibliography of some earlier nontechnical books.

Lucas, Henry C., Jr. *Computer Based Information Systems in Organizations.* Chicago, Science Research Associates, 1973.

Designed to provide managers and management students with some of the technological background basic to understanding information systems and to working effectively with systems technicians. In 4 parts: introduction; technical background; systems analysis and design; advanced systems and problems. Includes a glossary; also recommended readings (annotated) at end of chapters. Some computer background is presumed. Professor Lucas has also written a useful monograph *Toward Creative Systems Design* (New York, Columbia University Press, 1974), which discusses techniques for systems design for overcoming organizational behavior problems that have kept many present-day systems from realizing their potential for improving organizational performance and decision-making.

Meadow, Charles T. *The Analysis of Information Systems.* 2d ed. Los Angeles, Calif., Melville Publishing Co., 1973.

A book concerned primarily with information retrieval and meant to bridge the communications gap among information users, librarians and data processors. It assumes some knowledge of computers and programming and a little elementary mathematics. There are 4 main sections: language and communication; retrieval of information; organization of information; computer processing of information. Includes bibliographies at end of chapters.

Mockler, Robert J. *Information Systems for Management.* Columbus, Ohio, Charles E. Merrill, 1974.

Designed to give managers and potential managers the basic "know-how" to understand information systems and data processing and to be able to work effectively with systems technicians. Chapters 4 through 10 discuss the development of basic information systems in finance and accounting, marketing, operations, project management. There is also a chapter on organizing information systems functions.

Murdick, Robert G. and Joel E. Ross. *Information Systems for Modern Management.* 2d ed. Englewood Cliffs, N.J., Prentice-Hall, 1975.

An attempt to blend a study of the concepts and practices of management with those of information systems in order to help close the gap separating the manager from the computer specialist and to improve the art of managing. There are 4 parts: management and systems; planning, design, and implementation of MIS; concepts for decision-making with MIS; the future of MIS. Suggested readings at end of chapters and 6 cases at end of book.

Nolan, Richard L., ed. *Managing the Data Resource Function.* St. Paul, Minn., West Publishing Co., 1974.

A selection of readings on the data resource function — its evolution, how to assess it, how to manage it, and speculation about the future.

Prince, Thomas R. *Information Systems for Management Planning and Control.* 3d ed. Homewood, Ill., Irwin, 1975.

This latest edition of a basic upper level or graduate text "reflects the significant changes and developments in information systems and the system analyst's function in recent years," and the coverage is expanded to include nonprofit organizations, especially health care institutions. Includes a few cases with each chapters. Presumes some understanding of computer programming language, mathematical methods and an introductory course in cost accounting.

COMPUTER BIBLIOGRAPHIES

"Books Useful in Teaching Business Applications of the Computer." In *Computing Newsletter for Schools of Business,* Colorado Springs, School of Business Administration, University of Colorado (annual, January issue).

This is a simple listing of books that is revised each year. It is arranged by curriculum specialization: introduction to EDP (books for students, for managers, for laymen); computer programming (both introductory and advanced books; those on 9 specific programs, and on special machines); systems analysis (decision tables, flowcharting, etc.); systems design; computer-based management information systems; computer applications (for each of 12 fields); computer simulation; special subjects (such as computers and society); computer math; hardware; computer references. No descriptive notes are given but a code specifies whether each book is a text, whether it has cases, readings, problems or programmed instruction.

Carter, Ciel. *Guide to Reference Sources in the Computer Sciences.* New York, Macmillan Information, 1974.

An excellent, descriptive guide that is worldwide in scope and covers the following kinds of computer sources: bibliographies, abstracts, indexes, encyclopedias, dictionaries, directories, handbooks, periodicals, professional organizations, trade associations, research centers, conference literature.

Pritchard, Alan. *A Guide to Computer Literature.* 2d ed., rev. and expanded. London, England, Bingley; Hamden, Conn., Shoe String Press, 1972.

A bibliographic essay about various kinds of computer reference works: periodicals, abstracts, indexes, bibliographies, dictionaries, directories, libraries, etc. It is worldwide in scope, with discussions in each chapter arranged by country. Useful but not as easy to check as Carter above because of its prose style and relatively short index.

INDEXES AND ABSTRACTS

Computer & Information Systems. Riverdale, Md., Cambridge Scientific Abstracts (semi-annual).

Abstracts of the world's literature in this rapidly growing field, with items classified by very specific topics under the following headings: computer software; computer applications; computer mathematics; computer electronics (hardware). Mentions in which language the publication is written.

Computing Reviews. New York, Association for Computing Machinery (monthly).

Good, signed reviews of books and articles on computer sciences, classified by specific topics within 8 broad fields. Includes computer applications, software, hardware, mathematics. Lengthy bibliographies on a specific computer topic are at end of occasional issues.

New Literature on Automation. Amsterdam, Netherlands Centre for Informatics (monthly).

An international abstracting journal on automatic data processing, classified by detailed subjects. Abstracts are in either English, German, French or Spanish, with one-sentence summaries in the other three languages.

Quarterly Bibliography of Computers and Data Processing. Phoenix, Ariz., Applied Computer Research (quarterly, with annual cumulation).

A good, annotated subject index to nonacademic books, reports and articles of interest to computer users, manufacturers and consultants. Covers a wide range of journals, over 200 subject classifications, and includes an author index in each issue.

Among several useful foreign abstracting services is the monthly *Computer Abstracts* (St. Helier, British Channel Islands, Technical Information Co., Ltd.), a classified list of articles, conference proceedings, government reports, patents and a few books.

COMPUTER DICTIONARIES

Jordain, Philip B. and Michael Breslau, eds. *Condensed Computer Encyclopedia.* New York, McGraw-Hill, 1969.

This is more than a straight dictionary because the definitions are often longer than just one paragraph and occasionally they run to several pages. Meant for the nonspecialist businessman, so definitions are clear and relatively simple. Many helpful diagrams are included, and there is also a short index and a bibliography.

Meek, C. L. *Glossary of Computing Terminology.* New York, CCM Information Corp., 1972.
Concise definitions of terms on a wide range of computer-related subjects, and taken from other published sources.

Sippl, Charles J. and Charles P. Sippl. *Computer Dictionary and Handbook.* 2d ed. Indianapolis, Ind., Howard W. Sams, 1972.
A dictionary and handbook rolled into one and "designed to aid in identifying, classifying, and interpreting terms and concepts concerned with electronic data processing, information technology, computer science, and many types of automation." The handbook section, pp. 491–778, includes data on mathematical and statistical definitions, flowcharting, acronyms, abbreviations, etc.

Weik, Martin H. *Standard Dictionary of Computers and Information Processing.* New York, Hayden Book Co., 1969.
A good, comprehensive dictionary by an information systems expert, with definitions reflecting the best current usage. Includes some diagrams, many useful cross-references, and a bibliography of the many dictionaries and glossaries that were checked in the preparation of this volume.

PERIODICALS

American Federation of Information Processing Societies. *AFIPS Conference Proceedings.* Montvale, N.J., AFIPS Press (annual).
These proceedings offer an excellent means of keeping up to date on new developments in computer science and technology and their applications. AFIPS is a federation of 13 computer, statistical and information science societies; the conference is also called the "National Computer Conference & Exposition."

Communications of the ACM. New York, Association for Computing Machinery (monthly).
Technical articles on computer science and also news from ACM members. This association also publishes a quarterly *Journal,* which reports on scientific and mathematically oriented research, and is indexed in ASTI.

Computers and People. Newtonville, Mass., Berkeley Enterprises, Inc. (monthly).
One of the oldest and most widely read trade journals, this was formerly called *Computers and Automation.* It is devoted to "the design, applications, and implications of information processing systems — and the pursuit of truth in input, output, and processing, for the benefit of people." A monthly feature is its "Computer Census," also listings of "New Contracts" and "New Installations." Indexed in BPI, F&S. An annual *Computer Directory and Buyers' Guide* is published separately as their "Midyear Directory Issue."

Data Management. Park Ridge, Ill., Data Processing Management Association (monthly).
Short articles for managers on a wide range of data processing topics. Former title was *Journal of Data Management.* Indexed in BPI.

Datamation. Barrington, Ill., Technical Publishing Co. (monthly).

A trade journal for managers, with short timely articles on data processing and related subjects. An annual "Survey of DP Budgets" is in February issue each year, and an "EDP Salary Survey" appears in May. Indexed in BPI, F&S.

EDP Analyzer. Vista, Calif., Canning Publications (monthly).

Each issue is a short, professional report (about 15 pages) on one specific topic of interest to data processing management. Several 1974 titles were: "Improving the Systems Building Process;" "The Upgrading of Computer Operators;" "Charging for Computer Services."

Infosystems. Wheaton, Ill., Hitchcock Publishing Co. (monthly).

Short, practical articles for systems managers. Annual features include a "Salary Survey" for DP employees, currently in September issue; a table of "Computer Characteristics" in May 1974. This journal was formerly called *Business Automation.* Indexed in BPI, F&S, PAIS.

Journal of Systems Management. Cleveland, Ohio, Association for Systems Management (monthly).

The articles in this journal are also quite short and are aimed at advancing information systems knowledge. Indexed in BPI.

COMPUTER DIRECTORIES

Directories listing computerized data bases, selective dissemination of information services, information centers, etc., can be found in Chapter 2.

Computer Directory and Buyers' Guide. Published annually as the "Midyear Directory Issue" of *Computers and People.*

An annually revised roster of computer and data processing firms. Includes officers, description of principal activities, approximate number of employees. This issue also has a list of associations; information about college and university computer facilities; computer users groups; tabular list of characteristics of digital computers; a "World Computer Census."

Computer Yearbook. Detroit, Mich., Computer Yearbook Co. (triennial).

A handbook-like volume. The 1972 issue is in 5 sections, with the major parts covering: state-of-the-art; computer applications in 13 areas such as banking, government, transportation. Includes descriptive information about principal manufacturers on pp. 57–111.

World-Wide Directory of Computer Companies. Ed. by Marie B. Waters. Orange, N.J., Academic Media, 1973.

A comprehensive list of public, private and nonprofit computer firms, giving officers, product information and occasionally sales and approximate number of employees. Includes geographic, sector and personnel indexes.

Computer Review. Lexington, Mass., GML Corp. (loose-leaf annual, with two updates during each year).

This is not a directory of companies but rather a list of the characteristics and prices of many central processors and of peripheral devices (magnetic tape, line printers, etc.) of manufacturers in the United States, in Canada, in 8 European countries, in Israel and in Japan.

ASSOCIATIONS

Association for Computing Machinery, 1133 Avenue of the Americas, New York, N.Y. 10036.

Association for Systems Management, 24587 Bagley Road, Cleveland, Ohio 44138.

Business Equipment Manufacturers Association, 1828 L Street, N.W., Washington, D.C. 20036.

Data Processing Management Association, 505 Busse Highway, Park Ridge, Ill. 60068.

Society for Management Information Systems, One First National Plaza, Chicago, Ill. 60670.

OFFICE MANAGEMENT

Office work in any organization is involved primarily with information processing, so it is useful to include in this chapter several recent texts on the administrative management of information.

Handbooks

Fetridge, William H. *Office Administration Handbook.* Chicago, Dartnell Corp., 1975.

This new handbook on the practices and procedures of office administration is over 1,000 pages in length. Its 36 chapters are divided into the following major sections: administrative management — the basics; office personnel — recruiting and selection; office personnel — administration; guides through the paperwork jungle; office practices and procedures; the office environment; how to improve administrative skills. An appendix includes management, computer, word-processing terms; sources of information.

Heyel, Carl, ed. *Handbook of Modern Office Management and Administrative Services.* New York, McGraw-Hill, 1972.

A comprehensive reference source on office management and administration applicable not only to companies of all sizes but also to governmental and institutional administration. Seventy-six chapters and eighty-one experts provide "how to" information for the efficient organization and conduct of office operations, with one of the ten sections covering data processing. Short bibliographies are at end of some chapters.

Books

Neuner, John J. W., B. Lewis Keeling and Norman F. Kallaus. *Administrative Office Management.* 6th ed. Cincinnati, Ohio, South-Western, 1972.

This latest edition of a standard text places added emphasis on information as the major product of the office. It covers 5 basic areas of administrative office management: administrative office management in modern business; organizing and planning administrative office services; leadership and human relations; controlling office administrative operations; business information processing systems.

Place, Irene, Charles B. Hicks and Robin L. Wilkinson. *Office Management.* 3d ed. Boston, Allyn and Bacon, 1971.

Two professors and an industrial expert collaborated to produce this text on the management of information processing, which stresses an analytical and administrative approach. It is in 5 parts: office management (management and office management functions); data processing (computing, duplicating, correspondence, records management, etc.); systems analysis (includes work simplification, work measurement, analysis of forms, layout); managerial functions (planning, organization, control); office personnel (job analysis, selection, development, motivation, etc.). Includes problems and a glossary.

Terry, George R. *Office Management and Control: The Administrative Managing of Information.* 6th ed. Homewood, Ill., Irwin, 1970. (The 7th edition is scheduled for publication in 1975.)

Another standard text presenting basic principles and successful practices used in getting office work accomplished. Organized around the 4 basic functional areas of planning, controlling, organizing, and actuating, and it also has chapters on systems and procedures, computers, records management.

Periodicals

Administrative Management. New York, Geyer-McAllister Publications (monthly).

A trade journal covering business systems, equipment and personnel. Indexed in BPI, F&S, F&SI.

The Office. Stamford, Conn., Office Publications (monthly).

A trade journal with articles covering office management, equipment and systems. Includes annotated booklists in most issues. Indexed in BPI, F&S.

Associations

Administrative Management Society, Willow Grove, Pa. 19090.

14

CORPORATE FINANCE AND BANKING

Financial Handbooks — Books on Corporate Finance — Capital Budgeting and Capital Expenditures — Public Stock Offerings — Directories of Venture Capital Companies — Acquisitions and Mergers — Finance Bibliographies — Finance Dictionaries — Finance Periodicals — Finance Associations — *MONEY AND BANKING* **— Basic Texts — Financial Institutions and the Money Market — Bank Management — Credit Management — Mortgage Banking — Personal Finance — Banking Law and Financial Legal Services — Banking and Financial Tables — Banking Bibliographies — Banking Dictionaries — Financial Manuals and Bank Directories — U.S. Banking and Financial Statistics — Banking Newspapers and Periodicals — Bank and Credit Associations**

The broad area of business finance can be divided into three interrelated parts: corporate finance, banking and investments. This chapter concentrates on two of these: corporate finance; money, banking and credit. Although a distinction in the literature is sometimes difficult to make, it seems logical to consider investment sources following the chapter covering industry statistics, and so investment management books are described separately in Chapter 7. Books and reference sources on international finance are in Chapter 16; insurance and real estate sources are discussed in Chapter 15; several books on the mathematics of finance are included in Chapter 17.

FINANCIAL HANDBOOKS

Bogen, Jules I. and Samuel S. Shipman. *Financial Handbook.* 4th ed. New York, Ronald, 1968.

Ever since its original publication Bogen's handbook has been *the* indispensable, comprehensive guide to corporate finance, money and banking. Now it is somewhat out of date but still of value for background financial information.

Prentice-Hall, Inc. *Corporate Treasurer's and Controller's Encyclopedia.* Rev. by Sam R. Goodman. Englewood Cliffs, N.J., Prentice-Hall, 1975.

This revises Lillian Doris's excellent 4-volume encyclopedia of useful information for the effective performance of corporate treasurers and controllers. Its coverage is comprehensive, with 32 lengthy chapters on such topics as costs, inventories, cash management, financial reports, payroll activities.

Vancil, Richard F., ed. *Financial Executive's Handbook.* Homewood, Ill., Dow Jones-Irwin, 1970.

An excellent compendium of current knowledge on the responsibilities of financial executives — in 66 chapters, each written by a practicing businessman. Includes planning, accounting, information technology, financial structure, external relations, etc.

Baughn and Walker's *Bankers' Handbook* is listed in the "Bank Management" section of this chapter.

BOOKS ON CORPORATE FINANCE

Cohan, Avery B. *Financial Decision Making — Theory and Practice: Text and Problems.* Englewood Cliffs, N.J., Prentice-Hall, 1972.

A "problem oriented" book on modern theory of corporation finance, using capital budgeting as a framework. After an introductory section, Cohan discusses tools and techniques (present value, rates of return, probability distributions) and then sources of funds and cost of capital. Includes brief compound interest and present value tables, a bibliography and short glossary.

Diener, Royce. *How to Finance a Growing Business.* Rev. ed. New York, Frederick Fell, 1974.

A practical and readable book for the businessman/borrower on techniques of business finance, including specialized procedures for acquisition and for international financing.

Goodman, Sam R. *Financial Manager's Manual and Guide.* Englewood Cliffs, N.J., Prentice-Hall, 1973.

Designed as a practical guide to effective methods in financial planning and control. Covers such topics as cash management for small- and medium-sized companies, cost control, discounted cash flow, use of mathematical models, long-range planning, the finance function.

Helfert, Erich A. *Techniques of Financial Analysis.* 3d ed. Homewood, Ill., Irwin, 1972.

A good, concise presentation of "the more important tools and techniques of financial analysis, without delving into their broad theoretical and institutional background." Covers: business as a system of funds flow; measurement of business results; projection of business results; analysis of capital investment decisions; analysis of financial funds sources; business as a dynamic system; sources of financial information.

Hunt, Pearson, Charles M. Williams and Gordon Donaldson. *Basic Business Finance: Text.* Homewood, Ill., Irwin, 1974.

This introductory text appears for the first time without the cases that have been included in the 4 previous editions. Instead it contains questions and problems at the end of each chapter. The text is the same, with primary emphasis still on financial decision-making and administration in a going concern. There are 10 parts including: the management of issues and the need for funds; capital budgeting; long- and short-term sources of funds; financing growth and development; business failure.

Husband, William H. and James C. Dockeray. *Modern Corporation Finance.* 7th ed. Homewood, Ill., Irwin, 1972.

Latest edition of a standard text that "attempts to develop a 'policy approach' to finance in the context of the political and social environment of the day." It covers all the essentials in 31 chapters and the following 7 parts: finance and the corporation; instruments of corporation finance; promotion, capitalization, ownership and management; sale and regulation of securities; income and working capital; corporate expansion, failure and reorganization; public policy. Includes suggested readings with each chapter.

Johnson, Keith B. and Donald E. Fischer. *Readings in Contemporary Financial Management.* Glenview, Ill., Scott, Foresman, 1969.

A good selection of older basic readings by well-known authorities, such as Solomon, Donaldson, Weston.

Another selection of articles on techniques and problems of interest to financial managers is *Frontiers of Financial Management: Selected Readings* by William J. Serraino, S. S. Singhvi and Robert M. Soldofsky (2d ed., Cincinnati, Ohio, South-Western, 1976).

Johnson, Robert W. *Financial Management.* 4th ed. Boston, Allyn and Bacon, 1971.

An introductory text on the theory and concept of financial management, in 6 parts: introduction; planning and managing assets (cash, accounts receivable, inventory, capital budgeting); planning the financial structure (cost of capital); management of short- and intermediate-term funds; managing long-term funds; valuing business enterprises (valuation, mergers, failure). Includes suggested readings and present value tables.

Lerner, Eugene M. *Managerial Finance: A Systems Approach.* New York, Harcourt Brace Jovanovich, 1971.

Designed as a stimulating and practical text rather than one emphasizing theory. "The particular activities and relationships stressed . . . are the information flows that a manager receives, the cash flows through the firm, the growth of the enterprise, the market valuation placed upon the firm, and the environment within which the system as a whole operates." Includes suggested readings, a glossary and present value tables.

Van Horne, James C. *Fundamentals of Financial Management.* 2d ed. Englewood Cliffs, N.J., Prentice-Hall, 1974.

The purpose of this excellent, introductory text is "to provide the reader with a basic understanding of the allocation of funds within a business firm and the raising of funds." It presumes some knowledge of elementary algebra. This edition has been thoroughly revised to reflect many changes and to give greater emphasis to risk and valuation and to financial decision-making. There are 7 parts: introduction; the management of current assets; capital budgeting and the acceptance criterion; capital structure and dividend policy; short- and intermediate-term financing; long-term financing; external growth and contraction. Bibliographies are at end of chapters;

present value tables are at end of book. Professor Van Horne has also recently revised his standard text on *Financial Management and Policy* (3d ed., Prentice-Hall, 1974), which aims to develop an understanding of financial theory and the application of analytical techniques to problems involving financial decisions.

Weston, J. Fred and Eugene F. Brigham. *Essentials of Managerial Finance.* 3d ed. Hinsdale, Ill., Dryden, 1974.

A well-established introductory text on the fundamentals of business finance, with an emphasis on decision rather than on theory. After introductory and overview sections, the authors study: working capital management; decision involving long-term assets; sources and forms of long-term financing; financial structure and the cost of capital; integrated topics in financial management, (timing, external growth, firms facing financial difficulties). A glossary and a few mathematical tables are at end. This is an abbreviated version of the authors' *Managerial Finance* (5th ed., Dryden, 1975), which explores conceptual problems in depth and includes bibliographies. Professor Brigham has compiled a book of *Readings in Managerial Finance* (New York, Holt, Rinehart and Winston, 1971), which can be used with these texts.

CAPITAL BUDGETING AND CAPITAL EXPENDITURES

Abdelsamad, Moustafa H. *A Guide to Capital Expenditure Analysis.* New York, American Management Association, 1973.

A practical guide to the theory and practice of capital expenditure analysis for managers at all levels. It incorporates material on the practices of business firms based on questionnaires and interviews with financial officers, and it includes 5 chapters on specific methods — payback, accountant rate of return, discounted cash flow rate of return, net present value, MAPI (Machinery and Allied Products Institute). Appendixes include excerpts from 3 company financial manuals and a short selected reading list.

Bierman, Harold, Jr., and Seymour Smidt. *The Capital Budgeting Decision: Economic Analysis and Financing of Investment Projects.* 4th ed. New York, Macmillan, 1975.

These authors advocate the present value method in their well-established study on how to evaluate investment proposals. Part 1 treats decisions under certainty in a perfect capital market; Parts 2 and 4 introduce complications of imperfect capital markets and uncertainty, with Part 4 being somewhat more mathematical; Part 3 discusses miscellaneous topics that facilitate the application of capital budgeting techniques (buy or lease, inflation, investment timing, etc.). Present value tables are at end.

Johnson, Robert W. *Capital Budgeting.* Belmont; Calif., Wadsworth, 1970.

A concise "treatment of the issues that must be faced in any capital budgeting program." Includes a bibliography and present value tables.

Smith, Gerald W. *Engineering Economy: Analysis of Capital Expenditures.* 2d ed. Ames, Iowa State University Press, 1973.

"Deals with the concepts, principles, techniques, and reasoning by which the planner can be guided in his decisions pertaining to long-term facilities." Section headings include: time and money; methods of comparing alternatives; income tax considerations; multioutcome considerations: risk and uncertainty; capital budgeting considerations. Includes tables of random digits and compound interest, a bibliography and other useful data.

An earlier standard text is *Principles of Engineering Economy* by Eugene L. Grant and W. Grant Ireson (5th ed., New York, Ronald, 1970). For current articles devoted to applied and theoretical problems of capital investment see the quarterly journal *Engineering Economist* (Ephrata, Pa., American Society for Engineering Education). It includes book reviews and is indexed in PAIS.

Vaughn, Donald E., Richard L. Norgaard and Hite Bennett. *Financial Planning and Management: A Budgetary Approach.* Pacific Palisades, Calif., Goodyear Publishing Co., 1972.

Studies the management of a capital budgeting system, in 5 parts: organization and budget origination; evaluation approaches (as they apply to replacement planning, expansion, new product development, cost-saving, risk evaluation); working capital management; cost of capital; capital rationing and budget control. This is followed by a selected bibliography, 28 case problems and appendixes explaining several mathematical procedures. Assumes some knowledge of basic business statistics.

Expenditures for New Plants and Equipment

Conference Board. *Capital Appropriations.* New York (quarterly).

Brief quarterly statistics on manufacturers' capital appropriations by industry in both current and constant dollars; also seasonally adjusted figures, from 1973, for durable and nondurable goods industries, and proportion of appropriations for plant.

McGraw-Hill Publications Co. Economic Department. *Business Plans for New Plants and Equipment.* New York (annual).

This is a short summary of an annual questionnaire survey on company plans for new plants and equipment, with figures giving actual plans for one year and preliminary plans for 3 years in the future. Statistics are by broad industry and include plans for capital spending, expansion vs. modernization, index of industrial capacity, sales expectations, planned capital spending by region; also tables on how much companies expect their prices and employment will increase. McGraw-Hill also publishes an annual release on their fall survey covering *Preliminary Plans for Capital Spending.*

U.S. Bureau of the Census. *Census of Manufactures.* Washington, D.C.

Statistics on expenditures for new plants and equipment are included in this census and also in the *Annual Survey of Manufactures* taken in the years between each census. These give total expenditures and expenditures for new structures and additions to plants, new machinery and equipment.

Each issue of the Department of Commerce *Survey of Current Business* includes quarterly statistics on expenditures for new plants and equipment, arranged by broad industry. Separate tables accompany several special articles each year (for example, June, September and December 1974). Another semi-annual article with statistics is on "Property, Plant and Equipment Expenditures by Majority-Owned Foreign Affiliates of U.S. Companies" (for instance, March and September 1974).

PUBLIC STOCK OFFERINGS

Winter, Elmer L. *Complete Guide to Making a Public Stock Offering.* 2d ed. Englewood Cliffs, N.J., Prentice-Hall, 1972.

A practical and useful guide for managers covering all important techniques, plans and procedures, from the first consideration of a public stock offering to planning the first annual meeting of stockholders. Includes a glossary and sample agreements.

Another good, recent book that gives more consideration to the legal, accounting and financial aspects is *Going Public: A Practical Handbook of Procedures and Forms* by Daniel S. Berman (Prentice-Hall, 1974).

Sources for lists of new securities offerings are described in Chapter 7.

DIRECTORIES OF VENTURE CAPITAL COMPANIES

Rubel, Stanley M. *Guide to Venture Capital Sources.* Chicago, Capital Publishing Corp. (biennial).

Most of this useful guide consists of a directory of over 600 American, Canadian and a few international venture capital companies. Information for each includes projects of interest, minimum operating data, industry and geographical preferences, preferred size of investment. The third edition, 1974, also has a bibliography and the digested views of 17 venture capitalists who participated in seminars on "How to Raise Venture Capital."

S. M. Rubel & Co. publishes a monthly loose-leaf journal, *Venture Capital,* which contains brief news of the industry and of venture companies, a feature profile of one or more companies, financial statistics of publicly held SBICs and venture companies, a list of "venture backed publicly held growth companies." An index of reports and special studies in this monthly is included in Rubel's *Guide.*

Venture Capital. Ed. by Leroy W. Sinclair. 3d ed. New York, Technimetrics, 1973.

A "sourcebook of small business financing" in 3 parts. Part 1 is a directory of corporations and partnerships that make high risk funds available to businessmen. Information for each is similar to that in the guide above. Part 2 has information about securities underwriters that sell new issues; Part 3 gives data on the new business development departments of major industrial corporations.

There is a list of 816 firms in John R. Dominguez's *Venture Capital* (Lexington, Mass., D.C. Heath, 1974), giving only brief information about each. His first 79 pages are a textual discussion of venture capital financing, with case studies of two specific firms, and it also has a bibliography.

ACQUISITIONS AND MERGERS

Baumer, William H. and Leo J. Northart. *Buy, Sell, Merge: How to Do It.* Englewood Cliffs, N.J., Prentice-Hall, 1971.

This is a practical book focusing on the step-by-step merger process, with emphasis on personal rather than on legal factors. A "Business Appraisal Check List" is at end.

Eglit, Howard C., ed. *Creative Acquisition Techniques.* (Creative Business Library, Vol. 3.) Ann Arbor, Mich., Institute of Continuing Legal Education, 1969.

A useful compilation of 10 speeches presented at 2 panel discussions aimed at highlighting the knowledge that a corporate attorney must have to operate successfully in the area of corporate acquisitions. It covers corporate reorganization, corporate and securities considerations, stock-for-stock tender offers, drafting and technical problems, etc.

Guardino, Joseph R. *Accounting, Legal and Tax Aspects of Corporate Acquisitions.* Englewood Cliffs, N.J., Prentice-Hall, 1973.

The title pretty well describes the scope of this practical guide, which covers not only acquisitions but also reorganizations and liquidations. Appendixes include model agreements.

Harvey, John L. and Albert Newgarden, eds. *Management Guides to Mergers and Acquisitions.* New York, Wiley-Interscience, 1969.

A good selection of the older readings representing various viewpoints and considerations involving effective merger planning. For the many more recent articles check in *Business Periodicals Index* and other periodical indexes described in Chapter 2.

Scharf, Charles A. *Acquisitions, Mergers, Sales and Takeovers: A Handbook with Forms.* Englewood Cliffs, N.J., Prentice-Hall, 1971.

A practical guide on acquiring and merging businesses written by a specialist-lawyer and including rules governing the legal, tax, securities and accounting aspects. Portions of this book first appeared in Scharf's *Techniques for Buying, Selling and Merging Businesses* (Prentice-Hall, 1964).

Vance, Stanley C. *Managers in the Conglomerate Era.* New York, Wiley-Interscience, 1971.

Discusses the merger-conglomeration movement, the impact of managers on mergers and, in turn, the impact of mergers on tomorrow's managers.

A book on *Mergers: Motives, Effects, Policies* by Peter O. Steiner has just been published in late 1975 by the University of Michigan Press. It concentrates principally on conglomerate mergers.

Bibliographies and Periodicals

Mergers and Acquisitions: A Comprehensive Bibliography. Comp. by Robert Sperry. McLean, Va., Mergers & Acquisitions, 1972.

A topical listing of books, theses, documents and articles on all aspects of mergers and acquisitions, and also on other forms of corporate combining. Includes a section by country, listing foreign sources, and a section on mergers in specific industries.

Mergers & Acquisitions: The Journal of Corporate Venture. McLean, Va., Mergers & Acquisitions (quarterly).

Two to three good articles in each issue; also several regular features including rosters of mergers and acquisitions, joint ventures and foreign acquisitions.

Lists of Mergers and Acquisitions

The Federal Trade Commission in Washington, D.C., publishes an annual *F.T.C. Statistical Report on Mergers and Acquisitions,* which is a listing of large mergers and acquisitions, new joint ventures and foreign mergers recorded during the year. This is sometimes reprinted in part in the periodical *Mergers & Acquisitions* which also includes a roster of mergers and acquisitions in each issue. The Conference Board in New York City publishes a short monthly called *Announcements of Mergers and Acquisitions*. See also the "Capital Changes Services" section of Chapter 7.

FINANCE BIBLIOGRAPHIES

Brealey, Richard A. and Connie Pyle, comps. *A Bibliography of Finance and Investment.* London, Elek Books; Cambridge, Mass., MIT Press, 1973.

A comprehensive (but not annotated) list of over 3,600 books, articles and dissertations on corporate finance and on the securities and other speculative markets. Well arranged in 150 subject areas of which 30 are in the following areas of finance: money market and international capital markets; corporate finance; capital structure; dividend policy; asset management; mergers, bankruptcies and reorganizations.

FINANCE DICTIONARIES

Garcia, F. L. ed. *Glenn G. Munn's Encyclopedia of Banking and Finance.* 7th ed., rev. and enl. Boston, Bankers Publishing Co., 1973.

The latest edition of an excellent one-volume encyclopedia on banking and finance, with entries varying in length from one paragraph to several pages. Well-written definitions, often with discussion of uses and examples; also occasional statistics and bibliographies for persons who wish to read about any topic in more depth.

Moffat, Donald W., ed. *Concise Desk Book of Business Finance.* Englewood Cliffs, N.J., Prentice-Hall, 1975.

A good, concise dictionary for financial terms, concepts, theories and formulas which is easy to use and includes useful cross-references.

Ryder, F. R. and D. B. Jenkins, eds. *Thomson's Dictionary of Banking.* 12th ed. London, Pitman, 1974.

This encyclopedic dictionary on banking and finance has a British focus. Definitions range from one sentence to several pages with the longer articles containing illustrative examples, references to British court cases, legislation, etc. Includes many cross-references.

FINANCE PERIODICALS

Banking periodicals are listed elsewhere in this chapter; investment magazines are in Chapter 7.

Financial Executive. New York, Financial Executives Institute (monthly).

Authoritative and readable articles for the busy financial manager. Covers areas of related interest such as accounting and control as well as corporate financial management. Includes occasional book reviews. Indexed in BPI, F&S, PAIS.

Financial Management. Albany, N.Y., Financial Management Association (quarterly).

Instructive, scholarly articles on financial management and financial accounting, written primarily by academicians. Indexed in PAIS.

Institutional Investor. New York, Institutional Investor Systems (monthly).

A practical journal with articles of interest to money managers, including corporate financing, pension fund management, investor relations, profiles of specific money managers. Each issue includes a "Financing Record," which describes new securities offerings; also a table for "Performance" of bank pooled funds and mutual funds. Indexed in F&S. They also publish a separate *Annual Corporate Financing Directory,* which includes tables, by corporation, for all public financings of $5 million that took place during the year.

Journal of Business Finance & Accounting. Oxford, England, B. Blackwell (quarterly).

Authoritative articles on a wide spectrum of interrelated financial matters, including accounting as it relates to finance. Most of the articles are by academic persons. Includes book reviews.

Journal of Finance. New York, American Finance Association (5/yr.).

Professional journal covering technical articles on all phases of finance. Includes a good book review section and also abstracts of doctoral dissertations. May issue contains "Papers and Proceedings" of the annual AFA meeting. Indexed in BPI, PAIS.

Journal of Financial and Quantitative Analysis. Seattle, University of Washington, Graduate School of Business Administration in conjunction with the Western Finance Association (5/yr.).

An academic journal for theoretical articles on the title subject. March issue contains "Paper and Proceedings" of WFA annual meeting. Indexed in PAIS.

FINANCE ASSOCIATIONS

American Finance Association, Graduate School of Business Administration, New York University, New York, N.Y. 10006.

Financial Management Association, State University of New York at Albany, N.Y. 12222.

MONEY AND BANKING

BASIC TEXTS

Carson, Deane, ed. *Money and Finance: Readings in Theory, Policy and Institutions.* 2d ed. New York, Wiley, 1972.

Readings from a wide range of sources, meant to supplement a money and banking text.

Chandler, Lester V. *The Economics of Money and Banking.* 6th ed. New York, Harper & Row, 1973.

One of the best introductory texts on money and banking. Professor Chandler focuses on what he feels are the most important principles, processes and problems. His basic sections cover: commercial banking; central banking; monetary theory; international monetary relations; American monetary policy. Includes lists of suggested readings.

Duesenberry, James S. *Money and Credit: Impact and Control.* 3d ed. Englewood Cliffs, N.J., Prentice-Hall, 1972.

An excellent, short introduction to money and banking by a leading authority. Especially useful for the busy person who wants the essentials but not necessarily a long, comprehensive discussion. Includes a good suggested reading list for further study.

Einzig, Paul. *A Textbook on Monetary Policy.* 3d ed. London, Macmillan; New York, St. Martin's Press, 1972.

The meat of this book, by a well-known British financial writer, is in 2 of its 4 parts: the ends of monetary policy; the means of monetary policy. Includes a bibliography.

Ritter, Lawrence S. and William L. Silber. *Principles of Money, Banking, and Financial Markets.* New York, Basic Books, 1974.

A good, introductory text in 9 parts: the basics; monetary theory; the monetarist-Keynesian debate and its policy implications; Federal Reserve policy-making; financial markets and interest rates; the banking business; money and national priorities; international finance; the past and the future. Includes suggestions for further reading at end of most chapters. For persons who do not want a comprehensive text the authors have also written a clear, witty and readable elementary book on the intricacies of money and monetary policy called *Money* (2d ed., Basic Books, 1973).

FINANCIAL INSTITUTIONS AND THE MONEY MARKET

Beckhart, Benjamin H. *Federal Reserve System.* New York, American Institute of Banking and American Bankers Association; distributed by Columbia University Press, 1972.

A good, comprehensive treatise on the operations and policies of the Federal Reserve System from its establishment in 1913 to the early 1970s. Includes bibliographic notes and a glossary.

Dougall, Herbert E. and Jack E. Gaumnitz. *Capital Markets and Institutions.* 3d ed. Englewood Cliffs, N.J., Prentice-Hall, 1975.

This new edition aims "to present a careful but uncomplicated study of the institutions that funnel long-term funds into the capital markets and to assess the demand for funds in these markets so that the resulting yield can be noted and analyzed." It includes chapters on the major sources of capital market funds (banks, insurance companies, pension and retirement plans, investment companies) as well as chapters on the uses of funds (federal securities, state and local government bonds, corporate securities, mortgages). Includes a bibliography at end. Professor Dougall is best known for his popular introductory text on *Investments,* which is described in Chapter 7.

Gies, Thomas G. and Vincent P. Apilado, eds. *Banking Markets and Financial Institutions.* Homewood, Ill., Irwin, 1971.

A wide selection of readings by experts on monetary management, chosen both for academic and managerial audiences. Thirty-eight selections in nine chapters and arranged in three parts: structure and competition in banking; new directions in asset, liability and capital management; regulation and allocative efficiency.

Jacobs, Donald P., Loring C. Farwell and Edwin H. Neave. *Financial Institutions.* 5th ed. Homewood, Ill., Irwin, 1972.

An introductory text on the operations of financial institutions and their interrelations with economic activity. The authors examine money and credit flow in "6 major sections which deal respectively with the money and capital markets from the suppliers' (savers') side, with the markets for business and consumer loans from the demanders' (borrowers') side, with governmental taxing and spending activities, and with international finance." Descriptive bibliographies at end of most chapters.

Lindow, Wesley. *Inside the Money Market.* New York, Random House, 1972.

A practical book based on the author's personal experience. Lindow's purpose is "to bring out the relationship of the money market to our whole financial structure." He describes the types of paper used, the needs and objectives of money market participants, forces affecting the money market, some glimpses into possible future developments. Includes a bibliography and glossary.

Nicols, Alfred. *Management and Control in the Mutual Savings and Loan Association.* Lexington, Mass., Lexington Books, D.C. Heath, 1972.

In 4 parts: characteristics of mutual savings and loan associations; development and regulatory climate; theory of managerial decision; regressive results with respect to expenses and returns. Includes bibliographic notes.

Robinson, Roland I. and Dwayne Wrightsman. *Financial Markets: The Accumulation and Allocation of Wealth.* New York, McGraw-Hill, 1974.

The whats, hows, and whys of money and capital markets. Includes a bibliography. A glossary is incorporated in the index.

Woodworth, G. Walter. *The Money Market and Monetary Management.* 2d ed. New York, Harper & Row, 1972.

Well-written, basic text for an advanced course on the short-term money market and on monetary/fiscal management, with an emphasis "on the theoretical framework and on the analytical approach to policy determination." Includes references to other books and articles.

BANK MANAGEMENT

Bank Administration Institute. Technical Division. *Bank Administration Manual.* Park Ridge, Ill., 1974. 2 volumes.

This "Golden Anniversary Edition" provides encyclopedic coverage on bank administration, with heavy emphasis on accounting, auditing and control. It is arranged alphabetically by subject, and there are topical indexes in both volumes.

Baughn, William H. and Charls E. Walker. *The Bankers' Handbook.* Homewood, Ill., Dow Jones-Irwin, 1966.

Ninety contributors, mostly practicing bankers, have written chapters covering eighty-seven individual topics on all the important aspects of banking, including organization, systems and control, credit, funds management, special bank management problems, external influences. This is now very out of date, but because of its comprehensive coverage it is still of use as background reference.

Berry, Leonard L. and L. A. Capaldini, eds. *Marketing for the Bank Executive.* New York, Petrocelli Books, 1974.

A selection of 19 "classic" pieces and 11 original papers meant to provide "an overall, organized, cohesive view of the bank marketing field." It is arranged in 8 parts and includes a good, short, annotated bibliography of both marketing and bank marketing books.

Corns, Marshall C. *The Practical Operations and Management of a Bank.* 2d ed. Boston, Bankers Publishing Co., 1968.

A complete study on all important aspects of bank management, written both for prospective bankers and for bank employees. Includes a bibliography.

Crosse, Howard D. and George H. Hempel. *Management Policies for Commercial Banks.* 2d ed. Englewood Cliffs, N.J., Prentice-Hall, 1973.

The title subject is well treated in this revision, which is divided into 4 major sections: the banking environment; basic considerations in banking (risks, bank capital adequacy, bank earnings); balance sheet management; other bank policy areas (such as audit and control, personnel policies, marketing and community relations).

McKinney, George W., Jr., and William J. Brown. *Management of Commercial Bank Funds.* New York, American Institute of Banking and American Bankers Association, 1974.

A good, up-to-date text on the principles of funds management, based on the practical experience of a banker and the classroom experience of a teacher, and meant to be useful to bankers in institutions of all sizes. Includes a bibliography of books and selected articles.

Nadler, Paul S. *Commercial Banking in the Economy.* 2d ed. New York, Random House, 1973.

A readable, informative paperback that examines the role of banking in the economy, with special emphasis on new trends.

Prochnow, Herbert V. and Herbert V. Prochnow, Jr., eds. *The Changing World of Banking.* New York, Harper & Row, 1974.

Essays by 23 competent bankers and academicians who study "actual American banking practices which reflect the vast changes of recent years." Includes such topics as the role of the Eurodollar, bank deposits, control systems, marketing, social responsibility.

CREDIT MANAGEMENT

Handbooks

Redding, Harold T. and Guyon H. Knight III. *The Dun & Bradstreet Handbook of Credits and Collections.* New York, T. Y. Crowell, 1974.

This handy reference guide to credit management is arranged in a concise outline format that is classified by topic. It includes sections on organization, credit investigation, sources of credit information, credit systems, financial analysis, etc. There are charts and forms throughout the volume.

Books

Beckman, Theodore N. and Ronald S. Foster. *Credits and Collections: Management and Theory.* 8th ed. New York, McGraw-Hill, 1969.

A basic text on the theory, principles and practices of credit and collection management, with increased attention given to its role in the economic and social environment. Includes sections on both the consumer and the business credit-granting function, on the analysis of risk in different types of mercantile and financial institutions, on the management of the collection function.

Cole, Robert H. *Consumer and Commercial Credit Management.* 5th ed. Homewood, Ill., Irwin, 1976.

What credit is, what it does, and what it can and cannot do — for persons involved in the management of credit and collection activities. Brought up to date to include economic and social implications and to cover new federal legislation, new trends such as credit card plans, ramifications of a "checkless society," and related topics. Includes bibliographies.

Kreps, Clifton H., Jr., and Richard F. Wacht. *Credit Administration.* New York, American Institute of Banking and the American Bankers Associations, 1972.

Written to assist in the training of lending officers and bank credit administrators, with the major parts discussing lending policies and bank credit administration. Includes a selected bibliography, sample forms and agreements.

MORTGAGE BANKING

De Huszar, William I. *Mortgage Loan Administration.* New York, McGraw-Hill, 1972.

This study seeks "to establish and define the principles of mortgage loan administration and to describe the duties and responsibilities of the mortgage loan administrator." Two of its three sections cover: mortgage office operations; mortgage loan servicing. It was sponsored by the Mortgage Bankers Association of America and represents the thoughts and views of many individuals. Includes a glossary.

PERSONAL FINANCE

Cohen, Jerome B. *Personal Finance: Principles and Case Problems.* 5th ed. Homewood, Ill., Irwin, 1975.

Standard text covering all aspects of personal finance, from income and basic expenditures to long-term investing and estate planning. It has been brought up to date in this latest edition to "reflect important developments in many fields from consumer credit protection to health care to tax matters to investment innovations." Includes useful charts, statistical tables, and suggested readings at end of chapters.

Donaldson, Elvin F. and John K. Pfahl. *Personal Finance.* 5th ed. New York, Ronald, 1971.

A readable college text "designed to help students to understand better how to plan their financial affairs, how to spend intelligently, how to save, and to invest." Includes charts and statistical tables. Its treatment is thorough, nontechnical, and it does not presuppose the reader possesses large sums of money.

Lyons, John T., ed. *Personal Financial Planning for Executives.* New York, American Management Association, 1970.

Twelve expert contributors discuss various elements of effective financial planning, such as planning for spending, the business of credit, the economic need for life insurance, your income and your employer.

Wiltsee, Joseph L. *Business Week's Guide to Personal Business.* New York, McGraw-Hill, 1970.

A practical and chatty book on personal business planning by the editor of *Business Week*'s "Personal Business" column. In 2 parts: Part 1 covers what to do with your dollars; Part 2 discusses family considerations.

BANKING LAW AND FINANCIAL LEGAL SERVICES

Beutel, Frederick K. *Bank Officer's Handbook of Commercial Banking Law.* 4th ed. Boston, Warren, Gorham & Lamont, 1974.

Good for its nontechnical coverage of information on the ordinary legal problems that arise in the regular course of the banking business.

Commerce Clearing House. *Bankruptcy Law Reports.* Chicago. 2 volumes (biweekly).

This loose-leaf service spans the whole field of bankruptcy and debt relief law embodied in the federal Bankruptcy Act and related federal statutes. Gives explanations, text of laws, interpretative reports of congressional committees, general orders, specimen forms.

Commerce Clearing House. *Federal Banking Law Reports.* Chicago. 5 volumes (loose-leaf).

Comprehensive, continuing coverage of federal banking laws, regulations, rulings, explanations, forms. Includes data on the Federal Reserve System, National Banking Acts, deposit insurance, monetary regulations, federal lending agencies.

Prentice-Hall, Inc. *Banking Service.* Englewood Cliffs, N.J. 2 volumes (loose-leaf).

One volume, *Control of Banking,* reports on federal laws regulating operations and financial practices of banks, including rules, regulations, interpretations and opinions of federal agencies, latest court decisions. The other volume, *Federal Aids to Financing,* gives rules, regulations, etc., about federal loan insurance and guaranty programs of financial institutions.

BANKING AND FINANCIAL TABLES

Bracken, Jerome and Charles J. Christenson. *Tables for Use in Analyzing Business Problems.* Homewood, Ill., Irwin, 1965.

Contains tables for analyzing problems involving capital investments and financial expenditures (present value tables, for example); also tables of probability functions and of random numbers.

Ellwood, L. W. *Ellwood Tables for Real Estate Appraising and Financing.* 3d ed. Chicago, American Institute of Real Estate Appraisers, 1970. 2 volumes.

Vol. 1 is "Explanatory Text"; Vol. 2, "Tables," includes compound interest tables, amortization tables, capitalization rate tables, etc.

Financial Publishing Co. *Monthly Payment Direct Reduction Loan Amortization Schedules.* 12th ed. Boston, 1970.

A comprehensive set of tables "showing equal monthly payments necessary to amortize a loan of $1,000; also the amount of interest and principal in each payment, and the balance outstanding at any time during the life of the loan." Among the several other books of tables by this publisher are: *Expanded Payment Table for Monthly Mortgage Loans* (1969); *Financial Compound Interest and Annuity Tables* (5th ed., 1970).

Johnson, Irvin E. *The Instant Mortgage-Equity Technique.* Lexington, Mass., D.C. Heath, 1972.

This book was written by an appraiser for appraisers and other nonmathematicians, and it was published for the Society of Real Estate Appraisers. The first part discusses and explains mortgage-equity theory, techniques and procedures, with problems and solutions. The major part of the book contains OAR tables (Precomputed Mortgage-Equity Over-All Rates) for the valuation of income property.

Thorndike, David. *The Thorndike Encyclopedia of Banking and Financial Tables.* Boston, Warren, Gorham & Lamont, 1973.

Contains "tables for real estate and depreciation; compound interest and annuity; interest and savings; installment loans and rebates; bond and mortgage values, stock yields." A supplement, "1975 Yearbook," is in 2 parts, with Part 1 containing general information to reflect changing economic conditions and new developments, and Part 2, new tables.

BANKING BIBLIOGRAPHIES

American Bankers Association. Bank Education Committee. *A Basic Reading List on Banking Topics.* Rev. ed. New York, 1975.

This is a good, short list arranged in 15 subject sections.

American Bankers Association. Marketing Division. *A Selective, Annotated Bank Marketing Bibliography.* 2d ed. Washington, D.C., 1971.

Covers 9 broad areas of bank marketing as well as books on marketing in general. It also lists journals and has a two-page "basic bank marketing library." Annotations add to its value.

American Bankers Association. Stonier Graduate School of Banking. *Cumulative Catalog of Theses.* Washington, D.C. (Base volumes cover 1937–1961, and 1962–1970; annual supplements, 1971 to date.)

This is a descriptive list of theses accepted for deposit in the ABA library. It is a useful source to check when researching any bank management topic, especially those where no published books are found. Prior to 1973 ABA theses were deposited in only a few libraries, but now they are available for anyone to purchase through Xerox University Microfilms in Ann Arbor, Michigan.

BANKING DICTIONARIES

Two encyclopedic dictionaries, including the useful Garcia/Munn *Encyclopedia of Banking and Finance,* are described in the "Finance Dictionaries" section of this chapter.

FINANCIAL MANUALS AND BANK DIRECTORIES

Moody's Bank and Finance Manual. New York, Moody's Investors Service (annual, with semi-weekly supplements).

This basic financial manual covers not only U.S. and some foreign banks and trust companies but also insurance, investment and finance companies, U.S. real estate companies, real estate investment trusts, savings and loan associations. Information usually includes a brief financial history of each company; officers and directors; comparative income statements; balance sheets; information on capital stock; record of dividend payments; recent stock price range. Center blue pages include 10-year price range of stocks and bonds; also lists of largest banks, mutual savings banks, S&Ls.

The three principal directories of banks are:

Bankers' Almanac and Year Book. London, T. Skinner.

A directory of British and international banks, giving officers, correspondents, balance sheet statistics; also a comprehensive geographic listing of banks without any details. General information at end includes list of British banking associations; U.K. amalgamations, absorptions, liquidations; Bank of England statistics; currencies of the world.

Polk's World Bank Directory. North American Section. Nashville, Tenn., R. L. Polk (semi-annual and bimonthly supplements).

Geographic list of world banks, giving officers and directors, correspondents, out-of-town branches, assets and liabilities. Supplementary information includes maps for each state, state banking officials, legal holidays, list of bank holding companies, transit numbers.

Rand-McNally International Bankers Directory. Chicago, Rand McNally (semi-annual and bimonthly supplements).

Geographic list of U.S. and the principal foreign banks, with information similar to Polk above. Includes also data on Federal Reserve Banks, Federal Home Loan Banks, lists of associations, holding companies, 400 largest commercial banks, bank holidays, digest of laws. Basic marketing statistics at end of each state section (population, households, total retail trade and Ranally city ratings).

Several specialized directories are:

Directory of American Savings and Loan Associations. Baltimore, Md., T. K. Sanderson Organization (annual).

Geographic list, giving officers, branches, total assets, interest rate for each S&L.

National Association of Mutual Savings Banks. *Directory and Guide to the Mutual Savings Banks of the United States.* Washington, D.C. (annual).

Geographic list, giving officers, total assets, reserves and accounts, types of savings accounts offered, interest rates.

Who Owns What in World Banking. London, Banker Research Unit (annual).

A list of 245 of the major world banks, with subsidiaries and affiliated interests, and percentage figures for holdings when available. A companion volume, *Who is Where in World Banking,* is a guide to the overseas representation of the major world banks, classified by financial center.

Who's Who in Banking. 3d ed. New York, Business Press, 1972.

Biographical sketches of U.S. financial executives.

The annual *Hambro Euromoney Directory* (London, Euromoney Publications, Ltd.) lists banks, brokers, and other organizations in the international money and bond markets. *Investor's Chronicle* in London publishes a *World Banking: Annual Survey* giving balance sheet statistics for specific banks, by country.

U.S. BANKING AND FINANCIAL STATISTICS

International financial statistics are listed in Chapter 6; statistics on government finance in Chapter 4.

Bankers Trust Co. *Credit and Capital Markets.* New York (annual).
Statistics on funds raised and funds supplied for the financing of government securities, mortgages, corporate securities, open market paper; also sources and uses of funds for specific financial intermediaries such as insurance companies and pension funds, thrift institutions, investment companies, commercial banks. Annual figures are for past 7 years and a one-year projection.

Dun & Bradstreet, Inc. *The Business Failure Record.* New York (annual).
Statistics are by location, industry, age, size of company, cause. For current statistics see D&B's *Monthly Failures.*
The U.S. Administrative Office of the United States Courts publishes annual *Tables of Bankruptcy Statistics* based on bankruptcy cases commenced and terminated in the U.S. District Courts.

Federal Home Loan Bank Board. *Journal.* Washington, D.C., U.S. Government Printing Office (monthly).
Articles on savings and home finance by FHLBB staff members and others, with monthly statistics on mortgage and housing markets, the FHLBB, Savings and Loan Associations; also general financial data. Indexed in PAIS.

Mortgage Banking: Financial Statements & Operating Ratios. Washington, D.C., Mortgage Bankers Association of America (annual).
Operating ratios and balance sheet statistics, based on the experience of over 200 mortgage banking companies. Statistics are by size of servicing portfolio, type of business, etc.; also sources and uses of income tables. The MBA's monthly *Mortgage Banker* includes current statistics on mortgage market activity.

National Association of Mutual Savings Banks. *National Fact Book of Mutual Savings Banks.* New York (annual).
Statistics are in 7 sections to cover the structure and operations of the savings bank industry and its role in savings and mortgage markets. Brief current statistics are also in each issue of their monthly *Savings Bank Journal.*

National Consumer Finance Association. *Finance Facts Yearbook.* Washington, D.C.
Brief text, with statistics and charts, on consumers — their income, spending, finance and credit management, as well as the consumer installment credit industry. Includes a bibliography.

Salomon Brothers. *Supply and Demand for Credit in (year).* New York (annual).
Credit flow statistics for 5 years plus estimates for 2 years. The demand factor is covered by figures for corporate, municipal and foreign bonds, short-term private demands, privately held Treasury and federal agency debt. The supply factor covers nonbank investing institutions, commercial banks, finance companies and other sources.

Savings and Home Financing Source Book. Washington, D.C., Federal Home Loan Bank Board (annual).
Financial statistics for FHLBBs and for savings association; also flow of savings, statistics of mortgage foreclosures, loans held, mortgage lending activity. Current statistics are in the Federal Home Loan Bank Board *Journal.*

U.S. Board of Governors of the Federal Reserve System. *Banking and Monetary Statistics.* Washington, D.C., 1943. And supplementary pamphlets.

A useful compilation of historical statistics, largely for the period 1914–1941 and including separate series on bank assets and liabilities, bank debits and deposit turnover, bank earnings, suspensions, money rates and security markets, gold, consumer credit, and international financial statistics. An incomplete series of supplements were published for Sections 1-2, 5-6, 9-12, 14-16, which bring some of these figures up to 1960 and a few years beyond. Another historical volume the board published in 1959 is *All Bank Statistics, 1896–1955,* which gives state-by-state statistics on assets, liabilities and number, for all commercial banks, for national banks, state commercial banks, unincorporated banks and mutual savings banks.

U.S. Board of Governors of the Federal Reserve System. *Federal Reserve Bulletin* Washington, D.C. (monthly).

The "Financial and Business Statistics" section in each issue of this bulletin is the best single source for current U.S. banking and monetary statistics. It includes Federal Bank statistics, financial statistics for commercial banks, money market rates, government securities, credit, flow of funds, etc.; also international financial statistics, and basic business statistics such as the Federal Reserve Board's index of industrial production. Several of these are continuations of the tables in *Banking and Monetary Statistics* listed above. The most important statistics from the bulletin are published in chart form in the FRB *Monthly Chart Book* and their annual *Historical Chart Book.* More detailed flow of funds figures are in their *Flow of Funds Account: Annual Total Flows & Year-End Assets and Liabilities, 1945–72,* with annual supplements and preliminary quarterlies. There are other FRB statistical releases published on specific financial subjects.

United States League of Savings Associations. *Savings & Loan Fact Book.* Chicago. (annual).

Brief text with statistics and charts on savings, home ownership, residential construction and financing; also data on the savings and loan business and on related federal government agencies.

There are many other sources for U.S. banking statistics. At the federal level the Federal Deposit Insurance Corp. publishes statistics as Part 4 of its *Annual Report* (number of banks and branches, bank assets and liabilities, income of insured banks, banks closed, etc.). They also publish an annual *Bank Operating Statistics* and several other statistical series on accounts and deposits for commercial banks and for mutual savings banks. The U.S. Comptroller of the Currency in its *Annual Report* includes such statistics as assets, liabilities, capital accounts, and loans of national banks, income and expenses, mergers, new branches. Monthly bulletins of the 12 Federal Reserve District banks and also bank letters of specific U.S. banks include current data on financial as well as regional economic conditions.

BANKING NEWSPAPERS AND PERIODICALS

American Banker. New York, American Banker, Inc. (5/wk.).

This daily banking newspaper covers news about bank developments, pending legislation, national and international monetary affairs, bank stock quotations, etc. The "Required Reading" section in each issue contains the text of speeches by leading bankers on current topics of wide interest. Various issues include annual lists of largest banks. See, for example, last July issue for list of largest banks in the free world and separate lists of largest banks in the U.S.; last January, for largest mutual savings banks; late February, for largest savings and loan associations; mid-February, for year-end ranking of top banks and economic forecast of banking and industry; last May, for largest finance companies. *American Banker* now publishes an Index (monthly, with quarterly and annual cumulations) in 3 sections: by corporation and bank; by general subject; by personal name.

Bank Marketing. Chicago, Bank Marketing Association (monthly).

Short articles on advertising, marketing and public relations, of interest to bank managers.

Bankers Magazine. Boston, Warren, Gorham & Lamont (quarterly).

Excellent selection of practical, readable articles on banking and money management in this journal, which has been in existence since 1846. Includes book reviews on a wide range of subjects. Indexed in BPI, PAIS.

Bankers Monthly. Northbrook, Ill., Bankers Monthly, Inc.

A national trade magazine for banking and investments. An annual "Finance Industry Survey" in Apr. 15 issue includes a roster of the major finance companies.

Banking. New York, American Bankers Association (monthly).

This official publication of the ABA is a good source of information for banking trends, new and improved banking techniques, news of interest to bankers. Indexed in BPI, PAIS.

Burroughs Clearing House. Detroit, Mich., Burroughs Corp. (monthly).

Trade journal for bank and financial officers, in existence since 1916. Indexed in BPI, F&S.

Credit and Financial Management. New York, National Association of Credit Management (monthly).

Short articles and news for credit managers. Includes book reviews. Indexed in BPI, F&S.

Journal of Bank Research. Park Ridge, Ill., Bank Administration Institute (quarterly).

Authoritative research papers on banking, accounting and finance. Indexed in PAIS.

Journal of Commercial Bank Lending. Philadelphia, Pa., Robert Morris Associates (monthly).

Practical articles of interest to bank loan and credit officers. Indexed in BPI, PAIS.

Journal of Money, Credit and Banking. Columbus, Ohio State University Press (quarterly).

Research studies on monetary policy, banking and credit, written primarily by professors and economists. Includes book reviews. Indexed in PAIS, SSI.

Magazine of Bank Administration. Park Ridge, Ill., Bank Administration Institute (monthly).

Practical articles on bank operations. Indexed in PAIS.

Money. Chicago (monthly).

A relatively new journal of popularly written articles on personal finance. Indexed in PAIS.

Money Manager. New York, Bond Buyer (weekly).

A financial weekly for the money and capital markets. Includes some articles, but is especially useful for its news and statistical coverage on mortgage, corporate, international, and U.S. financial markets. Includes good statistics on money market rates, U.S. government securities, etc.

Mortgage Banker. Washington, D.C., Mortgage Bankers Association of America (monthly).

Articles and news of interest to MBA members. Current statistics in each issue in a section for "Mortgage Market Trends" include mortgage market activity, activity in government, housing starts. Includes book reviews. Indexed in PAIS.

Savings and Loan News. Chicago, United States League of Savings Associations (monthly).

About 4 or 5 feature articles in each issue on topics relating to S&L, also regular feature columns for financial news, business trends. List of top 200 S&Ls in February issue. Indexed in PAIS.

Savings Bank Journal. New York, National Association of Mutual Savings Banks (monthly).

Information on trends in savings banking field and current news of interest to savings bank officers. Each issue contains "Savings Bank Statistics"; a list of 100 largest savings banks is in August issue.

Many of the largest U.S. banks publish bank letters or bulletins, which are useful sources for current regional financial and economic information. Several examples are listed in Chapter 8. The monthly *Federal Reserve Bulletin* usually contains one to three articles on recent financial trends as well as Federal Reserve Board announcements, statements and publications. It is described in the "U.S. Banking and Financial Statistics" section of this chapter.

Several good foreign periodicals are:

Banker. London, Bankers Division, Financial Times, Ltd. (monthly).

Articles on banking and monetary policy of worldwide interest. An annual survey on "International Banking" appears in August each year; a ranked list of the top 300 world banks is in June issue. Indexed in BPI, PAIS.

Bankers' Magazine. London, Arben Publishing Co., Ltd. (monthly).

"The practical magazine for the practising banker," of special interest to British and European bankers. Includes book reviews. Indexed in PAIS.

Canadian Banker & ICB Review. Toronto, Canadian Bankers' Association (bimonthly).

Articles on Canadian and international bank management and monetary policy. Aims to be a forum for discussion rather than a medium for association news. Includes book reviews. Indexed in PAIS.

Institute of Bankers. *Journal.* London (bimonthly).

Articles on banking and finance of special interest to British bank managers. Includes some book reviews. Indexed in PAIS.

Savings Banks International. Geneva, Switzerland, International Savings Banks
Institute (quarterly).

Articles on savings banking and finance, many of which are on practices in a specific
country. Includes book reviews and various statistics in most issues.

BANK AND CREDIT ASSOCIATIONS

American Bankers Association, 1120 Connecticut Avenue, N.W., Washington,
D.C. 20036. (The American Institute of Banking is a Division of ABA.)

American Savings and Loan Institute, 111 East Wacker Drive, Chicago, Ill.
60601.

American Savings and Loan League, 5505 5th Street, N.W., Washington, D.C.
20011.

Association of Registered Bank Holding Companies, 730 15th Street, N.W.,
Washington, D.C. 20005.

Bank Administration Institute, 303 South Northwest Highway, Park Ridge, Ill.
60068.

Independent Bankers Association of America, P.O. Box 267, Sauk Centre,
Minn. 56378.

National Association of Credit Management, 475 Park Avenue South, New
York, N.Y. 10016. (Credit Research Foundation is a research affiliate.)

National Association of Mutual Savings Banks, 200 Park Avenue, New York,
N.Y. 10017.

National Consumer Finance Association, 1000 16th Street, N.W., Washington,
D.C. 20036.

Robert Morris Associates, the National Association of Bank Loan and Credit
Officers, 1432 Philadelphia National Bank Building, Philadelphia, Pa. 19107.

United States League of Savings Associations, 111 East Wacker Drive, Chicago, Ill. 60601.

15

INSURANCE AND REAL ESTATE

INSURANCE — Risk and Insurance Books — Life/Health Insurance — Property/Liability Insurance — Insurance Bibliographies and Indexes — Insurance Dictionaries — Insurance Law and Legal Services — Information About Insurance Companies — Insurance Statistics — Insurance Periodicals — Insurance Directories — Insurance Associations — *REAL ESTATE* — Real Estate Principles and Practices — Real Estate Management and Appraisal — Real Estate Finance and Investing — Real Estate Law — Housing and Real Estate Bibliographies — Real Estate Dictionaries — Information About Real Estate Companies — Real Estate Operating Statistics — Housing and Real Estate Statistics — Real Estate Periodicals — Real Estate Directories — Real Estate Associations

INSURANCE

Insurance companies have developed into big business today due to the fact that risk and misfortune are daily possibilities and most individuals and businesses are prudent enough to want to plan ahead either to avoid a loss entirely or to reduce it significantly by sharing the burden with someone else. However most people know very little about the industry itself. The first half of this chapter attempts to help correct this situation by suggesting a selection of recent books and reference sources on risk and insurance in general and also on several major insurance lines.

RISK AND INSURANCE BOOKS

Bickelhaupt, David L. *General Insurance.* 9th ed. Homewood, Ill., Irwin, 1974.
This is the latest edition of a popular textbook that was formerly written by the author in collaboration with John H. Magee. It aims to provide the fundamental and

applied concepts of insurance and risk in 5 parts: risk, risk management, insurance; the structure and operations of the insurance business; life and health insurance; property and liability insurance; the future of insurance.

Greene, Mark R. *Risk and Insurance.* 3d ed. Cincinnati, Ohio, South-Western, 1973.

Professor Greene's textbook is designed "to cover basic ideas, problems, and principles found in all types of modern-day insurance and other methods of handling risk." Part 4 covers major property and liability insurance contracts; Part 5 discusses life and health insurance; Parts 6-7 are on government regulation and international insurance. Appendixes contain Best's ratings, interest tables and a bibliography. The author has also compiled (with Paul Swadener) a selection of 37 readings on risk and insurance called *Insurance Insights* (South-Western, 1974).

Mehr, Robert I. and Emerson Cammack. *Principles of Insurance.* 5th ed. Homewood, Ill., Irwin, 1972.

The object of this popular and comprehensive textbook is "to present basic insurance principles (illustrated by practices) to the beginning insurance student in a language he can understand." Its 8 parts (32 chapters) are: introduction; insurer; law; the insurance contract; fields of insurance (9 chapters); buying insurance; company organization and operation; the insurance industry.

Mehr, Robert I. and Bob A. Hedges. *Risk Management: Concepts and Applications.* Homewood, Ill., Irwin, 1974.

Studies risk from the management approach rather than the theoretical approach as it applies to all kinds of organizations, not solely to business. It covers objectives, after which there are 4 chapters on means to objectives, 6 chapters on various aspects of risk analysis (including 2 on employee benefit plans); also chapters on selecting risk management devices, insurance coverage, administering insurance purchases. Mathematics is discussed in an appendix.

Pfeffer, Irving and David R. Klock. *Perspectives on Insurance.* Englewood Cliffs, N.J., Prentice-Hall, 1974.

This book offers a multi-disciplinary approach that studies the subject of risk and insurance in the light of historical, legal, psychological, economic, actuarial, managerial and consumerist perspectives. Mortality tables are at end.

Williams, C. Arthur, Jr., and Richard M. Heins. *Risk Management and Insurance.* 3d ed. New York, McGraw-Hill, 1976.

Presents a balanced introduction to the 2 title subjects. Major consideration is given to business risk management, with 28 of its chapters covering the risk function, risk identification, tools, insurance contracts (by line), implementing an insurance decision. A shorter section discusses family risk management. Bibliographies are at end of chapters. Professor Williams also did most of the writing for the latest edition of *Insurance: Its Theory and Practice in the United States* by Albert Mowbray, Ralph H. Blanchard and C. Arthur Williams, Jr. (6th ed., McGraw-Hill, 1969). This has been a standard text on risk and on all lines of insurance.

LIFE/HEALTH INSURANCE

A few reference sources on unemployment insurance are included in Chapter 19 under "Pension Plans and Social Security."

Handbooks

Gregg, Davis W., and Vane B. Lucas, eds. *Life and Health Insurance Handbook.* 3d ed. Homewood, Ill., Irwin, 1973.

"A comprehensive reference source on all major phases of life and health insurance, including the increasingly important fields of pensions, profit sharing, and estate planning." Its 75 chapters, each by an insurance authority, are arranged in 10 basic sections: economic security and insurance; individual life insurance and annuities; variable life insurance, variable annuities, mutual funds; individual health insurance; group life and health insurance; pensions and other qualified deferred compensation plans; business uses of life and health insurance; government benefits — protection and retirement; planning small and large estates; company operations and institutional aspects. Bibliographies are at end of each chapter for persons interested in studying any subject in more detail. Appendixes contain sample contracts, forms and other useful information.

Books

Huebner, S. S. and Kenneth Black, Jr. *Life Insurance.* 8th ed. New York, Appleton-Century-Crofts, 1973.

This is the best known life insurance textbook. It covers all important aspects in its 9 parts, including a study of types of life insurance contracts, analysis of the contract, the mathematics of life insurance and of health insurance, life and health risks, special forms of life and health insurance, organization and management of life insurance companies. Bibliographies are at end of sections. Appendixes include sample copies of policies; also interest tables.

Mehr, Robert I. *Life Insurance: Theory and Practice.* 4th ed. Austin, Tex., Business Publications, 1970.

Another comprehensive, well-established text integrating theories and practices developed in the 1960s, and approaching the subject of life and health insurance as a risk management device.

White, Edwin H. and Herbert Chasman. *Business Insurance.* 4th ed. Englewood Cliffs, N.J., Prentice-Hall, 1974.

This text has been revised to encompass the expanded definition of business insurance, a term "used to identify any life and health insurance policies that are owned by and payable to a business." There are 4 principal sections, 3 of which cover the subject as it relates to proprietorships, partnerships and corporations. Within each of these there are 3 parts to consider: fundamental facts; plans used in attempts to avoid liquidation; buy-sell agreements. Following all this there is a fourth and new section on other uses of life and health insurance to benefit the business organization (containing chapters on: disability buy-sell agreements and salary continuation plans; key man insurance; design and tax aspects of nonqualified deferred compensation; split-dollar insurance plans).

For persons who need further study on the fundamental concepts underlying the mathematics of insurance, consult *Fundamental Mathematics of Life Insurance* by Floyd S. Harper and Lewis C. Workman (Irwin, 1970).

PROPERTY/LIABILITY INSURANCE

Until after this list was originally prepared there were no recently published books on property and liability insurance. The newly revised Riegel/Miller/Williams text has now been added, but all the other books below are very old. To find further up-to-date information one can use pertinent chapters in general books covering all lines of insurance and supplement this with articles in current periodicals.

Handbooks

Long, John D. and Davis W. Gregg, eds. *Property and Liability Insurance.* Homewood, Ill., Irwin, 1965.

This handbook represents the work of 132 insurance authorities, both as authors and as expert consultants. There are 76 chapters arranged in the following 9 sections: risk and insurance; fire and allied lines insurance; marine and aviation insurance; inland marine insurance; liability insurance and related lines; multiple line insurance; suretyship; the institution of property-liability insurance; risk management. Appendixes include sample policies; bibliographies are at end of chapters.

Books

Huebner, S. S., Kenneth Black, Jr., and Robert S. Cline. *Property and Liability Insurance.* New York, Appleton-Century-Crofts, 1968.

Attempts to give the underwriter, student, and insurance buyer an understanding of the nature of property and liability insurance, the ways it can be used and the implications of new developments. Second edition to be published in 1976.

Kulp, C. A. and John W. Hall. *Casualty Insurance.* 4th ed. New York, Ronald, 1968.

This textbook offers an analytic treatment of casualty hazards and policies in 3 parts: risk, insurance and casualty insurance; casualty hazards, perils and policies; insurers, rates and regulation. Includes a bibliography.

Michelbacher, G. F. and Nestor R. Roos. *Multiple-Line Insurers: Their Nature and Operation.* 2d ed. New York, McGraw-Hill, 1970.

A discussion of the nature and function of multiple-line insurance operations and the management of this operation. Assumes a basic knowledge of insurance principles and contracts. Several contributors helped with the writing of this book.

Riegel, Robert, Jerome S. Miller and C. Arthur Williams, Jr. *Insurance Principles and Practices: Property and Liability.* 6th ed. Englewood Cliffs, N.J. Prentice-Hall, 1976.

This revision of a standard book is the only recent full-length text on this subject. The first of its 5 parts (6 chapters) covers insurance in general; this is followed by 9 chapters on property insurance, 2 on liability insurance, 5 on combined property and liability insurance, and one on government programs. Suggested readings are at end of chapters.

Rodda, William H. *Marine Insurance: Ocean & Inland.* 3d ed. Englewood Cliffs, N.J., Prentice-Hall, 1970.

A book on the principles and practices of marine insurance for persons with a basic knowledge of insurance. More attention is given to inland than to ocean marine insurance. This author also wrote a book on the principles of *Property and Liability Insurance* (Prentice-Hall, 1966).

Services

Fire, Casualty and Surety Bulletin. Cincinnti, Ohio, National Underwriter Co. 4 volumes (loose-leaf service, with monthly supplements).

A comprehensive loose-leaf service providing good background information and explanations on all types of property/liability insurance. The volumes cover: casualty/surety; fire/marine; sales; companies and coverages.

A somewhat similar service is *Monthly Policy, Form & Manual Analysis Service.* Indianapolis, Ind., Rough Notes Co. 4 volumes (loose-leaf).

INSURANCE BIBLIOGRAPHIES AND INDEXES

Institute of Life Insurance. *List of Worthwhile Life and Health Insurance Books.* New York, Institute of Life Insurance and the Health Insurance Institute (annual).

This is a good, first place to check when looking for books, reference sources or periodicals on life and health insurance. It is an annotated list, arranged by subject, and is updated each year.

Insurance Periodicals Index. New York, Insurance Division, Special Libraries Association (annual).

A subject index to articles in insurance periodicals, compiled by a group of insurance librarians. This is a cumulation of monthly lists that appear first in each issue of both editions of *Best's Review.* This annual includes an index by author.

Insurance Society of New York. *Books in Insurance: Property, Liability, Marine, Surety.* 8th ed. New York, 1974.

This is a companion bibliography to the one above, for the property/liability field. It also is an annotated list, arranged by subject, and it is updated about once every 3 years.

Special Libraries Association. Insurance Division. *Insurance Literature* (monthly). (Subscriptions handled in 1975 by W. J. Mortimer, Life Insurance Marketing and Research Association, Hartford, Conn.)

A continuing, annotated list of selected books, pamphlets, reference works and a few articles in noninsurance periodicals, arranged by broad line of insurance.

INSURANCE DICTIONARIES

Davids, Lewis E. *Dictionary of Insurance.* 2d ed. Totowa, N.J., Littlefield, Adams & Co., 1970.

A dictionary of terms in insurance and related fields for laymen, students and insurance people.

Osler, Robert W. and John S. Bickley. *Glossary of Insurance Terms.* Santa Monica, Calif., Insurors Press, 1972.

A useful glossary of insurance terms, abbreviations and acronyms; also a short appendix containing pension and profit sharing terms.

INSURANCE LAW AND LEGAL SERVICES

Keeton, Robert E. *Basic Text on Insurance Law.* St. Paul, Minn., West Publishing Co., 1971.

A book that aims to contribute to a reader's understanding of insurance law generally and to suggest some of the principles, policies and practices bearing upon any legal problem at hand. Specimen forms and excerpts from laws are in an appendix.

Commerce Clearing House. *Insurance Law Reports.* Chicago. 2 volumes (loose-leaf).

This service reports on new decisions in major insurance areas handed down by higher federal and state courts. One volume contains "Fire and Casualty Insurance Law Reports" and the other, "Life-Health and Accident Insurance Reports." Prior bound volumes of cases for each are available. CCH publishes a separate service for decisions involving motor vehicles, called *Automobile Law Reports.*

Prentice-Hall, Inc. *Insurance Guide.* Englewood Cliffs, N.J. (loose-leaf).

Describes personal and business insurance sales plans and ideas, including employee plans and trusts, self-employed retirement plans, social security benefits, tax information.

There are two complete, multi-volume treatises covering all types of insurance law and including the substance of the law, with practical illustrations and also appellate court cases. These are: George J. Couch's *Couch Cyclopedia of Insurance Law* (2d ed. by Ronald A. Anderson, Rochester, N.Y., Lawyers Cooperative Publishing Co. 1959, 24 volumes); and *Insurance Law and Practice* by John A. Appleton and Jean Appleman (Kansas City, Mo., Vernon Law Book Co., 1965, 26 volumes in 38). Annual pocket supplements at the back of every volume in both services keep these services up to date.

INFORMATION ABOUT INSURANCE COMPANIES

Argus F. C. & S. Chart. Cincinnati, Ohio, National Underwriter Co. (annual).

Financial statement figures in tabular format for companies writing fire, casualty and surety lines. For some 1,000 companies there are financial and operating statistics covering each of the last 3 years, with 5-year totals for operating results. Data on 320 additional companies is given only for one year. Includes also group totals, classification of business by lines written, list of corporate relationships. A companion volume is *Argus Chart of Health Insurance* (annual) containing financial statistics for over 1,100 insurers and also giving data on Blue Cross and Blue Shield plans.

Assecuranz-Compass: Year Book for International Insurance. Vienna, Austria, A. I. Ediziun S.A.

A worldwide financial manual for insurance companies and organizations, arranged by country and including names of officers and directors, income and financial statistics for each.

Best's Aggregates & Averages: Property-Liability. Oldwick, N.J., A. M. Best Co. (annual).

Statistics are by company for stock, mutual, reciprocal, and "Lloyds" organizations and contain balance sheet and operating data, underwriting expenses incurred, by-line underwriting experience, all in tabular form; also various aggregate figures and a list of 100 leading companies and groups.

Best's Flitcraft Compend. Oldwick, N.J., A. M. Best Co. (annual).
Gives information on the policies, rates, values and dividends of most U.S. life insurance companies. At end is annuity data on over 50 companies, settlement options, cash value tables, mortality tables, compound interest and discount tables, mortgage amortization tables, text of the Federal Social Security Act, analysis of Medicare.

Best's Insurance Reports: Life-Health. Oldwick, N.J., A. M. Best Co. (annual).
Financial manual for U.S. and Canadian life/health companies, giving brief corporate history, management and operation, assets and liabilities, investment data, statistics on growth of company, insurance in force, new business issued.

Best's Insurance Reports: Property-Liability. Oldwick, N.J., A. M. Best Co. (annual).
A financial manual for U.S. and Canadian stock companies, mutual companies, "Lloyds" organizations, reciprocal and interinsurance exchanges, state funds. Information given is similar to that in the preceding volume.

Best's Key Rating Guide: Property-Liability. Oldwick, N.J., A. M. Best Co. (annual).
Provides ratings and comprehensive financial and operating statistics for U.S. stock property/liability companies, also mutual companies, "Lloyds" organizations, reciprocal insurance exchanges.

Life Reports: Financial and Operating Results of Life Insurers. Cincinnati, Ohio, National Underwriter Co. (annual).
Basic financial information on over 1,200 life insurers plus detailed corporate and operating statistics on more than half of these companies. A companion volume is their *Life Rates & Data* (annual), which gives premium rates, cash values, dividends, costs and policy conditions for the life plans of insurers.

Moodys' Bank and Finance Manual. New York, Moody's Investors Service (annual).
This basic financial manual includes U.S. and large Canadian insurance companies. The information for each company usually covers brief financial history, officers and directors, income and balance sheet statistics, total insurance written, recent stock price range. Center blue pages give 10-year price range of stocks and bonds; also lists of largest life companies ranked by total assets.

The Spectator Handy Guide. Radnor, Pa. (annual).
This is a comprehensive guide "to standard and special life insurance contracts, nonforfeiture values." It gives summaries or reproduces insurance policies, and includes annual premium rates for each company.

INSURANCE STATISTICS

Health Insurance Institute. *Source Book of Health Insurance Data.* New York (annual).
Statistics with explanatory text, including coverage trends in benefits and premiums, U.S. medical care cost, trends in morbidity. Contains a glossary.

Insurance Facts. New York, Insurance Information Institute (annual).
Brief text with basic statistics and facts on the property and liability business.

Life Insurance Fact Book. New York, Institute of Life Insurance (annual).
  Statistics, charts and brief interpretative text on the U.S. life insurance business. The Canadian Life Insurance Association in Toronto publishes a similar annual called *Canadian Life Insurance Facts.*

Life Insurance Marketing and Research Association. *Monthly Survey of Life Insurance Sales in the United States and Canada.* Hartford, Conn.
  This is an example of one of several brief statistical reports of this association.

Metropolitan Life Insurance Co. *Statistical Bulletin.* New York (monthly).
  Text and brief statistics on accidents, mortality, birth trends and other topics of interest to the life insurance industry.

U.S. National Center for Health Statistics. *Vital Statistics of the United States.* Washington, D.C., U.S. Government Printing Office (annual).
  This is the definitive publication for U.S. vital statistics, containing extensive data and analysis on marriage, divorce, nationality, fetal mortality and mortality. Vol. 1 covers natality; Vol. 2, in 2 parts, covers mortality. Current statistics appear in their *Monthly Vital Statistics Report.* Statistics for other countries are included in the UN's *Demographic Yearbook.*

INSURANCE PERIODICALS

All of the periodicals in this list, with the exception of the Institute of Actuaries' *Journal,* are indexed in *Insurance Periodicals Index,* which is described elsewhere in this chapter.

American Society of Chartered Life Underwriters. *CLU Journal.* Bryn Mawr, Pa. (quarterly).
  Research papers on nonselling problems of the life insurance business. Includes book reviews and a list of "Recent Publications." Indexed in PAIS.

Best's Review: Life/Health Insurance Edition. Oldwick, N.J., A. M. Best Co. (monthly).
  Short, practical articles of special interest to life/health insurance executives and agents, with recent news about companies and industry developments. Includes frequent annual statistical tables for companies, e.g., leading life companies (June 1974), sales results of leading companies (November 1974), 20-year dividend comparisons (December 1974). An "Insurance Periodicals Index" is in each issue; also "life sales" and stock prices. Indexed in BPI.

Best's Review: Property/Liability Insurance Edition. Oldwick, N.J., A. M. Best Co. (monthly).
  Similar journal to the one preceding, but meant for property/liability executives and agents. Special annual issues include list of leading property/liability companies (August 1974), insurance company investments (October 1974), operating expenses (December 1974). The "Insurance Periodicals Index" is in each issue, as are stock prices. Indexed in BPI.

Business Insurance. Chicago, Crain Communications (semi-monthly).
  A news magazine for buyers of employee, property and liability protection and financial services.

Institute of Actuaries. *Journal.* London (3/yr.).

Research papers and reports, with an emphasis on those using quantitative methods. Includes annotated list of publications of actuarial interest.

Journal of Risk and Insurance. Bloomington, Ill., American Risk and Insurance Association (quarterly).

Contains authoritative, original research on all aspects of risk and insurance, with the articles written primarily by academic persons. Includes book reviews. Indexed in PAIS.

Life Association News. Washington, D.C., National Association of Life Underwriters (monthly).

Articles on selling methods and news of interest to NALU members.

National Underwriter: Life & Health Insurance Edition. Chicago (weekly).

A weekly newspaper for life/health agents, brokers and executives providing news about companies, agency activity, business trends, legislation, associations, etc. A similar weekly for the property/casualty field is *National Underwriter: Property & Casualty Insurance Edition.*

Risk Management. New York, Risk and Insurance Management Society (monthly).

Articles cover new developments, regulation and news of interest to the professional risk manager. Includes book reviews.

Rough Notes. Indianapolis, Ind. (monthly).

A journal for insurance agents and brokers covering selling techniques, agency management, office management.

Society of Chartered Property and Casualty Underwriters. *CPCU Annals.* Media, Pa. (quarterly).

In-depth studies on current problems and issues, analysis of legislation, management, marketing, etc.

Two journals containing insurance news that is worldwide in scope are: *International Insurance Monitor* (New York, Monitor Trade Publications, monthly); and *The Review* (London, Guildhall Publishing Co., fortnightly), which is international but with special emphasis on U.K. countries.

INSURANCE DIRECTORIES

Insurance Almanac. Englewood, N.J., Underwriting Printing and Publishing Co. (annual).

A company directory for the 6 principal lines of insurance, giving for each, officers, type of insurance written, territory covered and, for a few of the larger companies, corporate history and company statistics. Includes also a directory of agents and brokers, adjusters, organizations, state officials, management and insurance groups.

Life Insurance Marketing and Research Association. *Member Roster.* Hartford, Conn. (annual).

This directory of members is arranged by company and does not have an index by individual name.

Society of Actuaries. *Year Book.* Chicago.
> Directory of officers and members; also other data such as constitution and by-laws.

Who's Who in Insurance. Englewood, N.J., Underwriter Printing and Publishing Co. (annual).
> Brief biographical sketches of U.S. insurance leaders. The same publisher also compiles a *Who's Who in Risk Management* (1974).

INSURANCE ASSOCIATIONS

American Council of Life Insurance (formed in January 1976 by a merger of ALIA and ILI, but each will continue to operate separately). Probable address is same as that of ALIA.

American Insurance Association, 85 John Street, New York, N.Y. 10038.

American Life Insurance Association, 1730 Pennsylvania Avenue, N.W., Washington, D.C. 20006.

American Society of Chartered Life Underwriters, 270 Bryn Mawr Avenue, Bryn Mawr, Pa. 19010.

Health Insurance Association of America, 1701 K Street, N.W., Washington, D.C. 20006.

Institute of Life Insurance, 277 Park Avenue, New York, N.Y. 10017.

Insurance Information Institute, 110 Williams Street, New York, N.Y. 10038.

Life Insurance Marketing and Research Association, 170 Sigourney Street, Hartford, Conn. 06105.

National Association of Insurance Agents, 85 John Street, New York, N.Y. 10038.

National Association of Life Underwriters, 1922 F Street, N.W., Washington, D.C. 20006.

Risk and Insurance Management Society, 205 East 42d Street, New York, N.Y. 10017.

REAL ESTATE

This second half of the chapter is concerned with listing selected recent books on real estate as a business — principles and practices, management and appraisal, finance and investing and the basic reference sources including statistics on housing. There has been no attempt to cover the many books being written on the increasingly important problem of urban development and urban renewal, although several abstracting services and periodicals on urban affairs are included in Chapter 11.

REAL ESTATE PRINCIPLES AND PRACTICES

Atkinson, Harry G. and Percy E. Wagner. *Modern Real Estate Practice: An Introduction to a Career in Real Estate Brokerage.* Homewood, Ill., Dow Jones-Irwin, 1974.
> The subtitle adequately describes the purpose of this book. It covers principles and

policies, organization, personnel, and sales force, with chapters also on condominiums, management of real property, financial control. Includes a code of ethics, real estate license law and a bibliography.

Kinnard, William N., Jr., and Stephen D. Messner. *Industrial Real Estate.* 2d ed. Washington, D.C., Society of Industrial Realtors of the National Association of Real Estate Boards, 1971.

A comprehensive study of the principles and practices of industrial real estate. Its 17 chapters are in 4 parts: the economics of industrial real estate (site selection, space, real estate as an investment); major functions of the broker; supplementary activities (for example, real estate lending, leasing, valuation); industrial real estate development (industrial districts and parks, aids to industrial development, etc.). Bibliographies are at end of each chapter.

Prentice-Hall, Inc. *Real Estate Guide.* Englewood Cliffs, N.J. (monthly).

Designed for investors and dealers in real estate to give them quick access to information on all important phases of real estate and also to give beginners a practical understanding of the problems and practices of the real estate business. Covers management, appraising, financing, federal regulations, federal taxation, federal aids to financing, selling and advertising.

Ring, Alfred A. *Real Estate Principles and Practices.* 7th ed. Englewood Cliffs, N.J., Prentice-Hall, 1972.

A standard introductory text on the real estate business. It includes a discussion of real estate financing, real estate investment and counseling, real estate management and development, regional planning and property appraising. Appendixes include interest and amortization tables, a glossary; bibliographies are at end of chapters. Mr. Ring has also written a teaching and training guide on *The Valuation of Real Estate* (2d ed., Prentice-Hall, 1970).

Semenow, Robert W. *Questions and Answers on Real Estate.* 8th ed. Englewood Cliffs, N.J., Prentice-Hall, 1975.

This is the "bible" for applicants preparing for state licensing examinations, and it is also a reference guide for the everyday real estate practitioner. It covers all important aspects including agreements, deeds, financing, mortgages, judgments, landlord and tenant, valuation and appraisal, license laws, condominiums, syndicates. Each chapter consists of a concise text followed by questions and answers.

Smith, Halbert C., Carl J. Tschappat and Ronald L. Racster. *Real Estate and Urban Development.* Homewood, Ill., Irwin, 1973.

An excellent upper-level text focusing on real estate decision-making, and "attempting to shed some light from the micro decision-making point of view upon the macro problems of cities, and from the macro problems point of view upon the investment decision-making process." Its 6 basic parts cover: framework for analysis; value and investment analysis; investment opportunity and constraint; development functions; real estate administration in the public sector. Appendixes include interest tables, a glossary of terms; bibliographies are at end of chapters.

Unger, Maurice A. *Real Estate: Principles & Practices.* 5th ed. Cincinnati, Ohio, South-Western, 1974.

The latest edition of a traditional text on "theories and practices of real estate that have a significant influence on the real estate market locally and nationally." It is in 7 parts: an overview; property rights; property ownership; financing real estate; real estate brokerage; property evaluation; planning for the future. Suggested books are at end of chapters.

Weimer, Arthur M., Homer Hoyt and George F. Bloom. *Real Estate.* 6th ed. New York, Ronald, 1972.

A popular, decision-oriented introduction to real estate, in 4 parts: introduction (physical and legal aspects); analysis for real estate decisions (political and economic trends, location factors, appraising methods); real estate decision areas (practical problems in production, marketing, financing); special properties and problems (housing, urban trends, international trends, etc.). Includes a glossary, interest and annuity tables, code of ethics; bibliographies are at end of chapters.

REAL ESTATE MANAGEMENT AND APPRAISAL

Clurman, David. *The Business Condominium: A New Form of Business Property Ownership.* New York, Wiley, 1973.

Concentrates on studying the legal, management and financing problems involved in the formation and operation of this new form of business property ownership. Clurman has also written (with Edna L. Hebard) an introduction to condominiums and their legal structure called *Condominiums and Cooperatives* (Wiley, 1971).

Downs, James C., Jr. *Principles of Real Estate Management.* 11th ed. Chicago, Institute of Real Estate Management, 1975.

A standard text on real estate management, newly revised and expanded and arranged in 3 basic parts: the real estate process; the marketing process (chapters on managing various kinds of houses and commercial buildings, commercial leases, etc.); the administrative process (such as operating a management office, personnel, records). Short bibliographies are at end of chapters.

Hanford, Lloyd D., Sr. *Analysis and Management of Investment Property.* 3d ed. Chicago, Institute of Real Estate Management, 1970.

A nontechnical overview of the management and ownership of investment property. It is in 3 parts: basic concepts for investment property management; techniques and applications to various types of property; the management business. Mr. Hanford has also written a brief but useful guide for new property managers called *The Property Management Process* (Institute of Real Estate Management, 1972).

Wendt, Paul F. *Real Estate Appraisal: Review and Outlook.* Athens, University of Georgia Press, 1974.

Professor Wendt's newest book on real estate appraisal has 2 objectives — "first, to provide a review of the development of appraisal theory and practice, and second to evaluate the present state of the appraisal art and to project its future." The first 3 chapters review the major contributions in value theory, and the rest of the book focuses on new techniques and approaches. Includes a bibliography.

REAL ESTATE FINANCE AND INVESTING

The basic sources on mortgage banking and financing (including savings and loan statistics, mortgage lending, amortization tables and income capitalization techniques) are described in the "Money and Banking" section of Chapter 14.

Bagby, Joseph R., *Real Estate Finance Desk Book*. Englewood Cliffs, N.J., Institute for Business Planning, 1975.

Intended as a reference source and a guide for persons interested in property ownership and development. Part 1 is a step-by-step guide to techniques, with chapters on specific kinds of real estate such as office buildings, shopping centers, mobile home parks. Part 2 discusses sources of finance and how to use them, and most chapters include useful lists of largest firms: S&Ls, banks, insurance companies, savings banks, mortgage bankers, money managers, finance companies, mortgage trusts (REITs), equity trusts and limited partnerships, investors and buyers, bank holding companies, SBICs, foreign investors in the United States. Part 3 is a glossary covering the language of real estate and finance.

Beaton, William R. *Real Estate Finance*. Englewood Cliffs, N.J., Prentice-Hall, 1975.

An introductory, nontechnical text on the principles and practices of real estate finance, with an emphasis on residential mortgage financing. Includes bibliographies, and a glossary is at end. Professor Beaton has also written a book on the principles and practices of *Real Estate Investment* (Prentice-Hall, 1971). This covers income tax considerations, ownership forms, financing, and it also has chapters on specific types of investment properties. Bibliographies are at end of chapters.

Campbell, Kenneth D. *Real Estate Trusts: America's Newest Billionaires*. New York, Audit Investment Research, 1971.

Part 1 (247 pages) is a text on "The Trust Business" based on a series of lectures the author gave on real estate investment trusts at New York University. It includes discussions of the historical development, framing an underwriting proposal, liability and asset management, tax and accounting issues. Part 2 contains "Profiles of Individual Trusts," which is now too old to be of much use. More recent data on trusts can be found in the NAREIT *Handbook of Member Trusts* listed elsewhere in this chapter.

Casey, William J. *Real Estate Desk Book*. 4th ed. Englewood Cliffs, N.J., Institute for Business Planning, 1972.

A handy volume of facts and techniques on such topics as tax planning, sale-leasebacks, financing, syndication, cooperatives, depreciation, property management. "Real Estate Investment Tables" are at end. This is a shortened version of much of the material in the institute's service noted below. Another one-volume guide by this specialist is *Real Estate Investments and How to Make Them* (4th ed., Institute for Business Planning, 1972).

Hoagland, Henry E. and Leo D. Stone. *Real Estate Finance*. 5th ed. Homewood, Ill., Irwin, 1973.

The latest edition of a well-known text begins with several chapters devoted to basic legal concepts, then discusses each of the major institutional sources of funds, procedures and problems of originating and servicing loans, financing development projects, the secondary mortgage markets. It ends with a discussion of the expanding roles of the federal government. Includes a bibliography.

Institute for Business Planning. *Real Estate Investment Planning*. Englewood Cliffs, N.J., 1975. 2 volumes.

A loose-leaf service covering techniques and strategies for real estate investment planning, including such topics as financing, leasing, depreciation, form of ownership, syndicates, land development, various kinds of property, brokerage, valuing and appraisal. Vol. 1 has a section for "Real Estate Investment Tables"; Vol. 2 contains checklists and forms. Included with this service is a semi-monthly *Real Estate Investment Ideas.*

Mair, George. *Guide to Successful Real Estate Investing, Buying, Financing and Leasing.* Englewood Cliffs, N.J., Prentice-Hall, 1971.

A practical, readable book for the beginner meant to answer the most important questions on real estate investing as well as on buying, selling, financing and leasing.

REAL ESTATE LAW

Kratovil, Robert. *Real Estate Law.* 6th ed. Englewood Cliffs, N.J., Prentice-Hall, 1974.

The standard work on real estate law enlarged and updated. It is comprehensive but made easy to use by a numbered paragraph format within 39 chapters, and also by frequent comments and examples. Kratovil has also written a good book on *Mortgage Law and Practice* (Prentice-Hall, 1972) and a nontechnical guide to *Modern Real Estate Documentation* (Prentice-Hall, 1975).

HOUSING AND REAL ESTATE BIBLIOGRAPHIES

Society of Industrial Realtors. Reference Library. *List of Books, Periodicals, Proceedings, Articles on Subjects Related to Industrial Real Estate.* Washington, D.C., 1971.

This bibliography, not annotated, is arranged by topic.

U.S. Department of Housing and Urban Development. *Housing and Planning References.* Washington, D.C., U. S. Government Printing Office. (bimonthly).

A continuing subject list of selected publications and articles on housing and planning received in the library at HUD. Each issue also includes a list of planning reports arrranged by state, and several book reviews at front.

U.S. Small Business Administration. *Real Estate Business.* (Small Business Bibliography, No. 65). Washington, D.C., 1969.

A short, annotated list of government and nongovernmental publications on real estate, including appraisal, brokerage management, finance, law and taxation.

REAL ESTATE DICTIONARIES

Boyce, Byrl N., comp. *Real Estate Appraisal Terminology.* Cambridge, Mass., Ballinger, 1975.

A good, up-to-date dictionary on real estate sponsored jointly by the American Institute of Real Estate Appraisers and the Society of Real Estate Appraisers, and including terms that were in earlier dictionaries published by both organizations. Supplementary data in an appendix includes symbols, measures, valuation models, rates and relationships; also a section on depreciation methods, and a list of books, articles and reference sources.

Collison, Koder M. *The Developers' Dictionary and Handbook.* Lexington, Mass., D. C. Heath, 1974.

A dictionary, with a short handbook section containing useful facts, mileage tables, sample forms, etc.

Another dictionary published too late to be available for examination is *Modern Real Estate Dictionary* by John R. Johnsich (San Francisco, Canfield Press, 1975).

INFORMATION ABOUT REAL ESTATE COMPANIES

Statistics on the major homebuilders are included in Chapter 5.

National Association of Real Estate Investment Trusts. *Handbook of Member Trusts.* Washington, D.C. (annual).

Financial manual for NAREIT member trusts, giving brief history, officers, trustees, investment policy, property owned, range of stock price; also balance sheet and income statistics. NAREIT also publishes a separate semi-annual *Membership Directory.*

Real Estate Syndication Digest. San Francisco, Calif. (monthly).

Information about real estate limited partnership and condominium offerings registered with the SEC and the California Department of Corporations. Data for each includes policy, objectives, and property description of the investments, names of general partners, parent company, management, compensation, prior offerings, offering amounts.

Moody's Bank and Finance Manual includes financial information on U.S. real estate companies and real estate investment trusts. See listing in the "Insurance" section of this chapter.

REAL ESTATE OPERATING STATISTICS

Building Owners and Managers Association International. *Office Building Exchange Report.* Chicago (annual).

Gives income and expense statistics by age of building in cents per square foot, relating to the total building rentable area, to the office rentable area, to the actual rented office area. Includes statistical analysis also for regions and for 45 U.S. and Canadian cities.

Institute of Real Estate Management. Experience Exchange Committee. *A Statistical Compilation and Analysis of Actual (year) Income and Expenses Experienced in Apartment, Condominium, and Cooperative Building Operation.* Chicago, (annual).

Apartment building income/expense data for elevator buildings, low-rise buildings, garden type buildings, furnished buildings — based on reports from over 2,800 buildings in the United States and Canada. For each, statistics include average income and operating costs, both by selected metropolitan areas and by age groups. Includes also statistics for cooperatives, condominiums, rate of tenant turnover, heating and fuel costs by region, etc.

National Institute of Real Estate Brokers. *Percentage Leases: Commercial Rental Survey.* 13th ed. Chicago, 1973 (published irregularly).

Rates and terms for over 3,100 individual lease contracts, arranged by 97 retailing store categories. Data given includes percentage rental rate, square feet of gross selling area, annual minimum rent in dollars and also per square foot, etc. The introduction states that this is meant as a guide to current practices and not as a model of exact terms and conditions.

Urban Land Institute. *Dollars & Cents of Shopping Centers: A Study of Receipts & Expenses in Shopping Center Operations.* Washington, D.C. (triennial).

Detailed operating statistics for 4 categories of U.S. shopping centers (super-regional, regional, community, neighborhood) and also for Canadian shopping centers, arranged by specific kind of shop. The statistics in the 1975 edition are based on data from 550 centers.

HOUSING AND REAL ESTATE STATISTICS

The first two governmental series listed below are the best sources for U.S. housing statistics. Statistics on the building and construction industry are included in Chapter 5.

U.S. Bureau of the Census. *Census of Housing.* Washington, D.C., U.S. Government Printing Office.

The Census of Housing is taken every 10 years on the year ending in zero. It consists of a series of 7 volumes, each with many parts, that provide detailed statistics on the number and characteristics of houses in the United States, including block statistics. The basic volumes in the 1970 *Census* are:

Vol. 1: HC (1): *Characteristics for States, Cities and Counties.* Part A of this series gives general characteristics. Part B gives detailed statistics, including tenure, vacancy status, number of persons per room, type of structure, condition and plumbing facilities, financial characteristics — for states, counties, for urbanized areas, SMSAs, and places of 1,000 inhabitants or more.

Vol. 2: HC (2): *Metropolitan Housing Characteristics.*

Vol. 3: HC (3): *Block Statistics.*

Vol. 4: HC (4): *Components of Inventory Change.*

Vol. 5: HC (5): *Residential Finance.*

Vol. 6: HC (6): *Estimates of "Substandard" Housing.*

Vol. 7: HC (7): *Subject Reports.* These special subject reports cover such topics as housing of senior citizens and selected racial groups, mobile homes, cooperative and condominium housing.

U.S. Department of Housing and Urban Development. *HUD Statistical Yearbook.* Washington, D.C., U.S. Government Printing Office.

Comprehensive housing statistics covering such subjects as community planning and management, equal opportunity, housing management, housing production and mortgage credit; also general statistics relating to housing and urban activities including population and households, housing sales, occupancy, construction costs, mortgage financing. Current statistics on housing production and financing as well as on program activities of HUD are in their quarterly *Housing and Urban Development Trends.*

National Association of Real Estate Investment Trusts. *REIT Fact Book.* Washington, D.C. (annual).

Information and basic facts about REITs, mostly in brief text form with a few statistics at end. Includes data on types of mortgage loans by REITs, construction loans, ownership of property, sources of funds.

National Association of Realtors. *Spring Real Estate Market Report.* Chicago (annual).

Brief text with statistics on trends in three segments of the real estate market (single-family home sales, residential rental properties, land for nonfarm use). Two other short statistical releases published by this association are: *Existing Home Sales Series* (annual); *Mortgage Market Report* (semi-annual).

U.S. Bureau of the Census. *Census of Governments.* Washington, D.C., U.S. Government Printing Office.

This census is taken every 5 years in the years ending with 2 and 7. The 1972 census was in 8 volumes, and Vol. 2 is of special interest for its statistics on "Taxable Property Values and Assessment-Sales Price Ratios."

U.S. Housing Markets. Detroit, Mich., Advance Mortgage Corp. (semi-annual).

A short statistical survey of 17 metropolitan areas and 8 regions, with statistics for each area covering housing starts and permits, apartment completions, vacancy trends, employment trends, mortgage price trends, insured loan activity.

REAL ESTATE PERIODICALS

American Institute of Real Estate Appraisers. *Appraisal Journal.* Chicago (quarterly).

Authoritative articles on real estate appraisal and real estate financing, with news about recent legal cases, rulings on matters affecting real property valuation. Indexed in BPI.

Condominium World. Boston, Warren, Gorham & Lamont (quarterly).

A new (1974) professional journal for in-depth coverage of topics relating to condominiums. Includes book notes and selected lists of articles. This same publisher issues a monthly reporting service for persons who need the latest developments in laws, regulations and other news. It is called *The Condominium Report.*

Journal of Housing. Washington, D.C., National Association of Housing and Redevelopment Officials (11/yr.).

Primarily news about new developments, government programs, legislation, court decisions and NAHRO members.

Journal of Property Management. Chicago, Institute of Real Estate Management (bimonthly).

Articles cover management practices, procedures and related topics on property management. Indexed in PAIS.

National Real Estate Investor. New York, Communication Channels, Inc. (monthly).

Each issue includes articles discussing real estate developments in 3 different cities. There are also regular columns and news about various kinds of buildings, legislation, etc. Their annual "Directory Issue" is described under "Directories" below.

Real Estate Law Journal. Boston, Warren, Gorham & Lamont (quarterly).

Research articles on the legal and tax aspects of real estate; also news about legislation, case digests. Includes book reviews, a subject survey of articles, digests of significant articles.

Real Estate Review. Boston, Warren, Gorham & Lamont (quarterly).
Short, readable articles by real estate, legal and accounting experts, on all aspects of real estate and related subjects. Includes a good book review section. Indexed in BPI.

Real Estate Today. Chicago, Realtors National Marketing Institute (bimonthly).
Covers articles on real estate management. Includes book reviews.

REIT Review. Mequon, Wisc., J. T. Hall, Inc. (quarterly).
A new journal (1973) covering articles on real estate investment trusts and related topics. Each issue contains financial tables for specific REITs.

Shopping Center World. New York, Communication Channels, Inc. (monthly).
Short articles on such topics as shopping center trends, financing, leasing, operations, and also news of interest to shopping center managers and real estate developers.

REAL ESTATE DIRECTORIES

Employee Relocation Council. *ERREAC Directory.* Chicago (annual).
A geographical list of real estate appraisers and brokers. ERREAC stands for "Employee Relocation Real Estate Advisory Council."

National Institute of Real Estate Brokers. *Membership Roster.* Chicago (biennial).
Directory of individual members of the NIREB, arranged by state.

National Real Estate Investor. "Directory Issue." (annual, e.g. July 15).
Useful geographic lists of appraisers, developers, consultants, corporate real estate managers, development agencies, industrial parks, land companies, mortgage sources, real estate management firms, REITs, realtors/brokers, sale-leasebacks, urban renewal agencies, etc.

Site Selection Handbook. Atlanta, Ga., Conway Research, Inc. 3 volumes (annual).
Vol. 1, "Real Estate Investment and Development," includes a directory, by state, of lending sources for land development; Vol. 2, "Industry's Guide to Geo-Economic Planning," lists development organizations and industrial sites; Vol. 3, "The Environmental Planning Guide," has a list of environmental control agencies, checklist of site selection factors, etc.

REAL ESTATE ASSOCIATIONS

International Council of Shopping Centers, 445 Park Avenue, New York, N.Y. 10022.

National Association of Corporate Real Estate Executives, 7799 S.W. 62d Avenue, South Miami, Fla. 33143.

National Association of Realtors, 155 East Superior Street, Chicago, Ill. 60611 (This is a federation of state and local real estate boards and was formerly the National Association of Real Estate Boards. Several institutes affiliated with this association are: American Institute of Real Estate Appraisers; Institute of Real Estate Management; and National Institute of Real Estate Brokers.)

National Center for Housing Management, 1133 15th Street, N.W., Washington, D.C. 20005.

National Property Management Association, P.O. Box 375, Camden, N.J. 08101.

Society of Industrial Realtors, 935 15th Street, N.W., Washington, D.C. 20005. (Affiliated with National Association of Realtors.)

16

INTERNATIONAL MANAGEMENT

International Economics (including Finance) — International Management — International Financial Management — International Marketing — International Business Bibliographies — Dictionaries — Tax and Trade Guides for Specific Countries — Reference Data for Exporters — International Management Periodicals — Directories — Associations

The rapid development of international business in the period following World War II has brought with it many new and important challenges for management. Added to the usual problems of managing a domestic company the international or multinational corporation must concern itself with many complex questions in connection with political, economic and social differences between nations. The literature has lagged behind this growth in international business for several reasons: the wide range of complicated factors that must be considered, rapidly changing events and diversity of opinion, to name a few. Although the time lag in book publishing has lessened, the reasons for it point up the particular importance of periodicals in this field. Current articles offer the most up-to-date information on global economic and governmental activity, on continuing management efforts to adjust to changing environments, and they also have the advantage of being able to present various opinions on how to solve specific business problems. Not only are business and economic periodicals of value but it is assumed the person with international interest also reads current U.S. and foreign affairs journals and one or more U.S. and foreign newspaper.

This chapter describes a selection of recent books, periodicals and a few reference sources on the topics listed above. The following reference materials are covered elsewhere in this book: directories of foreign companies in Chapter 3; foreign statistical sources and foreign economic trends in Chapter 6; financial manuals for foreign companies in Chapter 7.

INTERNATIONAL ECONOMICS (INCLUDING FINANCE)

Bell, Geoffrey. *The Euro-dollar Market and the International Financial System.* New York, Wiley, 1973.

The purpose of this short, readable book "is to examine the growth of the euro-dollar market and its relationship to the functioning of the international financial system as a whole. The aim has been to blend economic analysis with the practical problems of international monetary relations and the field of international banking and finance." Includes a bibliography.

Caves, Richard E. and Ronald W. Jones. *World Trade and Payments: An Introduction.* Boston, Little, Brown, 1973.

This introductory text integrates descriptive material with the theory of world trade and balance of payments, and it is geared for undergraduates with limited mathematics. Its main sections cover: commodity exchange and balance of payments; the theory of trade and production; the theory and practice of commercial policy; macroeconomic concerns — international external balance; international factor movements. Includes bibliographies.

Einzig, Paul. *The Euro-Dollar System: Practice and Theory of International Interest Rates.* 5th ed. New York, St. Martin's Press, 1973.

A respected British monetary expert updates his thoughtful study of the Eurodollar system, covering both theoretical and practical aspects and considering also its various policy aspects. Includes a bibliography.

Farmer, Richard N., Robert W. Stevens and Hans Schöllhammer. *Readings in International Business.* Encino, Calif., Dickenson Publishing Co., 1972.

A selection of readings covering both the macro environmental problems and the micro firm problems of international business. The 7 parts cover: balance of payments and trade policy; international and comparative management; regional economic groups; economic planning; development questions in international business; international investment; special aspects of international management.

Gilpin, Robert. *U.S. Power and the Multinational Corporation: The Political Economy of Foreign Direct Investment.* New York, Basic Books, 1975.

Professor Gilpin attempts to further an understanding of the relationship between international economics and international politics by analyzing the multinational corporation and foreign investment from the general perspective of international relations and by showing the significance of foreign investment in the larger context of international politics. In doing so he raises important questions about the costs and benefits of foreign direct investment. Bibliographical notes are at end.

Goodsell, Charles T. *American Corporations and Peruvian Politics.* Cambridge, Mass., Harvard University Press, 1974.

Presents "the results of several years' study of political implications for Peru of the presence of sizable American business investments in the country." Although this is limited to a study of just one country, it presents much of serious interest to all international businessmen. There are 4 parts: theory and setting; the challenge to national independence; implications for community and society; conclusions. It includes a selected bibliography and bibliographical "notes."

Kenen, Peter B. and Raymond Lubitz. *International Economics.* 3d ed. Englewood Cliffs, N.J., Prentice-Hall, 1971.

This book is for persons who want a short overview, in paperback, by 2 leading authorities. There are 6 chapters, 4 of which cover trade and resource allocation, trade policy, balance of payments, foreign exchange, and financial policy. A selected bibliography suggests sources for further reading.

Kindleberger, Charles P. *International Economics.* 5th ed. Homewood, Ill., Irwin, 1973.

The latest edition of Professor Kindleberger's classic text is in 5 parts: Parts 1-3 deal with microeconomic aspects of international economics (theory of international trade, commercial policy, factor movements); Part 4 discusses the macroeconomic problems of money, income, price, foreign exchange market, balance of payments; Part 5 discusses balance of payments adjustment and international monetary arrangements. Includes bibliographies at end of chapters. A thought-provoking series of lectures by Kindleberger is his *American Business Abroad: Six Lectures on Direct Investment* (New Haven, Conn., Yale University Press, 1969). He has also edited an excellent collection of papers that were presented at a Seminar in Spring 1969, titled *The International Corporation: A Symposium* (Cambridge, Mass., MIT Press, 1970). In addition, an impressive collection of essays has been published in his honor, called *Trade, Balance of Payments and Growth: Papers in International Economics in Honor of Charles P. Kindleberger* edited by Jagdish N. Bhagwati et al. (Amsterdam, North Holland Publishing Co., 1971).

Lees, Francis A. and Maximo Eng. *International Financial Markets: Development of the Present System and Future Prospects.* New York, Praeger, 1975.

Parts 2-6 of this recent study on the changing structure and scope of activities in international financial markets describe and analyze the financial markets in 14 countries that have strategic importance in the international flow of funds. The first part provides an historical and conceptual framework; Part 7 analyzes the structure and scope of operations (including Eurodollar, Eurobond, and the international market for foreign exchange); and Part 8 covers comparisons and future prospects. References at end of chapters. Mr. Lees has also written a recent textbook on *International Banking and Finance* (New York, Wiley, 1974).

Mason, R. Hal, Robert R. Miller and Dale R. Weigel. *The Economics of International Business.* New York, Wiley, 1975.

An economic analysis of international business in 3 parts: Part 1 discusses the international economic environment (including balance of payments, foreign exchange, international monetary system); Part 2 examines key decision areas that the international firm must deal with (selection of entry form and expansion vehicle, selection of technology, project analysis, financing, organization); the final section explores conflicts between host countries and the international enterprise. Bibliographies are at end of chapters.

Meier, Gerald M. *Problems of a World Monetary Order.* London and New York, Oxford University Press, 1974.

A study of the 3 basic international monetary policy problems: the currency crisis in connection with the evolution of the post-war international monetary system; the dollar problem in connection with the balance of payments policy; international monetary reform and exchange-rate flexibility. Includes frequent excerpts from source material, and there are bibliographies at end of each section.

Scammell, W. M. *International Trade and Payments.* New York, St. Martin's Press, 1974.

This comprehensive text concentrates on the theoretical aspects of international trade and balance of payments. Its 3 principal parts are: the pure theory of international trade; commercial policy; the economics of the balance of payments. For persons who want to read further there is a good, short list of texts, treatises and some articles on international economics in general and also on the theory of international trade, commercial policy and the balance of payments.

Stern, Robert M. *The Balance of Payments: Theory and Economic Policy.* Chicago, Aldine Publishing Co., 1973.

A thorough treatise on the theory of balance of payments and how it may be influenced by governmental economic policy, with a bibliography of sources used that lists not only books but also a selection of articles.

Vernon, Raymond. *The Economic Environment of International Business.* Englewood Cliffs, N.J., Prentice-Hall, 1972. (A major revision is in progress, with Louis T. Wells, Jr., as joint author and publication planned for 1976.)

Professor Vernon borrows from the concepts of economic theory but states that this book should be thought of as a standard textbook on international economics, with the objective "to introduce the student to the fields of international payments, international trade and international investment." He emphasizes problems encountered both by enterprises that operate across international boundaries from a base in a single country and also those with subsidiaries and affiliates in a number of countries. This useful paperback edition has also been published as a bound textbook titled *Manager in the International Economy* (3d ed., Prentice-Hall, 1976), which he expanded for teaching purposes to include a second part containing 13 cases. A collection of 7 informative articles on the multinational enterprise written by Vernon in 1968–1971 is *The Economic and Political Consequences of Multinational Enterprise: An Anthology* (Boston, Division of Research, Graduate School of Business Administration, Harvard University, 1972; now distributed by Harvard University Press).

Wasserman, Max J., Andreas R. Prindl and Charles C. Townsend, Jr. *International Money Management.* New York, American Management Association, 1972.

"Attempts to give a practical description of the foreign exchange markets and provide a framework for managerial decisions in the foreign exchange area." It begins with a discussion of theoretical framework, then follows with a section on foreign exchange markets, rates and transactions, another section on international money management, and ends with 2 chapters on foreign exchange exposure and protection. Includes a glossary and bibliography.

INTERNATIONAL MANAGEMENT

Aitken, Thomas. *The Multinational Man: The Role of the Manager Abroad.* New York, Wiley; London, G. Allen & Unwin, 1973.

A short, readable book focusing on managers in foreign subsidiaries of international companies — who these men are and what their role is. Includes a bibliography.

Barnet, Richard J. and Ronald E. Müller. *Global Reach: The Power of the Multinational Corporations.* New York, Simon and Schuster, 1974.

Two critics of the power of large multinational corporations have teamed up to write this readable and persuasive indictment of MNCs, which they base on an extensive search of published materials listed in a lengthy "Notes for Text and Tables" section at end. Parts of this book originally appeared in a 2-part article in *New Yorker* magazine, Dec. 2 and 9, 1974.

Brooke, Michael Z. and H. Lee Remmers. *The Strategy of Multinational Enterprise: Organisation and Finance.* London, Longman; New York, American Elsevier, 1970.

This excellent book is the result of a 6-year research project on the organization and finance of the multinational company during which time (1964–1969) these 2 British scholars studied over 80 manufacturing companies and 30 banks in 7 European countries and in the United States. Part 1 analyzes the processes and pressures influencing company organization; Part 2 covers the sources and methods of financing foreign investments used by MNCs; Part 3 deals with performance motives and the environment. Notes and a bibliography are at end. These authors have also edited a collection of research papers on *The Multinational Company in Europe: Some Key Problems* (London, Longman, 1972; Ann Arbor, University of Michigan Press, 1974).

Dymsza, William A. *Multinational Business Strategy.* New York, McGraw-Hill, 1972.

"This book strives to present a relatively concise and conceptual approach to international business strategy, organizational structure, and control arrangements." Emphasis is on strategic planning and strategy in international marketing, production/logistics, finance, international investment/acquisitions, ownership and international control. A bibliography is at end.

Haner, F. T. *Multinational Management.* Columbus, Ohio, C. E. Merrill, 1973.

"The purpose of this book is to give Americans a greater understanding of the differences between business in the United States and in other countries, and to elaborate on the strategies needed to improve our performance in these operations." It is in 2 parts: Part 1 covers fundamentals of establishing multinational businesses; Part 2 consists of individual chapters on specific aspects of managing MNCs (organization, personnel, finance, marketing, production). Includes 11 cases based on the author's personal experience; bibliographies are at end of chapters.

Hays, Richard D., Christopher M. Korth and Manucher Roudiani. *International Business: An Introduction to the World of the Multinational Firm.* Englewood Cliffs, N.J., Prentice-Hall, 1972.

A broad "survey of both levels of the international businessman's world: the environment (economic, political, and social) within which he will be operating, and the new dimensions of his traditional business operations." In 4 parts: the nature of international business; the environment of international business; multinational business operations; a look forward. Several readings are with each chapter, as well as bibliographies.

Heck, Harold J. *International Trade: A Management Guide.* New York, American Management Association, 1972.

Designed as a practical guide for private practitioners of exporting and importing, to give them information on important aspects of international trade in a concise and simple format.

Jonnard, Claude M. *Exporter's Financial and Marketing Handbook.* 2d ed. Park Ridge, N.J., Noyes Data Corp., 1975.

Written to serve as a methods manual on the fundamentals of exporting and selling overseas for managers of small sales-oriented firms. There are 14 chapters covering particular areas of concern such as the mechanics of export operation, selling terms, researching export statistics, export financing programs, international licensing, free trade zones.

Kapoor, Ashok and Phillip D. Grub, eds. *The Multinational Enterprise in Transition: Selected Readings and Essays.* Princeton, N.J., Darwin Press, 1972.

An excellent anthology of 34 papers selected to give a better understanding of the changing context in which business is conducted on a global basis. The authors are all well-known names such as Robinson, Stobaugh, Vernon, and the selection provides a wide range of issues and varying points of view. It is arranged in 3 parts: introduction; the functions — a managerial approach (17 chapters covering organizational structure and management, marketing, accounting/finance, manufacturing); environment and future evolution (12 chapters, with an emphasis on nationalism and government relations).

Kapoor, Ashok. *Planning for International Business Negotiation.* Cambridge, Mass., Ballinger, 1975.

"This book discusses the subject of international business negotiations with particular focus on negotiations between the international company (IC) and the host governments of developing countries." Chapter 1 discusses the background and nature of negotiation; Chapters 2-5 present 4 case studies that give a detailed picture of the process and the dynamics of negotiations. Chapter 6 is an analysis based on the 4 studies. Includes a bibliography.

Kolde, Endel J. *International Business Enterprise.* 2d ed. Englewood Cliffs, N.J., Prentice-Hall, 1973.

Professor Kolde's book on the concepts, environments and management of international business is in 7 parts: background; international trade; the multinational company (10 chapters on organization, joint ventures, foreign licensing, taxation, etc.); financial structures and processes of international business; marketing in the multinational context; environmental dynamics — international integration; environment dynamics — modernization of developing areas. A bibliography is at end. Kolde has also written an in-depth, interdisciplinary analysis of *The Multinational Company: Behavioral and Managerial Analysis* (Lexington, Mass., D. C. Heath, 1974). It includes chapters on such topics as "financial motivites," structural models, communication, development of multinational executives, labor conflict; it also has a bibliography.

Kujawa, Duane, ed. *American Labor and the Multinational Corporation.* New York, Praeger, 1973.

A selection of 11 essays by experts representing both the prolabor and probusiness positions on the interaction between American labor and the U.S. multinational enterprise (concentrating mainly in the economic and industrial relations spheres).

Massie, Joseph L. and Jan Luytjes. *Management in an International Context.* New York, Harper & Row, 1972.

A comparative study of management, with each chapter written by a management specialist from a selected country (in Europe, Asia, Africa or South America) who describes and explains the critical environmental factors that affect managerial approaches in his country. Bibliographies are at end of chapters.

Phatak, Arvind V. *Managing Multinational Corporations.* New York, Praeger, 1974.

This book is about the role of the headquarters of a multinational company in managing its worldwide operations, and it is meant as a handy desk reference for the practitioner and student. There are 4 main parts: introduction; the multinational environment (economic, legal, business tax, political and cultural); managing multinational operations (planning, organizing, staffing, compensating, controlling); strategic decision areas (evaluating foreign direct investment opportunities, licensing and exporting, joint ventures, etc.). Includes bibliographical notes.

Robinson, Richard D. *International Business Management: A Guide to Decision Making.* New York, Holt, Rinehart and Winston, 1973.

Focuses on strategy decisions with which the international firm is faced. Chapters cover strategy in each of the following areas: sales, supply, labor, management, ownership, financial, legal, control. Several short cases and a bibliography are at end of each chapter; a glossary is at end.

Robock, Stefan and Kenneth Simmonds. *International Business and Multinational Enterprises.* Homewood, Ill., Irwin, 1973.

This excellent introductory text is the result of 10 years of teaching international business courses, and the authors aim to write a book that is both intellectually challenging and that focuses on the development of management skills in handling the problems of multinational business. Its 5 principal sections follow a logical progression: the nature and scope of international business; the framework for international transactions; international business and the nation-state; assessing and forecasting the business environment; managing the multinational enterprise. Cases, problems and a bibliography are at end.

Sethi, S. Prakash and Jagdish N. Sheth. *Multinational Business Operations.* Pacific Palisades, Calif., Goodyear Publishing Co., 1973. 4 volumes.

A 4-volume paperback set of readings, with Vol. 1 covering "Environmental Aspects of Operating Abroad"; Vol. 2, "Long-Range Planning, Organization, and Management"; Vol. 3, "Marketing Management"; Vol. 4, "Financial Management." Selected annotated bibliographies of articles are at back of each volume.

Stopford, John M. and Louis T. Wells, Jr. *Managing the Multinational Enterprise: Organization of the Firm and Ownership of the Subsidiaries.* New York, Basic Books, 1972.

"The primary purpose of this study is to explore a few of the choices that businessmen have been making in dealing with the challenges posed by the multinational enterprises, the difficulties that they have encountered with these choices, and the directions in which they are moving." The first part deals with ways multinational structures have been altered as they develop new and more complex strategies; the second part, "Strategy and Ownership Policies," is concerned with decisions about the inclusion of local partners in the foreign operations of the firm. Includes bibliographical notes at end. This book was one of the major studies published in connection with the Harvard Multinational Enterprise Project, which is described briefly under the entry for Vaupel below.

U.S. Congress. Senate. Committee on Finance. *Implications of Multinational Firms for World Trade and Investment and for U.S. Trade and Labor: Report . . .* Washington, U.S. Government Printing Office, 1973.

In over 900 pages, this provides both a summary and the text of the Tariff Commission's study on the multinational firm. Chapters 2-5 of the text deal with such subjects as implications of the MNCs for balance of payments, and also for world trade, investment and international finance. Chapters 6-8 cover implications for technology transfers, labor and certain aspects of legal issues. Statistical tables are included throughout.

Vaupel, James W. and Joan P. Curhan. *The Making of Multinational Enterprise: A Sourcebook of Tables Based on a Study of 187 Major U.S. Manufacturing Corporations.* Boston, Division of Research, Graduate School of Business Administration, Harvard University, 1969. Also a later volume: *The World's Multinational Enterprises: A Sourcebook of Tables Based on a Study of the Largest U.S. and non-U.S. Manufacturing Corporations* (same publisher, 1973). Both of these volumes are now being distributed by Harvard University Press. The latter volume has also been published in Geneva by the Research Unit of the Center for Education in International Management (1974).

These are valuable tabulations of statistical data collected in connection with a long-term Multinational Enterprise Project at the Harvard Business School. The first volume represents data collected for the first phase of the project, which was devoted to an in-depth study (conducted during 1965–1969) of the problems and practices of large U.S.-based multinational manufacturing enterprises. There are over 500 tables showing details of the expansion and development of some 10,000 subsidiaries of 187 U.S. parent companies traced from 1900 through 1967. The massive data on which these tables are based was collected principally from published sources such as Securities and Exchange Commission 10-K Reports, annual corporate reports, books, articles, as well as from company interviews. The second volume contains data collected for the second phase of the study, which was extended to cover the operations of multinational enterprises based in Canada, Europe and Japan and to probe some larger questions relating to the effects of MNCs on international trade, capital movements and other areas of public policy. This data traced foreign subsidiaries of the largest manufacturing enterprises based *outside* the United States from 1900 to 1970. All of this data has been stored on computer tapes for easy access by researchers. In Summer 1975 an effort was begun to carry forward the statistics collected for the first phase of the study to include the years 1968 through 1974. This data will also be stored on tapes, but there are no plans as yet for publishing a third sourcebook of tables.

In addition to the compilation of this vast statistical data, the Multinational Enterprise Project has contributed (as of December 1974) to the completion of 13 books, 24 doctoral dissertations and 146 articles in various journals and other publications.

Vernon, Raymond. *Sovereignty at Bay: The Multinational Spread of U.S. Enterprises.* New York, Basic Books, 1971.

This thought-provoking treatise, written by the coordinator of Harvard's Multinational Enterprise Project, is a synthesis of the research on U.S.-controlled multinational enterprises in manufacturing and extractive industries — their personality, their economic causes and influence, their threat to local élites, ideologies and culture. Several other books resulting from this long-term research project are described elsewhere in this chapter. Professor Vernon has also edited an excellent collection of essays discussing relationships between big business and the state in 5

European countries and in 5 important European industries, titled *Big Business and the State: Changing Relations in Western Europe* (Cambridge, Mass., Harvard University Press, 1974).

Wilkins, Mira. *The Emergence of Multinational Enterprise: American Business Abroad from the Colonial Era to 1914.* Cambridge, Mass., Harvard University Press, 1970. And a later volume: *The Maturing of Multinational Enterprise: American Business Abroad from 1914 to 1970* (Harvard Studies in Business History, 27). Harvard University Press, 1974.

An excellent 2-volume comprehensive study of the history of American multinational enterprise from colonial times to 1970, carefully researched from published literature, archival records and interviews with many businessmen. The author confines her study "to foreign investments by U.S. businessmen and business organizations which involved managerial responsibility, the possibility of a voice in management, and direct business purpose." Each book is an independent work and each includes a lengthy bibliography and bibliographical notes.

INTERNATIONAL FINANCIAL MANAGEMENT

Eiteman, David K. and Arthur I. Stonehill. *Multinational Business Finance.* Reading, Mass., Addison-Wesley, 1973.

An excellent book in the relatively new field of managing financial decisions within multinational business enterprises that presupposes a basic business finance course and some knowledge of international economics. After an introductory section, the authors devote 6 chapters to a discussion of the international monetary environment and to institutional factors (internal and external sources of funds, import and export financing, taxation); then 5 chapters deal with financial decision-making (the foreign investment decision, cost of capital and financial structure, adapting to political interference, risk of foreign exchange loss, management of working capital); and 2 chapters on accounting, reporting and control. Bibliographies are at end of chapters.

Manser, W. A. P. *The Financial Role of Multinational Enterprises.* London, Associated Business Programmes, 1973.

This is an important study on the impact that financial transactions of MNCs may have upon the countries in which they operate, and it includes factual data gathered from U.K. and European companies, interviews, and an examination of published and unpublished material. Part 1, "Financial Decisions," studies the effects on the countries in relation to balances of payments, capital resources, and financial markets. Part 2, "Financial Management," considers the effects on the companies themselves. Includes a short bibliography.

Nehrt, Lee C., ed. *International Finance for Multinational Business.* 2d ed. Scranton, Pa., Intext Educational Publishers, 1972.

A wide selection of readings on the international monetary environment, financing foreign trade and investment, and multinational financial management. Includes lists of additional readings with each of the 12 chapters.

Reuber, Grant L. *Private Foreign Investment in Development.* Oxford, England, Clarendon Press, 1973.

A useful study "principally concerned with describing and evaluating some of the main characteristics and economic effects of private foreign direct investment in manufacturing industries in LDCs" (less-developed countries). Chapters cover: host and home country interests; the determinants of investment and investor; determinants of direct investment; 2 chapters on effects on host countires. The study was undertaken for the Development Centre of the OECD and was based not only on existing material from a wide variety of sources but on data collected from a survey of companies.

Robbins, Sidney M. and Robert B. Stobaugh. *Money in the International Enterprise: A Study of Financial Policy.* New York, Basic Books, 1973.

This informative book reports on a study of the financial practices and policies of 187 multinational companies, undertaken in an effort to help U.S. firms better resolve the financial problems they encounter abroad. In connection with this research the authors employed a model of a multinational firm, which enabled them to show the outcome of alternative courses of action. This book, one of the major products of Harvard's Multinational Enterprise Project, includes chapters on withdrawing funds from abroad, managing current assets, protecting against exchange risks. Bibliographical notes are at end.

Schneider, Gerhard W. *Export-Import Financing: A Practical Guide.* New York, Ronald, 1974.

An international banker has written this book to give practical guidance and orientation to international traders, executives, bankers and students. It is in 3 parts: facilitating institutions and services; executing the transactions; financing techniques and vehicles. "Revised American Foreign Trade Definitions" are included in an appendix.

Weston, J. Fred and Bart W. Sorge. *International Managerial Finance.* Homewood, Ill., Irwin, 1972.

The first part of this text emphasizes the foundation, framework and tools of international finance; the second applies this background to important areas of management policy and decision-making, and includes chapters on the foreign investment decision, working capital management, the multinational firm. Short bibliographies are with each chapter; a glossary and present value tables are at end.

Zenoff, David B. and Jack Zwick. *International Financial Management.* Englewood Cliffs, N.J., Prentice-Hall, 1969.

An older textbook on the theory and practice of international financial management, with an emphasis "on the environmental forces that distinguish international transactions from purely domestic business." Includes chapters on evaluating direct investment opportunities, working capital management, sources and instruments of international finance, import and export financing, management control of foreign operations. Bibliographies and one or more cases are with each chapter.

INTERNATIONAL MARKETING

Cateora, Philip R. and John M. Hess. *International Marketing.* 3d ed. Homewood, Ill., Irwin, 1975.

This third edition of a comprehensive text still focuses on the environment but puts greater emphasis on management problems, techniques and strategies for competing in markets with different cultures. It is in 6 parts: an overview; the world marketing environment; world market patterns; international marketing management (in 2 parts, covering planning and developing consumer and industrial products, advertising, pricing, distribution system, logistics, export trade techniques); corporate context of marketing (financing, manpower, control). One or two readings are with each chapter and interesting notes from other sources are in "boxes" scattered throughout the text. Cases are at end of each section, and a bibliography is at end.

Fayerweather, John. *International Marketing.* 2d ed. Englewood Cliffs, N.J., Prentice-Hall, 1970.

A concise paperback meant as a simple overview of the various aspects of adapting to foreign markets. It includes chapters on consumers, product policy, distribution and promotion, and market research. A bibliography is at end.

Grub, Phillip D. and Mika Kaskimies, eds. *International Marketing in Perspective.* Helsinki, Finland, Kirja Oy, 1971.

A good selection of 40 articles written by both American and European authorities on the methods and techniques of international marketing.

Another selection of 31 readings in 8 parts is *International Marketing Strategy: Selected Readings* edited by H. B. Thorelli (Harmondsworth, Middlesex, England, Penguin Books, 1973).

Keegan, Warren J. *Multinational Marketing Management.* Englewood Cliffs, N.J., Prentice-Hall, 1974.

Attempts to introduce students and practitioners to a systematic treatment of marketing on a global scale. Part 1 is on the environment of international marketing; Part 2 is devoted to systematic approaches to the identification of global opportunities and threats; Part 3 focuses on key decision elements (product, pricing, channel and communications decisions); Part 4 examines planning, organizing and controlling the multinational program. One case and a bibliography is with each chapter; an appendix includes a descriptive list of "Documentary Sources of Information."

Two other introductory texts are *International Marketing* by Roland L. Kramer (3d ed., Cincinnati, Ohio, South-Western, 1970) and *International Marketing* by Vern Terpstra (Hinsdale, Ill., Dryden Press, 1972).

INTERNATIONAL BUSINESS BIBLIOGRAPHIES

See also bibliographies listed in Chapter 6.

Business International Corp. *Master Key Index.* New York (quarterly, with annual cumulations).

This up-to-date index of BI publications is available to subscribers and covers their periodicals, research reports, management reports and reference services in the field of international business. The index is arranged by country (white pages), by company (blue pages), and a short section (yellow) indexes their reports on management techniques. These BI publications are usually short studies of practical interest to firms actively concerned with foreign management and markets; others may find them too expensive to purchase but possibly can locate them in a large business library that subscribes. BI periodicals and their 2 reference services are described elsewhere in this chapter; their Compensation Surveys are listed in Chapter 19; their new computer service, *BI/DATA,* in Chapter 6. Several examples of their research reports are: "Solving Accounting Problems for Worldwide Operations" (1974); "Worldwide Executive Compensation" (1974); "Germany in the 70's" (1973). Their *Management Monographs* are brief analyses of how companies solve particular problems, e.g., No. 54, "Solving Joint Venture Problems" (1972); No. 57, "Improving Capital-Liability Structure (1972). For further information contact the publisher.

Foreign Commerce Handbook. 17th ed. Washington, D.C., Chamber of Commerce of the United States, 1975 or early 1976.

This is a useful and inexpensive guide to foreign commerce sources and to basic information, recently updated to include all the new material published since the earlier (1967) edition. The bibliographic section is a list (by title) of books, periodicals and reference works on foreign trade and related economic matters. The other sections describe the foreign trade service of governmental and nongovernmental organizations; provide information on kinds and sources of information by specific topic; list chambers of commerce, embassies, and other useful data.

Goldstucker, Jac L. and Jose R. de la Torre, Jr. *International Marketing.* (AMA Bibliographic Series, 19). Chicago, American Marketing Association, 1972.

A selected, annotated bibliography of articles published 1960–1972, arranged by topic. Three out of the seven sections cover environmental influences, multinational marketing management, area studies. A short list of basic books is at end.

Hostettler, Pierre and Vincent P. Luchsinger. *Bibliography of International/Comparative Business: Management and Organizations.* (Exchange Bibliographies, Nos. 706–708). Monticello, Ill., Council of Planning Librarians, 1974. 2 volumes.

Comprehensive bibliography of books, proceedings, theses, articles, written both in English and in foreign languages, 1960 to mid-1972, usually with brief key-word annotations. The first volume is the author listing; Vol. 2 lists reference works, periodicals, and has a subject and geographic index.

International Executive. Hastings-on-Hudson, N.Y., Foundation for the Advancement of International Business Administration (3/yr.).

An important continuing bibliography and abstracting journal in 2 parts. The first part abstracts current books of note, selected articles, published research projects useful for international management. The second half is an annotated "Reference Guide," which describes books, pamphlets, articles of interest to the international businessman. It is arranged by broad management function, with the last section listing background sources on specific regions and countries.

Lall, Sanjaya. *Foreign Private Manufacturing Investment and Multinational Corporations: An Annotated Bibliography.* New York, Praeger, 1975.

A useful, annotated bibliography of books and articles on private foreign direct investment in the manufacturing sector. It is arranged in 15 subject categories, including conflict between MNCs and nation-states, government policies, organization and management, labor relations, industry and firm studies, area studies.

The Conference Board, in New York City, publishes a number of studies on international economics and international management, for example: *Conference Board Report* No. 597, "Organization and Control of International Operations" (1973); No. 635, "Evolving Corporate Policy and Organization for East-West Trade" (1974); No. 656, "Foreign Investment and Employment: An Examination of Foreign Investments to Make 58 Products Overseas" (1975). An index of their publications is described in Chapter 11 of this book.

DICTIONARIES

Schultz, Harry D. *Financial Tactics and Terms for the Sophisticated International Investor.* New York, Harper & Row, 1974.

Definitions run from one sentence to several pages, and they include basic investment terms and descriptions of organizations as well as international terms.

TAX AND TRADE GUIDES FOR SPECIFIC COUNTRIES

Several of the largest accounting firms compile information guides about those countries in which they do business. These are described below along with a few other similar services. The basic sources for international statistics and current economic trends in foreign countries are listed in Chapter 6.

Arthur Andersen & Co. *Tax and Trade Guide Series.* Chicago.

Separate guides for over 20 countries giving basic information on the government of each, types of business organizations, taxes, labor and social laws, banking, finance and incentives.

Bureau of National Affairs. *International Trade Reporter: Export Shipping Manual.* Washington, D.C. 2 volumes (weekly service).

A compendium of useful shipping facts concerning 180 countries, including ports and shipping routes, principal imports and exports, tariff system, shipping regulations, postal information and rates, labeling, warehousing, government information offices, major banks, travel requirements.

Business International. *Investing, Licensing & Trading Conditions Abroad.* New York (loose-leaf service, with monthly supplements).

For each country, these analyses usually give current information on the state's role in industry, organizing for foreign investments, rules of competition, price controls, licensing, corporate and personal taxes, incentives, capital sources, labor, foreign trade.

Commerce Clearing House. *Doing Business in Europe.* Chicago (loose-leaf service).

For each European country this gives information on foreign investment, forms of doing business, tax provisions, business incentives, industrial property (including patents and trademark law), basic labor legislation, arbitration procedures, environmental rules, competitive rules, court systems. This is published as Vol. 3 of the CCH *Common Market Reporter.*

Coopers & Lybrand. *International Reference Manual.* New York (loose-leaf).

Brief information on foreign countries, giving descriptions of those factors (business, political, social and economic) that affect the operations of international business in that country. Includes accounting requirements, tax systems.

Diamond, Walter H. *Foreign Tax and Trade Briefs.* New York, Matthew Bender. 2 volumes (loose-leaf).

Basic data on taxation and trading laws for the principal countries of the world where American capital is frequently invested.

Ernst & Ernst. *International Business Series.* New York.

Separate booklets on 22 countries summarizing various factors that affect trade and investment in each country, with special attention given to the national profile, characteristics of business entities, principal taxes. There are also special reports, bulletins and tax bulletins published periodically to supplement these country booklets.

Europa Year Book. London, Europa Publications (annual).

An international encyclopedia, with Vol. 1 covering international organizations and Europe; Vol. 2 covering Africa, the Americas, Asia and Australasia. For each country, data includes recent history, basic economic statistics, constitution, government, political parties, religion; also lists of the various media (newspapers, periodicals, publishers, radio and TV stations), financial institutions (banks, insurance companies, stock exchanges), trade and industrial organizations (chambers of commerce, trade associations, employer's associations, trade unions, trade fairs), railroads, shipping companies, airlines, universities. Europa also publishes 3 regional yearbooks: *Africa South of the Sahara*; *The Far East and Australasia*; *The Middle East and North Africa*. These give much the same sort of directory information as well as concise data about the geography, the government, basic economic statistics, and a "Who's Who" section for information on prominent people in the countries covered by each yearbook.

Price Waterhouse & Co. *Information Guide for Doing Business in (name of country)*. New York.

Separate booklets giving concise information about the commercial entities, accounting methods, taxes, labor legislation, etc., in about 60 countries.

Touche Ross International. *Business Study*. New York.

Covers only 10 countries but the pamphlets for each are longer than several of the series above, and they include general information, investment factors, labor conditions, business practices and customs, forms of business entities, accounting and auditing, taxation. A separate series called *Executive Digest* contains brief reference data on labor conditions, accounting and auditing, tax structure for 9 countries.

U.S. Domestic and International Business Administration, Department of Commerce. *Overseas Business Reports*. Washington, D.C., U.S. Government Printing Office.

A series of useful reports for about 100 countries, with varying titles such as "Marketing in (name of country)"; Selling in . . . "; "Doing Business in . . . ." The data in each varies but usually includes information about form of business organization, trade regulations, tariff, taxation, trademarks, credit, labor force, foreign trade outlook, market outlook; also sources of economic and commercial information.

Tax Guides and Services

Auderieth, Steven and Elmer M. Pergament. *Tax Guide to International Operations*. Greenvale, N.Y., Panel Publishers, 1971. 2 volumes (loose-leaf, with 3/yr. supplements).

Vol. 1 contains important information on the U.S. tax system as applied to international operations (foreign tax credit, controlled foreign corporations, foreign exchange, employment abroad, etc.); Vol. 2 covers methods of operating abroad (DISCs, foreign direct investment, foreign tax havens, etc.).

European Taxation. Amsterdam, International Bureau of Fiscal Documentation (monthly).

A journal for articles "designed to present basic and objective studies of the tax structure of European countries." A biweekly loose-leaf *Tax News Service* is received with this monthly. The IBFD also publishes: *Supplementary Service to European Taxation* (7 loose-leaf volumes, with monthly supplements), which gives tax rates, tax treaties, abstracts from official reports, a worldwide bibliography of new tax documents and publications; *Guides to European Taxation* (loose-leaf); *Bulletin for International Fiscal Documentation* (monthly).

Institute for International Research. *International Tax Report.* London (bi-weekly).

A short news report on recent developments in international taxation.

Prentice-Hall, Inc. *U.S. Taxation of International Operations.* Englewood Cliffs, N.J. (semi-monthly).

Analyses written by leading international tax practitioners to give practical ideas and techniques for a tax-saving program. The principal sections are for tax ideas, planning, operations.

Commerce Clearing House publishes a number of Canadian, Mexican and Venezuelan tax guides as well as a 3-volume *British Tax Guide.* In March 1976 CCH will begin publication of a 5-volume loose-leaf *Income Taxes Worldwide,* which will contain an overview of the income tax structure of more than 100 countries, revised periodically. Both CCH and PH have loose-leaf services giving the text of *Tax Treaties,* the former in 2 volumes and the latter in one volume.

REFERENCE DATA FOR EXPORTERS

Sources for foreign statistics and foreign economic trends are described in Chapter 6.

Bureau of National Affairs. *International Trade Reporter: U.S. Export Weekly.* Washington, D.C.

Current news about legislation, regulations, international negotiations, court decisions, tariff, tax, foreign investment, international monetary developments, etc. Gives text of legislation and other documents and includes periodic "Special Reports." The other part of this service, *Export Shipping Manual,* is described in the previous section.

Business International. *Financing Foreign Operations.* New York (loose-leaf, with semi-monthly supplements).

Section 3 covers domestic financing for each country that lends funds, and it includes information on the monetary system, sources of capital, long-, medium-, and short-term financing techniques, capital incentives, public stock and bond financing, export insurance and credit. Part 1 covers general financial techniques; Part 2 deals with cross-border financing. A bimonthly "FFO Updater and Forecasts of Interest Rates" is included.

Commerce Clearing House. *Balance of Payments Reporter.* Chicago (loose-leaf).

Up-to-date information about developments in the various phases of the administration's Balance of Payments Program, including foreign investment, repatriation of earnings, overseas lending, import-export measures, government overseas spending, interest equalization tax, travel.

Commerce Clearing House. *Common Market Reporter.* Chicago. 3 volumes (loose-leaf).

Vols. 1-2 provide information on the pertinent laws, regulations, rulings and decisions needed to guide firms doing business in Common Market countries. Vol. 3, "Doing Business in Europe," is described in the previous section.

Croner's Reference Book for World Traders. Comp. by Ulrich H. E. Croner. New York, Croner Publications, Inc. 2 volumes (loose-leaf, with monthly supplements).

This service is designed as a handy guide to information about foreign countries for persons in international trade and market research. Data for each country includes facts about the economy and commerce, lists of consulates, banks, commercial periodicals, associations, market research organizations, statistics sources, trade directories, export documents. The first part of Vol. 1 contains information sources in the United States, foreign import and export controls, postal information, shipping and airline directories.

Custom House Guide. New York (annual).

A basic reference volume in 6 parts. Part 1, "Ports Section," gives data for the principal U.S. ports (customs and port authority officials, description of the port, directory of custom house brokers, steamship lines and agents, truckmen, warehouses, etc.). Part 2, "General Information," includes a directory of foreign freight forwarders, bonded common carriers, airlines, etc. Part 3 is an alphabetical import commodity index, giving TSUS item number and rate of duty for each commodity. Part 4 gives the text of the Tariff Schedules of the U.S. Annotated (TSUSA); Parts 5-6 have U.S. Customs regulations. Included with this volume is a monthly *American Import & Export Bulletin,* which contains current customs regulations, news of important export activities and a few short feature articles.

Exporter's Encyclopedia. New York, Dun & Bradstreet (annual, with semi-monthly supplements).

A comprehensive world marketing reference guide, in 5 sections. Section 2, "Export Markets," gives important market information for specific countries (import and exchange regulations, shipping services, communications data, postal information, currency, banks, embassies, and so forth). Other sections contain general export information (for example, laws, legal aspects); export and shipping practice; reference data (communications information, weights and measures, time charts, description of U.S. ports); names of government agencies, trade associations, chambers of commerce, overseas ports and trade centers. A semi-monthly news sheet, *World Marketing,* is received with this annual.

Rand McNally & Co. *Commercial Atlas & Marketing Guide.* Chicago (annual).

A popular atlas, with maps for each state in the United States and a shorter section for maps of foreign countries. Includes useful marketing statistics for states and some worldwide data, such as population, airline and steamship distances. A *Road Atlas* covering the United States, Canada and Mexico is received with this and includes city and metropolitan area maps.

The Times, London. *The Times Atlas of the World.* Comprehensive ed.: 2d ed., rev. London, Times Newspaper Ltd.; Boston, Houghton Mifflin, 1971.

This atlas is especially good for its coverage of foreign countries.

U.S. Department of State. *United States Treaties and Other International Agree-*

ments. Washington, D.C., U.S. Government Printing Office. Vol. 1, 1950 to date.

Compilation of text for individual treaties and international agreements, arranged in the numerical order in which they were originally published in pamphlet form in the *Treaties and Other International Acts Series* (TIAS). The Department of State also publishes an annual *Treaties in Force* and other related publications.

U.S. International Trade Commission. *Tariff Schedules of the United States Annotated.* Washington, D.C., U.S. Government Printing Office (issued irregularly, with supplementary sheets).

A classified list of commodities, giving rates of duty. An alphabetical index is at end. The ITC (formerly the Tariff Commission) has also published *The Tariff Schedules of the United States Converted into the Format of the Brussels Tariff Nomenclature* (Washington, D.C., 1973, 9 volumes), useful for comparative purposes because the BTN is the standardized product classification system used by most trading nations of the world.

U.S. Office of Export Administration, Department of Commerce. *Export Administration Regulations.* Washington, D.C., U.S. Government Printing Office (annual, with irregular updates).

A loose-leaf compilation of official export control regulations, with instructions, interpretations and explanatory material. Current changes are announced in their *Export Administration Bulletins.*

INTERNATIONAL MANAGEMENT PERIODICALS

Several foreign management journals, such as *The Director, European Business,* and *Management International Review,* are included in Chapter 10.

Business International. New York (weekly).

An 8-page weekly report for managers of worldwide operations, providing current news about companies; recent developments in laws and practices relating to such topics as taxes, licensing, capital sources, politics, and profitability; worldwide and regional trends and news about specific countries; checklists and occasional statistical tables. BI publishes similar weeklies for managers in particular regions: *Business Asia*; *Business Europe*; *Business Latin America*; also *Eastern Europe Report* (semi-monthly). Their new weekly for international financial executives, *Business International Money Report,* is an 8-page news sheet about the international capital market, currency exchange rates, interest rates, credit controls, and related subjects.

Columbia Journal of World Business. New York, Columbia University (quarterly).

A good selection of articles on current issues and trends of interest to anyone with responsibilities and interests in international business. Current issues usually focus on a particular area, e.g., energy, finance, manpower. Indexed in BPI, F&S, PAIS.

Commerce America. Washington, D.C., U.S. Department of Commerce (biweekly). Order from U.S. Government Printing Office.

Current news on the economy, domestic and international business, energy management. Each issue contains an "International Commerce Report" and also data on "Worldwide Business Opportunities" (licensing and joint venture proposals, direct sales, future construction abroad, exhibitions). An annual "Special World Trade

Outlook Issue" (e.g., Jan. 20, 1975) gives brief information about individual countries. Indexed in BPI, F&S. Former title was *Commerce Today.*

Euromoney. London, Euromoney Publications, Ltd. (monthly).

Articles and news about the European money market, with statistics on Eurodollar rates, interest rates, exchange rates. Contains a quarterly currency review; also short, annotated booklists in each issue. Indexed in PAIS.

Finance and Development. Washington, D.C., International Monetary Fund and the International Bank for Reconstruction and Development (quarterly).

This periodical is published in English, French, German and Spanish editions. It contains short articles on the title subjects and includes book reviews. Indexed in BPI, F&S, PAIS.

Financial Times. London (daily).

An important British financial newspaper covering financial and investment news, world trade, labor news, etc., for the United Kingdom and Europe. Includes current commodity prices, statistics on the money market, stock prices.

International Currency Review. London (bimonthly).

Specializes in economic and monetary affairs, with every issue including currency reviews for each of the principal currencies. Indexed in PAIS.

International Management. London, McGraw-Hill International Publications Co. (monthly).

Short, practical articles on current problems in a wide range of management topics, many detailing experiences of specific companies or techniques used in one country. Indexed in BPI, PAIS.

International Monetary Fund. *IMF Survey.* Washington, D.C. (semi-monthly).

Each issue usually contains information on IMF activities, national economies, brief notes about financial and economic news developments, and one article on a topic of interest. It is published in English, French and Spanish. The IMF also publishes *Staff Papers* (3/yr.), which contains lengthy research papers on international monetary policies and problems. The 2 statistical publications of the IMF are described in Chapter 6.

Journal of International Business Studies. Atlanta, Academy of International Business and the School of Business Administration, Georgia State University (semi-annual).

Excellent, scholarly articles, primarily by academicians and focusing on issues in management, public policy, research and education in international business.

Journal of International Economics. Amsterdam, North Holland Publishing Co. (quarterly).

"The principal outlet for analytical work in the pure theory of international trade and in balance of payments analysis, and also for institutional, empirical and econometric work of high quality." Includes book reviews. Indexed in SSI.

Journal of World Trade Law. Twickenham, Middlesex, England (6/yr.).

Well-documented research papers of wide interest on international trade, monetary policies, antitrust policy, environmental problems, etc.

Law and Policy in International Business. Washington, D.C., Georgetown University Law Center (quarterly).

Scholarly articles on a broad range of topics, with a legal focus. Includes also recent legislative developments and book reviews. Indexed in PAIS.

Multinational Business. London, Economist Intelligence Unit (quarterly).

About 2 or 3 articles in each issue on international management, foreign investments, finance, etc.; also news of interest to the international businessman, and occasional charts. The EIU also publishes quarterly or monthly reviews of specific countries and industries, which are described in Chapter 6.

Trade and Industry. London, H.M. Stationery Office (weekly).

This incorporates the former *Board of Trade Journal* and gives trade and tariff news, news about exhibitions and fairs, the European Communities as well as "home news." Current basic economic statistics are in each issue and include U.K. balance of payments figures. Indexed in F&S.

World Financial Markets. New York, Morgan Guaranty Trust Co. of New York (monthly).

A short newsletter, with up-to-date statistics, by country, for international government and corporate bond yields, new international bond issues, rates for Eurodollar deposits, Treasury bills, etc.

DIRECTORIES

Most directories of interest to the international businessman are described elsewhere in this book. Chapter 3 includes directories of U.S., multinational, and foreign subsidiaries of U.S. companies. Financial manuals for foreign companies are in Chapter 7; directories of foreign banks in Chapter 14; directories for foreign market research firms in Chapter 18. *Europa Year Book,* an international encyclopedia described elsewhere in this chapter, includes for each country the names of chambers of commerce, trade associations, trade fairs, as well as banks, railways, shipping companies and airlines. It also lists the most important international organizations.

U.S. Department of State. *Foreign Service List.* Washington, D.C., U.S. Government Printing Office (3/yr.).

A directory, by country, of U.S. personnel in foreign service, including consuls, attachés, U.S. Information Agency, Agency for International Development, Armed Forces.

Yearbook of International Organizations. Brussels, Union of International Associations.

A useful, descriptive directory of international organizations, usually giving top officers, aim, structure, activities, funding, publications, total staff members. Includes several indexes (by subject, key word, English or French name). Available also in a French edition.

ASSOCIATIONS

American Importers Association, 420 Lexington Avenue, New York, N.Y. 10017.

American Society of International Executives, 734 Land Title Building, Philadelphia, Pa. 19110.

Bankers Association for Foreign Trade, 1101 16th Street, N.W., Washington, D.C. 20036.

International Council for Scientific Management, 1 rue de Varembé, 1211 Geneva, Switzerland (an international federation of management associations in 40 countries, U.S. affiliate of which is: Council for International Progress in Management, 135 West 50th Street, New York, N.Y. 10020).

International Executives Association, One World Trade Center, New York, N.Y. 10048.

National Foreign Trade Council, 10 Rockefeller Plaza, New York, N.Y. 10020.

United States Council of the International Chambers of Commerce, 1212 Avenue of the Americas, New York, N.Y. 10036.

17

MANAGEMENT SCIENCE AND STATISTICAL METHODS

Mathematics for Management — Mathematical Tables — Probability and Statistics — Decision-Making and Decision Theory — Statistical Abstracting Services — Statistical Dictionaries — Mathematical and Statistical Periodicals — Directories of Statisticians — Mathematical and Statistical Associations — Quantitative Methods and Operations Research — Operations Research Abstracts — Operations Research Periodicals — Operations Research Associations

The importance of quantitative techniques and statistical analysis in making managerial decisions is already well known. Use of this scientific approach in solving business problems developed rapidly following World War II. As computer capabilities increased, new and more sophisticated mathematical and statistical techniques were devised, and the application of these techniques brought revolutionary changes in all areas of business where decisions are made. In today's fast-paced business world probably the most important factor in effective corporate performance is the quality of decisions made. Thus, the administrator who is unfamiliar with the concepts, techniques and language of mathematics and statistics is at a decided disadvantage. This chapter lists a selection of books and reference sources that executives may find useful in learning how to solve problems and to make decisions. First are the names of several basic mathematics books that may be useful before reading books on the subjects that follow — probability and statistics, decision-making and decision theory and, finally, operations research (sometimes called "management science"). Many of these books include problems with each chapter as a teaching aid. For books on computers, systems analysis and management information systems see Chapter 13.

MATHEMATICS FOR MANAGEMENT

Bashaw, W. L. *Mathematics for Statistics.* New York, Wiley, 1969.

"Written to provide the arithmetic and mathematics background that is essential to the learning of introductory applied statistics." Can be used for self-study by a highly motivated person. Its 5 parts cover: basic arithmetic refresher; basic algebra refresher; basic matrix algebra; set algebra and probability; miscellaneous skills.

Childress, Robert L. *Mathematics for Managerial Decisions.* Englewood Cliffs, N.J., Prentice-Hall, 1974.

Provides "an introduction to the important quantitative tools of sets, matrices, linear programming, calculus, and probability in a manner that permits the nonmathematically inclined students to . . . grasp the basic mathematical concepts." Includes examples that apply to business administration, suggested readings, and has logarithms and mathematical tables in an appendix. Professor Childress has also written a book on *Calculus for Business and Economics* (Prentice-Hall, 1972). Both books presume a knowledge of college algebra.

Cissell, Robert and Helen Cissell. *Mathematics of Finance.* 4th ed. Boston, Houghton Mifflin, 1973.

A recently revised standard introduction to mathematics used in modern business administration, for students of economics or business. Requires either a college or a good high school algebra course. The authors begin by discussing simple and compound interest and then proceed to bank discount annuities, amortization and sinking funds, bonds, capital budgeting and depreciation, life insurance and stocks. Practical problems are used throughout to illustrate the applications of formulas and tables. A good selection of mathematical tables is at end.

A similar book is *Mathematics of Finance* by Paul M. Hummel and Charles L. Seebeck, Jr. (3d ed., New York, McGraw-Hill, 1971), although it lacks a chapter on capital budgeting.

Dyckman, Thomas R. and L. Joseph Thomas. *Algebra and Calculus for Business.* Englewood Cliffs, N.J., Prentice-Hall, 1974.

An "introduction to the basic mathematical skills required for the study of managerial problems." Can be used either as a text or as a refresher course for self-study. Presumes a knowledge of high school algebra.

Howell, James E. and Daniel Teichroew. *Mathematical Analysis for Business Decisions.* Rev. ed. Homewood, Ill., Irwin, 1971.

Written for the student or business practitioner who needs to learn enough about the possible uses of modern mathematics to read the literature and understand recent developments in the several fields of business.

Kemeny, John G., Arthur Schleifer, Jr., J. Laurie Snell and Gerald L. Thompson. *Finite Mathematics, with Business Applications.* 2d ed. Englewood Cliffs, N.J., Prentice-Hall, 1972.

An introduction to finite mathematics and its applications to business and administration problems. Covers statements and sets, counting problems, probability theory, vectors and matrices, linear programming, decision theory and analysis, mathematics of finance, Markov decision processes, theory of games. Includes mathematical tables and suggested readings. Presupposes at least 2½ years of high school mathematics.

Martin, E. Wainright, Jr. *Mathematics for Decision Making: A Programmed Basic Text.* Homewood, Ill., Irwin, 1969. 2 volumes.

An excellent programmed text for the motivated but nonmathematical student who wants "to learn the mathematics that is most important in making decisions, in studying topics associated with decision making, and in communicating with specialists in model building." Vol. 1 covers linear mathematics, and Vol. 2, calculus. It is "designed to require a background of two years of high school algebra in which you didn't do too well." A few bibliographic references are at end of each chapter.

Snyder, Llewellyn R. and William F. Jackson. *Essential Business Mathematics.* 6th ed. New York, McGraw-Hill, 1972.

Covers the mathematical essentials needed for subsequent courses in accounting, finance, retailing, etc. Part 1 covers basic business arithmetic, and Part 2, the essentials of business mathematics.

MATHEMATICAL TABLES

These are just two of the many reference volumes devoted exclusively to providing mathematical and statistical tables and mathematical formulas. A few useful tables and formulas are also found in the appendixes of some textbooks listed in this chapter. For several books of banking and financial tables see Chapter 14.

Burington, Richard S. *Handbook of Mathematical Tables and Formulas.* 5th ed. New York, McGraw-Hill, 1973.

Designed as an aid in any field where mathematical reasoning, processes and computations are required. Formulas, definitions and theorems from elementary mathematics are in Part 1; Part 2 contains tables of logarithms, square root, interest, etc. Includes a bibliography and glossary of symbols. This book serves as a companion to *Handbook of Probability and Statistics with Tables* by Burington and Donald C. May (2d ed., McGraw-Hill, 1970).

Selby, Samuel M., ed. *CRC Standard Mathematical Tables.* 23d ed. Cleveland, Ohio, Chemical Rubber Co., 1975.

Covers a wide range of formulas and tables, including algebra of sets, determinants and matrices, logarithm tables, calculus, probability and statistics, binomial distribution, and financial tables.

PROBABILITY AND STATISTICS

Since this author is far from an expert on the contents of books in this chapter, much reliance has been placed on book prefaces in describing contents and especially in stating the degree of mathematical expertise necessary for understanding each. For persons who may be confused by some of the terms used, all of these books explain the various techniques. Professor Hamburg in his *Basic Statistics,* for example, gives a short, simple explanation (pp. 4–5) of the difference between descriptive statistics and statistical inference (or inductive statistics), and he also explains such terms as "Bayesian decision theory."

Anson, Cyril J. *Profit from Figures: A Manager's Guide to Statistical Methods.* London and New York, McGraw-Hill, 1971.

A clearly written book by a British consultant, which is "designed as a simple guide to the practising manager on how he can make figures talk, how he can use them to make a bigger profit." Includes a glossary and a short reading list.

Boot, John C. G. and Edwin B. Cox. *Statistical Analysis for Managerial Decisions.* 2d ed. New York, McGraw-Hill, 1974.

An introduction to statistical reasoning and the primary statistical techniques used in solving managerial problems, with only a good knowledge of high school mathematics required. Organized in 3 sections: basic concepts of descriptive statistics, probability, and principal probability distributions in statistics; important concepts and techniques of inferential statistics, including discussion of Bayesian inference; topics relevant to business and economic research (time series analysis, index numbers, statistical methods for quality assurance, design of sample surveys, nonparametric statistics). Appendix includes mathematical tables and a short but useful annotated bibliography.

Freund, John E. and Frank J. Williams. *Elementary Business Statistics: The Modern Approach.* 2d ed. Englewood Cliffs, N.J., Prentice-Hall, 1972.

Expanded edition of a good basic text on the techniques, theories and tools of statistics in decision-making and operations analysis, requiring only an elementary mathematical background. There are chapters on probability, sampling, decision-making employing various statistical techniques (6 chapters); also a chapter on planning business research and on operations research. Includes statistical tables and a bibliography. Professor Freund has also written an *Introduction to Probability* (Encino, Calif., Dickenson Publishing Co., 1973).

Hamburg, Morris. *Basic Statistics: A Modern Approach.* New York, Harcourt Brace Jovanovich, 1974.

This first course in statistics is a shortened and more informal version of Professor Hamburg's *Statistical Analysis for Decision Making* (Harcourt, Brace & World, 1970). It covers descriptive statistics, probability, statistical inference and statistical decision theory. It was written for students of business and public administration and assumes only a modest mathematical background. Includes mathematical tables and a bibliography.

Neter, John, William Wasserman and G. A. Whitmore. *Fundamental Statistics for Business and Economics.* 4th ed. Boston, Allyn and Bacon, 1973.

A good, standard introductory text for students of business, public administration and economics, with only a knowledge of high school algebra required. Coverage is similar to other beginning texts, and many actual case applications are used in explaining specific statistical methods. Includes mathematical tables.

Schlaifer, Robert. *Probability and Statistics for Business Decisions: An Introduction to Managerial Economics Under Uncertainty.* New York, McGraw-Hill, 1959.

This is a classic nonmathematical introduction to probability and statistics that is Bayesian and decision oriented. "The analysis which it recommends is based on the modern theory of utility and what has come to be known as the 'personal' definition of probability; the author believes, in other words, that when the consequences of various possible courses of action depend on some unpredictable event, the *practical* way of choosing the 'best' act is to assign values to consequences and probabilities to events and then to select the act with the highest expected value." Professor Schlaifer, who pioneered the development of decision-making for the business manager, has also written an *Introduction to Statistics for Business Decisions* (McGraw-Hill, 1961), which covers both classical and Bayesian statistics.

Spurr, William A. and Charles P. Bonini. *Statistical Analysis for Business Decisions.* Rev. ed. Homewood, Ill., Irwin, 1973.

Another good, standard text that emphasizes the use of scientific method in analyzing practical business and economic problems. The authors divide the text roughly into 6 parts: basic tools of analysis (ratios, averages, dispersion measures); probability theory and the principal probability distributions; tests of hypotheses; Bayes' theorem and sampling; regression and correlation techniques; index numbers, time series and seasonal variations. Includes annotated bibliographies, mathematical tables. Most of this book requires only elementary algebra.

Two other introductory texts are: *Basic Statistics* by Dick A. Leabo (4th ed., Homewood, Ill., Irwin, 1972); and *Statistical Techniques in Business and Economics* by Robert D. Mason (Homewood, Ill., Irwin, 1974).

DECISION-MAKING AND DECISION THEORY

Benton, John B. *Managing the Organizational Decision Process.* Lexington, Mass., D. C. Heath, 1973.

Examines "the keys to a successful organizational experience with the newer techniques of planning, analysis, and decision making" in such a way as to clarify some of the difficulties encountered and to give more awareness to the "human and institutional environment in which organizational decision-making takes place." Includes theory but also has many real examples to describe and support key arguments, and it also has a bibliography.

Marvin, Philip. *Developing Decisions for Action.* Homewood, Ill., Dow Jones-Irwin, 1971.

A concise and practical discussion of factors that make for effective decision-making, based on lessons Marvin learned from long experience as an administrator. His style is informal and he includes many examples to support his thesis.

Newman, Joseph W. *Management Applications of Decision Theory.* New York, Harper & Row, 1971.

"Written for the student of management, in school or out, who would like to find out what Bayesian decision theory is and what is involved in applying it. The focus is on practical applications under real-life circumstances, a feature that distinguishes the book from most writings on the subject." The main portion describes applications of the Bayesian approach, some requiring use of a computer. Presupposes a course in basic algebra.

Odiorne, George S. *Management Decisions by Objectives.* Englewood Cliffs, N.J., Prentice-Hall, 1969.

A practical guide to help managers make better decisions, written by a pioneer in developing the management by objectives technique. Surveys theory, methods and tools in simple language; includes a short, annotated reading list.

Raiffa, Howard. *Decision Analysis: Introductory Lectures on Choices Under Uncertainty.* Reading, Mass., Addison-Wesley, 1968.

Professor Raiffa's informal style and studied effort to keep the mathematical demands to a minimum make this an excellent book for independent reading by anyone who has to make important decisions. His approach is that of Bayesians who, in their analysis, take explicit account of the risk inherent in any possible course of action (expressed as "subjective probabilities") and the decision maker's attitude toward taking risk (expressed as "utilities"). This book starts with a simple noncontroversial problem and proceeds by introducing complicated features into this decision problem one at a time.

Schlaifer, Robert. *Analysis of Decisions Under Uncertainty.* New York, McGraw-Hill, 1969.

An excellent nonstatistical introduction to logical analysis of the problems of decision under uncertainty, intended for the business decision maker, not the mathematician. Primarily concerned with large-scale problems and emphasizes the use of digital computers to solve many problems. It is in 3 parts: basic principles; basic methods for arriving at preferences and probabilities; special problems involving acquisition and use of information obtained by sampling or experimentation. Includes mathematical tables. Professor Schlaifer's 2 earlier books are listed in the previous section of this chapter.

Weisselberg, Robert C. and Joseph G. Cowley. *The Executive Strategist: An Armchair Guide to Scientific Decision-Making.* New York, McGraw-Hill, 1969.

"This is not a technical text but an easy-to-read guide to scientific decision-making, written by authors who are themselves management-oriented rather than technical specialists, for the executive who is assumed to have little or no specialized training in the subject." It is written with a light touch and includes diagrams and a bibliography.

STATISTICAL ABSTRACTING SERVICES

Quality Control and Applied Statistics. Whippany, N.J., Executive Sciences Institute (monthly loose-leaf service).

A digesting service for articles on applied statistics, classified by specific topic. Includes statement of purpose for each article, also summary and results obtained.

Statistical Theory and Method Abstracts. Edinburgh, published for International Statistical Institute by Longman Group Ltd. (quarterly).

Abstracts, in English, of articles in worldwide journals, reports, proceedings, and classified within 12 main sections: mathematical methods; probability; frequency distributions; sampling distributions, estimation; hypothesis testing; relationships; variance analysis; sampling design; design of experiment; stochastic processes and time series; miscellaneous and special topics. Each issue is printed so as to allow users either to split issues according to section (each is a different color) or to clip the abstracts for filing in a loose-leaf binder by author or by subsection.

STATISTICAL DICTIONARIES

Kendall, Maurice G. and William R. Buckland. *A Dictionary of Statistical Terms.* 3d ed., rev. and enl. New York, Hafner; Edinburgh, Oliver & Boyd, 1971.

A useful, authoritative dictionary defining statistical terms in current usage. Compiled by 2 British statistical experts and published under the auspices of the International Statistical Institute.

MATHEMATICAL AND STATISTICAL PERIODICALS

American Statistical Association. *Journal* (also called *JASA*). Washington, D.C. (quarterly).

Excellent, authoritative articles by professors and statisticians, with most articles giving bibliographic citations. Each issue is in 2 parts: "Applications"; and "Theory and Methods" — with greater attention given the latter part. Includes good, critical book reviews, and a list of technical reports available. Indexed in BPI, PAIS.

American Statistician. Washington, D.C., American Statistical Association (quarterly).

Short, practical articles on statistics of special interest to statistical educators. Indexed in PAIS.

Annals of Probability and **Annals of Statistics.** Baltimore, Md., Institute of Mathematical Statistics (bimonthly).

Each of these bimonthlies publishes original contributions, one on the theory of probability and the other on the theory of statistics.

Decision Sciences. Atlanta, Ga., American Institute for Decision Sciences (quarterly).

Research papers by academic persons covering concepts, theory and techniques of decision sciences; applications and implementation; education; communications.

Industrial Mathematics. Detroit, Mich., Industrial Mathematics Society (semi-annual).

Usually 4 to 6 technical articles in each issue on the application of mathematics in industry.

International Statistical Review. Edinburgh, published for the International Statistical Institute by Longman Group Ltd. (3/yr.).

Each issue is in 2 parts: the first contains about 6 to 8 research papers and an occasional bibliography; the second covers news of statistical activity of organizations and societies, statistical training and research, calendar of meetings, book reviews, and so forth.

Royal Statistical Society. *Journal.* Series A,B,C. London.

"Series A (General)" is a quarterly containing scholarly articles by academicians. It includes book reviews, table of contents for other statistical journals, a list of library accessions. Indexed in PAIS.

"Series B (Methodological)" covers methodological research of interest to statisticians (3/yr.).

Series C is published separately as *Applied Statistics* (3/yr.). It contains authoritative papers reporting on statistical research of interest to science, industry, agriculture, etc., and it includes book reviews.

Society for Industrial and Applied Mathematics. *SIAM Review.* Philadelphia, Pa., (quarterly).

Devoted primarily to expository and survey papers in applied mathematics. Includes book reviews; also sections on problems and solutions. This society publishes 7 other journals including *SIAM Journal of Applied Mathematics* (8/yr.).

DIRECTORIES OF STATISTICIANS

Statisticians and Others in Allied Professions. Washington, D.C., American Statistical Association (triennial).

A directory of the combined memberships of the ASA, the Biometric Society, and the Institute of Mathematical Statistics.

MATHEMATICAL AND STATISTICAL ASSOCIATIONS

American Institute for Decision Sciences, University Plaza, Atlanta, Ga. 30303.

American Statistical Association, 806 15th Street, N.W., Washington, D.C. 20005.

Industrial Mathematics Society, P.O. Box 159, Roseville, Mich. 48066.

International Statistical Institute, 428 Prinses Beatrixlaan, Voorburg, Netherlands.

Royal Statistical Society, 21 Bentinck Street, London W1M 6AR, England.

Society for Industrial and Applied Mathematics, 33 South 17th Street, Philadelphia, Pa. 19103.

QUANTITATIVE METHODS AND OPERATIONS RESEARCH

The terms "management science" and "operations research" are often used interchangeably in the literature that studies the application of quantitative methods to solving management problems. This is a selection of several general books on the subject. A few books that discuss quantitative methods in marketing are in Chapter 18; for those in production and operations management see Chapter 20.

Ackoff, Russell L. and Maurice W. Sasieni. *Fundamentals of Operations Research.* New York, Wiley, 1968.

An introductory text that attempts "to reconcile a rigid mathematical treatment of the subject with a conceptually oriented qualitative treatment." Includes bibliographies. These authors are well-known authorities on operations research, having both been involved in the writing of early introductory works. Ackoff was joint author of the classic *Introduction to Operations Research* by C. West Churchman, Russell L. Ackoff and E. Leonard Arnoff (Wiley, 1957). He also wrote, with Patrick Rivett, an early nontechnical work called *A Manager's Guide to Operations Research* (Wiley, 1963). Sasieni wrote, with Arthur Yaspan and Lawrence Friedman, an early textbook on *Operations Research — Methods and Problems* (Wiley, 1959). Both this book and the Churchman text presume a knowledge of calculus.

Anderson, David R., Dennis J. Sweeney and Thomas A. Williams. *Linear Programming for Decision Making: An Applications Approach.* St. Paul, Minn., West Publishing Co., 1974.

As the title implies, this is an applications oriented introduction to linear programming, with college algebra a prerequisite. Problems and a glossary are at end of each chapter, and a selected, annotated bibliography is at end of book.

Bierman, Harold, Jr., Charles P. Bonini and Warren H. Hausman. *Quantitative Analysis for Business Decisions.* 4th ed. Homewood, Ill., Irwin, 1973.

An introduction to the use of quantitative techniques in dealing with difficult problems of business. Includes chapters on specific techniques and mathematical models such as linear programming, game theory, simulation, Markov processes. There are also problems, mathematical tables and a bibliography. Requires a general mathematical background.

Brinkloe, William D. *Managerial Operations Research.* New York, McGraw-Hill, 1969.

"Presents a wide range of quantitative management techniques in easily understood style, and aims at practical problems the real-life executive encounters every day."

Loomba, Narendra P. and Efraim Turban. *Applied Programming for Management.* New York, Holt, Rinehart & Winston, 1974.

The main focus of this introductory text on mathematical programming is on allocation models and their applications, and the algebra and math required is contained within the book. Chapters describe various linear, integer, nonlinear, and dynamic programming methods and include specific examples and applications. Bibliographies are with each chapter.

Miller, David W. and Martin K. Starr. *Executive Decisions and Operations Research.* 2d ed. Englewood Cliffs, N.J., Prentice-Hall, 1969.

Comprehensive examination of the structure of decision problems, written for the uninitiated, the business student and the executive. Some mathematics is required. It is in 5 parts: organizations and decisions; the theory of decision; the nature of models; decision-problem paradigms; the executive and operations research. Includes a bibliography arranged by specific topic.

Paik, C. M. *Quantitative Methods for Managerial Decisions.* New York, McGraw-Hill, 1973.

A text for graduate students in business and public administration, requiring only a high school level mathematics background. Paik's objective is "to provide an appreciation of the scientific, mathematical, and quantitative methods as 'formal' aids to managerial decision making."

Plane, Donald R. and Gary A. Kochenberger. *Operations Research for Managerial Decisions.* Homewood, Ill., Irwin, 1972.

The fundamentals of operations research, emphasizing techniques most useful in their application to managerial problems (decision theory, linear programming, waiting lines, simulation, etc.). Includes bibliographies. Requires algebra and some computer programming knowledge.

Siemens, Nicolai, C. H. Marting and Frank Greenwood. *Operations Research: Planning, Operating, and Information Systems.* New York, Free Press, 1973.

An upper-level or graduate systems text emphasizing "the pragmatic application of OR concepts to the solution of a broad range of problems in government, industry, health, urban planning, etc." In 3 parts: planning systems (discusses OR concepts in long-range planning and decision-making); operating systems (short-range decision-making techniques); management information systems. Includes problems and bibliographies at end of most chapters. Presumes a proficiency in algebra.

Wagner, Harvey M. *Principles of Management Science: With Applications to Executive Decisions.* 2d ed. Englewood Cliffs, N.J., Prentice-Hall, 1975.

This thorough, introductory book is written for potential managers, not for specialists, and it aims to answer the question "what are the *fundamental ideas* of management science?" Its chapters are organized by standard mathematical techniques including linear models, dynamic models, stochastic models. It assumes a standard college-level introductory calculus course and a finite math course. A short bibliography is at end, but a more complete bibliography is in Professor Wagner's newly revised and excellent *Principles of Operations Research: With Applications to Managerial Decisions* (2d ed., Prentice-Hall, 1975).

OPERATIONS RESEARCH ABSTRACTS

International Abstracts in Operations Research. Amsterdam, published for International Federation of Operational Research Societies by North Holland Publishing Co. (quarterly).

Abstracts (in English) of articles in worldwide journals, arranged by topic within 4 broad subject areas: models of common processes; experiment and special applications; theoretical; professional. Also includes sources for book reviews and a few books.

Operations Research/Management Science. Whippany, N.J., Executive Sciences Institute (monthly loose-leaf service).

A classified digesting service for articles on operations research that are in the most important journals. Includes statement of purpose for each article, also summary and results obtained.

OPERATIONS RESEARCH PERIODICALS

Interfaces. Providence, R.I., Institute of Management Sciences in cooperation with the Operations Research Society of America (quarterly).

Articles on the operational problems of using management science and operations research, meant to encourage interaction between managers and management science people. Includes occasional interviews, state-of-the-arts, book reviews.

Management Science. Providence, R.I., Institute of Management Sciences (monthly).

Significant articles reporting both on new methodological developments in management science and on the problems of developing and converting management theory to practice. Each issue concentrates either on theory or on application in rotating order. Indexed in BPI.

OMEGA. The International Journal of Management Science. Oxford, England, Pergamon (bimonthly).

Reports developments in management science, operational research and managerial economics, including research results and applications. Includes also abstracts of selected reports and theses.

Operational Research Quarterly. Oxford, England, published for Operational Research Society by Pergamon Press.

Contains both theoretical and case oriented papers with an emphasis on the former. Includes occasional review and survey papers, general papers, technical notes and book reviews. Indexed in BPI.

Operations Research. Baltimore, Md., Operations Research Society of America (bimonthly).
Covers a broad range of OR topics, including summaries of observations, models, descriptions of how specific problems were solved, papers reporting inventions and designs. Includes book reviews. Indexed in BPI.

Several other foreign periodicals are: *Cahiers du Centre d'Études de Recherche Opérationnelle* (Bruxelles, Institut de Statistique de l'U.L.B, quarterly); *INFOR* (Ottawa, Ontario, Canada — a Canadian journal of operational research and information processing, 3/yr.); and *Zeitschrift Für Operations Research* (Würzburg, Wien, Physica Verlag Für Deutschen Gesellschaft Für Operations Research, quarterly).

OPERATIONS RESEARCH ASSOCIATIONS

Institute of Management Sciences, 146 Westminster Street, Providence, R.I. 02903.
Operational Research Society, Neville House, Waterloo Street, Birmingham, B2 5TX, England.
Operations Research Society of America, 428 East Preston Street, Baltimore, Md. 21202.

18

MARKETING

Marketing Handbooks — Marketing Books — Marketing Systems and Quantitative Methods — Consumer Behavior — Channels of Distribution — Industrial Marketing — Marketing Research — Pricing — Product Development — Public Policy and Marketing — Sales Management — Salesmanship — Marketing Bibliographies — Marketing Dictionaries — Marketing Guides — Marketing Reports on Industries and Locations — Consumer Expenditure Studies — Marketing Periodicals — Marketing and Market Research Directories — Marketing Associations — Sales Promotion — Advertisng Handbooks and Books — Advertising Statistics — Advertising Dictionaries — Advertising Periodicals — Advertising Directores — Advertising Associations — Retailing — Retailing Statistics — Retailing Periodicals — Directories of Retail Stores — Retailing Associations

The same new forces that have brought about changes in other areas of business are also evident in business activities concerned with the marketing of goods and services to consumers and industry. A more systematic, analytic approach to solving complex marketing problems (aided by rapidly developing data processing techniques); increased importance given to knowledge about what the consumer wants and how he behaves; an awakening concern for the environment — these topics are all receiving much more attention in the current literature on marketing and advertising.

This chapter describes a selection of recent books, periodicals and reference guides on major marketing subjects. Advertising and retailing materials are described at the end in order to list their reference sources separately rather than to interfile them with the statistics, periodicals and directories pertaining to the whole area of marketing. Related topics described in other chapters are: physical distribution, or logistics (including purchasing and transportation), in

Chapter 20; public relations and social responsibilities, in Chapter 9; and international marketing, in Chapter 16.

MARKETING HANDBOOKS

These handbooks cover the whole field of marketing. Several more specialized handbooks are listed in the sections for marketing research, sales management, sales promotion and advertising.

Britt, Steuart H., ed. *The Dartnell Marketing Manager's Handbook.* Chicago, Dartnell Corp. 1973.

Each of its 73 chapters is written by a team consisting of a marketing professor and a marketing executive, with a total of 150 experts collaborating on this comprehensive reference volume. Covers all important topics: 5 chapters on organization and staffing; 6 chapters on establishing objectives; 12 on marketing research; 11 on developing the marketing plan; 12 on putting the marketing plan into action for consumer products and services; 4 on planning for industrial products; 10 on promoting products and services; 3 on international marketing; and 2 on appraising and controlling the marketing program. Useful suggestions for reading are at end of each chapter for persons wanting to read further on any topic.

Buell, Victor P., ed. *Handbook of Modern Marketing.* New York, McGraw-Hill, 1970.

Another comprehensive single source for concise data on all important aspects of marketing, in 120 chapters, each written by an authority. This handbook is in 20 sections: modern marketing concept; classification of markets; planning the product line; distribution; pricing; marketing research; planning the marketing program; organization and staffing; controlling; marketing management; marketing mix; selling and sales management; communications; customer services; financing; packaging; ethical and legal aspects; application of the sciences to marketing; specialty marketing; international marketing. Selective bibliographies at end of most chapters.

MARKETING BOOKS

Beckman, Theodore N., William R. Davidson and W. W. Talarzyk. *Marketing.* 9th ed. New York, Ronald, 1973.

A popular introductory text analyzing the whole marketing process and its environment, the various markets, institutional structure, functions and goals.

Britt, Steuart H. and Harper W. Boyd, Jr. *Marketing Management and Administrative Action.* 3d ed. New York, McGraw-Hill, 1973.

An excellent selection of 45 articles and essays designed to help the reader understand marketing problems better and also to solve them. In 5 sections, with over half of the book (26 selections) covering topics related to "Putting the Marketing Plan into Action." Many of the authors are well-known marketing names, such as Kotler, Levitt, Luck.

Buzzell, Robert D., Robert E. M. Nourse, John B. Matthews, Jr., and Theodore Levitt. *Marketing: A Contemporary Analysis.* 2d ed. New York, McGraw-Hill, 1972.

An introduction to marketing, with the focus on problem-solving and decision-making. Of its 6 parts, the most attention is given to "Marketing Management" (Part

4), with 12 chapters on the major functional areas of policy and decision, such as product policies, pricing, channels, advertising, logistics. Other parts cover: customer and marketing behavior; retail and wholesale distribution; marketing information and analysis; the public environment of marketing.

Carman, James M. and Kenneth P. Uhl. *Phillips and Duncan's Marketing: Principles and Methods.* 7th ed. Homewood, Ill., Irwin, 1973.
This latest edition of a classic marketing text has been thoroughly revised by 2 new authors. It emphasizes the marketing system and environmental forces that have caused rapid changes in marketing. Comprehensive, and includes annotated bibliographies at end of chapters.

Corey, E. Raymond and Steven H. Star. *Organization Strategy: A Marketing Approach.* Boston, Division of Research, Harvard University, Graduate School of Business Administration, 1971. Distributed by Harvard University Press.
This is an exploratory study based on the authors' in-depth research on the organization and organizational changes in 13 large, innovative businesses representing various industries. Their aim is "to provide a conceptual scheme which will be useful to top corporate managers and to teachers and students of business in dealing with organization problems at the division (or the 'business') level." The authors further tested their hypotheses by a mail survey of more than 500 other large companies. The bulk of this book consists of the 13 informative case studies, each of which is followed by an analytical commentary.

Enis, Bon M. and Keith K. Cox. *Marketing Classics: A Selection of Influential Articles.* Boston, Allyn and Bacon, 1969.
A selection of 34 widely quoted articles, chosen because of their enduring significance to marketing thought.

Kelley, Eugene J. and William Lazer. *Managerial Marketing: Policies, Strategies, and Decisions.* Homewood, Ill., Irwin, 1973.
Another selection of articles, this one "designed to present the most current perspectives on marketing management while highlighting the changing environmental forces influencing and shaping marketing policy and strategy." Covers 4 major areas: a conceptual framework of managerial marketing; consumers and marketing action; the systems approach; managing the marketing mix. A bibliography is at end of each of these sections. A companion volume called *Social Marketing: Perspectives and Viewpoints* (Irwin, 1973) contains a selection of articles on the evolving societal approach to marketing. Professor Kelley has also written a concise treatise in paperback called *Marketing Planning and Competitive Strategy* (Englewood Cliffs, N.J., Prentice-Hall, 1972).

Kotler, Philip. *Marketing Management: Analysis, Planning and Control.* 3d ed. Englewood Cliffs, N.J., Prentice-Hall, 1976.
The major portion of Kotler's graduate-level text covers the marketing administration processes of analysis, organization, planning and control. A beginning section develops the concepts of marketing and the marketing systems; a last section looks ahead to the broadening role of marketing in societal and international affairs. This latest edition is updated, "streamlined" and gives increased attention to formulating product strategy. A book of *Readings in Marketing Management* by Kotler and Keith J. Cox (Prentice-Hall, 1972) follows the same section headings as does the

book. Professor Kotler has also written a book on *Marketing for Non-Profit Organizations* (Prentice-Hall, 1975), which is largely based on his marketing management text.

Levitt, Theodore. *Marketing for Business Growth.* New York, McGraw-Hill, 1973.

A practical, readable book whose purpose is "to talk with the chief executive . . . about what he ought to know about marketing, how to manage his marketing chief, and how to balance the opportunities and threats of his *external environment . . .* with the resources and aims of his *internal environment.*" It is also meant for marketing executives — to give them new insights regarding their jobs. This is a revised version of the author's *Marketing Mode* (1969).

McCarthy, E. Jerome. *Basic Marketing: A Managerial Approach.* 5th ed. Homewood, Ill., Irwin, 1975.

A widely used, beginning marketing text that "takes an integrated, analytical approach to both macro- and micro-marketing problems," but with primary emphasis on micro-marketing. After an introduction the principal parts cover: developing marketing mixes; marketing management in action; marketing reappraised. Bibliographic notes are at end of sections; marketing arithmetic and a few cases are at end. Professor McCarthy (with John F. Grashof and Andrew A. Brogowicz) has recently compiled a good selection of 35 *Readings in Basic Marketing* (Irwin, 1975). It is designed to parallel the topical development of his book.

Stanton, William J. *Fundamentals of Marketing.* 4th ed. New York, McGraw-Hill, 1975.

Professor Stanton has substantially revised his introductory text to reflect new challenges concerning the role of marketing in our socioeconomic system. The central theme remains the same — that marketing is a "total system" of business action, and the emphasis is on marketing problem-solving and decision-making from the viewpoint of management in an individual firm. His major sections are: modern marketing; the market; the product; the pricing system; distribution structure; promotional activities; marketing in special fields (service, international); planning and evaluating the marketing effort. A few cases are at end of each section; an appendix contains marketing arithmetic; bibliographic footnotes appear throughout the text.

Webster, Frederick E., Jr. *Marketing for Managers.* New York, Harper & Row, 1974.

Because Professor Webster felt many marketing texts were too descriptive, too consumer oriented, and overly theoretical, he has written this book in an attempt "to stress the ideas and problems of interest and usefulness for *practicing* marketing managers, in a variety of industrial and multinational contexts." There are 15 chapters, which cover all the important areas of marketing management and decision-making. A short list of suggested readings for each chapter is at end.

Wilson, Aubrey. *The Marketing of Professional Services.* London and New York, McGraw-Hill, 1972.

This book fills a gap in the literature by providing a practical study on the marketing of professional services. Wilson, who is a British industrial market researcher, covers all important aspects, from basic concepts and the buying/selling interface, on to the selection of a professional service company, implications and marketing opportunities, strategy, planning and functions, and finally pricing. Includes a bibliography and an outline checklist.

Several other marketing texts worth mentioning are: *Marketing Management: Operating, Strategic and Administrative* by John A. Howard (3d ed., Homewood, Ill., Irwin, 1973); *Marketing Strategy and Structure* by David J. Rachman (Englewood Cliffs, N.J., Prentice-Hall, 1974); and *Essentials of Marketing* by Richard R. Still and Edward W. Cundiff (2d ed., Englewood Cliffs, N.J., Prentice-Hall, 1972).

MARKETING SYSTEMS AND QUANTITATIVE METHODS

These books concentrate on systems analysis and quantitative methods in marketing. Several books in the "Marketing Research" section also discuss quantitative techniques. For a list of the more general books on management science and statistical methods see Chapter 17.

Day, Ralph L. and Leonard J. Parsons, eds. *Marketing Models: Quantitative Applications.* Scranton, Pa., Intext Educational Publishers, 1971.

Thirty-four articles by well-known marketing authorities, selected to represent a variety of model structures and marketing problem situations. A companion volume is their *Marketing Models: Behavioral Science Applications* (Intext Educational Publishers, 1971), which has thirty-five selections.

Jolson, Marvin A. and Richard T. Hise. *Quantitative Techniques for Marketing Decisions.* New York, Macmillan, 1973.

Designed as a short, supplementary text in a basic marketing management course to introduce students to 4 important quantitative tools that can be used in solving many marketing problems (Bayesian decision theory, simulation and Markov process, linear programming, differential calculus). A grasp of algebra and probability theory are prerequisites. Includes exercises and bibliographies at end of chapters; illustrative examples are used throughout.

Kotler, Philip. *Marketing Decision Making: A Model Building Approach.* New York, Holt, Rinehart and Winston, 1971.

Professor Kotler is well known for his excellent marketing texts. This one "seeks to construct a systematic and self-contained theory of marketing analysis and decision making." It is in 4 parts: macromarketing decision theory; micromarketing decision models (covers chapters on distribution, pricing, sales force, advertising); models of market behavior; moving from theory to practice. Assumes elementary courses in calculus, linear programming and probability theory.

Montgomery, David B. and Glen L. Urban. *Management Science in Marketing.* Englewood Cliffs, N.J., Prentice-Hall, 1969.

An excellent background text presenting an "integrated discussion of the uses of management science in analyzing and solving marketing problems," and a description of the state of the art as of 1969. After an introduction, the authors discuss models as applied to 5 marketing areas: advertising, pricing, distribution, personal selling, new products. They end with chapters on implementation and on future developments. Requires some knowledge of calculus and statistical theory. A companion volume of 26 readings edited by Montgomery and Urban is *Applications of Management Science in Marketing* (Prentice-Hall, 1970).

Ramond, Charles. *The Art of Using Science in Marketing.* New York, Harper & Row, 1974.

Ramond's book attempts to show how scientific knowledge and methods can help the consumer marketing practitioner plan and evaluate the marketing of consumer products. Part 1 discusses obstacles to the use of science in marketing and how to get around them; Part 2 shows how science has aided product planning; Part 3 reports examples used in the evaluation of marketing expenditures; Part 4 summarizes and looks to the future. Includes an annotated list of "Ten Key Paperbacks," a list of ten useful anthologies, and an annotated list on the future as it relates to marketing and planning.

CONSUMER BEHAVIOR

Engel, James F., David T. Kollat and Roger D. Blackwell. *Consumer Behavior.* 2d. ed. New York, Holt, Rinehart and Winston, 1973.

A comprehensive text on the concept of consumer behavior, with practical implications for its various processes and facets. The main sections cover: group influences on consumer behavior; the nature and influence of individual predispositions; persuasive communication and attitude change; decision process; additional dimensions. A final section studies consumerism as well as the current status of consumer behavior research. Includes bibliographical footnotes.

Kassarjian, Harold H. and Thomas S. Robertson. *Perspectives in Consumer Behavior.* Rev. ed. Glenview, Ill., Scott, Foresman, 1973.

A wide collection of readings selected to represent the current state of the field of consumer behavior.

Walters, C. Glenn. *Consumer Behavior: Theory and Practice.* Rev. ed. Homewood, Ill., Irwin, 1974.

A textbook in 5 parts: foundation for consumer behavior; the individual — basic determinants of consumer behavior; environmental influences on consumers; business effects on consumer behavior; consumer purchase decisions. Includes bibliographical footnotes.

Ward, Scott and Thomas S. Robertson, eds. *Consumer Behavior: Theoretical Sources.* Englewood Cliffs, N.J., Prentice-Hall, 1973.

This book acquaints "the reader with some of the more prevalent conceptual, theoretical, and empirical research traditions, which have been particularly useful to researchers interested in consumer behavior, and to review and illustrate some applications of these traditions in consumer behavior research." In 13 chapters, each by an academic authority.

CHANNELS OF DISTRIBUTION

Most of the recent material in book form on channels of distribution consists of collections of readings. Outside of the several books listed below one must rely on chapters in marketing texts and handbooks as well as on articles in current journals for material on channels of distribution and on wholesaling. Good statistics on wholesaling are published every 5 years in the *Census of Wholesale*

Trade and in the Census *Enterprise Statistics* volumes, described in Chapter 4. Financial and operating ratios for wholesaling lines are included in the ratio studies described in Chapter 5. Associations of wholesalers in specific industries may also publish ratio studies or other information.

Lewis, Edwin H. *Marketing Channels: Structure and Strategy.* New York, McGraw-Hill, 1968.

An overview of marketing channels — their development; control, distribution policies and channel decision-making processes; concepts and theories. Includes a bibliography.

Stern, Louis W. *Distribution Channels: Behavioral Dimensions.* Boston, Houghton Mifflin, 1969.

Original essays and related readings selected to provide discussions of channels of distribution as conceptual entities rather than those using the descriptive approach. It covers 4 important dimensions of social systems: role, power, conflict, communication.

Walker, Bruce J. and Joel B. Haynes, eds. *Marketing Channels and Institutions: Readings in Distribution Concepts and Practices.* Columbus, Ohio, Grid, 1973.

A collection of 41 readings to give a broad view of distribution channels and of wholesaling and retailing institutions. Each includes a brief introduction, and there is a bibliography at end.

Another recent selection of 49 readings, also with a bibliography at end, is *Marketing Channels* by Louis E. Boone and James C. Johnson (Morristown, N.J., General Learning Press, 1973).

Walters, C. Glenn. *Marketing Channels.* New York, Ronald, 1974.

This book offers an integrated, managerial approach to the study of major marketing institutions. Its 20 chapters are in 5 parts: channels management (concept, opportunity, responsibility); channel structure; management of channel operations (channel purchasing decisions, pricing, logistics); management of channel communications; decisions of channel leadership (including motivation, team effort, conflict management and special decisions of international channels).

INDUSTRIAL MARKETING

Fisher, Lawrence. *Industrial Marketing: An Analytical Approach to Planning and Execution.* London, Business Books, 1969; Princeton, N.J., Brandon/ Systems Press, 1970.

A good, practical discussion on what industrial marketing is, how it fits into the business world, how it can be used to generate turnover and profit. Includes a bibliography. This book was written by a British economist and industrial marketing expert, and was sponsored by the Industrial Marketing Council, in England.

Hill, Richard M., Ralph S. Alexander and James S. Cross. *Industrial Marketing.* 4th ed. Homewood, Ill., Irwin, 1975.

This is a substantial revision of a standard text, with the newer material putting greater emphasis on marketing applications of quantitative techniques. Of the 8 sections, 4 are on important components of industrial marketing strategy (products and services, channels, pricing, promotion), and the others discuss: basic considerations;

the demand for industrial goods; marketing intelligence; marketing control. Cases comprise about a third of this revision.

Risley, George. *Modern Industrial Marketing.* New York, McGraw-Hill, 1972.

Professor Risley stresses practical applicability to decision-making in an interesting treatise on industrial marketing. He has written this for the industrial manager, and much of it is based on the thinking of 16 expert contributing authors. Includes bibliographies at end of chapters.

Vinson, Donald E. and Donald Sciglimpaglia, comps. *The Environment of Industrial Marketing.* Columbus, Ohio, Grid, 1975.

A selection of readings from a wide variety of academic and trade press sources to reflect the nature and scope of the industrial market environment. They are arranged in 8 sections: introduction; organizational buying behavior; industrial market research; product planning and management; channels of distribution; pricing industrial products; promotion in the industrial market; industrial reciprocity. Short lists of additional readings are at end of each section.

MARKETING RESEARCH

Handbooks

Ferber, Robert, ed. *Handbook of Marketing Research.* New York, McGraw-Hill, 1974.

A concentrated one-volume reference source on marketing research methods and applications, in over 80 chapters by 89 expert collaborators. Includes 38 chapters on specific statistical and mathematical techniques, 10 on behavioral science techniques, 25 on major areas of application (new product development, sales analysis, advertising research, industrial marketing, retail research, international marketing). References are at end of each chapter.

Worcester, Robert M., ed. *Consumer Market Research Handbook.* London and New York, McGraw-Hill, 1972.

Twenty-six chapters, each by a practicing consumer market researcher, and covering both the techniques and the uses of consumer market research. This handbook has a British focus.

Books

Boyd, Harper W., Jr., and Ralph Westfall. *Marketing Research: Text and Cases.* 3d ed. Homewood, Ill., Irwin, 1972.

This basic text is in 3 parts: introduction; market research procedures (including sampling, statistical design, data collection); selected applications (chapters on motivation, advertising, product, and sales control research). Includes cases with each chapter. The chapter on "Secondary Data" describes principal census data, a few guides to books, to articles, to commercial marketing information.

Engel, James F., Henry F. Fiorillo and Murray A. Cayley, eds. *Market Segmentation: Concepts and Applications.* New York, Holt, Rinehart and Winston, 1972.

A good selection of 27 readings reflecting "the economic, behavioral, mathematical and managerial facets of market segmentation." Suggested readings are at end of each of the 5 sections and a longer bibliography is at end of book.

Frank, Ronald E., William F. Massy and Yoram Wind. *Market Segmentation.* Englewood Cliffs, N.J., Prentice-Hall, 1972.

Reviews the findings and implications of segmentation studies; discusses the alternative methodology of segmentation research; and develops normative models for the application of segmentation research findings to marketing decisions. Includes a comprehensive bibliography. This text assumes some skill in mathematics.

Govoni, Norman A. P. *Contemporary Marketing Research: Perspectives and Applications.* Morristown, N.J., General Learning Corp., 1972.

A selection of 35 articles most of which deal with practical applications of marketing research to the following areas: product, sales, advertising, distribution, price, consumer behavior, industrial marketing, and international marketing. Bibliographies at end of each of 9 sections.

Green, Paul E. and Donald S. Tull. *Research for Marketing Decisions.* 3d ed. Englewood Cliffs, N.J., Prentice-Hall, 1975.

Presents the basic methodology and techniques for a quantitatively designed course in market research. This text presumes some background in statistics. Includes mathematical tables.

Luck, David J., Hugh G. Wales and Donald A. Taylor. *Marketing Research.* 4th ed. Englewood Cliffs, N.J., Prentice-Hall, 1974.

Another standard text revised to reflect the many changes that have taken place in such areas as information systems and analytical methods. In 5 parts: introduction; defining and planning research; gathering the data; analysis, interpretation and utilization; applications (forecasting, new product research, advertising research). Chapter on "Secondary Data" describes basic guides to marketing literature and statistics. Includes 24 cases and a bibliography.

Wentz, Walter B. *Marketing Research: Management and Methods.* New York, Harper & Row, 1972.

Designed to introduce practitioners to the tools of marketing research. Its 8 basic sections cover: research management; data acquisition and management; sampling; experimentation; consumer-behavior analysis; regression analysis; prediction and forecasting; simulation. Bibliographies at end of sections; mathematical and statistical tables in appendix.

Bibliographies

Ferber, Robert, et al. *A Basic Bibliography on Marketing Research.* (A.M.A. Bibliography No. 20.) 3d ed. Chicago, American Marketing Association, 1974.

A useful, annotated list of articles and a few books, arranged in 31 subject areas within 5 broad categories: background; techniques; areas of research; communication and administration; miscellaneous aspects.

PRICING

Most of the information on pricing can be found in older books, in chapters of general books on marketing, or in journal articles. Following are two relatively recent books.

Oxenfeldt, Alfred R. *Pricing Strategies.* New York, AMACOM, American Management Associations, 1975.

Since 1951 Professor Oxenfeldt has specialized in the study of industrial pricing, and he has written several well-known books on this subject. Here he directs his study to the needs of the executive in a private profit-oriented firm — to develop for him a general approach in setting prices by drawing maximum direction and guidance from what he knows about his market.

Palda, Kristian S. *Pricing Decisions and Marketing Policy.* Englewood Cliffs, N.J., Prentice-Hall, 1971.

A concise paperback outlining "the conceptual scheme that serves as a basis for making the firm's pricing decisions." Includes bibliographical notes. This book belongs to the "Prentice-Hall Foundations of Marketing Series," which aims to offer authoritative yet short overviews of important marketing topics in a convenient format.

PRODUCT DEVELOPMENT

Butrick, Frank M. *How to Develop New Products for Sale to Industry.* Englewood Cliffs, N.J., Prentice-Hall, 1971.

"A working manual for the successful development, introduction and management of new products — specifically those intended for sale to industry or to businesses," written by a consultant specialist. It is in 3 parts: the new product development function; the process; details about specific subjects and departments involved in new product development (patents, finance, producing, promoting, etc.). Includes a short, annotated bibliography.

Gisser Philip. *Launching the New Industrial Product.* New York, American Management Association, 1972.

A concise treatment of the title subject by a marketing and advertising consultant.

Another short guide for management, with a European focus, is *New-Product Strategy: Innovation and Diversification Techniques* by Bruno Hake (London and New York, Pitman, 1971).

Karger, Delmar W. and Robert G. Murdick. *New Product Venture Management.* New York, Gordon and Breach, 1972.

This useful text for would-be entrepreneurs emphasizes the nature of risk and cost in all decisions relating to the management of new product ventures. Bibliographies at end of chapters.

Luck, David J. *Product Policy and Strategy.* Englewood Cliffs, N.J., Prentice-Hall, 1972.

One of the "Foundations of Marketing Series," which are concise paperbacks — this one giving an overview of recent research and developments in product policies, strategies and management. Includes a bibliography.

McGuire, E. Patrick. *Evaluating New-Product Proposals.* (Conference Board Report No. 604). New York, Conference Board, 1973.

A short but useful report describing "the various methods managements use to judge the relative merits of new products and services proposed for development and marketing by their companies." It is based on a survey of the practices of 203 manufacturing and service firms, and it includes a bibliography at end. Their Conference Board Report No. 613 is on *Options in New-Product Organization* by David S. Hopkins (1974).

Marvin, Philip. *Product Planning Simplified.* New York, American Management Association, 1972.

Marvin presents his study on the management of product planning in 4 parts: finding and screening; funding and auditing; organizing; staffing.

Another recent AMA book, *Product Management* by George S. Dominguez (1971), is a practical guide on the organization and responsibilities of product management. It includes a bibliography.

Scheuing, Eberhard E. *New Product Management.* Hinsdale, Ill., Dryden, 1974.

A text covering the latest concepts, practices and techniques of new product management and emphasizing its role within the broader area of marketing management. It is in 5 parts: the job of new product management; the evolution of new products; the introductory marketing program; the diffusion of innovation; the product life cycle. Includes bibliographical footnotes.

Watton, Harry B. *New-Product Planning: A Practical Guide for Diversification.* Englewood Cliffs, N.J., Prentice-Hall, 1969.

This guide for managers and persons in charge of new product programs is written by a practitioner. The first part contains 3 chapters on establishing a new product program. A much longer second part deals with the various aspects of operating the program (collecting and evaluating ideas, testing new products, etc.). Includes a glossary of terms.

PUBLIC POLICY AND MARKETING

This section contains a few books and legal services on antitrust and trade regulation, also several books on consumerism and how this new concern is affecting business. Refer to Chapter 9 for names of books and reference sources in the general area of business and society, including a few books on business and government and on business law.

Allvine, Fred C., ed. *Public Policy and Marketing Practices. Proceedings of Workshop* . . . Chicago, American Marketing Association, 1973.

This collection of 26 thoughtful papers presented by well-known marketing experts is about the only recent full-length study of note published as of 1975 on public policy and marketing. They were presented at a workshop held at Northwestern University in 1972 to stimulate thinking and research on this important subject. An effort was made to present several papers on the same issues to represent different points of view.

The American Marketing Association has also published selected papers from a conference on *Advertising and the Public Interest* held in Washington, D.C., in May 1973. It was edited by S. F. Divita and published by the AMA in 1974.

Ferrell, O. C. and Raymond La Garce, eds. *Public Policy in Marketing.* Lexington, Mass., D. C. Heath, 1975.

Another collection, this one containing 12 essays, primarily by marketing professors, on the emerging public policy issues that are influencing marketing practices. With each essay is a commentary by an academic person. There are 4 parts: public policy structure; advertising truthfulness; business responsibilities; future dimensions.

Consumerism

Aaker, David A. and George S. Day, eds. *Consumerism: Search for the Consumer Interest.* 2d ed. New York, Free Press, 1974.

A good selection of recent readings on this increasingly important subject. After a preliminary section covering perspectives on consumerism, the editors have organized the discussions of issues according to the steps of the purchasing process — the prepurchase phase (the availability and quality of information); the purchase transaction (selling practices, pricing, constraints on choice); the post-purchase experience (warranties, safety, consumer recourse, etc.). A final section is devoted to "broadening the perspective" (ecology, social issues).

Commerce Clearing House. *Consumerism.* Chicago (weekly).

This weekly service and newsletter informs and alerts companies as to how consumer demands from both public and government sources affect their business interests and decisions in production, advertising, sales and related areas.

Cron, Rodney L. *Assuring Customer Satisfaction: A Guide for Business and Industry.* New York, Van Nostrand Reinhold, 1974.

Attempts to guide business in translating consumers' needs into effective organization and response, with 3 of its 5 parts exploring the differences as they pertain to small, to medium-sized and to large businesses.

Antitrust and Trade Regulation

Commerce Clearing House. *Trade Regulation Reports.* Chicago. 5 volumes (loose-leaf, with weekly supplements).

A comprehensive service covering important federal and state laws, court decisions, Federal Trade Commission decisions, rules, controls, guides, FTC complaints and orders, advisory opinions, etc., relating to trade regulation, antitrust and pricing. Vol. 5 contains current trade cases, which give recent court decisions and consent decrees. There is a separate set of bound volumes for past *Trade Cases.*

Persons who do not need such detailed coverage may want to investigate a similar 2-volume service of the Bureau of National Affairs called *Antitrust & Trade Regulation Reports.* It covers activities of the FTC and the Antitrust Division of the Department of Justice concerning antitrust and trade regulation; also legislative court decisions and special analyses of current developments.

Howard, Marshall C. *Legal Aspects of Marketing.* New York, McGraw-Hill, 1964.

A useful source for a concise analysis of important laws and their application to specific marketing policies, but special note should be made of the fact that this book will not include legal changes after 1964. Bibliographies at end of chapters.

Kintner, Earl W. *An Antitrust Primer: A Guide to Antitrust and Trade Regulation Laws for Businessmen.* 2d ed. New York, Macmillan, 1973.

A useful guide for background reading to help businessmen familiarize themselves with antitrust and trade regulation laws — why these laws were enacted, what they provide, who enforces them, and how they are enforced. Includes a bibliography, selected FTC guides, summaries of principal antitrust statutes. Kintner, who is a lawyer and former chairman of the FTC, has also written several other related guides on antitrust and trade regulation law. These are: *A Primer on the Law of Deceptive Practices: A Guide for the Businessman* (Macmillan, 1971); *Primer on the Law of Mergers: A Guide for Businessmen* (Macmillan, 1973), which emphasizes the antitrust aspects of mergers; *A Robinson-Patman Primer: A Businessman's Guide to the Law Against Price Discrimination* (Macmillan, 1970). His fifth book in the series, written with Mark T. Joelson, is *An International Antitrust Primer: A Businessman's Guide to* the *International Aspects of United States Antitrust Law and to Key Foreign Antitrust Laws* (Macmillan, 1974).

Periodicals

Antitrust Bulletin. New York, Federal Legal Publications (quarterly).

Lengthy research articles, usually by lawyers or academicians, on American and foreign antitrust and trade regulation. Includes book reviews. Indexed in PAIS.

SALES MANAGEMENT

Handbooks

Riso, Ovid, ed. *The Dartnell Sales Manager's Handbook.* 12th ed. Chicago, Dartnell Corp. To be published in 1976.

Since its first appearance in 1934 J. C. Aspley's *Sales Management Handbook* has been an essential and practical one-volume reference source about the sales policies and practices of American companies. Its many chapters cover all important topics from the evolution of sales management to the operations of the sales force. Its "Ready-Reference Section" (which we assume will also be in this new edition) includes such useful information as a bibliography, a glossary, legal data, contract forms, a directory of sales-training aids and of business directories, a few marketing statistics, transportation fares.

Books

Dunn, Albert H., Eugene M. Johnson and David L. Kurtz. *Sales Management: Concepts, Practices and Cases.* Morristown, N.J., General Learning Press, 1974.

Designed as a "complete learning/teaching tool" for students in personal selling and in sales management classes. It is in 5 parts: the personal selling function; planning and organizing for sales management; developing the sales force; directing the sales force; the future of selling and sales management. Case problems are at end of each section.

Stanton, William J. and Richard H. Buskirk. *Management of the Sales Force.* 4th ed. Homewood, Ill., Irwin, 1974.

A standard text on the management of an outside sales force and its activities, brought up to date to reflect many changing conditions. Its 4 major sections cover sales organization, operation, sales planning, sales analysis and evaluation. Cases are with each chapter.

Still, Richard R., Edward W. Cundiff, and N. A. P. Govoni. *Sales Management: Decisions, Policies and Cases.* 3d ed. Englewood Cliffs, N.J., Prentice-Hall (forthcoming).

Revision of this standard book is in progress with publication scheduled for early 1976. Section headings for the 1969 edition are: sales management — the setting; sales force management; information for sales management; sales management and marketing decison-making.

Wotruba, Thomas R. *Sales Management: Planning, Accomplishment and Evaluation.* New York, Holt, Rinehart and Winston, 1971.

An introductory text in 3 parts: development of personal selling goals (sales potential, forecasting, budgeting, territories, quotas); accomplishment of goals through the sales organization (including motivation, recruiting and training sales personnel); evaluation of sales management goals and accomplishment. Annotated lists of readings at end of each part.

SALESMANSHIP

Baer, Earl E. *Salesmanship.* New York, McGraw-Hill, 1972.

A concise text "designed to provide the framework for a successful career in any field of salesmanship." Its 4 parts cover: the selling system; development of the salesman within the sales organization; salesmanship in action; sales management. Includes some case studies.

Haas, Kenneth B. and John W. Ernest. *Creative Salesmanship: Understanding Essentials.* 2d ed. Beverly Hills, Calif., Glencoe, 1974.

This text has been brought up to date to include changes that have occurred in personal salesmanship. It covers 4 important aspects: the nature of selling; getting ready to sell; basic sales techniques; special sales situations.

Pederson, Carlton A. and Milburn D. Wright. *Selling: Principles and Methods.* 6th ed. Homewood, Ill., Irwin. To be published in 1976.

A good, traditional text arranged according to 5 phases of selling: the field of selling (and its role in the economy); knowledge and skill requirements for successful selling; the sales process; the salesman's personal, customer and social responsibilities; introduction to sales management. Case problems and bibliographies with each chapter. This note is based on an examination of the 5th edition.

Russell, Frederick A., Frank H. Beach and Richard H. Buskirk. *Textbook of Salesmanship.* 9th ed. New York, McGraw-Hill, 1974.

The latest edition of this popular textbook emphasizes industrial selling more than consumer-specialty selling and is brought up to date to give increased attention to behavioral material and the legal aspects of selling.

Stroh, Thomas F. *Training and Developing the Professional Salesman.* New York, AMACOM, American Management Associations, 1973.

This practical guide to planning sales training and to dealing with training problems is written for first-level sales managers. It examines continuous training processes, new techniques such as video instant replay, and includes annotated bibliographies.

MARKETING BIBLIOGRAPHIES

American Marketing Association. *A.M.A. Bibliography Series.* Chicago.

A series of 20 annotated bibliographies have been published to date on important marketing topics. Several of the latest are: No. 2: *A Basic Bibliography on Marketing Research,* comp. by Robert Ferber et al., 3d ed., 1974; No. 18: *Brands: A Selected and Annotated Bibliography,* comp. by Ernest B. Uhr and William A. Wallace, 1972; No. 19: *International Marketing,* comp. and ed. by Jac L. Goldstucker and Jose de la Torre, Jr., 1972.

Journal of Marketing. "Marketing Abstracts" section. Chicago, American Marketing Association (quarterly).

Each issue has a useful, annotated bibliography describing selected articles and a few special studies of interest to marketers. It is arranged in 23 broad subject areas such as "Consumer Behavior," "Industrial Marketing," "International Marketing."

The Marketing Information Guide. Garden City, N.Y., The Trade Marketing Information Guide, Inc. (monthly).

A continuing, annotated bibliography of selected marketing studies and statistics published by organizations such as government agencies, universities, associations, publishing firms. Basic sections are: marketing functions, policy, methodology, operations; areas and markets; industries and commodities. Cumulated indexes are in issues for March, June, September and December.

U.S. Small Business Administration. *Small Business Bibliography Series.* Washington, D.C. (irregular).

These short, annotated bibliographies are on subjects of interest to the small businessman, and they usually list a few books, government publications, directories, journals and associations. Several 1974/1975 revisions of interest to market researchers are: No. 3, "Selling by Mail Order"; No. 9, "Marketing Research Procedures"; No. 12, "Statistics and Maps for National Market Analysis"; No. 15, "Recordkeeping Systems — Small Store and Service Trade"; No. 31, "Retail Credit and Collections"; No. 55, "Wholesaling." Other recently revised numbers are on specific retail or service businesses, such as: No. 42, "Bookstores"; No. 66, "Motels."

Two British associations publish marketing abstract services. The Market Research Society publishes a semi-annual *Market Research Abstracts,* which covers articles on marketing and advertising, arranged by broad topic. The Industrial Marketing Research Association publishes a complementing semi-annual *Industrial Marketing Research Abstracts,* arranged by number with a subject index. Also the British *Anbar Management Services* publishes a section for "Marketing + Distribution Abstracts," described in Chapter 10.

MARKETING DICTIONARIES

American Marketing Association. *Marketing Dictionary.* Ed. by Claire Corbin. Chicago. To be published in 1976.

This promises to be a good, up-to-date dictionary for the generalist covering marketing and marketing related definitions and including explanations and comments with most terms. In addition there is a bibliography of books, dictionaries and other marketing sources.

Audit & Surveys, Inc. *A Dictionary for Marketing Research.* New York, 1974.

A small volume of marketing and quantitative definitions for persons not technically trained, often with name of a publication where one can find a more detailed discussion.

Graham, Irvin. *Encyclopedia of Advertising.* 2d ed. New York, Fairchild Publications, 1969.

An encyclopedic dictionary of "more than 1,100 entries relating to advertising, marketing, publishing, law, research, public relations, publicity and the graphic arts."

Shapiro, Irving J. *Marketing Terms: Definitions, Explanations, and/or Aspects.* 3d ed. West Long Branch, N.J., S-M-C Publishing Co., 1973.

Concise definitions of nearly 3,000 terms of interest to marketers.

MARKETING GUIDES

The market researcher has a wide variety of statistical sources at his disposal when undertaking any research project. Chapters 4 through 6 in this book describe the more important U.S. and foreign statistical volumes and also statistics on individual manufacturing and on agricultural and mining industries. Statistics for retail and wholesale businesses, as well as advertising expenditures, can be found elsewhere in this chapter. Here are listed several annual guides that provide recent statistical estimates for such important marketing barometers as population, households, income, buying power and retail sales.

Editor & Publisher. *Market Guide.* New York (annual).

Market data for more than 1,500 U.S. and Canadian newspaper cities covering facts and figures about: location, transportation, population, households, banks, autos, gas & electric meters, principal industries, climate, tap water, retailing, retail outlets, newspapers. Also gives the following statistics with each state: E & P estimates by county, newspaper city, and SMSA (Standard Metropolitan Statistical Area) for population, personal income, households, value of farm products, total retail sales, number of retail stores, sales estimates for 9 retail store groups (lumber/hardware, general merchandise, food, auto, gasoline, apparel, furniture, eat/drink, drugs). Rankings by SMSA are at front of volume. This annual guide has been published since 1924.

European Marketing Data and Statistics. London, Euromonitor Publications, Ltd. (annual).

Statistics are for: basic economic indicators by European country; standard of living (earnings, taxation, prices, expenditures, industrial consumption); the consumer; statistics covering European society (education, health, mass media, leisure, communications , r&d, etc.). For other sources of foreign statistics see Chapter 6.

Financial Post. *Survey of Markets.* Toronto, Ontario, Canada, Maclean-Hunter (annual).

Statistical data on more than 400 Canadian consumer markets, including estimates of population, retail sales (by specific type of store), personal disposable income; statistics on housing, employment, household income (by income size), taxation statistics by income size, number of banks, circulation of newspapers, etc. Overall tables at front give buying power index, population, personal disposable income, farm cash income — by province, county and major urban area. Also at front is a directory of market research firms and a list of market research studies.

A Guide to Consumer Markets. New York, Conference Board (annual).

A useful compilation of U.S. statistics and graphs, from a wide range of government and trade sources, on the consumer and his behavior in the marketplace. Covers population, employment, income, consumer expenditures, production and distribution, prices.

Marketing Economics Guide. New York, Marketing Economics Institute. (annual).

Part 2 of this 3-part guide gives estimates for population, households and income (by income size), for U.S. counties and cities. Part 3 has retail sales estimates for 1,500 cities, 3,100 counties, metropolitan areas and the 13 newly designated SCSAs (Standard Consolidated Statistical Areas). These estimates are for 9 retail groups (food and eating stores; drinking places; drug and proprietary stores; gasoline service stations; general merchandise; apparel and accessory stores; furniture/home furnishings equipment; automotive dealers; building materials/hardware/farm equipment). Part 1 ranks SMSAs in population, disposable income, total retail sales and sales for the 9 store groups.

Plant Location. Chicago, Simmons-Boardman (annual).

For each U.S. state, for Canadian provinces and for Puerto Rico, this gives population of larger cities, hours and earnings by industry, employment and unemployment statistics for cities, cost of living, climate, raw materials, names of transportation facilities, utilities, industrial development organizations, pollution control commissioner.

Rand McNally & Co. *Commercial Atlas & Marketing Guide.* Chicago (annual).

This atlas includes, with each state, census statistics for counties and principal cities on population, and total manufacturing and business statistics. Most of the marketing data is at the front, and includes: statistics by SMSA (population; households; total retail sales; sales for shopping goods, food stores, drugstores; passenger car registration; total manufacturing; land area); also such data as railroad and air distances, postal regulations, etc.

Sales & Marketing Management. New York (semi-monthly).

This trade journal publishes 4 useful, annual statistical issues:

(1) "Survey of Buying Power" (in a July issue each year, e.g., July 21, 1975). Marketing and economic researchers usually turn to this important issue first when they seek current estimates showing U.S. and Canadian geographic variations in population, income and retail business. It is arranged in 5 sections (A to E): Section C gives metropolitan county area estimates (SMSAs and SCSAs) for population by age group, households, EBI (Effective Buying Index), percentage of households by cash income groups, graduated buying power indexes, retail sales for 9 retail store groups, merchandise line sales for 7 lines. Section D covers estimates, by county and city, for population, households, percentage of households by cash income groups, EBI, retail sales for 5 major retail store groups. Section B has national, regional and state summaries and metropolitan area rankings; Section E gives similar marketing estimates for Canadian provinces, counties and cities. This special issue has been published every year since the 1930s; for many years it appeared as the May 10 issue, then it was changed to a June issue, and in 1974 it was changed again to July. Market Statistics, New York, which generates the data for this survey, maintains an up-to-date data bank for these demographic and sales statistics.

(2) "Survey of Buying Power, Part II" (last October issue each year). This special issue combines 2 marketing surveys that were formerly published separately. Section B, "Metropolitan Market Projections," gives a 5-year projection and percentage of change for population, EBI, and total retail sales in U.S. counties and metropolitan areas; similar tables for Canada are in Section F. Section C through E, "Annual Surveys of TV, Newspaper, and Radio Markets," contain — for each TV market — estimates for TV homes, population, black population, EBI, and total retail sales. For each newspaper market the tables include percentage of households covered; also population, EBI, and sales for the 5 major retail store groups. For radio markets, statistics cover only listening by age and sex.

(3) "Survey of Industrial Purchasing Power" (last April issue, beginning in 1974). These statistics are by county for all counties in the United States that have at least

one manufacturing plant with 20 or more employees. It gives total number of manufacturing plants, total also for 4-digit SIC industries having at least 1,000 employees, total large plants of 100 or more employees, total shipments, percentage of United States.

(4) "Survey of Selling Costs" (first issue each year). Another new annual issue, this one giving statistics on "Metro Sales Costs" (lodging, food, drink costs for 77 markets; also per diem index, taxi and auto-rental rates); compensation of salesmen; data on sales meetings and sales training; transportation (auto allowances, air/train/bus fares); sales-support activities (audio-visual equipment rental, moving costs, etc.); international data (cost of living abroad, air fares).

Standard Rate & Data Service. Skokie, Ill.

In 3 of the SRDS monthly publications (those for newspapers; spot radio; spot television) marketing statistics are included at the beginning of each state section. These give state, county, metropolitan area estimates for population, households, consumer spendable income (percentage distribution of families by income size), retail sales for 7 retail store groups (food, drug, general merchandise, apparel, home furnishings, automotive, service stations), number of passenger cars, farm population, gross farm income. Metropolitan area rankings are at front. The SRDS annual "Newspaper Circulation Analysis" also has these figures.

MARKETING REPORTS ON INDUSTRIES AND LOCATIONS

The publishers of some trade journals issue marketing research reports or surveys for their industry that are either published separately or are included as an annual issue of their journal. A few commercial firms also publish marketing guides for a specific industry. References to several of these guides and annual issues are in Chapter 5. Newspaper publishers in several large cities publish periodic "consumer analyses" that give buying habits and brand preferences of families in their market area; a few newspaper publishers issue market or media studies that include statistics for the market area.

Advertising Age formerly published an annual descriptive listing of over 1,000 items available from media, trade associations and other sources, arranged by market categories: national, farm, regional and local, Canadian, international, distribution, professional, industrial. Unfortunately AA stopped issuing this useful list after 1972. However, checking the latest "Available Market Data" issue (May 22, 1972) can still be of some use to the market researcher, because although now out of date, it still gives a good idea of the many possible sources one can contact for current marketing data, and of course some of the items listed are still being published.

The journal *Industrial Marketing* has a continuing "Guide to Special Issues of Business Publications," which describes special issues of trade journals in over 30 industry categories. This lists not only statistical issues but also directory issues, conference issues, equipment issues, etc. Its one drawback is that there is no cumulated listing.

Special Libraries Association, in New York City, will publish (in late 1975 or early 1976) a second edition of the *Guide to Special Issues and Indexes of Periodicals* by Charlotte M. Devers, Doris B. Katz and Mary M. Regan. It will list many special issues of trade journals of interest to marketers. A few statistical issues and market guides can also be found in a short subject list compiled by librarians of SLA's Advertising and Marketing Division, called *What's New in Advertising and Marketing* (10/yr.).

Several other possible sources for finding market reports are in the "Marketing Bibliographies" section of this chapter.

CONSUMER EXPENDITURE STUDIES

The principal U.S. government source for current personal consumption expenditures by specific types of products is the "National Income Issue" of the Department of Commerce's *Survey of Current Business* (July issue each year). This is described in Chapter 4. Current quarterly consumer expenditures for major goods and services categories are in each monthly issue of the *Survey*.

Periodically the Bureau of Labor Statistics conducts comprehensive surveys of consumer expenditures, savings and income. These give detailed information for the largest U.S. cities, by income size, by size of family, by age of family head, by occupation of family head. The seventh major *Survey of Consumer Expenditures, 1960–61: Consumer Expenditures and Income* was issued in 93 parts as *BLS Report* No. 237. The eighth survey is in progress, with present plans calling for publication to begin in 1976 and the complete survey results ready for distribution in April 1977. This new survey will be based on statistics compiled in 1972–1973.

British statistics are in *Family Expenditure Survey,* published annually by the Great Britain Department of Employment; also in *National Income and Expenditure of the United Kingdom,* an annual publication of their Central Statistical Office. National account statistics for UN and OECD countries include consumer expenditure statistics, and these publications are described in Chapter 6.

MARKETING PERIODICALS

Advertising and retailing periodicals are listed elsewhere in this chapter.

American Marketing Association. *Combined Proceedings.* Chicago (annual).

Although this is not a periodical, these combined proceedings of the spring and fall marketing conferences do offer a good source for current thinking on the themes of each conference. For 1972 these were "Dynamic Marketing in a Changing World" and "Marketing Education and the Real World"; For 1973, "Increasing Marketing Productivity" and "Conceptual and Methodological Foundations of Marketing." The AMA has compiled an index to these proceedings: see *AMA Bibliography Series* No. 20: "Conferences, 66/71: An Annotated Index to the Proceedings" (1973). *AMA Bibliography Series* No. 10 indexed the proceedings for 1955–1965.

Industrial Distribution. New York, Buttenheim Publishing Corp. (monthly).

Special issues of this trade journal include: "Annual Survey of Distributions Operations" in March each year; "Census of Industrial Distributors" in May issue. Indexed in BPI, F&S.

Industrial Marketing. Chicago, Crain Communications, Inc. (monthly).

A trade journal on advertising and selling to business, industry and the professions.

The June issue each year has the "ABP's Annual 'Info/File,'" which shows graphic and tabular results from an annual survey conducted by the American Business Press. The April issue contains an annual IM survey of "Agency Billings in Business-to-Business and Corporate Advertising." A continuing feature is its "Guide to Special Issues of Business Publications," listing journals by primary market classification; also a short column called "Market Info," which describes new market studies and pamphlets of interest to industrial marketers. Lists of "Ad Volume in Business Publications" (in number of pages) appear quarterly. This journal is indexed in BPI, F&S.

Industrial Marketing Management. Amsterdam, The Netherlands, Elsevier Scientific Publishing Co. (semi-monthly).

An international journal of industrial marketing and marketing research published jointly with the European Association for Industrial Marketing Research. Indexed in F&S.

Journal of Consumer Research. Chicago (quarterly).

This is a new journal (1974), which publishes empirical research on consumer behavior with special emphasis on articles having interdisciplinary content or interest.

Journal of Marketing. Chicago, American Marketing Association (quarterly).

This is the leading academic marketing journal, with articles on concepts, theory and techniques in a wide range of marketing topics. Each issue also contains marketing notes and communications and the following useful regular features: brief information on current legal cases, arranged by topic; a "Marketing Abstracts" section (see bibliographies section for description); a good critical book review section. Indexed in BPI, F&S, PAIS.

Journal of Marketing Research. Chicago, American Marketing Association (quarterly).

Another more specialized journal of the AMA for professional articles on statistical and quantitative methods used in solving marketing research problems. Each issue also describes several computer programs, has a section on "Research Notes and Communications," and includes a book review section. Indexed in BPI, F&S, PAIS.

Sales & Marketing Management. New York (semi-monthly).

This is the new title (1976) of a widely read magazine, published for many years (1918–1975) as *Sales Management.* It is best known for its excellent special issues, which are described in the "Marketing Guides" section of this chapter. Indexed in BPI, F&S, PAIS.

Several British and Canadian marketing periodicals are: *European Journal of Marketing* (Bradford, Yorkshire, England, MCB Ltd., 3/yr.); *Marketing* (London, Haymarket Publishing, Ltd. for Institute of Marketing, monthly); *Marketing* (Toronto, Maclean-Hunter, a trade weekly); and Market Research Society, *Journal* (London, quarterly).

MARKETING AND MARKET RESEARCH DIRECTORIES

American Marketing Association. *Directory of Marketing Services and Membership Roster.* Chicago, R. F. Clancy Co., 1973.

List of AMA members and index of affiliation. A section in front lists firms providing marketing services, e.g., advertising agencies, consultants, market research, public relations firms, etc.

American Marketing Association. New York Chapter. *International Directory of Marketing Research Houses and Services.* New York (annual).

This list, also called the "Green Book," is arranged alphabetically with a geographical index. Gives top officers and brief description of scope of activity for each firm.

Bradford's Directory of Marketing Research Agencies and Management Consultants in the United States and the World. Fairfax, Va. (biennial).

Arranged geographically with an alphabetical index. Gives brief description of scope of activity for each agency and frequently the names of top officers. A list, classified by type of service offered, is at end.

Marketing Research in Europe: Handbook. Amsterdam, The Netherlands, European Society for Opinion and Marketing Research (annual).

A list of European market research societies and organizations, arranged by country. Includes officers and activities or services offered.

MARKETING ASSOCIATIONS

American Marketing Association, 222 South Riverside Plaza, Chicago, Ill. 60606.

SALES PROMOTION

Several books on promotion management are included in the following section on "Advertising Handbooks and Books."

Riso, Ovid, ed. *The Dartnell Sales Promotion Handbook.* 6th ed. Chicago, Dartnell Corp. 1973.

A comprehensive, recently revised reference volume meant to give sales promotion practitioners all the information they need to evaluate the probable success of a promotion and then to develop a plan. In 4 parts: 5 chapters are on the responsibilities and organization; 24 chapters on techniques and tools, such as catalogs, letters, manuals, mailing lists, displays, contests; 10 chapters on channels of distribution; 7 chapters on special related topics, such as controlling expenditures, measuring results, computers, international sales promotion. Very practical, with many illustrations, charts, examples; lists of business directories, business and professional publications, media, and so forth.

ADVERTISING HANDBOOKS AND BOOKS

Handbooks

Barton, Roger, ed. *Handbook of Advertising Management.* New York, McGraw-Hill, 1970.

Brings together a broad view on the management of advertising, in 9 parts, and 32 chapters, and written with the collaboration of 37 authorities. Includes a glossary of advertising terms.

Hodgson, Richard S. *The Dartnell Direct Mail and Mail Order Handbook.* 2d ed. Chicago, Dartnell Corp. 1974.

A one-volume compendium (49 chapters and over 1,500 pages) covering methods, techniques and important problems of direct mail and mail order. Includes practical illustrations and examples throughout. An appendix has useful reference data, such as a direct mail bibliography, a glossary, a list of business directories, postal rates and regulations.

Riso, Ovid. *Advertising Cost Control Handbook.* New York, Van Nostrand Reinhold, 1973.

Covers advertising cost practices and is based on actual experiences of executives in both large and small companies, agencies and media. In 5 sections: management responsibilities; creators and producers; the media; legal and international aspects; evaluation and control.

Stansfield, Richard H. *The Dartnell Advertising Managers' Handbook.* Chicago, Dartnell Corp. New edition to be published in 1976.

The 1969 edition of this extensive compilation is oriented toward industrial advertising but can also be applied to consumer advertising. It covers all important topics in 21 chapters, with case histories and other data contributed by over 300 specialists.

Books

Boyd, Alvin. *The Business Owner's Advertising Handbook.* Austin, Tex., Boyd Co., 1974.

This book, unlike most books on advertising, is meant as a practical guide for the small businessman — to give him the basics and to tell him where to go or whom to ask if he needs further help with advertising problems. Includes a glossary.

Caples, John. *Tested Advertising Methods.* 4th ed., rev. and enl. Englewood Cliffs, N.J., Prentice-Hall, 1974.

A practical book on how to write advertising that produces sales, based on the author's 49 years of experience in writing and researching advertising. This is a classic. Includes illustrations and many examples.

Dirksen, Charles J. and Arthur Kroeger. *Advertising Principles and Problems.* 4th ed. Homewood, Ill., Irwin, 1973.

A standard introduction to advertising that emphasizes "what advertising is, how it functions, and its advantages and disadvantages." Includes cases with each chapter.

Dunn, S. Watson and Arnold M. Barban. *Advertising: Its Role in Modern Marketing.* 3d. ed. Hinsdale, Ill., Dryden, 1974.

Another standard text combining theory and practice and focusing on general principles and on decision-making rather than on techniques. It is organized around the major problems of modern advertising and promotion: background and environment; planning the campaign; creating the message; media; special purposes and special publics (retail advertising, public relations, multinational advertising and promotion). Extensive use of charts, tables and illustrations, with bibliographies at end of most chapters.

Engel, James F., Hugh G. Wales and Martin R. Warshaw. *Promotional Strategy.* 3d ed. Homewood, Ill., Irwin, 1975.

This text "builds on a rigorous base of consumer psychology and then proceeds to treat advertising, reseller stimulation, personal selling and other communication tools as part of an overall promotional mix." Includes bibliographical footnotes.

Kleppner, Otto. *Advertising Procedure.* 6th ed. Englewood Cliffs, N.J., Prentice-Hall, 1973.

This is a well-established, nontechnical text on the management, planning, creation and use of advertising. Includes many illustrations; also reading suggestions, a glossary, names of periodicals, associations, services.

Nicosia, Francesco M. *Advertising, Management, and Society: A Business Point of View.* New York, McGraw-Hill, 1974.

Studies the 2 major facets of advertising: (1) the micro view of advertising as a managerial function in business firms; (2) the macro view, as an entire institution in society and the economy. Nicosia does this by quoting the testimony of corporate executives at the extensive hearings on modern advertising practices held by the Federal Trade Commission in 1971, and this, with commentaries, comprises the bulk of his study. A bibliography is at end.

Quera, Leon. *Advertising Campaigns: Formulation and Tactics.* Columbus, Ohio, Grid, 1973.

Quera's book fills a gap in the advertising literature by offering a study on one important aspect — the advertising campaign. Includes chapters on measuring effectiveness and on selecting an agency.

Sandage, C. H. and Vernon Fryburger. *Advertising Theory and Practice.* 9th ed. Homewood, Ill., Irwin, 1975.

A popular introduction "intended to give the student broad perspective and penetrating understanding of advertising — its social and economic functions, its role in business, how it works, how it is planned and created, its challenge and opportunities."

Simon, Julian L. *Issues in the Economics of Advertising.* Urbana, University of Illinois Press, 1970.

Simon's study is not a comprehensive survey but rather a useful investigation of those problems in the economics of advertising that he felt would benefit from attention. As he states in his introduction, nothing as yet has taken the place of Neil H. Borden's comprehensive and classic *The Economic Effects of Advertising* (Irwin, 1942). Simon's book is in 2 parts: microeconomics of advertising; advertising in the economy and society. Appendix includes a bibliography, "a bibliographical essay on some sources of data in advertising," and a list of "needed research."

Tillman, Rollie and C. A. Kirkpatrick. *Promotion: Persuasive Communication in Marketing.* Rev. ed. Homewood, Ill., Irwin, 1972.

An introductory overview of promotion management. After a section that provides a behavioral foundation for the promotional processes, the authors concentrate on the 4 major elements of persuasion: personal selling, advertising, sales promotion, indirect promotion (public relations, publicity and institutional advertising). A final section discusses management of the promotion program. Includes occasional illustrations.

Wright, John S., Daniel S. Warner and Willis L. Winter, Jr. *Advertising.* 3d ed. New York, McGraw-Hill, 1971.

This long (over 800 pages) standard text represents the various views of its 3 authors who are professors in the fields of marketing, communications and journalism, respectively. It focuses on general principles and broad viewpoints rather than on specific techniques. It includes many illustrations; has short bibliographies at end of each chapter and a glossary at end of book. Professor Wright (with John S. Mertes) has also compiled a book of readings on *Advertising's Role in Society* (St. Paul, Minn., West Publishing Co., 1974).

Bibliographies

Advertising Research Foundation. *Measuring Payout: An Annotated Bibliography on the Dollar Effectiveness of Advertising.* New York, 1973.
An annotated list of books, parts of books, and articles on the sales effect of advertising, arranged by year of publication, 1965–1972.

See also the more general marketing bibliographies and abstracts listed elsewhere in this chapter.

ADVERTISING STATISTICS

Advertising Age. Chicago (weekly).
This important advertising weekly publishes several annual surveys or features of special interest:
(1) "Marketing Reports" (mid- to late August issue each year). For each of the top 100 U.S. national advertisers this provides useful facts about sales and earnings, leading product lines and brands, advertising expenditures; also names of marketing personnel and agency account executives, both for parent company and for principal divisions. It also includes 2 tables: "100 Leaders' Advertising as Per Cent of Sales," [listing companies by industry]; "100 Leaders' Media Expenditures," also by industry.
(2) "Top 100 National Advertisers in (year)" for 6 media (mid- to late April each year, for example Apr. 29, 1974); and "The Top 100 National Advertisers of (year)" in 8 or 9 media (in a summer issue each year, for example, Aug. 18, 1975). The 6 media are: magazines, newspaper supplements, network TV, spot TV, network radio, outdoor media. The 9 media include also: farm publications, business publications, spot radio.
(3) "National Expenditures in Newspapers for (year)" (Section 2 of first June issue each year). This special issue gives a tabulation for brands of those U.S. companies spending $10,000 or more for national newspaper space. It also lists the "Top 100 National Newspaper Advertisers" and total "National Ad Investments in Newspapers" by industry classification.
(4) "U.S. Agency Section" (4th February issue each year); and "International Agency Section" (4th March issue each year). The first of these special issues contains profiles of over 650 U.S. advertising agencies, with facts concerning billings for each agency by media, accounts won and lost. Includes a list of agencies ranked by gross income and also by billings. The international issue has profiles of over 700 agencies outside the United States, arranged by country and giving similar data. It includes a list of "World's Biggest Agencies."
(5) Two other useful tables that usually appear annually are: "Percentage of Sales Invested in Advertising," totals by industry, not by company (annual, e.g., Sept. 30, 1974); "Four A's Agencies Cost, Profits" for 10 years (annual, for example, Aug. 5, 1974).
(6) "Profiles of Top 100 Markets in the U.S." (Dec. 15, 1975). Short descriptions of each of the top 100 SMSAs, including significant business and economic

developments in the area, and forecasts of some probabilities for the coming year. This is the first time these profiles have appeared, and it is not known whether or not it will be an annual feature.

Critchley, R. A. *U.K. Advertising Statistics: A Review of the Principal Sources and Figures.* London, Advertising Association, 1974.

This is in 3 parts: U.K. advertising expenditures; U.K. advertising rates and audiences; advertising agency data. Includes a bibliography of statistical sources. Current advertising expenditure statistics are in summer issue, each year, of the AA's *Advertising Quarterly.*

LNA Multi-Media Report Service. New York, Leading National Advertisers. 3 volumes (quarterly).

The 3 titles are: *Company/Brand $* (U.S. advertising expenditures in 6 media by company and brands); *Class/Brand Qtr $* (arranges the statistics by product class); *Ad $ Summary* (an index of brands with year-to-year total advertising expenditures). This latter publication also has a ranking of the top 1,000 advertisers.

World Advertising Expenditures. New York, Starch INRA Hooper (biennial).

This statistical survey is sponsored jointly by Starch INRA Hooper and the International Advertising Association. It gives estimates of advertising expenditures, by media, for 63 countries.

Magazine and Newspaper Advertising

American Business Press, Inc. *Leading Advertisers in Business Publications.* New York (annual)

Ranks over 600 leading advertisers in business journals. Includes also an alphabetical list of over 2,000 companies that spend $35,000 or more in business publications.

Media Records, Inc. *Expenditures of National Advertisers in Newspapers.* New York (annual).

Advertising expenditures by national brand, by company. List of "Top 100 Newspaper Advertisers" is at front. Compiled by Media Records, Inc., for the Newspaper Advertising Bureau.

Media Records: Newspaper and Newspaper Advertising. New York, Media Records, Inc. (annual).

Part 1 gives "advertising linage record of over 200 daily and Sunday newspapers in over 70 cities, showing totals on 215 industry classifications and subclassifications of advertising for each newspaper." It is arranged alphabetically by city. Parts 2-3, "Newspaper Advertisers," give individual linage record of 6,530 automotive and general advertisers in newspapers, arranged alphabetically by industry classification and name of advertiser.

Radio and Television Advertising

Blair, John, & Co. *Statistical Trends in Broadcasting.* New York (annual).

Television and radio station revenues, expenses and income by individual market; also ranking of TV and radio markets.

Television Factbook. Washington, D.C., Television Digest. 2 volumes (annual).

The "Services" volume includes statistics on radio and TV production, TV households, TV station income and expenditures, etc.; also lists of equipment manufacturers, community antenna systems, television program sources and services, associations, and other data. The "Stations" volume is described under "Advertising Directories," below.

ADVERTISING DICTIONARIES

Graham's *Encyclopedia of Advertising* is described in the "Marketing Dictionaries" section of this chapter.

ADVERTISING PERIODICALS

Advertising Age. Chicago (weekly).

An important weekly advertising newspaper containing current news of interest to marketing and advertising people. Several of its most useful special issues and statistical tables are described in the "Advertising Statistics" section of this chapter. Indexed in BPI, F&S.

Advertising Quarterly. London, Advertising Association.

A professional review containing short research articles and papers on a broad range of advertising topics. The summer issue, each year, contains "Statistical Tables of Advertising Expenditures" in the United Kingdom, for a 12-year period. Includes book reviews.

Journal of Advertising. De Kalb, Ill., American Academy of Advertising (quarterly).

"A professional journal devoted to the advancement of advertising as a communication industry." Articles are quite short and cover specific topics on theory, research, creativity, international advertising and so forth. Includes occasional book reviews.

Journal of Advertising Research. New York, Advertising Research Foundation (bimonthly).

Covers original research on advertising and marketing, with papers written primarily by academic persons. Indexed in BPI.

Media Decisions. New York, Decisions Publications (monthly).

Short articles on specific media, agencies, media research, experiences of particular companies, etc. An annual article on "Cost Trends" (for example, August 1974) includes "Media Cost Indices" by type of media for 10 years. Their annual "Top 200 Millionaire Brand Directory" (December) contains a ranking by total advertising expenditures and also media profiles for each brand.

ADVERTISING DIRECTORIES

Largest Advertisers

Information about the largest U.S. advertisers is in *Standard Directory of Advertisers*. It includes name of agency, advertising appropriations, media used, etc. A similar directory for Canadian companies is *National List of Advertisers*. Both of these directories are described in Chapter 3. See also the annual "Marketing Reports" issue of *Advertising Age* mentioned in the "Advertising Statistics" section of this chapter.

Media Directories

The basic directories of newspapers and periodicals are described in Chapter 3.

Advertiser's Annual. London, Admark Directories.

A directory of British newspapers, trade journals, outdoor sign firms, TV, radio and cinema firms, advertising agencies, public relations firms, British advertisers, who's who, etc.

Broadcasting. *Yearbook.* Washington, D.C.

Directory of U.S. and Canadian television and radio stations, advertising agencies, equipment manufacturers, and other useful information. Brief TV market data is at front.

Standard Rate & Data Service. Skokie, Ill.

This service offers separate directories giving advertising rates, specifications, and circulation for publications, broadcast stations, etc., in the following advertising media: *Business Publication Rates & Data* (monthly); *Consumer Magazine and Farm Publication Rates & Data* (monthly); *Direct Mail List Rates & Data* (semi-annual); *Medical/Paramedical Publication Rates & Data* (bimonthly); *Network Rates & Data* (bimonthly); *Newspaper Rates & Data* (monthly); *Print Production Data* (quarterly); *Spot Radio Rates & Data* (monthly); *Spot Television Rates & Data* (monthly); *Transit Advertising Rates & Data* (quarterly); *Weekly Newspaper Rates & Data* (semi-annual); *Newspaper Circulation Analysis* (annual). The 4 sections for newspapers, newspaper circulation, spot radio, spot television include marketing statistics for states, counties, cities, and metropolitan areas.

SRDS also publishes several international editions that give data for each type of media in one volume. These are: *British Rates & Data* (monthly); *Canadian Advertising Rates & Data* (monthly); and foreign language editions for France, Italy, Mexico and West Germany.

Television Factbook. Washington, D.C., Television Digest. 2 volumes (annual).

The "Stations" volume is a directory of U.S. and Canadian television and radio stations, arranged geographically, and including such data as personnel and rates; also a separate listing of educational television stations, and lesser information about stations in other countries. The "Services" volume is described in section for "Advertising Statistics," above.

Advertising Agencies

Advertising Age. "U.S. Agency Section" (4th February issue each year) and "International Agency Section" (4th March issue each year).

For descriptive note see listing in "Advertising Statistics" section of this chapter.

Standard Directory of Advertising Agencies. Skokie, Ill., National Register Publishing Co. (3/yr. and supplements).

For each agency, this directory gives officers, account executives, approximate annual billings, names of accounts, media used.

A list of Canadian advertising agencies is in *National List of Advertisers,* which is described in Chapter 3.

Biographical Dictionaries

Who's Who in Advertising. 2d ed. Rye, N.Y., Redfield Publishing Co., 1972.

Biographies of U.S. and Canadian executives in advertising and allied fields.

ADVERTISING ASSOCIATIONS

American Association of Advertising Agencies, 200 Park Avenue, New York, N.Y. 10017.

Association of National Advertisers, 155 East 44th Street, New York, N.Y. 10017.

International Advertising Association, 475 Fifth Avenue, New York, N.Y. 10017.

RETAILING

Corbman, Bernard P. and Murray Krieger. *Mathematics for Retail Merchandising.* 2d ed. New York, Ronald, 1972.

Discusses the various mathematical procedures necessary· for making effective decisions in the marketing, buying and selling of merchandise. Chapters are on specific techniques, such as markon, turnover, price lining. Includes many practical exercises and illustrative problems, and has a bibliography.

Davidson, William R., Alton F. Doody and Daniel J. Sweeney. *Retailing Management.* 4th ed. New York, Ronald, 1975.

Substantial revision of a standard text to reflect the many changes and new influences in the retailing industry. Its 26 chapter are divided into 7 parts: the environment of retailing management; retailing management and strategy; merchandise management; sales promotion and customer services; facilities and organization management; expense and productivity management; review and prospect. Cases and problems are at end of book.

Duncan, Delbert J., Charles F. Phillips and Stanley C. Hollander. *Modern Retailing Management: Basic Concepts and Practices.* 8th ed. Homewood, Ill., Irwin, 1972. (The 9th edition is scheduled for publication in 1976.)

An excellent, popular text revised to reflect an emphasis on management responsibilities under current changing conditions and to highlight newer concepts and practices. Annotated bibliography is at end.

Gist, Ronald R. *Management Perspectives in Retailing.* 2d ed. New York, Wiley, 1971.

A wide selection of articles, published prior to 1971, organized into 11 subject categories. Professor Gist has also written a good, simple text called *Basic Retailing: Text and Cases* (Wiley, 1971).

Rachman, David J. *Retail Strategy and Structure: A Management Approach.* 2d ed. Englewood Cliffs, N.J., Prentice-Hall, 1975.

"This text takes a broad overview of the firm and one particularly related to the management activities of decision making and the role of change in the firm's environment." It is in 4 parts: introduction; the uncontrollable factors (competition, legal restraints, the consumer); the controllable factors (buying, pricing, communicating, selling, etc.); controlling the firm. Includes a selected bibliography. Rachman has also published *Retail Management Strategy: Selected Readings* (Prentice-Hall, 1970).

Wingate, John W., Elmer O. Schaller and F. Leonard Miller. *Retail Merchandise Management.* Englewood Cliffs, N.J., Prentice-Hall, 1972.

This is a complete revision of the classic *Techniques of Retail Merchandising*. It examines the philosophy, concepts and techniques in management's planning, pricing, and controlling inventory in retail stores. Includes a bibliography. Wingate and Schaller have also written (with I. Goldenthal) a book of *Problems in Retail Merchandising* (6th ed., Prentice-Hall, 1973), which contains problems primarily of a mathematical nature and has sections corresponding to their text. A companion volume by Wingate (and J. Friedlander) is *The Management of Retail Buying* (Prentice-Hall, 1963).

RETAILING STATISTICS

Statistics published every fifth year by the Bureau of the Census provide valuable data on 100 kinds of retail and 150 service businesses. These volumes of the *Census of Retail Trade*, the *Census of Selected Service Industries*, and *Enterprise Statistics* are described in Chapter 4. Current but very general statistics are in the Census Bureau's *Annual Retail Trade Report* and *Monthly Retail Trade*. Annual estimates of sales for 7 or 9 basic retail store categories by geographic area are found in publications listed in the "Marketing Guides" section of this chapter. Operating ratio figures for many other retail businesses are described in Chapter 5. Listed below are a few trade journals and annual operating studies for three important categories of retail business. For data on other store groups, consult trade journals, publications of trade associations, indexes such as *F & S Index of Corporations and Industries*.

Department, Specialty and Discount Stores

Discount Merchandiser. New York, Macfadden-Bartell Corp. (monthly).

An annual statistical issue, "The True Look of the Discount Industry," appears in June. In 1974 this was followed in the July issue by profiles of "The $100 Million Club." Statistics giving "Sales of Health and Beauty Aids in Discount Stores" are in the September issue. A few financial figures for leading companies appear in each issue. Articles from this journal are selectively indexed in PAIS.

Discount Store News. New York, Lebhar-Friedman (biweekly).

Of special interest is the annual "Census of Discount Stores" issued in 1974 as a 2-part September 23 issue.

Fairchild's Financial Manual of Retail Stores. New York, Fairchild Publications (annual).

Financial manual for general mechandising chains, discount chains, mail order firms, drugstores, food stores, shoe stores, etc. Includes names of officers and directors; number of stores; sales and earnings; income account, assets and liabilities.

National Retail Merchants Association. Financial Executives Division. *Department Store and Specialty Store Merchandising and Operating Results* and *Financial and Operating Results of Department and Specialty Stores*. New York (annual).

Useful operating statistics in 8 sales volume categories of department stores and 3 for specialty stores. The first of these 2 annuals includes sales, merchandise and earnings data; expenses by expense center, by natural division; advertising media costs, etc. The second gives merchandise and inventory data (markon, markdown, stock shortage, gross margin, etc.) for each store department.

New York State College of Agriculture and Life Sciences, Cornell University. *Operating Results of Self-Service Discount Department Stores.* Ithaca, N.Y. (annual).

Financial and merchandising statistics for discount department stores by 3 sales volume categories.

Retail Distributors' Association. *Report on Departmental Trading and Operating Costs and Results of Department Stores.* London (annual).

Statistics for British department stores are in 2 parts: sales, stockturns, gross-margin percentage by department; operating costs and results (usually in 4 size categories).

Drugstores

American Druggist. New York, Hearst Corp. (semi-monthly).

"Annual Survey of Drug Store Sales by Departments" is in first July issue. Articles in this trade journal are indexed in BPI.

Chain Store Age. Drug Edition. New York, Lebhar-Friedman (monthly).

A trade journal for managers of drug chains. An "Annual Report of the Chain Drug Industry" appears in one issue (e.g., May 1974) and is also published separately. This has brief text, tables and charts on the growth of drug chains, performance of specific departments, and it also has profiles for about 30 pace-setting chains.

Drug Topics. Oradell, N.J., Medical Economics Co. (semi-monthly).

This trade journal now publishes a separate annual *Marketing Guide,* which gives 3-year comparative figures covering amount spent in drugstores for over 300 product lines. A summary is in first October issue.

Product Management. Oradell, N.J., Medical Economics Co. (monthly).

A trade journal for the drug and cosmetics industry. Their "Annual Survey: What the Public Spent for Drugs, Cosmetics, Toiletries in (year)" appears in a late summer or fall issue, for example, August 1974. It give statistics on consumer expenditures for specific products in all outlets for a 3-year period. Their "Ad Expenditures for Health and Beauty Aids" is in a summer issue (for example, July 1974) and gives statistics by media, brands and companies.

Food Stores

Chain Store Age. Supermarket Headquarters Edition. New York, Lebhar-Friedman (monthly).

Their "Supermarkets Sales Manual" is issued as Part 1 of the July issue each year. It give performance reports on 35 product categories. Articles in this trade journal are indexed in BPI, PAIS.

New York State College of Agriculture and Life Sciences, Cornell University. *Operating Results of Food Chains.* Ithaca, N.Y. (annual).

Gross margin, expenses, earnings, assets, liabilities, net worth, etc., for food chains by sales size categories.

Progressive Grocer. New York (monthly).

Their "Annual Report of the Grocery Industry" is in the April issue; "How Products Perform in the Big New Stores" is in the July issue. Articles in this trade journal are indexed in BPI, F&S.

Super Market Institute. *The Super Market Industry Speaks.* Chicago (annual).
  Brief text, charts and a few statistics on the state of the supermarket industry. This institute also publishes an annual *Facts About New Super Markets Opened in (year).*

Supermarket News. New York, Fairchild Publications (weekly).
  This weekly trade newspaper publishes a separate annual *Distribution Study of Grocery Store Sales in 287 Cities,* which is in 3 sections: (1) a statistical profile of the top 50 metropolitan areas ranked by supermarket sales; (2) information on grocery store business in other major areas; (3) summary figures on grocery store numbers and sales. In 1973 this journal prepared a short *Grocery Store Fact Book,* which contains statistics from Part 3 of the *Distribution Study* and also from other sources, such as the census and the Super Market Institute.

Supermarketing. New York, Gralla Publications (monthly).
  Their "Annual Consumer Expenditures Study" is in the September issue. It gives 3-year comparative figures on amount spent in grocery stores for many product lines. An annual table for "Sales and Net Income, 55 Top Publicly-Owned Food Chains Ranked by Sales Volume" is in October issue.

The Super Market Institute publishes a *Monthly Index Listings,* which consists of abstracts of articles on food retailing arranged by major subject classification.

RETAILING PERIODICALS

Journal of Retailing. New York University Institute of Retail Management (quarterly).
  An academic journal containing research papers on retailing and marketing subjects of interest to retailers, and written primarily by academic persons. Includes book review, and a "Retailing Abstracts" section. Indexed in BPI, PAIS.

Stores. New York, National Retail Merchants Association (monthly).
  Short articles and also news about the NRMA. Indexed in BPI.

DIRECTORIES OF RETAIL STORES

Fairchild's Financial Manual of Retail Stores is described in the "Retailing Statistics" section of this chapter. For directories of U.S. department and specialty stores, food stores, and the many other types of retail stores consult *Guide to American Directories* described in Chapter 3.

RETAILING ASSOCIATIONS

There are trade associations for almost every type of retail business. A good list is in *Encyclopedia of Associations,* which is described in Chapter 3. Following are the names of just three of the best known associations.

Mass Retailing Institute, 570 Seventh Avenue, New York, N.Y. 10018.
National Retail Merchants Association, 100 West 31st Street, New York, N.Y. 10001.
Super Market Institute, 200 East Ontario Street, Chicago, Ill. 60611.

19

PERSONNEL MANAGEMENT AND
INDUSTRIAL RELATIONS

PERSONNEL MANAGEMENT — Handbooks — Personnel
Management Books — Managerial Performance — Manage-
ment Development — Supervision — Wage and Salary Ad-
ministration — Personnel Bibliographies and Abstracts —
Personnel Dictionaries — Personnel Services — Personnel
Periodicals — Personnel Directories — Personnel Manage-
ment Associations — *INDUSTRIAL RELATIONS* — Labor
Economics and Labor Relations — Arbitration and Collective
Bargaining — Industrial Relations Bibliographies and
Abstracts — Industrial Relations Dictionaries — Labor Services
— Labor Statistics — Industrial Relations Periodicals — Labor
Directories — Industrial Relations Associations — Pension
Plans and Social Security

The well-known behavioral theorist Rensis Likert said in his
Human Organization (New York, McGraw-Hill, 1967, p. 1): "Every aspect of a
firm's activities is determined by the competence, motivation and general effectiveness of its human organization. Of all the tasks of management, managing
the human component is the central and most important task, because all else
depends on how well it is done."

The field of personnel and industrial relations is well documented, and information can be located not only in the publications in this chapter but also in
many of the books and periodicals on management in general (Chapter 10). Of
special interest is the section in that chapter on "Human Factors in Organizations." Personnel management draws upon many of the theories and techniques
used in the behavioral sciences, and the dividing line in listing books is often
hazy. Users are urged to check the material in both of these chapters when
researching any topic relating to human resources management.

PERSONNEL MANAGEMENT

HANDBOOKS

American Society for Personnel Administration. *ASPA Handbook of Personnel and Industrial Relations.* Washington, D.C., Bureau of National Affairs, 1974– . To be published in 8 volumes.

This is planned as a comprehensive handbook to cover the gamut of personnel and industrial relations (PAIR). It will be issued first in 8 paperback volumes and then will be published in a single bound volume. It aims to combine the best in theory and practice and to emphasize the "how" and "why." Each of its 55 chapters will be written by a recognized authority and will include references to useful sources for further information. The first volume is on "Staffing Policies and Strategies" by Dale Yoder and Herbert G. Heneman, Jr. (1974). The others will cover: "Manpower Management Systems"; "Planning and Auditing"; "Administration and Organization"; "Training and Development"; "Motivation and Commitment"; "Employment and Labor Relations"; "Professional PAIR."

Famularo, Joseph J., ed. *Handbook of Modern Personnel Administration.* New York, McGraw-Hill, 1972.

A practical, comprehensive, one-volume handbook covering all important aspects of personnel administration in 81 chapters, each written by a qualified personnel practitioner. The 18 parts include: organization; recruitment; training and development; wage and salary administration; employee benefits; employee appraisal and assessment; employee services, safety and health; government controls; labor relations; international personnel management; acquisitions and mergers; communications; records, reports and statistics; personnel research. Bibliographies are at end of chapters.

PERSONNEL MANAGEMENT BOOKS

Beach, Dale S. *Personnel: The Management of People at Work.* 3d ed. New York, Macmillan, 1975.

"This work seeks to provide a sound foundation in theory, principles, and practice for all those whose careers will require knowledge of and skills in management." It covers not only traditional personnel topics and functions but also the closely related area of organizational behavior. It is in 6 parts: management, employees, unions and organization; employment and development of people; understanding and managing people; financial compensation; security; perspective. Bibliographies are at end of chapters. Professor Beach has also compiled a book of readings called *Managing People at Work: Readings in Personnel* (2d ed., Macmillan, 1975).

Chruden, Herbert J. and Arthru W. Sherman, Jr. *Personnel Management.* 5th ed. Cincinnati, Ohio, South-Western, 1976.

Chruden and Sherman direct their personnel textbook toward managers rather than toward personnel staff, and they give increased attention to social responsibilities and to the application of behavioral science principles. There are 7 parts: the personnel management system; staffing the organization; maximizing employee potential; organizational behavior; management-labor relations; remuneration and security; assessment and research. Bibliographies are at end of chapters; 14 short case problems are at end. The authors compiled a companion book of *Readings in Per-*

sonnel Management (4th ed., South-Western, 1976); also the results of a research study on the *Personnel Practices of American Companies in Europe* (New York, American Management Association, 1972), which is based on interviews with managers from 40 American subsidiaries in the United Kingdom and in 7 European countries.

Flippo, Edwin B. *Principles of Personnel Management.* 4th ed. New York, McGraw-Hill, 1976.

The approach in this newly revised introductory text is a functional one, concentrating on the important processes and philosophies of personnel procurement (recruiting, hiring, testing), development, compensation, integration (motivation, communication, etc.), maintenance (safety and health, benefits, etc.). Lists of supplementary readings are at end of chapters; cases are at end of sections.

Greenman, Russell L. and Eric J. Schmertz. *Personnel Administration and the Law.* Washington, D.C., Bureau of National Affairs, 1972.

This book "is designed to alert personnel and labor administrators to situations in which legal advice may be required to arrive at sound management decisions." Each chapter concentrates on a specific topic: wages and hours; equal employment opportunity and civil rights; employee benefits and insurance; workmen's compensation, safety, and health; employees' personal rights; arbitration and the law. There are frequent references to legal cases throughout, and a good topical index.

Jucius, Michael J. *Personnel Management.* 8th ed. Homewood, Ill., Irwin, 1975.

The latest edition of this good, standard text was not available in time to examine its contents. The 1971 edition is "organized around the functions which management must perform in order to build, and cooperate with, an effective and satisfied group of people." Includes chapters on selecting, developing, compensating employees; also on morale, union-management relations. There is a balance of descriptive and interpretative material in this book, which also has brief case studies and a short bibliography.

Lopez, Felix M. *Personnel Interviewing: Theory and Practice.* 2d ed. New York, McGraw-Hill, 1975.

This is a completely revised book, which provides a "bottoms up" review of personnel administration by focusing on the interview and relating it to other personnel techniques. It is in 4 parts: some basic considerations; decision-making interviews (selection, employment, assessment); problem-solving interviews (job effectiveness, performance-evaluation, career-counseling, problem-employee); information-exchange interviews (including the termination interview). Includes a bibliography.

Megginson, Leon C. *Personnel: A Behavioral Approach to Administration.* Rev. ed. Homewood, Ill., Irwin, 1972.

Professor Megginson states that he undertook this revision primarily to recognize and critically evaluate the effects upon personnel management of what he feels are the most pressing problems facing management today (technical change, social responsibility, movement to international operations). Emphasis is given to the behavioral science approach, and he concentrates on philosophical and theoretical concepts rather than on techniques. His section divisions are: managing human resources; personnel management in perspective; manpower development; using compensation to improve performance; using managerial leadership to improve performance; changing dimensions of personnel management. Short case problems are at end of each of the 6 sections.

Pigors, Paul and Charles A. Myers. *Personnel Administration: A Point of View and a Method.* 7th ed. New York, McGraw-Hill, 1972. (The 8th edition will be published in spring 1976.)

One of the most popular, basic personnel texts, written at the policy level and brought up to date to include important recent developments and new findings, especially those drawn from the behavioral sciences. Includes bibliographies at end of chapters. Professors Pigors and Myers (with F. T. Malm) were compilers of *Management of Human Resources: Readings in Personnel Administration* (3d ed., McGraw-Hill, 1973. [4th edition scheduled for publication in 1976.]

Strauss, George and Leonard R. Sayles. *Personnel: The Human Problems of Management.* 3d ed. Englewood Cliffs, N.J., Prentice-Hall, 1972.

Another excellent text, integrating contributions from the behavioral sciences and meant to deal with management problems in nonbusiness as well as in business organizations. The titles of the 7 major divisions indicate how this book varies from the traditional personnel approach: individuals, jobs, and groups; motivation and leadership; managerial skills (communications, interviewing, introducing change, discipline); organization; manpower and employee development; management and organization development; reward systems.

Yoder, Dale. *Personnel Management and Industrial Relations.* 6th ed. Englewood Cliffs, N.J., Prentice-Hall, 1970.

Yoder's well-established textbook "emphasizes goals, objectives, and understanding — the 'why' of employment behavior and manpower management — rather then the 'how' of programs, practices, and techniques," and it is written for all management rather than solely for personnel and industrial relations managers. Its 7 sections cover: policy and theory in manpower management; organization and administration; staffing; training and development; labor relations management; maintaining commitment; audits and research. Very short case problems are at end of chapters.

MANAGERIAL PERFORMANCE

Campbell, John P., Marvin D. Dunnette, Edward E. Lawler III, and Karl E. Weick, Jr. *Managerial Behavior, Performance, and Effectiveness.* New York, McGraw-Hill, 1970.

A consideration of managerial effectiveness in all its aspects. The authors surveyed firms and government agencies to learn about prevailing practices. They evaluate these practices in light of knowledge about managerial effectiveness contained in the behavioral science and business literature, and they suggest strategies for developing improved practices in the future. Includes a bibliography.

Cummings, L. L. and Donald P. Schwab. *Performance in Organizations: Determinants & Appraisal.* Glenview, Ill., Scott, Foresman, 1973.

"The major objective of this book is to aid the reader in understanding how people perform in organizations with the expectation that this understanding will be of value in improving the organizational performance of employees." The first part elaborates on a model to show how employee performance can be increased in an organizational setting; the second part discusses how effective performance appraisal systems are constructed and implemented. A useful annotated bibliography is on pp. 131–168.

Finkle, Robert B. and William S. Jones. *Assessing Corporate Talent: A Key to Managerial Manpower Planning.* New York, Wiley-Interscience, 1970.

This book describes an assessment process used at Standard Oil Company of Ohio. "Primary attention is devoted to explaining how the program uses present-day assessment technology in ways that help the management of the organization understand and build confidence in the results and how these results affect manpower planning decisions."

Koontz, Harold. *Appraising Managers as Managers.* New York, McGraw-Hill, 1971.

A practical book setting forth "an appraisal program that emphasizes both appraisal against objectives and appraisal of managers by managers." Includes a bibliography. Based on the wide experience of this management professor, writer and consultant.

Rothery, Brian. *Survival by Competence.* Philadelphia, Pa., Auerbach, 1973.

A British systems engineer presents a short, sharp discourse on leadership and competence, and he includes several "leadership and balance tests" at end.

Rowland, Virgil K. *Evaluating and Improving Managerial Performance.* New York, McGraw-Hill, 1970.

"This book is an attempt to pull together the management practices of many thousands of successful managers and to classify, explain, evaluate, and illustrate these practices so that they may be used by other managers who desire to improve their own managerial skills." Parts 1 and 6 discuss management philosophies and problems; Parts 2–5 are devoted to specific management tools or techniques.

Wortman, Max S., Jr., and Joann Sperling. *Defining the Manager's Job: A Manual of Position Descriptions.* 2d ed. New York, AMACOM, American Management Associations, 1975.

This book is not on managerial performance but seems to fit best in this section. It is an up-to-date revision of a very useful manual on current organization practices in preparing and using managerial position descriptions. There are 3 parts: Part 1 is a survey of 136 organizations that already have position descriptions; Part 2 provides information on techniques, methods and procedures; Part 3, comprising over half of the book, contains descriptions of individual top management and middle management positions, thus serving as a good source for typical examples of their content, style and format. A bibliography is at end.

MANAGEMENT DEVELOPMENT

Kaufman, H. G. *Obsolescence and Professional Career Development.* New York, AMACOM, American Management Associations, 1974.

A useful book for the practicing manager about the obsolescence of knowledge and skills among professionals in business, industrial and governmental organizations. Professor Kaufman integrates up-to-date empirical knowledge from research (some of it his own) with the practical experiences of managers and professionals. Includes bibliographical notes at end.

Lopez, Felix M. *The Making of a Manager: Guidelines to His Selection and Promotion.* New York, American Management Association, 1971.

A book about the manager — who he is, what he does, how he is selected and developed. It is written by the president of a psychological consulting firm to stimulate other presidents to more creative thinking in planning for future management development. There are 2 parts: theories, models, and facts; programs, procedures and practices.

Mahler, Walter R. and William F. Wrightnour. *Executive Continuity: How to Build and Retain an Effective Management Team.* Homewood, Ill., Dow Jones-Irwin, 1973.

A personnel consultant and a practitioner recommend a systems approach for building a management team. They consider the 10 basic requirements for the systems approach (such as effective staff contribution, anticipating future needs, objective data), and they give examples of methods, procedures and policy statements from organizations in a lengthy appendix.

Tracey, William R. *Managing Training and Development Systems.* New York, AMACOM, American Management Associations, 1974.

Studies the management of training and development in all types of enterprises according to the 5 basic managerial functions (planning, organizing, staffing, directing and controlling). Bibliographies at end of chapters.

Bibliographies

Hanson, Agnes O., comp. and ed. *Executive and Management Development for Business and Government: A Source Book* (Management Information Guide, No. 31). Detroit, Mich., Gale Research Co. To be published in late 1975 or early 1976.

This annotated bibliography covers much more than just books and other sources on management development itself, and the emphasis is on those sources that discuss conceptual approaches and skills. The first 10 chapters cover the history of management thought, organizational theory, relations with society and government, management in general (principles, practices, functions), management by objectives and by results, human resource planning, executives (including administration, planning and decision-making), international management, management education and development. This is followed by a chapter describing books on executive and management development in government. The last 4 chapters list basic reference sources, including indexes, abstracts, periodicals, directories, management development guides and organizations. There are author, title, and subject indexes at end.

Directories of Executive Development Programs

Bricker, George W., comp. *Bricker's Directory of University-Sponsored Executive Development Programs.* South Chatham, Mass., Bricker Publications (annual).

Describes English-language programs in the United States, Canada, Europe, the United Kingdom and Australia.

Periodicals

Training and Development Journal. Madison, Wisc., American Society for Training and Development (monthly).

Short articles on all aspects of training and development, and news of interest to ASTD members. Includes book reviews.

SUPERVISION

Benton, Lewis R. *Supervision and Management.* New York, McGraw-Hill, 1972.
A basic text on effective supervision and management of human resources in all kinds of organizations. After an introductory section Benton considers: the process of recruitment; functional supervision (training, discipline, wage administration, etc.); management components (management development, performance evaluating, decision-making, etc.); elements of production (work measurement, wage incentives, productivity, etc.); "the long view" (recruitment and training of disadvantaged groups, and future perspectives).

Black, James M. *The Basics of Supervisory Management: Mastering the Art of Effective Supervision.* New York, McGraw-Hill, 1975.
This aims to be a practical "easy-to-read, easy-to-understand introduction to the responsibilities of the supervisory job together with clear explanations of the day-to-day problems supervisors face and how they go about solving them."

Cone, William F. *Supervising Employees Effectively.* Reading, Mass., Addison-Wesley, 1974.
A short, practical guide, in paperback, written by a personnel development expert primarily for new supervisors and concentrating on day-to-day work situations. Includes a short bibliography of basic organizational behavior books and articles at end.

Dowling, William F. and Leonard R. Sayles. *How Managers Motivate: The Imperatives of Supervision.* New York, McGraw-Hill, 1971.
This book on face-to-face supervision has 3 objectives: "first, to include a broad range of research findings from the leadership and organizational behavior field; second, to express these in ways that would appeal to the reader . . . ; and third, to emphasize the actual behavior and analytical thinking required of supervisors, not abstract 'principles' and traditional 'theories.'" Each chapter has 2 interesting features: (1) a brief selection from the ideas of one of 12 classic management thinkers such as Barnard, McGregor; (2) a continuing case study keyed to each chapter and recording the growth of a typical new supervisor. A few suggested books are also listed with each chapter.

Sartain, Aaron Q. and Alton W. Baker. *The Supervisor and His Job.* 2d ed. New York, McGraw-Hill, 1972.
Aims to give all persons involved in supervisory-related functions the background that may help them "in understanding the present situation of the supervisor's job, likely changes in it, and how it may be performed more efficiently and effectively." It includes sections discussing: studies of supervision; the basis for effective supervision; basic functions of the supervisor; the supervisor and day-to-day problems; the future. Includes short case problems and a bibliography.

Terry, George R. *Supervisory Management.* Homewood, Ill., Irwin, 1974.
Brings the study of the supervisory job up to date by emphasizing behavioral aspects. The material is organized in 4 main sections: the supervisor and his total management environment; the supervisor's management of himself; the supervisor and his relationship with his individual employees; the supervisor and his relationship with his work group. Includes short case problems.

Van Dersal, William R. *The Successful Supervisor in Government and Business.* 3d ed. New York, Harper & Row, 1974.

A book for practicing supervisors, with an emphasis on the behavioral aspects. Includes a list of 16 recommended books on management and human relations and also a few journals.

Periodicals

Supervisory Management. New York, AMACOM, American Management Associations (monthly).

About 5 short articles in each issue, on practical techniques and problems, written for supervisors and managers. Indexed in BPI.

WAGE AND SALARY ADMINISTRATION

Handbooks

Rock, Milton L., ed. *Handbook of Wage and Salary Administration.* New York, McGraw-Hill, 1972.

Intended as a practical reference work for managers, this handbook covers concepts, techniques and processes basic to good wage and salary administration. There are 51 chapters written by a large group of authors, and it is divided into the following 9 parts: job content; job measurement; surveys; pay structure; performance appraisal; noncash compensation; incentives; special compensation programs; the compensation program in action.

Books

Armstrong, Michael. *Principles & Practices of Salary Administration.* London, Kogan Page, 1974.

The aim of this book "is to review the whole range of salary administration practices and procedures available to management in an inflationary era." After first discussing the aims of salary administration, factors, motivation and salary policies, the author follows with chapters dealing with the various stages of an evaluation program (job analysis, job grading, conducting market rate surveys, designing salary structures). The last part of the book considers fringe benefits, such as bonus schemes, profit sharing, share ownership, and pensions. Although this book is based on practical experience in the United Kingdom, it is still of interest to all salary administrators wherever they may be located.

Belcher, David W. *Compensation Administration.* Englewood Cliffs, N.J., Prentice-Hall, 1974.

Professor Belcher's approach in this study of compensation policies, practices and problems is that employment is an exchange transaction "between the organization and employee in which each gets something and gives something." He divides the book into 6 parts: compensation models; contributions (both job-related and personal); rewards (job-related and personal); the comparison process; compensation problems of special employee groups (sales compensation and compensation of managers and professionals); system integration and control. Includes bibliographical footnotes.

Cheeks, James E. *How to Compensate Executives.* Homewood, Ill., Dow Jones-Irwin, 1974.

Meant as a practical guide for planning an effective compensation program that will attract, stimulate and help retain capable executives. The author, who is an attorney, focuses on the true cost to the company and the after-tax benefits to the executive.

Dunn, J. D. and Frank M. Rachel. *Wage and Salary Administration: Total Compensation Systems.* New York, McGraw-Hill, 1971.

An examination of compensation theory and practice applicable in all kinds of organizations. It is arranged in 5 major sections: compensation fundamentals; job design and analysis; compensation practices and programs; designing a compensation package; total compensation systems. Includes bibliographical footnotes; also case problems with each chapter.

Lawler, Edward E. III. *Pay and Organizational Effectiveness: A Psychological View.* New York, McGraw-Hill, 1971.

Professor Lawler focuses on the psychological issues concerned with pay in an effort to gain better understanding of human behavior at work. His research covers 3 areas: the importance of pay; the ability of pay to motivate employees; satisfaction with pay. A final section is an overview of pay and organizational effectiveness. Includes a bibliography.

Sibson, Robert E. *Compensation.* New York, AMACOM, American Management Associations, 1974.

This practical book gives line managers information about compensation administration, with an emphasis on compensation policies, practices and techniques. It is based on an earlier work and reflects the many years experience of this business consultant.

Zollitsch, Herbert G. and Adolph Langsner. *Wage and Salary Administration.* 2d ed. Cincinnati, Ohio, South-Western, 1970.

Presents "the philosophy and fundamental guiding principles essential for establishing and maintaining adequate compensation for all employees in an enterprise." Includes a bibliography. Professor Zollitsch is working on a third edition that he hopes will be published in 1977, perhaps with a different title.

An earlier work on executive compensation is *Financial Motivation for Executives* by Graef S. Crystal (New York, American Management Association, 1970). A practical study of the problems, the various options and alternatives of international compensation is *Worldwide Executive Compensation* (New York, Business International Corp., 1974).

Surveys of Executive Compensation

American Management Associations. *Executive Compensation Service.* New York (annual).

A comprehensive source of salary, bonus and benefit information available to companies on subscription by special arrangement with AMA. The "Domestic Compensation Service" contains 14 special reports on top management, middle management, directors, sales personnel, supervisory management, office personnel, etc. The "International Compensation Service" consists of 20 separate reports on individual countries. Can be purchased either as a whole or in parts; contact the AMA for further information.

Business International Corp. *European Compensation Survey* and *Asia/Pacific Regional Compensation Survey.* New York.

These are periodic country surveys of company compensation policies and practices. The European surveys are for 10 countries, the Asia/Pacific for 12 countries. Each country report contains 2 series: Series I covers "Expatriate Allowances and Fringe

Benefits," surveying the policies of major U.S. firms in the region; Series II, "Local Salaries and Compensation Policies," surveys major companies of all nationalities in the region and includes a monthly index of salaries/wages for about 70 specific job categories. These surveys are quite expensive but can be purchased for a specific country. Business International also publishes a series of *Survey of Living Costs* for 47 cities. They are usually 6-page statistical tables of costs for specific items of household supplies, personal care, clothing, transportation, education, etc.

Dartnell Survey of Executive Compensation. 10th Survey by R. J. Wytmar. Chicago, Dartnell Corp. 1973.

This latest survey of executive compensation was conducted in 1972 and is published in 12 sections covering top management and each basic functional area. It is based on compensation data from over 1,900 companies and includes statistics, charts, reprints of articles.

Top Executive Compensation. New York, Conference Board (annual).

This annual survey of the 3 highest paid executives in each of over 1,200 corporations is issued in the *Conference Board Reports* series. (The 1974 edition contains the 1973 survey and was *Report* No. 640.) It is arranged by broad industry and includes data on the prevalence of various elements in the executive compensation package, such as bonus and stock option plans.

Three annual surveys appear in periodicals. *Business Week's* "Annual Survey of Executive Compensation" is in the first May issue each year. It consists of a table arranged by industry, showing salaries of the 2 or 3 top officers of specific large U.S. companies. The *McKinsey Quarterly* publishes a "Top Executive Compensation Survey" in its Autumn issue each year. This is a short article based on a survey of almost 600 large companies. A roster of over 800 chief executives ranked by salary appears in the "Annual Directory Issue" of *Forbes* (May 15).

Abstracts and Bibliographies

Compensation Review. New York, AMACOM, American Management Associations (quarterly).

Useful not only for its several feature articles on compensation, pensions, etc., but especially as a source for keeping up to date on what is being published elsewhere on this subject. It includes condensations of noteworthy articles and also annotated lists of articles and a few books.

Tracy, Karen B., comp. *Executive Compensation: Selected References.* (Reference List, No. 28). Boston, Baker Library, Harvard Business School, 1976.

A short, partially annotated list of books and selected articles on executive compensation in general, and on stock options, incentives, pay practices abroad; also sources for salary surveys and statistics (some on specific industries) and for executive position descriptions.

PERSONNEL BIBLIOGRAPHIES AND ABSTRACTS

Several of the bibliographies listed in the "Industrial Relations" section of this chapter are also useful for locating current literature on personnel administration and human relations. The British *Anbar Management Services* publication "Personnel + Training Abstracts" is described in Chapter 10.

Institute of Personnel Management. *IPM Bibliography.* London, 1973–   To be published in 6 parts.

An annotated bibliography, with selection based on books added to the IPM library in London. Part 1, "Management and the Enterprizes; and Personnel Management, General," and also Part 2, "Manpower Studies and Labour Economics" have already been published as of spring 1975. The other parts will cover: "Education, Training and Development"; "Pay and Employment Conditions"; "Industrial Relations"; "The Behavioural Sciences."

Personnel Management Abstracts. Ann Arbor, Mich., Graduate School of Business Administration, University of Michigan (quarterly).

Each issue is in 2 parts: (1) an annotated subject listing of periodical articles that deal with the management of people and organizational behavior; (2) abstracts of a small selection of these articles and a few books.

U.S. Civil Service Commission. Library. *Personnel Literature.* Washington, D.C., U.S. Government Printing Office (monthly, with annual index).

A continuing list of new books, pamphlets, articles added to the CSC library, arranged by almost 100 subject headings and including subject descriptors with each entry. The annual index is by author and subject. Biennial cumulations of selected materials from this monthly are issued as their *Personnel Bibliography Series* (order also from GPO), with each bibliography covering one broad area. Several numbers published in 1974 are: No. 56, "Improving Employee Performance"; No. 57, "The Personnel Management Function — Organization, Staffing and Evaluation"; No. 58, "Self Development Aids for Supervisors and Middle Managers"; No. 59, "Labor-Management Relations in the Public Service"; No. 60, "Employee Benefits and Services."

Work Related Abstracts. Detroit, Mich., Information Coordinators (monthly).

A good comprehensive, annotated index of articles, dissertations and books covering labor, personnel and organizational behavior, in loose-leaf format. It is arranged in 20 broad sections for such subjects as: human relations and personnel concepts; personnel practices; education, training and vocational education; labor force and manpower. A detailed subject index is at front.

The American Management Associations publishes occasional practical treatises in the area of personnel and industrial relations. Several are included in this chapter. Others can be found by checking their annual list of publications, *AMACOM Resources for Professional Management.*

Conference Board. *Cumulative Index.* New York (annual).

The Conference Board publishes a number of useful reports on the personnel policies and practices of companies, and this is a cumulated subject index to all of their publications. Several examples of studies published 1973–1974 in their *Conference Board Reports* series are: No. 589, "Nondiscrimination in Employment"; No. 594, "Worker Participation: New Voice in Management"; No. 596, "Corporate Directorship Practices — Compensation"; No. 612, "Supervisory Training"; No. 640, "Top Executive Compensation."

PERSONNEL DICTIONARIES

Banki, Ivan S. *Dictionary of Supervision and Management.* Los Angeles, Calif., Systems Research, 1974.

A dictionary of terms and concepts in management, supervision and training; also descriptions of organizations. A list of dictionaries and encylopedias is at end.

PERSONNEL SERVICES

Bureau of National Affairs. *BNA Policy and Practice Series.* Washington, D.C. 8 volumes. And weekly supplements.

This is a comprehensive, loose-leaf reference guide providing up-to-date information on personnel policies, practices and procedures, and it is of value to anyone involved in employer-employee relations. There are 5 sections: *Personnel Management* (1 volume), which is a practical guide to everyday nonlegal problems of employer-employee relations, covering all important subjects, such as induction and orientation, training and employee education, absenteeism and turnover, community relations. (A useful feature is its inclusion of annotated lists of books and articles with each discussion.); *Labor Relations* (2 volumes), consisting of federal and state labor laws, explanations of National Labor Relations Board and court rulings; *Fair Employment Practices* (1 volume), covering federal and state laws dealing with equal employment opportunity; *Wages and Hours* (2 volumes), both federal and state wage-hour laws; *Compensation* (2 volumes), covering all aspects of compensation policies and plans, and also including occasional lists of books and articles with certain sections.

Bureau of National Affairs. *Personnel Policies Forum Surveys.* Washington, D.C. (3 or 4 numbers per year).

These survey pamphlets report on company policies and practices of BNA Personnel Policy Forum members, who represent all types of enterprises. There have been 110 surveys published up to mid-1975, with recent numbers covering such topics as: No. 101, "Employer Policies on Political Activity"; No. 102, "Employee Conduct and Discipline"; No. 103, "Pensions & Other Retirement Benefits"; No. 104, "Management Performance Appraisal Programs"; No. 106, "Employee Absenteeism and Turnover."

Commerce Clearing House. *Personnel Guide.* Chicago. 1 volume. And biweekly supplements.

This loose-leaf service reports on specific employer-employee problems and explains how each was handled or resolved. Includes a dictionary of personnel terms.

Prentice-Hall, Inc. *Personnel Management.* Englewood Cliffs, N.J. 2 volumes. And biweekly supplements.

One of these volumes, "Policies and Practices," gives concise, practical information on a wide range of personnel techniques used by employers, including employee selection, training, promoting, compensation, discipline. The other volume, "Communications," which can be purchased separately, covers methods, ideas, forms, etc., used in communicating company rules and policies to employees.

Prentice-Hall publishes a separate service on *Public Personnel Administration — Policies and Practices for Personnel* (biweekly), which is a practical guide on effective personnel policies as well as on new developments and trends in the public sector.

PERSONNEL PERIODICALS

All of these personnel periodicals are indexed in *Work Related Abstracts,* which is described elsewhere in this chapter.

Human Resource Management. Ann Arbor, School of Business Administration, University of Michigan (quarterly).

This journal aims to publish short, easy-to-read research reports on management topics relating to the development of practices that more effectively use the organization's human resources. There are usually 4 to 6 articles in each issue. Indexed in PAIS.

Personnel. Saranac Lake, N.Y., AMACOM, American Management Associations (bimonthly).

Short, practical articles for managers and behavioral scientists on topics related to organizational behavior, human relations, personnel administration. Annotated booklists are in most issues. Indexed in BPI.

The Personnel Administrator. Berea, Ohio, American Society for Personnel Administration (8/yr.).

Each issue usually concentrates on a specific topic in the human resources management area, such as motivation, communciations, labor negotiations. The articles are short and discuss recent developments, research studies, etc. A special directory issue is published each year.

Personnel Journal. Santa Monica, Calif. (monthly).

Billed as "the magazine of industrial relations and personnel management" this trade journal contains good, short and practical articles on a broad range of personnel topics. It also has book reviews, book notes; news about personnel research, conferences, new publications and films, employee magazines, personnel changes; help and positions wanted advertisements. Indexed in BPI.

Personnel Psychology. Durham, N.C. (quarterly).

A journal of applied research covering personnel psychology and organizational behavior. Excellent articles written primarily by academic authorities, often with bibliographic citations. Includes a good book review section.

Public Personnel Management. Chicago, International Personnel Management Association (bimonthly).

Articles are on industrial relations and personnel administration topics of special interest to personnel managers in the public sector. Indexed in BPI.

Two foreign journals are: *Canadian Personnel and Industrial Relations Journal* (Toronto, Council of Canadian Personnel Associations, 6/yr.); and *Personnel Management* (London, Institute of Personnel Management, monthly). This latter journal includes book reviews and is indexed in BPI.

PERSONNEL DIRECTORIES

Who's Who in Personnel Administration and Industrial Relations. Epping, Essex, England, Gower Press, 1973.

Brief biographical data on important British personnel managers and industrial relations officials, with an index by affiliation and field of activity.

PERSONNEL MANAGEMENT ASSOCIATIONS

American Society for Personnel Administration, 19 Church Street, Berea, Ohio 44017.

American Society for Training and Development, P.O. Box 5307, Madison, Wisc. 53707.

Institute of Personnel Management, 5 Winsley Street, London W1N 7AQ, England.

International Personnel Management Association, 1313 East 60th Street, Chicago, Ill. 60637.

Tavistock Institute of Human Relations, Tavistock Centre, Belsize Lane, London NW3 5BA, England.

INDUSTRIAL RELATIONS

LABOR ECONOMICS AND LABOR RELATIONS

Bloom, Gordon F. and Herbert R. Northrup. *Economics of Labor Relations.* 7th ed. Homewood, Ill., Irwin, 1973.

This latest edition of a popular text has been completely revised to include current key issues in labor relations, such as unemployment and poverty, race relations, wage controls. The authors' main objective is "the integration of economic facts and economic analysis so that the student may acquire not only an awareness of labor problems, but also an understanding of conflicting views concerning their causes and possible solutions." Annotated bibliographies are at end of chapters.

Bok, Derek C. and John T. Dunlop. *Labor and the American Community.* New York, Simon and Schuster, 1970.

A study of the characteristics and problems of the American labor movement, with particular emphasis on the nature of unions and their administration, the state of collective bargaining and how it relates to inflation, the special problems of labor relations in the public sector, and the political role of labor unions. Includes bibliographical notes at end.

Chamberlain, Neil W. and Donald E. Cullen. *The Labor Sector.* 2d ed. New York, McGraw-Hill, 1971.

Considers labor from various points of view: a seller of services; a movement; a factor of production; a market; a pressure group; as a subject of social protection; and in relation to the performance of the economy. Bibliographies are at end of most chapters.

Reynolds, Lloyd G. *Labor Economics and Labor Relations.* 6th ed. Englewood Cliffs, N.J., Prentice-Hall, 1974.

Another popular textbook covering both of the title subjects and brought up to date to include the many new trends of labor in today's industrial society. Reading suggestions are at end of chapters. Professor Reynolds (with Stanley H. Masters and Collette H. Moser) has also edited a book of *Readings in Labor Economics and Labor Relations* (Prentice-Hall, 1974).

Rowe, David K. *Industrial Relations Management for Profit and Growth.* New York, American Management Association, 1971.

This is not a "how-to" book but rather an informative treatise on the organization and on the ways industrial relations management relates to the organization's objectives — its contribution to profits, growth, resources, productivity, and its relation to operations, manpower planning, employee objectives, etc. A bibliography is at end.

Sloane, Arthur A. and Fred Witney. *Labor Relations.* 2d ed., Englewood Cliffs, N.J., Prentice-Hall, 1972.

A text on union-management relations, with Part 3, "collective bargaining," the longest of its 4 parts. Part 3 examines the negotiation, administration and major contents of the labor contract and includes 12 arbitration cases drawn from the authors' experience. Part 2 surveys the historical, legal and structural environments that influence labor relations behavior. Includes bibliographies.

ARBITRATION AND COLLECTIVE BARGAINING

Baer, Walter E. *The Labor Arbitration Guide.* Homewood, Ill., Dow Jones-Irwin, 1974.

This is a guide to the grievance arbitration process. It begins with selecting and researching the arbitrator, continues with restrictions placed upon him, the grievance procedure, interpreting the agreement, rules of evidence, etc., and ends with a discussion of critical issues of arbitral conclusions. Baer has also written a book on *Strikes: A Study of Conflict & How to Resolve It* (New York, AMACOM, American Management Associations, 1975).

Beal, Edwin F., Edward D. Wickersham and Philip Kienast. *The Practice of Collective Bargaining.* 4th ed. Homewood, Ill., Irwin, 1972.

A standard text that includes recent developments, with an added section on collective bargaining in the public sector. Annotated bibliographies are at end of most chapters; cases are on pp. 493–702.

Elkouri, Frank and Edna A. Elkouri. *How Arbitration Works.* 3d ed. Washington, D.C., Bureau of National Affairs, 1973.

An expanded guidebook and text dealing with essential principles of law and practice in the field of labor-management arbitration. It is written by 2 lawyers and includes frequent references to reported arbitration cases to illustrate and substantiate specific processes.

Marshall, Howard D. and Natalie J. Marshall. *Collective Bargaining.* New York, Random House, 1971.

A beginning textbook in 3 parts: the institutional and historical background; contract time (wages, hours, grievance procedures, strikes, etc.); collective bargaining and the economy. Includes an annotated bibliography.

Prasow, Paul and Edward Peters. *Arbitration and Collective Bargaining: Conflict Resolution in Labor Relations.* New York, McGraw-Hill, 1970.

"Focuses on the decision-making function of the arbitrator and on the dynamics of the arbitration process," with substantial material taken from actual arbitration opinions and awards. Includes a bibliography.

Simkin, William E. *Mediation and the Dynamics of Collective Bargaining.* Washington, D.C., Bureau of National Affairs, 1971.

Simkin draws on his long experience to write this useful and readable analysis of the philosophy of labor mediation. He begins with a discussion of the ABCs of collective bargaining, and then covers facts about mediation, mediation practice, crisis bargaining and extraordinary procedures.

Taylor, Benjamin T. and Fred Witney. *Labor Relations Law.* 2d ed. Englewood Cliffs, N.J., Prentice-Hall, 1975.

A text for persons with little legal background on "the major trends in the law of collective bargaining, the reasons for these trends, and their consequences on the overall function of collective bargaining." Includes text of important labor acts in an appendix; also a bibliography.

Trotta, Maurice S. *Arbitration of Labor-Management Disputes.* New York, AMACOM, American Management Associations, 1974.

Trotta, an arbitrator of long experience, intends this as a source of basic information rather than an exhaustive treatise. Part 1 is on principles and procedures; Part 2 gives actual arbitration cases; Part 3 is a lengthy appendix containing significant legislation.

INDUSTRIAL RELATIONS BIBLIOGRAPHIES AND ABSTRACTS

A. G. Bush Library Abstracts. Chicago, A. G. Bush Library, Industrial Relations Center, University of Chicago (biweekly).

An annotated subject listing of current literature on organizations, management, personnel, human behavior, the work force, industrial relations. Contains a quarterly index.

Industrial and Labor Relations Review. Ithaca, New York State School of Industrial Relations, Cornell University (quarterly).

A useful feature in this periodical is its "Recent Publications," a continuing list of books, pamphlets, theses and articles arranged by the following topics: labor-management relations; labor economics; labor conditions and problems; labor organizations; government and labor; social insurance and employees welfare; personnel; human relations. The current compiler (1975) is Gordon T. Law, Jr., reference librarian at this New York State school.

Industrial Relations Theses and Dissertations. Ottawa, Ontario, Canada, Department of Labour (annual).

A compilation of theses and dissertations accepted at 26 American and Canadian universities, including many in the personnel and organizational behavior area as well as in that of industrial relations. It is arranged alphabetically with a subject index and is compiled each year by an informal Committee of University Industrial Relations Librarians. The volume covering 1974 is being edited and published at the Industrial Relations Research Institute, University of Wisconsin.

International Labour Office. *International Labour Documentation.* Geneva, Switzerland (semi-monthly).

A descriptive subject listing, in English, based on current acquisitions in the ILO library, and covering the fields of industrial relations, management, manpower planning, vocational training and other areas of economics and social development. Difficult to use for searching since there is no cumulation; however the ILO does offer a computer search service for persons interested in a specialized list on any topic covered in their bibliography.

For the names of other ILO publications consult their *ILO Catalogue of Publications in Print.*

Massachusetts Institute of Technology. Industrial Relations Library. *Library Accessions Bulletin.* Cambridge, Mass. (bimonthly).

A good, descriptive list of selected books, pamphlets and articles added to this industrial relations library. It is arranged in over 40 subject areas and includes topics on personnel and industrial psychology as well as on industrial relations and labor.

Princeton University. Industrial Relations Section. *Selected References* (quarterly).

Instead of an accessions list, Princeton's Industrial Relations Section offers a series of 4-page annotated bibliographies, each on a topic of current interest. The March issue each year covers "Outstanding Books in Industrial Relations." Other 1974 titles are: No. 172, "Changing Schedules of Work"; No. 173, "Worker Participation in Industry: the European Experience"; No. 174, "Wage Determination in the Public Sector."

Work Related Abstracts. Detroit, Mich., Information Coordinators (monthly).

For a description of this important, comprehensive index see the section for "Personnel Bibliographies and Abstracts" in this chapter.

The U.S. Bureau of Labor Statistics publishes a semi-annual subject list of their *Publications.* They also publish an annual description of their *Major Programs: Bureau of Labor Statistics,* which includes the names of publications covering their research programs in employment, manpower, prices, wages and industrial relations, safety and health, and economic trends.

INDUSTRIAL RELATIONS DICTIONARIES

Roberts, Harold S. *Roberts' Dictionary of Industrial Relations.* Rev. ed. Washington, D.C., Bureau of National Affairs, 1971.

An encyclopedic dictionary not only for industrial relations terms but also for short summaries of decisions of the Supreme Court and NLRB, outlines of major labor laws, notes about international unions. References to sources of information are with most entries.

Seide, Katharine, ed. *A Dictionary of Arbitration and Its Terms.* Dobbs Ferry, N.Y., published for the American Arbitration Association by Oceana Publications, 1970.

This encyclopedic dictionary on arbitration also includes sources for further information with each definition. An appendix contains separate bibliographies (now rather outdated) on labor, commercial and international arbitration, U.S. and international arbitration rules and procedures.

LABOR SERVICES

Bureau of National Affairs. *Daily Labor Report.* Washington, D.C. (5/wk.).

Important for those executives and industrial relations specialists who must have immediate notification, analysis and interpretations of major U.S. labor developments. It covers news of congressional activity, important NLRB decisions, full text of important federal and state court rulings, arbitration awards, significant bargaining negotiations, equal employment opportunity developments, news of management and union strategy. It also includes basic statistics and economic data of use in bargaining.

Bureau of National Affairs. *Labor Relations Reporter.* Washington, D.C. 13 volumes. (loose-leaf, with semi-weekly supplements).

This comprehensive labor service gives full text coverage on current labor relations, state laws, fair employment practices, wages and hours, labor arbitration. The volumes are broken down as follows: *Master Index* (1 volume); *Labor Relations Expediter* (2 volumes), contains annotated discussions of the origin, development, and current status of all important labor relations topics, analyses of leading cases and rulings, text of federal labor laws, etc; *Analysis — News and Background Information* (1 volume); *Labor-Management Relations* (1 volume), covering all published decisions of the National Labor Relations Board, significant decisions of state labor boards, decisions of federal and state courts relating to labor-management issues; *State Laws* (2 volumes); *Fair Employment Practices* (2 volumes), provides text of federal and state laws, orders and regulations, etc.; *Wages and Hours* (3 volumes), full text of wage and hour cases, laws, etc.; *Labor Arbitration* (1 volume), weekly reports of labor dispute settlements, full text of awards, settlements.

Backing up this service are their several bound "Reference Library" series for past labor laws, decisions, etc., in the following sets: *Labor Relations Reference Manuals* containing digests of NLRB decisions and text of court decisions on labor relations; *Wage and Hour Cases,* covering both federal and state laws; *Labor Arbitration Reports*; *Fair Employment Practice Cases.* Cumulative digests and indexes provide easy access to these bound volumes. Their *Labor Relations Yearbook* is a one-volume summary of the year's major labor events, including conferences, studies, background and economic data.

Bureau of National Affairs. *Manpower Information Service.* Washington, D.C. 2 volumes.

The first volume is a biweekly report summarizing new developments in manpower activities, also text of reports, new acts, etc. The second volume is a permanent "Reference File" that contains: technical data for planners; information on contracts and grants; statistics on employment, training, manpower programs; directories of agencies and organizations; text of major federal manpower laws and regulations.

Several more specialized BNA labor services are: *BNA Policy and Practice Series* (described elsewhere in this chapter); *Collective Bargaining Negotiations & Contracts* (2 volumes, biweekly); *Government Employee Relations Report* (4 volumes, weekly); *Occupational Safety & Health Reporter* (5 volumes, weekly); *Union Labor Report* (2 volumes, weekly); and *White Collar Report* (weekly).

Commerce Clearing House. *Labor Law Reports.* Chicago. 14 volumes (looseleaf, with weekly or biweekly supplements).

A comprehensive, continuing guide to federal and state labor relations and wage-hour rules. It includes: laws, administrative interpretations, rulings, statutes, regulations, rules and forms; NLRB and court decisions; union contracts, arbitration procedures. The volume coverage is as follows: *Labor Relations* (5 volumes) contains federal labor relations and union control rules, statutes, regulations, etc.; *Wages-Hours* (2 volumes) covers federal controls, statutes, etc.; *State Laws* (3 volumes) gives a state-by-state breakdown of labor relations for employees in both industry and government; *Union Contract-Arbitration* (1 volume) explains arbitration principles; *Employment Practices* (3 volumes) covers federal and state fair employment rules.

Backing up this service are the following bound volumes for historical data: *Labor Cases,* which gives full-text federal and state court decisions; *NLRB Decisions,* which digests all board decisions; *Labor Arbitration Awards*; *Employment Practices Decisions* rendered both by federal and state courts.

Commerce Clearing House. *Labor Law Course.* Chicago (annual).

A one-volume reference or self-study course on the essentials of labor law, with an emphasis on broad federal statutes. It covers labor unions, labor relations, unfair labor practices, contract clauses, arbitration, wage-hour controls.

Commerce Clearing House. *Labor Law Guide.* Chicago. 2 volumes (loose-leaf, with weekly supplements).

This is a 2-volume summary of the comprehensive loose-leaf service described above that provides answers to many of the everyday problems arising under federal and state labor laws. It is arranged by topic and includes federal and state laws governing labor relations, wages and hours.

Two other CCH legal services are : *EEOC Compliance Manual*; and *Employment Safety and Health Guide* (3 volumes).

Prentice-Hall, Inc. *Labor Relations Guide.* Englewood Cliffs, N.J. 3 volumes (loose-leaf, with weekly supplements).

Volumes 1-2 contain explanations of labor laws, full texts of federal labor laws and regulations, pertinent data both parties should know about bargaining, and a cost-of-living index. The third volume covers "Occupational Safety and Health."

Two separate but closely related services are: *Wage-Hour Guide* (1 volume, with biweekly supplements), which contains wage and hour laws and regulations, with interpretations; *Industrial Relations Guide* (1 volume, with biweekly supplements), a guide for solving industrial relations problems, with emphasis on arbitration awards and union contract clauses, and including many actual examples.

Two other Prentice-Hall services are: *Payroll Guide* (biweekly); and *Personnel Management* (described elsewhere in this chapter).

U.S. National Labor Relations Board. *Decisions and Orders.* Washington, D.C., U.S. Government Printing Office. Vol. 1, Dec. 7, 1935 to date.

Although this is not a loose-leaf service, it is important to note here that the NRLB publishes this continuing series of its decisions and orders, and also, beginning on Dec. 31, 1939, a separate series of *Court Decisions Relating to the National Labor Relations Act.*

LABOR STATISTICS

U.S. Statistics

The Bureau of Labor Statistics publishes a variety of useful statistical publications, some quite general and indispensable as in the case of the two listed below, and others covering specialized labor subjects such as consumer prices (see section at end of Chapter 5), indexes of labor productivity and wages in specific industries. For a continuing bibliography consult their semi-annual, annotated subject list of *Publications* or their annual *Major Programs: Bureau of Labor Statistics,* which includes names of publications.

U.S. Bureau of Labor Statistics. *Handbook of Labor Statistics.* Washington, D.C., U.S. Government Printing Office (annual).

A valuable, one-volume compendium of major BLS statistics, with each table giving figures for as many years as they were compiled. Statistics cover: the labor force; employment; unemployment; hours; productivity; compensation; prices and living conditions; unions and industrial relations; occupational injuries and illnesses; foreign labor statistics. "Technical Notes" at front describe major statistical programs and identify the tables derived from each. This handbook is issued each year in the BLS *Bulletin* series, with the 1974 volume issued as *Bulletin* No. 1825.

Two other useful annual statistical volumes in the *Bulletin* series are: *Bulletin* No. 1312-9, "Employment and Earnings, 1909–72," which gives monthly historical statistics by SIC industry; *Bulletin* No. 1370-10, "Employment and Earnings, States and Areas, 1939–72," with figures for states and some cities by 2-digit SIC industries.

U.S. Bureau of Labor Statistics. *Monthly Labor Review.* Washington, D.C., U.S. Government Printing Office.

This is an indispensable publication for current labor statistics covering employment, unemployment, hours, earnings, consumer and wholesale prices, productivity, labor-management data (including work stoppages).

Several more specialized statistical monthlies of the BLS are: *Area Trends in Employment and Unemployment*; *Chartbook on Prices, Wages, and Productivity*; *CPI Detailed Report* (Consumer Price Index, U.S. and City Averages); *Employment and Earnings*; and *Wholesale Prices and Price Indexes.*

Labor statistics are found in other U.S. government publications. The various economic census volumes give number of employees and size of payroll by industry and by location. (These are described in Chapter 4.) The decennial *Census of Population* in its "Subject Reports," Series PC(2) for 1970, published special statistical reports on such subjects as "Employment Status and Work Experience" (Report PC[2] 6A); "Occupational Characteristics" (7A); "Occupation by Industry" (7C); "Government Workers" (7D); "Occupations of Persons with High Earnings" (7F); "Sources and Structure of Family Income" (8A); and "Earnings by Occupation and Education" (8B). The annual *Manpower Report of the President* also includes a statistical section.

Foreign Labor Statistics

International Labour Office. *Yearbook of Labour Statistics.* Geneva, Switzerland.

Statistics are for about 180 countries or territories for the past 10 years and cover: employment, unemployment, hours of work, productivity, wages, consumer prices, industrial accidents, industrial disputes, etc. "References and Sources" (at end) list, by country, the principal sources of national labor statistics. The ILO quarterly *Bulletin of Labour Statistics* contains current figures on employment, unemployment, hours of work, wages, consumer prices.

Organization for Economic Cooperation and Development. *Labour Force Statistics.* Paris (annual).

OECD country-by-country statistics on population, the labor force, employment and wages by broad industry, for the past 12 years. National sources for statistics are at front. A new *Quarterly Labour Force Statistics* is scheduled for publication in mid-1975.

Great Britain. Department of Employment. *British Labour Statistics Yearbook.* London, H.M. Stationery Office.

Statistics include wages and hours, earnings, retail prices, employment, unemployment, family expenditure, unions, work stoppages, accidents. For past figures see their *British Labour Statistics: Historical Abstract, 1886–1968* (1971). Current statistics are in their monthly *Department of Employment Gazette.*

Many other countries publish national labor statistics. For a list of these consult the "References and Sources" section in the ILO's *Yearbook of Labour Statistics,* mentioned above.

INDUSTRIAL RELATIONS PERIODICALS

Most of these industrial relations periodicals are indexed in *Work Related Abstracts* described elsewhere in this chapter.

Arbitration Journal. New York, American Arbitration Association (quarterly).
Scholarly articles on labor arbitration, with a "Review of Court Decisions" in each issue. Indexed in PAIS.

British Journal of Industrial Relations. London School of Economics and Political Science (3/yr.).
"A journal of research and analysis covering every aspect of industrial relations in Britain and overseas." Includes book reviews, and a "Chronicle" of recent statistics, government policies and activities.

Great Britain. Department of Employment. *Department of Employment Gazette.* London, H.M. Stationery Office (monthly).
Most useful for its continuing monthly British labor statistics. Includes also articles reporting on labor research, often with statistics. Its Canadian counterpart is *Labour Gazette,* published monthly in Ottawa by the Department of Labour.

Industrial and Labor Relations Review. Ithaca, New York State School of Industrial and Labor Relations, Cornell University (quarterly).
An outstanding academic journal, with research papers on a wide range of labor topics relating to both the public and private sector. Useful features in each issue include a good book review section, a bibliography of "Recent Publications" arranged by subject, and notes about research in progress. Indexed in BPI, PAIS.

Industrial Relations. Berkeley, Institute of Industrial Relations, University of California (3/yr.).
Articles and symposia on all aspects of the employment relationship, with special attention to pertinent developments in the fields of labor economics, sociology, psychology, political science, law. Indexed in BPI, PAIS.

Industrial Relations Journal. London, Mercury House Publications (quarterly).
Articles on industrial relations with a British and European focus. Summary in French at end of each article. Includes book reviews.

Industrial Relations Law Digest. Ann Arbor, Graduate School of Business Administration, University of Michigan (quarterly).
Each issue digests 4 to 6 articles relating to labor law. An "Index to Current Labor Law Literature" is in alternate issues.

International Labour Review. Geneva, Switzerland, International Labour Office (monthly).

A good source for current information about labor conditions in specific countries outside the United States. Authoritative articles also cover social and economic problems as they relate to labor. Includes book reviews, book notes, and list of ILO publications. Indexed in BPI, PAIS.

U.S. Bureau of Labor Statistics. *Monthly Labor Review.* Washington, D.C., U.S. Government Printing Office. Indexed in BPI, F&S, PAIS, RGPL.

An indispensable source for current U.S. labor information. Each issue contains 4 or 5 studies by BLS researchers, many with statistical tables. Useful features include: research summaries; significant labor decisions; major labor agreements expiring during the following month; recent developments in industrial relations; excellent current labor statistics; also book reviews, and a subject listing of selected books and articles received by the BLS.

LABOR DIRECTORIES

Fink, Gary M., ed. *Biographical Dictionary of American Labor Leaders.* Westport, Conn., Greenwood Press, 1974.

Career biographies for about 500 men and women who have had a significant impact on the American labor movement.

U.S. Bureau of Labor Statistics. *Directory of National Unions and Employee Associations.* Washington, D.C., U.S. Government Printing Office (biennial).

This directory gives top officers, total membership, names of publications for national and international union organizations, state labor organizations, professional and public employee associations. It also contains summaries of significant developments in the labor movement for the past few years, the structure of the labor movement, and a statistical appendix. This is issued in the BLS *Bulletin* series, and the 1973 edition is in a new loose-leaf format to enable periodic revisions during the 2-year interval.

Lists of labor unions, labor associations and federations are also included in the directories of U.S. associations described in Chapter 3.

INDUSTRIAL RELATIONS ASSOCIATIONS

American Arbitration Association, 140 West 51st Street, New York, N.Y. 10020.

Industrial Relations Counselors, P.O. Box 228, New York, N.Y. 10036.

Industrial Relations Research Association, Social Science Building, University of Wisconsin, Madison, Wisc. 53706.

International Industrial Relations Association, 154 rue de Lausanne, CH-1211, Geneva 22, Switzerland.

International Labour Office, CH-1211, Geneva 22, Switzerland.

Labor Research Association, 80 East 11th Street, New York, N.Y. 10003.

PENSION PLANS AND SOCIAL SECURITY

Books

Davey, Patrick J. *Financial Management of Company Pension Plans.* (Conference Board Report 611). New York, Conference Board, 1973.

Based on a survey of the trusteed pension plans of 117 companies, this briefly discusses current practices in such key areas as plan designs, financing of benefits, investment of pension fund assets, evaluation of investment performance. Includes a bibliography.

Melone, Joseph J. and Everett T. Allen, Jr. *Pension Planning: Pensions, Profit Sharing, and Other Deferred Compensation Plans.* Rev. ed. Homewood, Ill., Irwin, 1972.

Presents a comprehensive treatment of deferred compensation, with primary emphasis on *qualified* pension plans. There are 2 chapters on tax considerations and new chapters on inflation and variable annuities, thrift plans and survivor's benefits.

Turnbull, John G., C. Arthur Williams, Jr., and Earl F. Cheit. *Economic and Social Security.* 4th ed. New York, Ronald, 1973.

The authors' purpose "is to communicate the nature of economic insecurity, the factors that give rise to it, the responsive adjustments that society has made and the consequences of problems and remedial programs for the individual and the economy as a whole." This edition is expanded to include problems of poverty and substandard conditions. Annotated bibliographies are at end of chapters.

Services

The new Employee Retirement Income Security Act of 1974 (also called the Pension Reform Act) will bring about vast changes in pension and employee benefit planning as of December 31, 1975, when the new rules go into effect. All three of the principal legal service publishers have responded to industry's need for guidance with useful pension services described below. They each also publish separate handbooks giving the highlights of the new law.

Bureau of National Affairs. *Pension Reporter.* Washington, D.C. (weekly).

A weekly report of about 40 pages providing information on the latest developments in legislation, regulations, court decisions, industrial and union developments relating to pensions and employee benefit trust funds. A 6-week index cumulates quarterly.

Commerce Clearing House. *Pension Plan Guide.* Chicago. 6 volumes (loose-leaf, with weekly supplements).

This is the most comprehensive service to date, covering major aspects of pensions, profit sharing and other employee benefits, and blending planning and operating guidance with full information on the tax and legal rules in point. There are 4 numbered volumes and separate volumes covering "Plans and Clauses," "Pensions-Employee Benefits."

CCH also publishes a separate loose-leaf service for *Social Security — Unemployment Insurance* that subscribers can obtain in varying numbers of volumes according to whether they wish federal laws plus all states, selected state or just home state coverage.

Prentice-Hall, Inc. *Pension and Profit Sharing.* Englewood Cliffs, N.J. 3 volumes (loose-leaf, with weekly supplements).

Vols. 1-2 contain up-to-date information on the pension reform law, on pension and profit sharing planning, requirements for qualifying, taxation, legal considerations, etc. Vol. 3 provides "Pension and Profit Sharing Forms."

Another P-H service is *Social Security — Unemployment Compensation,* which consists of 1 volume covering general information and federal laws relating to social security (including medicare) and unemployment taxes, and 6 volumes to cover every state.

Statistics

U.S. Department of Labor. Manpower Administration. *Unemployment Insurance Statistics.* Washington, D.C. U.S. Government Printing Office (monthly).

Statistical data on benefit payment activities, employer contributions, appeals decisions, and disqualifications by issues — for selected industries and major occupational groups, also by claimant's age, sex and duration of unemployment.

U.S. Social Security Administration. *Social Security Bulletin.* Washington, D.C., U.S. Government Printing Office (monthly).

Current operating statistics for old-age, survivors, disability and health insurance (OASDHI) program, including cash benefits, supplementary security income for the aged, blind and disabled, public assistance, unemployment insurance. Usually several research studies with statistics are also in each issue. Includes an "Annual Statistical Supplement."

Periodicals

Pension and Profit Sharing Tax Journal. Greenvale, N.Y., Panel Publishers (quarterly).

A new professional journal that will aim to offer in-depth analyses concerning the problems and opportunities of private retirement plans, and also reports on current developments.

Pension & Welfare News. New York, Communication Channels, Inc. (monthly).

Practical articles on pension problems, developments and funding, also news of interest to financial and corporate pension managers. Includes special annual surveys on: bank pooled pension funds (May 1974), insurance company separate accounts (June 1974), state retirement systems (August 1974), municipal retirement systems (September 1974). Indexed in PAIS.

The *Institutional Investor* also includes articles on pension funds and funding. It is described in the "Finance Periodicals" section of Chapter 14.

Directories of Pension Funds

Bankers Trust Co. *Study of Corporate Pension Plans.* 10th ed. New York, 1975 (quinquennial).

A study of current practices in corporate pension plans. The major part (Section 4) is a comparison of the key provisions of 271 individual pension plans representing 190 large U.S. corporations and arranged in 56 industry categories. Section 3 summarizes amendments to these plans made within the 1970–1975 period. Section 1 is a summary of general pension practices and trends, and Section 2, a summary of the methods used to increase pensioners' retirement income.

Institutional Investor. *Pensions Directory.* New York (annual).

A directory of the 350 largest corporate pension and profit sharing funds, 50 state funds; also a list of real estate managers, money managers and consultants. The data on corporate pension funds was taken from *Money Market Directory.*

Money Market Directory. New York, Money Market Directories (annual).

This is a directory of over 12,500 institutional investors and their portfolio managers, with total assets given for each fund or firm. Part 1 covers "Tax-Exempt Funds" (company, union and government benefit funds, endowment funds, private foundation funds); Part 2 covers "Investment Services" (investment counsel firms, mutual funds, bank trust departments, insurance companies, and Canadian investment services). Each part is arranged geographically and has an alphabetical index.

U.S. Bureau of Labor Statistics. *Digest of Selected Pension Plans.* Washington, D.C., U.S. Government Printing Office 1970 ed., with 1972 supplements.

Summarizes the principal features of selected pension plans for employees under collective bargaining, and selected plans for salaried employees. They were selected to cover a large number of employees in major industries or to illustrate different approaches to pension planning.

U.S. Office of Labor-Management and Welfare-Pension Reports. *The 100 Largest Retirement Plans, 1960–1972.* Washington, D.C., 1974.

Charts, tables and brief explanatory text. This agency also publishes a quinquennial *Register of Retirement Benefit Plans,* which lists plans reported under the Welfare and Pension Plans Disclosure Act, by name of employer, association or organization; it gives codes for type of plan, type of employees covered, type of administrator.

20

PRODUCTION AND OPERATIONS MANAGEMENT

General Handbooks and Books — Production and Inventory Control — Industrial Engineering — Motion and Time Study — Quality Control — POM Bibliographies — Production Dictionaries — Production Periodicals — POM Assocations — Industrial Research — Materials Management (including Purchasing) — *BUSINESS LOGISTICS* **— General Texts — Materials Handling — Physical Distribution Bibliographies — Materials Dictionaries — Logistics Periodicals — Logistics Directories — Logistics Associations — Traffic and Transportation — Traffic and Transportation Bibliographies — Traffic and Transportation Dictionaries — Transportation Financial Manuals — Traffic and Transportation Periodicals — Traffic and Transportation Directories — Traffic and Transportation Associations**

Recent developments have brought profound changes in production and operations management, and much of the material written during the 1960s is now largely outdated. This chapter describes a selection of the newest books and reference sources on the whole POM field and also on some of its major components including the relatively new concepts of materials management and business logistics. There is some overlapping of coverage within this chapter because of variations in both terminology and subjects treated in the recent literature.

Basic statistical and quantitative books are described in Chapter 17; management information systems in Chapter 13; and books on business and technological forecasting in Chapter 8. Sources for production statistics of individual commodities and products are listed in Chapters 4 through 6.

GENERAL HANDBOOKS AND BOOKS

Handbooks

See also various sections of this chapter for more specialized handbooks on

331

production and inventory control, industrial engineering, quality control, industrial research, purchasing and materials handling.

Carson, Gordon B., Harold A. Bolz and Hewitt H. Young. *Production Handbook.* 3d ed. New York, Ronald, 1972.

"An encyclopedic distillation of the best experience in manufacturing systems and procedures, principles of organization and manpower utilization, and specialized techniques for achieving greater productivity and reduced costs." There were 40 contributing and consulting editors who cooperated on this extensive compilation, and the specific topics covered are: production systems, planning and control; materials management; inventory control; purchasing; inspection; quality control; statistical methods; operations research; process charts; work measurement; time and motion studies; work simplification; industrial research and development; plant layout and facilities planning; material handling; tools, jigs, fixtures; capital investment analysis; plant maintenance; industrial safety. There are useful outlines at the beginning of each of the 22 chapters; diagrams and charts throughout; many references to works consulted; and a list of books at end.

Maynard, H. B., ed. *Handbook of Modern Manufacturing Management.* New York, McGraw-Hill, 1970.

A practical handbook combining the older, tested manufacturing procedures with newer practices, in 81 chapters written by 86 authorities. Its 10 sections cover: the manufacturing function; organizational relationships; manufacturing planning; manufacturing control; manufacturing facilities; plant engineering and maintenance; products and materials; personnel; motivating employees; supporting services and activities. Includes useful diagrams, and bibliographies are at end of most chapters. Maynard is an experienced management engineer and author who has edited several other useful handbooks.

Zeyher, Lewis R. *Production Manager's Handbook of Formulas and Tables.* Englewood Cliffs, N.J., Prentice-Hall, 1972.

A handy reference volume for production managers that provides formulas, tables, charts, etc., arranged by the following topics: production control and inventory turnover; work measurement; production line techniques; formulas for materials handling, warehousing, industrial relations, inventory, cost/production, depreciation; capital investment decisions; queuing theory; sampling and correlation statistics. Useful appendixes on "make or buy" and on warehousing.

Books

Amrine, Harold T., John A. Ritchey and Oliver S. Hulley. *Manufacturing Organization and Management.* 3d ed. Englewood Cliffs, N.J., Prentice-Hall, 1975.

A nontechnical introduction to the principles, practices and functions of manufacturing management in 5 parts: manufacturing management — past, present and future; manufacturing systems design (plant location, design of manufacturing processes, methods engineering, work measurement, materials handling, plant layout); manufacturing control (including inventory control, purchasing, production planning and control, quality control); manufacturing relationships (relation to various functions such as personnel, research, financial management); appraisal of manufacturing results. Interest tables are at end.

Becker, Charles H. *Plant Manager's Handbook.* Englewood Cliffs, N.J., Prentice-Hall, 1974.

A "how-to" book by a plant manager, written for potential plant managers and covering plant organization, plant operations, costs/budgets/cost reductions, and plant equipment and facilities.

Buffa, Elwood S. *Modern Production Management.* 4th ed. New York, Wiley, 1973.

This revision of Professor Buffa's popular introductory text on production and operations management expands his discussion of analytical methods and includes new material emphasizing nonmanufacturing applications. The meat of the book is in 3 of its 6 parts: analytical methods (5 chapters); design of productive systems (process planning, plant location, layout, job design, etc.); operations planning and control (inventories, scheduling, maintenance, etc.). Includes charts and diagrams; bibliographies are at end of chapters. Several other recent books by Buffa are: *Basic Production Management* (2d ed., Wiley, 1975), an abridged, nonmathematical version of the book above; *Production-Inventory Systems* (written with William H. Taubert, rev. ed., Homewood, Ill. Irwin, 1972); *Operations Management: Problems and Models* (3d ed., Wiley, 1972).

Groff, Gene K. and John F. Muth. *Operations Management: Analysis for Decisions.* Homewood, Ill., Irwin, 1971.

This text emphasizes the designing, planning and controlling of operating systems. A basic acquaintance with mathematics, statistics and computer programming is a prerequisite. Exercises and bibliographies are at end of each chapter. These professors have also published *Operations Management: Selected Readings* (Irwin, 1969), a good selection of 33 older articles.

Johnson, Richard A., William T. Newell and Roger C. Vergin. *Operations Management: A Systems Concept.* Boston, Houghton Mifflin, 1972.

As the subtitle implies, this text uses the systems approach for providing a framework or model of analysis to which specific concepts, techniques and tools can be related. It is comprehensive and relates to management in all kinds of organizations, not just to those in manufacturing industries. Presumes some knowledge of college algebra, calculus, probability theory and computer technology. Annotated bibliographies are at end of chapters, and a few statistical tables are at end of book.

Levin, Richard I., Curtis P. McLaughlin, Rudolf P. Lamone and John F. Kottas. *Production/Operations Management: Contemporary Policy for Managing Operating Systems.* New York, McGraw-Hill, 1972.

A good, introductory text written from a policy approach and reflecting the total organization view as well as the POM view. Illustrations and examples cover both manufacturing and nonmanufacturing systems as well as many large operating systems in the public sector. The quantitative material can be mastered with an understanding of algebra and some differential calculus. It is in 4 parts: introduction and basic concepts; internal and external interfaces; designing the POM system; operating and controlling the POM system. Includes a bibliography.

Moore, Franklin G. *Production Management.* 6th ed. Homewood, Ill., Irwin, 1973.

A standard, traditional POM text brought up to date to include quantitative materials and problems. After a general section on production investment economics, the major subject divisions are for: production facilities; product development; economizing on work inputs; standards for pay and production; production control systems; materials inputs; quality control systems. Includes bibliographies. Professor

Moore has also written (with Ronald Jablonski) a book on *Production Control* (3d ed., New York, McGraw-Hill, 1969).

Starr, Martin K. *Production Management: Systems and Synthesis.* 2d ed. Englewood Cliffs, N.J., Prentice-Hall, 1972.

This is a good systems-oriented book on production management, presuming some knowledge of analytical tools and a minimal ability with algebra. It is in 3 parts: production-systems models; input-output management (management of information, product, process, materials, quality, facilities, manpower); synthesis of systems (the interacting roles of finance and marketing with production). Includes diagrams and tables; references at end of chapters. A closely related book, more quantitatively oriented, is Professor Starr's *Systems Management of Operations* (Prentice-Hall, 1971). He has also edited a paperback book of selected readings called *Management of Production* (Baltimore, Md., Penguin Books, 1970).

Vollmann, Thomas E. *Operations Management: A Systems Model-Building Approach.* Reading, Mass., Addison-Wesley, 1973.

An introductory text, with 3 goals: "To understand the basic operations functions, to gain a viable knowledge of the systems approach to the design of operations procedures, and to provide an applications forum where the skills gained in other areas of the curriculum can be utilized and applied." There are 6 major sections: the systems point of view; cost/value models; quantitative models; traditional operations management system design problems; materials flow systems; overview. Requires a minimal mathematics background. Bibliographies are at end of chapters.

PRODUCTION AND INVENTORY CONTROL

Greene, James H., ed. *Production and Inventory Control Handbook.* New York, McGraw-Hill, 1974.

A comprehensive desk-top reference book reflecting the work of over 90 contributing experts, most of whom are members of the American Production and Inventory Control Society, sponsors of this handbook. Its 8 principal sections cover: organization; supporting systems; planning; production control operations; inventory control; systems for production and inventory control; techniques and tools; report of a joint APICS/*Factory* survey. Bibliographies are with most of the 30 chapters. Professor Greene has also recently revised his text on *Production and Inventory Control: Systems and Decisions* (rev. ed., Homewood, Ill., Irwin, 1974).

Lipman, Burton E. *How to Control and Reduce Inventory.* Englewood Cliffs, N.J., Prentice-Hall, 1972.

A practitioner offers 6 basic steps to successful inventory control and reduction, which he bases on the learning experiences gathered from a number of companies. Includes a short bibliography and a glossary.

Mize, Joe H., Charles R. White and George H. Brooks. *Operations Planning and Control.* Englewood Cliffs, N.J., Prentice-Hall, 1971.

This introductory text on production planning and control is quantitatively oriented and presupposes a first course in calculus, with a knowledge of probability and statistics. Part 2 contains chapters on the 5 major operations planning and control functions (demand forecasting, operations planning, inventory planning and control, operations scheduling, dispatching and progress control); Part 5 is on control design. Includes bibliographies at end of most chapters, and exercises in an appendix.

O'Brien, James S., ed. *Scheduling Handbook.* New York, McGraw-Hill, 1969.
Each chapter discusses scheduling techniques, background and application in specific operational areas. The techniques include networks, PERT, line of balance; the applications include maintenance, systems, transportation, research and development, hospitals. There are diagrams, charts and illustrations throughout; short bibliographies are at end of each chapter.

Orlicky, Joseph. *Material Requirements Planning: The New Way of Life in Production and Inventory Management.* New York, McGraw-Hill, 1975.
This book is a "state-of-the-art" treatment of a new concept of growing importance in the field of manufacturing operations management — computer-based material requirements planning (MRP). It is written for users and potential users of MRP systems, and there are examples and illustrations used throughout to clarify important points. It is in 6 parts and there are a few bibliographical references at the end of most of its 12 chapters.

Plossl, George W. *Manufacturing Control: The Last Frontier for Profits.* Reston, Va., Reston Publishing Co. 1973.
Plossl wrote this short treatise for managers to outline for them in practical, easy-to-understand language what he feels they need to know to reach the 3 objectives of: good customer service, minimum capital investment, profitable operation. Includes a bibliography. He has also written (with O. W. Wight) a basic scientific approach to *Production and Inventory Control: Principles and Techniques* (Englewood Cliffs, N.J., Prentice-Hall, 1967).

INDUSTRIAL ENGINEERING

Ireson, W. Grant and Eugene L. Grant, eds. *Handbook of Industrial Engineering and Management.* 2d ed. Englewood Cliffs, N.J., Prentice-Hall, 1971.
Each of the 17 sections in this handbook is in essence a concise text — written by an authority, stressing general principles and the best current practice and including a bibliography for further study. It covers the traditional industrial engineering subjects of time and motion study, factory planning and materials handling, tool engineering, industrial safety. Increased coverage is given to quantitative methods in chapters on computers, industrial statistics, quality control, linear programming. The economic aspects are considered in chapters on managerial economics, engineering economics, capital budgeting. Includes many illustrations, forms and charts.

Maynard, H. B., ed. *Industrial Engineering Handbook.* 3d ed. New York, McGraw-Hill, 1971.
An essential one-volume reference work for industrial engineers. It is comprehensive (over 1,900 pages), is thoroughly revised to cover newer procedures, practices and techniques, and benefits from the contributions of 108 experts. The 87 chapters are divided into the following 13 sections: the industrial engineering function; methods; work measurement techniques; applied work measurement; predetermined time standards; wage and salary administration; behavorial science and human factors; planning and control procedures; computers and the industrial engineer; mathematical, statistical, and programming procedures; equipment and facilities; industrial engineering tools; industrial engineering applications. Includes illustrations and diagrams; most chapters have bibliographies for persons who wish to read further on any topic. Maynard's wide experience in industrial engineering and in editing several

other useful management handbooks makes him exceptionally well qualified to compile this useful work.

The *Engineering Index* abstracts technical articles on engineering and applied science and is described in Chapter 2.

MOTION AND TIME STUDY

Mundel, Marvin E. *Motion and Time Study: Principles and Practices.* 4th ed. Englewood Cliffs, N.J., Prentice-Hall, 1970.

An excellent text emphasizing the "how" of motion and time study. It includes many examples to show applications to government as well as to industrial organizations. There are illustrations and diagrams throughout; a bibliography is at end.

Niebel, Benjamin W. *Motion and Time Study.* 5th ed. Homewood, Ill., Irwin, 1972.

A good, standard text on methods engineering, time study and wage payment programs. Includes many illustrations, forms, and a glossary of terms.

QUALITY CONTROL

Handbooks

Juran, J. M., Frank M. Gryna, Jr., and R. S. Bingham, Jr., eds. *Quality Control Handbook.* 3d ed. New York, McGraw-Hill, 1974.

A comprehensive (about 1,800 pages) one-volume reference work, in 52 chapters written by 42 experts. The first 21 chapters are devoted to managing the quality functions; 8 chapters cover statistical methods; 20 chapters concentrate on quality in leading industries and in specific processes. Includes charts and diagrams, numerous bibliographic citations and footnotes, a few bibliographies with each section; also tables and charts in an appendix.

Books

Duncan, Acheson J. *Quality Control and Industrial Statistics.* 4th ed. Homewood, Ill., Irwin, 1974.

This latest revision of Professor Duncan's established text for engineering and business students is in 5 parts: fundamentals; lot acceptance sampling plans; rectifying inspection; control charts; some statistics useful in industrial research. Appendixes include a section for mathematical proofs and technical material; statistical tables and charts; a glossary; a bibliography of books and articles.

Grant, Eugene L. and Richard S. Leavenworth. *Statistical Quality Control.* 4th ed. New York, McGraw-Hill, 1972.

This is the best known quality control text. It is designed as a practical working manual for production supervisors, engineers and management to explain several techniques useful in improving product quality and in reducing costs. The majority of the book deals with various types of Shewhart control charts and also acceptance sampling systems and procedures. Includes descriptions of actual cases from a number of industries; there are some statistical tables and a bibliography at end.

An abstracting service on *Quality Control and Applied Statistics* is described in Chapter 17.

POM BIBLIOGRAPHIES

American Production and Inventory Control Society. *Bibliography of Articles, Books and Films on Production and Inventory Control and Related Subjects, 1968–1971.* 4th ed. comp. by Robert G. Ames. Washington, D.C., 1972.

The section listing books (pp. 29–53) is annotated and is arranged in 15 subject categories, including plant layout, physical distribution, purchasing, and also related topics of data processing, operations research and statistics. This was a project of the Los Angeles Chapter, APICS. More frequent updates are planned, with the first one edited by Alex L. Srbich and called *Bibliography of Articles, Books, Films, and Audio-Cassettes on Production and Inventory Control and Related Subjects, 1972–1973* (5th ed., 1975).

PRODUCTION DICTIONARIES

American Production and Inventory Control Society. *APICS Dictionary of Inventory Control Terms and Production Control Terms.* Ed. by Richard C. Sherrill. 3d ed. Washington, D.C., 1970.

This is a short glossary (45 pages) on production and inventory control that also covers related terms in data processing, operations research, industrial engineering and cost accounting.

Encyclopedic Dictionary of Production and Production Control. Englewood Cliffs, N.J., Prentice-Hall, 1964.

Explanations and illustrations of applications for basic terms in use at the time this dictionary was published. Still of value even though it is quite old.

Lindemann, A. J., Earl F. Lundgren and H. K. von Kaas. *Encyclopaedic Dictionary of Management and Manufacturing Terms.* 2d ed. Dubuque, Iowa, Kendall/Hunt Publishing Co., 1974.

"Technical terminology of engineering, manufacturing, organization, and business operational terms" arranged in 23 broad sections, e.g., operations research, plant location, materials handling, work design, inventory management, economic order quantity, value analysis. There is no index to the specific terms defined within each section.

PRODUCTION PERIODICALS

Automation. Cleveland, Ohio, Penton Publishing Co. (monthly).

Trade journal on automatic processing, control, etc., in the production engineering area. Indexed in ASTI, F&S, PAIS.

Factory. New York, Morgan-Grampian (monthly).

A leading trade journal on factory and operating management, with special emphasis on materials handling, systems, pollution control, maintenance, electrical equipment. Indexed in BPI.

Industrial Engineering. New York, American Institute of Industrial Engineers (monthly).

Short articles for the industrial engineer on such subjects as materials handling, management systems and control, production and inventory control. Includes book reviews. Indexed in ASTI. This society also publishes a quarterly that is more statistically oriented, called *AIIE Transactions.*

International Journal of Production Research. London, Taylor & Francis, Ltd. (bimonthly).

Publishes original research of university and research workers on the science of production. A few book reviews in alternate issue. This journal is sponsored by the American Institute of Industrial Engineers, the Institution of Production Engineers (U.K.), and the Society of Manufacturing Engineers.

Journal of Quality Technology. Milwaukee, Wisc., American Society for Quality Control (quarterly).

This journal publishes "papers which emphasize the practical applicability of new techniques, instructive examples of the operation of existing techniques, and results of historical research." Includes book reviews. Indexed in ASTI. Their *Quality Progress* is a monthly news magazine for ASQC members.

Manufacturing Engineering & Management. Dearborn, Mich., Society of Manufacturing Engineers (monthly).

News about specific machinery, tools, automatic systems, etc.

Production. Bloomfield Hills, Mich., Bramson Publishing Co. (monthly).

Articles and news to help managers and engineers improve manufacturing efficiency, costs and quality in production, metalworking plants and selected supplier industries.

Production & Inventory Management. Chicago, American Production and Inventory Control Society (quarterly).

Scholarly papers on planning, systems, control, etc., in production.

POM ASSOCIATIONS

American Institute of Industrial Engineers, 25 Technology Park/Atlanta, Norcross, Ga. 30071.

American Production and Inventory Control Society, Watergate Building, Suite 504, 2600 Virginia Avenue, N.W., Washington, D.C. 20037.

American Society for Quality Control, 161 West Wisconsin Avenue, Milwaukee, Wisc. 53203.

Institution of Production Engineers, 146 Cromwell Road, London SW7 4EF, England.

Society of American Value Engineers, 2500 Hargrove Drive, L-205, Smyrna, Ga. 30080.

Society of Manufacturing Engineers, 20501 Ford Road, Dearborn, Mich. 48128.

INDUSTRIAL RESEARCH

Handbooks

Heyel, Carl, ed. *Handbook of Industrial Research Management.* 2d ed. New York, Reinhold, 1968.

A handy reference volume for managers, operating heads and technical personnel to explain the concepts and techniques of industrial research. Each of the 24 chapters is by a competent contributor, and it is arranged in 6 parts: management perspectives; research perspectives (new product planning, patents); departmental operation; accounting, control and evaluation; personnel administration in research; research for governmental agencies.

Books

Books on new product development are listed in Chapter 18.

McLoughlin, William G. *Fundamentals of Research Management.* New York, American Management Association, 1970.

A book for managers on the concept of research and development within the organization. Position descriptions are in an appendix.

Morton, Jack A. *Organization for Innovations.* New York, McGraw-Hill, 1971.

Morton's thoughtful treatise describes the innovative process in terms of his own organization (Bell Telephone Systems), and his ecological-systems view that both the process and the organization are *living* systems.

Steele, Lowell W. *Innovation in Big Business.* New York, American Elsevier Publishing Co., 1975.

This book examines the interface between research and development and the sponsoring corporation, and it is written for r&d managers, for corporation executives concerned with planning and for students. Subjects covered include the environment for innovation, the role of technology in business strategy, strategic planning for r&d, transition to commercial use, communication with operating people, special problems of conducting r&d in a multinational framework. The author states that this book represents a distillation of 20 years' experience in industrial r&d, much of it with General Electric.

Twiss, Brian C. *Managing Technological Innovation.* London, Longman Group, 1974.

Designed for senior managers and corporate planners and focusing "on those areas of management where the technology of a company relates to the firm as a whole." The chapter titles give a good idea of its scope: the process of technological innovation; strategies for r&d; technological forecasting for decision-making; creativity and problem-solving; project selection and evaluation; financial evaluation of r&d projects; r&d program planning and control; organization for innovation. Includes reference at end of chapters.

Statistics

McGraw-Hill Publications Co. Economics Department. *Annual McGraw-Hill Survey: Business Plans for Research and Development Expenditures.* New York.

The 19th annual survey, published in 1974, covers the years 1974–1977. This is a very short pamphlet, with 7 statistical tables: r&d expenditures by broad industry; also percentage of sales in new products, total r&d pollution control expenditures, total energy in relation to r&d expenditures, r&d as percentage of capital spending — all by broad industry.

U.S. National Science Foundation. *Research and Development in Industry.* Washington, D.C., U.S. Government Printing Office (annual).

This gives: charts, statistics and brief interpretative text on federal and company funds for r&d, by industry and size of company, for over 10 years; employment of r&d scientists and engineers; r&d funds related to employment and net sales; funds for research and funds for development.

Two other NSF publications are: *An Analysis of Federal R & D Funding by Function* (annual, with statistics covering a 6-year period); *National Patterns of R & D Resources, Funds & Manpower in the United States,* 1953 to date (annual).

Periodicals

Industrial Research. New York (monthly).

About 4 articles are in each issue, usually on technical processes or equipment; also news of industries, materials, new products, and so forth. January issue contains an annual r&d forecast. Includes short book reviews. Indexed in BPI, F&S.

R & D Management. Oxford, England, B. Blackwell (3/yr.).

Presents research papers on current problem areas in r&d management, and on applications of new methods of management in those areas. Includes book reviews.

Research/Development. Barrington, Ill., Technical Publishing Co. (monthly).

Articles are primarily on technical developments in products, processes. Special section on vacuum technology in each issue. An annual forecast article is in January issue. Indexed in ASTI.

Research Management. Westport, Conn., Industrial Research Institute (bimonthly).

Informative, pragmatic articles on r&d management usually by practitioners. Includes descriptive reviews of books and articles. Indexed in BPI.

Research Policy. Amsterdam, The Netherlands, North-Holland Publishing Co. (quarterly).

An international journal written in English and devoted to authoritative papers on research policy, research management and planning.

Directories

American Council of Independent Laboratories. *Directory.* Washington, D.C. (triennial).

"A guide to the leading independent research and inspection laboratories of America," giving officers and scope of activities.

Industrial Research in Britain. 7th ed. Guernsey, British Isles, F. Hodgson, 1972.

A directory of British public corporations and government departments, associations, laboratories, universities, etc. that are engaged in industrial research. For each it gives name of executives, scope of research.

Industrial Research Laboratories of the United States. 14th ed. New York, R. R. Bowker, 1975.

This is an important directory of over 6,600 nongovernmental U.S. laboratories devoted to fundamental applied research, including development of products and processes. Gives names of executives, number of professional staff, statement of chief r&d activity. Includes indexes by name of executives, by geographic location, by subject.

Associations

Industrial Research Institute, 100 Park Avenue, New York, N.Y. 10017.

Research & Development Society, 47 Belgrave Square, London, SW1X 82X, England.

MATERIALS MANAGEMENT (INCLUDING PURCHASING)

Handbooks

Aljian, George W., ed. *Purchasing Handbook.* 3d ed. New York, McGraw-Hill, 1973.

A first-rate reference work (over 1,200 pages) on policies, practices and procedures in the many facets of purchasing and materials management, with each of its 32 sections by 3 or more of over 160 expert contributors. Besides the bibliographies with each section there is also a special chapter that lists books, periodicals and reference tools needed in a purchasing library. Other useful features are a glossary, conversion tables, tables of weights and measures, information on professional purchasing associations, purchasing forms.

National Association of Purchasing Management. *Guide to Purchasing.* New York, 1973.

A loose-leaf handbook on purchasing systems and procedures, purchasing management and related activities. Section 6.1A contains a good bibliography.

Books

Ammer, Dean S. *Materials Management.* 3d ed. Homewood, Ill., Irwin, 1974.

"The basic purpose of this book is to describe the nontechnical management-oriented skills needed for successful materials management" in both business and nonbusiness organizations. Chapters cover such management aspects as objectives, organization, forecasting, planning; also specialized subfunctions of materials management, such as production and inventory control, the buying process, traffic and physical distribution, negotiation. Several cases are with each chapter and a bibliography is at end of book.

Combs, Paul H. *Handbook of International Purchasing.* 2d ed. Boston, Cahners Books, 1976.

Designed as a practical guide for companies "seeking solutions to their business sourcing problems through international purchasing." Gives concise information on such topics as selecting foreign suppliers, shipping methods, trading regulations, foreign currencies, labor problems. Includes a glossary of import-export terms. For other books on international business see Chapter 16.

England, Wilbur B. and Michiel R. Leenders. *Purchasing and Materials Management.* 6th ed. Homewood, Ill., Irwin, 1975.

The latest edition of a combination text and casebook on the organization and operation of the procurement function, with an emphasis on the acquisition of material, parts, equipment and services for further manufacture or end use in the organization rather than on purchasing for resale. Cases and short bibliographies are at end of each chapter.

Gravereau, Victor P. and Leonard J. Konopa, eds. *Purchasing Management: Selected Readings.* Columbus, Ohio, Grid, 1973.

A selection of 48 articles written in the 1960s and early 1970s pertinent to the planning and execution of the purchasing function.

Heinritz, Stuart F. and Paul V. Farrell. *Purchasing: Principles and Applications.* 5th ed. Englewood Cliffs, N.J., Prentice-Hall, 1971.

A popular, beginning text on the fundamentals of the buying process. Covers purchasing functions, organization, personnel, systems, data processing, quality assurance, inventory management, price analysis, suppliers, make or buy, research, planning and forecasting, value analysis, negotiation, ethics, legal aspects, contract cancellations and purchasing performance. A brief case study is with each chapter; a bibliography is at end of book.

Kudrna, Dennis A. *Purchasing Manager's Decision Handbook.* Boston, Cahners Books, 1975.

Kudrna's book is meant to show how to apply purchasing considerations that are identified and defined in introductory texts, for more effective purchasing decision-making. Mathematical justifications for its various concepts appear in an appendix.

Peckham, Herbert H. *Effective Materials Management.* Englewood Cliffs, N.J., Prentice-Hall, 1972.

An industrial engineer wrote this book on important factors involved in an effective materials management system and on various means for arriving at solutions to problems. It is meant both for newcomers in the field and for experienced practitioners. Short bibliographies are at end of chapters.

Westing, J. H., I. V. Fine and Gary J. Zenz. *Purchasing Management: Materials in Motion.* 4th ed. New York, Wiley. To be published in 1976.

This standard text on traditional purchasing topics was written with the assistance of the Milwaukee Association of Purchasing Managers. It covers: organization and procedures; purchasing activities (quality, pricing, research, etc.); related purchasing activities (make or buy, transportation and traffic management, forward buying, legal aspects); control of purchasing activities (ethics, auditing, data processing, etc.). The last 77 pages contain purchasing cases. This note is based on an examination of the 3d edition.

Bibliographies

National Association of Purchasing Management. *A Bibliography of Purchasing Literature.* New York, 1969.

A useful, although now quite old, bibliography of books and selected articles arranged in about 40 subject areas such as inventory control, make or buy, negotiation, packaging, reciprocity. This list was compiled by the librarian, Helene S. Pandelakis, who also prepared a typed supplement in 1970 called "Current Books (& Booklets) in Purchasing and Related Fields."

Periodicals

Journal of Purchasing and Material Management. New York, National Association of Purchasing Management (quarterly).

Scholarly journal for articles covering theory and practice of purchasing and materials management. Includes book reviews. Indexed in BPI, PAIS.

Purchasing. Boston, Cahners Publishing Co. (semi-monthly).

This is the principal purchasing trade journal. It contains articles on policies and techniques, and news for purchasing managers. Indexed in BPI.

Purchasing World. Barrington, Ill., Technical Publishing Co. (monthly).

Articles, current news on purchasing, materials and products. Each issue has a page of current raw material prices and industrial prices. The January issue is a forecast issue.

Associations

International Material Management Society, 114-A Huron Towers, 2200 Fuller Road, Ann Arbor, Mich. 48105.

National Association of Purchasing Management, 11 Park Place, New York, N.Y. 10007.

BUSINESS LOGISTICS

The term "business logistics" (sometimes also called "physical distribution") is a relatively new concept for what Professor Bowersox defines as "the process of managing all activities required to strategically move raw materials, parts, and finished inventory from vendors, between enterprise facilities, and to customers" (see p. 1 of his book listed below). This encompasses activities relating to transportation, location analysis, inventory policy, order processing, materials handling, packaging, warehousing and communications.

GENERAL TEXTS

Ballou, Ronald H. *Business Logistics Management.* Englewood Cliffs, N.J., Prentice-Hall, 1973.

"This book is primarily about the management of business logistics activities in domestic firms with implications about the management of logistics activities in such areas as the military, service organizations, and nonprofit institutions." It focuses on a systems approach. After an introduction and overview, Professor Ballou studies the logistics environment (the product, transportation and storage systems), logistics decisions (decisions concerning facility location, inventory policy, transport, production scheduling, order processing, storage and materials-handling), logistics organization and control. Includes mathematical models and techniques and 2 cases; bibliographies are at end of chapters.

Bowersox, Donald J. *Logistical Management.* New York, Macmillan, 1974.

The subtitle of this book pretty well describes its scope: "A Systems Integration of Physical Distribution Management, Materials Management, and Logistical Coordination." Part 2 of this 4-part text covers the components of logistical systems (transportation, inventory, warehousing, material movement, communications). Appendixes include a physical distribution game; plant location factors and checklist; a short, selected bibliography. Portions of this text have been reprinted from earlier books Professor Bowersox has written in collaboration with other authors. One of these earlier texts had a companion book of *Readings in Physical Distribution: The Logistics of Marketing* by Bowersox, Bernard J. LaLonde and Edward W. Smykay (Macmillan, 1969).

Fair, Marvin L. and Ernest W. Williams, Jr. *Economics of Transportation and Logistics.* Dallas, Tex., Business Publications, 1975.

This book attempts to establish a background both for transport economics and for business logistics and to explore the relationships between these fields. The orientation is reflected in the titles of its 4 parts: spatial relations and economic and social organization; economics of transportation service in relation to logistics systems;

economics of transportation pricing and logistics management; public policy in transportation. Bibliographies are at end of chapters.

Heskett, James L., Nicholas A. Glaskowsky, Jr., and Robert M. Ivie. *Business Logistics: Physical Distribution and Materials Management.* 2d ed. New York, Ronald, 1973.

An excellent study of logistics systems design and management, in 5 parts: the scope and importance of logistics; elements of a logistics system; system relationships; logistics system design (the authors' use one company as an example to show the progress from theory to practical application); system management. Annotated bibliographies at end of most chapters; periodicals, associations and other information sources are listed at end. Professor Heskett has also written (with 3 other authors) a collection of *Case Problems in Business Logistics* (Ronald, 1973).

Smykay, Edward W. *Physical Distribution Management.* 3d ed. New York, Macmillan, 1973.

Examines physical distribution as a key element in the total corporate effort. Part 1 covers physical distribution and the market environment; Part 2 considers physical distribution activity centers (transportation, inventory allocations, etc.); and Part 3 is on system design and administration. A bibliography of books and articles is at end. The previous edition of this book was written by Donald J. Bowersox with Professor Smykay and Bernard J. LaLonde.

Taff, Charles A. *Management of Physical Distribution and Transportation.* 5th ed. Homewood, Ill., Irwin, 1972.

A substantial revision of a good, popular text, in 3 parts: management and organization of physical distribution; components and interfaces (transport system elements, inventory control, warehousing management, make-or-buy decisions, order processing, industrial packaging, material handling, location analysis, international distribution); the transport subsystem (commodity classification, transport pricing, tariff constraints, etc.). Selected bibliography is at end.

MATERIALS HANDLING

Handbooks

Bolz, Harold A. and George E. Hagemann, eds. *Materials Handling Handbook.* New York, Ronald, 1958.

A comprehensive handbook on materials handling principles, procedures and techniques, covering all important, time-tested aspects of this complex industrial problem. Its 47 chapters represent the work of a large corps of experts who drew not only from their own experience but also from the literature. Charts, diagrams and other illustrative material are included throughout. Although now quite old, this is still of value as concise background information both on policy and on daily operating problems.

Books

Apple, James M. *Material Handling Design Systems.* New York, Ronald, 1972.

Intended as a "practical reference" on the theory and practice of modern material handling for engineers, production managers, technicians. It includes a discussion of representative types of equipment, quantitative techniques, cost determination, storage and automated warehousing. Many illustrations, diagrams and charts appear throughout this book.

PHYSICAL DISTRIBUTION BIBLIOGRAPHIES

Brice, G., V. Knight and David Walters. *PDM: The IJPD Bibliography, 1965:1973.* Bradford, Yorkshire, England, International Journal of Physical Distribution, 1974.

A bibliography of 2,560 books, articles, theses, etc., in the field of physical distribution management and business logistics. It is arranged in 14 broad categories, including inventory, materials handling, warehouse location and management, transport management, EDP applications, channels & institutions, distribution systems.

National Council of Physical Distribution Management. *Bibliography on Physical Distribution Management.* Chicago, 1967. And annual supplements, 1968 to date.

A useful, continuing, loose-leaf, annotated bibliography of management-oriented books and articles, arranged in 9 topical sections. The first 2 volumes were compiled by Professors Smykay and LaLonde. Since then LaLonde has continued with various co-compilers.

MATERIALS DICTIONARIES

Brady, George B. *Materials Handbook: An Encyclopedia for Purchasing Managers, Engineers, Executives, and Foremen.* 10th ed. New York, McGraw-Hill, 1971.

An encyclopedic dictionary describing properties and uses of many materials, including metals, minerals, woods, chemicals, textiles.

LOGISTICS PERIODICALS

Distribution Worldwide. Radnor, Pa., Chilton Co. (monthly).

A trade journal covering current developments in physical distribution and published for traffic and distribution executives. The July issue each year is a "Distribution Guide Issue," which gives brief information about ports of the world and includes a geographic directory of public warehouses with name of top officer and description including number of square feet.

Handling & Shipping. Cleveland, Ohio, Industrial Publishing Co. (monthly).

"The Physical Distribution Magazine," covering transportation, management, warehousing, plant location, inventory control, materials handling, containerization, protective packaging. September issue is an "Annual Ports Directory"; December issue is an "Annual Directory of Traffic-Distribution Information."

International Journal of Physical Distribution. Bradford, West Yorkshire, England, MCB (3/yr.).

Research papers on problems and techniques in the field of physical distribution management (PDM). Received with this is *Physical Distribution Monograph* (3/yr.), which is a short pamphlet on specific topics of interest to PDM executives.

The Logistics and Transportation Review. Vancouver, Canada, Faculty of Commerce, University of British Columbia (quarterly).

An international journal for research papers on transportation and logistics, with an emphasis on the quantitative approach. Includes book reviews.

Material Handling Engineering. Cleveland, Ohio, Industrial Publishing Co. (monthly).

A trade journal for technical data and news on material management and flow. For their separately published directory see next section. Indexed in ASTI.

Modern Materials Handling. Boston, Cahners Publishing Co. (monthly, except semi-monthly in March and June).
Short articles on materials handling, also equipment news. Indexed in ASTI, F&S.

Modern Packaging. New York, McGraw-Hill (monthly).
Articles and current developments on technology and marketing in packaging. Indexed in BPI, F&S. The December issue each year is an "Encyclopedia and Planning Guide." This includes a classified and alphabetical buyers' directory for manufacturers of packaging materials, containers, machinery and equipment; also related service firms.

Traffic Management. Boston, Cahners Publishing Co. (monthly).
"The magazine for physical distribution/logistics/material control." The December issue includes an annual "Catalog of Physical Distribution Directories & Guides."

Transportation & Distribution Management. Washington, D.C., Traffic Service Corp. (bimonthly).
"The magazine of physical distribution plans and strategy."

LOGISTICS DIRECTORIES

American Warehousemen's Association. *Membership Directory.* Chicago (annual).
Short geographic list of warehouses, giving officers and size in square feet.

Material Handling Engineering Handbook & Directory. Comp. by Material Handling Engineering Magazine. Cleveland, Ohio, Industrial Publishing Co. (biennial).
The directory section contains an alphabetical list of over 1,000 manufacturers of material handling and packaging equipment, with a separate listing by specific product. Includes also a list of trade names, and names of consultants and associations.

The annual "Distribution Guide Issue" (July) of *Distribution Worldwide* includes a geographical directory of public warehouses. The December issue each year of *Traffic Management* is a descriptive "Catalog of Physical Distribution Directories & Guides."

LOGISTICS ASSOCIATIONS

American Warehousemen's Association, 222 West Adams Street, Chicago, Ill. 60606.
National Council of Physical Distribution Management, 222 West Adams Street, Chicago, Ill. 60606.

TRAFFIC AND TRANSPORTATION

Rapid changes have been occurring in the transport field in recent years and this trend is likely to continue in the future. The short list of recent books below makes no claim to being complete or to giving equal representation for each mode of transportation. Statistics on the various modes of transportation are described in Chapter 5.

Colton, Richard C. and Edmund S. Ward. *Practical Handbook of Industrial Traffic Management.* 5th ed., rev. by Charles H. Wager. Washington, D.C., Traffic Service Corp., 1973.

A broad overview, with practical information on such topics as freight classification, rates and routing, packaging, warehousing, organizing the traffic department, data processing in transportation, international shipments. Includes a glossary.

Farris, Martin T. and Paul T. McElhiney, eds. *Modern Transportation: Selected Readings.* 2d ed. Boston, Houghton Mifflin, 1973.

A good selection of 55 readings in 4 parts: the carriers; industrial traffic and distribution management; transportation rates and costs; transportation problems and issues.

Flood, Kenneth U. and F. V. Heinkel. *Traffic Management.* 3d rev. ed. Dubuque, Iowa, W. C. Brown Co., 1974.

This comprehensive text concentrates on an in-depth coverage of that material which is essential to the performance of the traffic management function. It includes Interstate Commerce Commission and other official interpretations of important rules, regulations and practices, with frequent citations to cases and other publications in footnotes.

Frankel, Ernst G. and Henry S. Marcus. *Ocean Transportation.* Cambridge, Mass., MIT Press, 1973.

A series of studies analyzing the development and status of ocean transportation and projecting future trends, based on a research project of the MIT Sea Grant Program, 1970–1972. It contains 9 parts to form a comprehensive work of over 800 pages: a world review of shipping demand and supply; ocean transportation technology; developing and using data on trade commodity flows; shipbuilding costs; ocean barging, a review; a review of maritime labor and a study of the longshore industry; financing of U.S. shipping; factors affecting shipping operations; a review of merchant marine subsidies.

Guandolo, John. *Transportation Law.* 2d ed. Dubuque, Iowa, W. C. Brown Co., 1973.

This lengthy volume on transportation law (1,159 pages) is arranged so that the reader can locate a discussion of the principles of law for any particular mode of transportation all in one place. The final chapters discuss practices and procedures before the Interstate Commerce Commission, the Civil Aeronautics Board, and the Federal Maritime Commission.

Locklin, D. Philip. *Economics of Transportation.* 7th ed. Homewood, Ill., Irwin, 1972.

The most widely used text on the economics of all modes of intercity transportation, well documented with bibliographies at end of each chapter. The coverage for rail transportation is in much greater depth than for other forms of transportation because Professor Locklin uses the study of railroad rate theory and rate-making and the evolution of railroad regulations as background for his later discussions of variations found in other modes of transportation.

Norton, Hugh S. *Modern Transportation Economics.* 2d ed. Columbus, Ohio, C. E. Merrill, 1971.

Another text on the economic aspects of transportation, not as detailed as Locklin's but still aiming to give a balanced treatment of the various modes. Parts 3–4 consider regulatory and policy issues. Bibliographies are at end of some chapters.

Pegrum, Dudley F. *Transportation: Economics and Public Policy.* 3d ed. Homewood, Ill., Irwin, 1973.

This text focuses "on the basic national questions and the various problems of policy that are of vital importance to the different modes in the task of rendering transport services." It is in 4 parts: the transport system; economics of transport pricing; the regulation of transport; national transportation policy. An annotated bibliography is at end.

Sampson, Roy J. and Martin T. Farris. *Domestic Transportation: Practice, Theory, and Policy.* 3d ed. Boston, Houghton Mifflin, 1975.

As the subtitle indicates this introductory text is a blend of theory and practice, meant for both business and economics students. It studies the various modes of domestic transportation as a whole rather than separately, and it is revised to reflect the many new developments and problems in the transportation field today. Suggested readings are at end of chapters.

Stratford, Alan H. *Air Transport Economics in the Supersonic Era.* 2d ed., rev. and extended. London and New York, Macmillan, 1973.

Attempts to stimulate interest in solving commercial air transport problems in connection with the development of aircraft, changing world markets, and operational systems. Bibliographies at end of chapters.

Taff, Charles A. *Commercial Motor Transportation.* 5th ed. Homewood, Ill., Irwin, 1975.

Professor Taff's text emphasizes the managerial and economic aspects of motor transportation, including financing motor carrier operations, equipment, rates, labor relations, and other pertinent areas. A selected bibliography is at end.

TRAFFIC AND TRANSPORTATION BIBLIOGRAPHIES

Canada. Ministry of Transport. Library. *List of Accessions.* Ottawa, Ontario (bimonthly).

A subject list of books and pamphlets added to this library. It includes material on management, data processing and the social sciences as well as the sections for each mode of transportation.

Northwestern University. Transportation Center Library. *Current Literature in Traffic and Transportation.* Evanston, Ill. (monthly).

A classified list of articles and books on all modes of transportation, and also on containerization, industrial distribution, travel, urban transportation. Includes foreign as well as American publications. This library also publishes *Doctoral Dissertations on Transportation: A Bibliography,* an annual or biennial list compiled from other sources such as *Dissertation Abstracts International,* and arranged by topic.

University of California. Institute of Transportation and Traffic Engineering. *Selected List of Recent Additions to the Transportation Library.* Berkeley (quarterly).

This is another subject list and includes books, pamphlets and microfiche on all modes of transportation; also covers environmental quality and planning.

TRAFFIC AND TRANSPORTATION DICTIONARIES

Bruce, Harry J. *Distribution and Transportation Handbook.* Boston, Cahners Books, 1971.

A reference book of transportation definitions, explanations and listings. Covers also warehousing, bills of lading, transport demurrage, shipper-carrier agreements, kinds of equipment, sources of information on federal regulation and control.

TRANSPORTATION FINANCIAL MANUALS

Carrier Reports. Old Saybrook, Conn. (quarterly).

Tabular listing of financial data about the nation's leading carriers, including truck, rail, bus, air, water carriers, REA Express, and freight forwarders.

Moody's Transportation Manual. New York, Moody's Investors Service (annual, with biweekly supplements).

The basic financial manual for all modes of transportation, covering U.S. and the larger Canadian companies. Information usually includes: a brief history of each company; officers and directors; subsidiaries; comparative income statements, balance sheets, selected financial ratios; description of outstanding securities. Center blue pages contain a good selection of statistics for railroads, air transport, trucking, urban transportation; also 10-year annual high/low stock price ranges of U.S. and Canadian transportation securities.

Trinc's Blue Book of the Trucking Industry. Washington, D.C., Trinc Transportation Consultants (annual).

Tabular listing of balance sheet statistics for the largest U.S. trucking firms, including revenues, expenses, manpower, ton-miles statistics; also alphabetical list of firms giving names of top officers. Trinc's also publishes a similar annual called *Trinc's Green Book of Air Freight and Freight Forwarders.*

TRAFFIC AND TRANSPORTATION PERIODICALS

Commercial Car Journal. Radnor, Pa., Chilton (monthly).

A trade journal for fleet management. October issue each year is a "Buyers' Guide & Specs Issue." Indexed in PAIS.

Traffic World. Washington, D.C., Traffic Service Corp. (weekly).

A news magazine of transportation management, including legislative news, current ICC decisions and orders, CAB and Federal Maritime Commission news, occasional statistics.

Transportation. Amsterdam, The Netherlands, Elsevier Scientific Publishing Co. (quarterly).

"An international journal devoted to the improvement of transportation planning and practice." Research papers are written in English and emphasize the systems approach. Includes book reviews.

Transportation Journal. Chicago, American Society of Traffic and Transportation (quarterly).

A professional journal for scholarly papers on practices and techniques in a wide range of transportation and physical distribution topics, written principally by academic persons. Indexed in BPI, PAIS.

Several foreign periodicals are: *Canadian Transportation & Distribution Management* (Don Mills, Ontario, Southam Business Publications, monthly); Chartered Institute of Transport *Journal* (London, bimonthly); and *Journal of Transport Economics and Policy* (London School of Economics, 3/yr., indexed in PAIS).

TRAFFIC AND TRANSPORTATION DIRECTORIES

Official Directory of Industrial and Commercial Traffic Executives. Washington, D.C., Traffic Service Corp. (annual).

A directory of U.S. and Canadian firms and their traffic executives. Includes also a list of transportation organizations; government departments, agencies, etc.; transportation consultants.

Who's Who in Railroading and Rail Transit. 17th ed. Frederick C. Osthoff, editor. New York, Simmons-Boardman, 1971.

Biographical dictionary of North American railroad leaders, including labor leaders, lawyers and other specialists.

For the many directories covering specific modes of transportation consult the guides to directories listed in Chapter 3.

TRAFFIC AND TRANSPORTATION ASSOCIATIONS

These are just a few of many associations. For other relating to specific modes of transportation consult the *Encyclopedia of Associations* described in Chapter 3.

American Society of Traffic and Transportation, 547 West Jackson Boulevard, Chicago, Ill. 60606.

American Trucking Associations, 1616 P Street, N.W., Washington, D.C. 20036.

Association of American Railroads, American Railroads Building, 1920 L Street, N.W., Washington, D.C. 20036.

National Industrial Traffic League, 425 13th Street, N.W., Suite 712, Washington, D.C. 20004.

Railway Systems and Management Association, 181 East Lake Shore Drive, Chicago, Ill. 60611.

Transportation Association of America, 1101 17th Street, N.W., Washington, D.C. 20036.

21

A BASIC BOOKSHELF

In assembling a reference collection for a personal, business or small public library one should start with a few essential works that are comprehensive in coverage and basic to almost any kind of business. This chapter suggests such a list and, although it is aimed more at a beginning collection for a company, it can easily be adapted for a small public library or to meet the more limited needs of a personal library.

It is assumed that all company collections will have the following: (1) a good dictionary (see Chapter 1); (2) an atlas — not necessarily an expensive one, but an up-to-date edition with print that is easy to read; (3) both a local newspaper and one for a major metropolitan area; (4) a weekly news magazine — either *Newsweek* or *Time*; (5) telephone directories for the immediate vicinity and perhaps for several large U.S. cities; (6) a zip code directory; (7) hotel and airline guides, if company personnel travel often; and (8) a small selection of trade journals, the important books and reference sources on the company's industry or business. Each source below is described elsewhere in this book. (Check the index for page references.)

Almanacs and Informational Yearbooks

Stateman's Year-Book. New York, St. Martin's Press (annual).

World Almanac & Book of Facts. New York, Newspaper Enterprise Association (annual).

Europa Year Book is more specialized but is worth considering for its comprehensive coverage on all countries.

Bibliographies

Business Books in Print. New York, R. R. Bowker (annual).

Encyclopedia of Business Information Sources. Vol. 1. Detroit, Mich., Gale Research Co., 1970. A revision is scheduled for 1976.

Guide to American Directories. 9th ed. Rye, N.Y., Klein Publications, 1975.

Harvard University. Graduate School of Business Administration. Baker Library. *Core Collection: An Author and Subject Guide.* Boston (annual); also their *New Books in Business and Economics: Recent Additions to Baker Library* (10/yr.).

Johnson, H. Webster. *How to Use the Business Library, With Sources of Business Information.* 4th ed. Cincinnati, Ohio, South-Western, 1972.

Statistics Sources. 4th ed. Detroit, Mich., Gale Research Co., 1974.

The company may also want to consider a subscription to the quarterly *Personnel Management Abstracts,* since it describes a good selection of current articles on management and organizational behavior (Ann Arbor, Division of Management Education, Graduate School of Business Administration, University of Michigan).

Biographical Dictionaries

Who's Who in America. Chicago, Marquis Who's Who (biennial).
Who's Who in Finance and Industry. Chicago, Marquis Who's Who (biennial).

Some companies may feel they can do without this latter volume if they usually need only the very brief biographical facts that are in *Standard & Poor's Register,* listed below.

Dictionaries

Garcia, F. L., ed. *Glenn G. Munn's Encyclopedia of Banking and Finance.* 7th ed., rev. and enl. Boston, Bankers Publishing Co., 1973.

Johannsen, Hano and G. Terry Page. *International Dictionary of Management: A Practical Guide.* Boston, Houghton Mifflin, 1975.

McGraw-Hill Dictionary of Modern Economics: A Handbook of Terms and Organizations. 2d ed. New York, McGraw-Hill, 1973.

Directories of Companies

Every collection should have one of the following two directories:

Dun & Bradstreet. *Million Dollar Directory* accompanied by their *Reference Book of Corporate Managements.* New York. 2 volumes (annual).

Standard & Poor's Register of Corporations, Directors and Executives. New York. 3 volumes (annual).

Consideration should be given to the need for including a more comprehensive directory of U.S. manufacturing firms, either *Thomas Register of American Manufacturers and Thomas Register Catalog File* (11 volumes, annual) or the *U.S. Industrial Directory* (4 volumes, annual); also a directory of industrial companies for the state in which the company is located.

If a company has frequent inquiries about the names of foreign manufacturers it should also have:

Kelly's Manufacturers and Merchants Directory. Kingston Upon Thames, Surrey, England. 2 volumes (annual).

Directories of Associations and Government Organizations
National Trade and Professional Associations of the United States and Canada and Labor Unions. Washington, D.C., Columbia Books, Inc. (annual).

If the firm regularly uses information on associations it may want to consider instead the more extensive *Encyclopedia of Associations* (Detroit, Mich., Gale Research Co., Vol. 1).

United States Government Manual. Washington, D.C., Office of the Federal Register, General Services Administration (annual). Purchase from U.S. Government Printing Office.

Directories of Periodicals
Select one of the following:

Ayer Directory of Publications. Philadelphia, Pa., Ayer Press (annual).
Standard Periodical Directory. New York, Oxbridge Publishing Co. (annual).

Financial Manuals
Moody's Investors Service. *Moody's Industrial Manual.* New York. 2 volumes (annual).

Statistical Compilations
Handbook of Basic Economic Statistics. Economics Statistics Bureau of Washington, D.C. (annual, with monthly supplements).
United Nations. *Statistical Yearbook.* New York. Also their *Monthly Bulletin of Statistics.*
U.S. Bureau of the Census. *Statistical Abstract of the United States.* Washington, D.C., U.S. Government Printing Office (annual).
U.S. Department of Commerce. *Business Statistics.* Washington, D.C., U.S. Government Printing Office (biennial).
U.S. Department of Commerce. *U.S. Industrial Outlook.* Washington, D.C., U.S. Government Printing Office (annual).

Current Statistical Monthlies
U.S. Board of Governors of the Federal Reserve System. *Federal Reserve Bulletin.* Washington, D.C.
U.S. Bureau of Economic Analysis, Department of Commerce. *Business Conditions Digest.* Washington, D.C., U.S. Government Printing Office.
U.S. Bureau of Labor Statistics. *Monthly Labor Review.* Washington, D.C., U.S. Government Printing Office.
U.S. Council of Economic Advisers. *Economic Indicators.* Washington, D.C., U.S. Government Printing Office.
U.S. Department of Commerce. *Survey of Current Business.* Washington, D.C., U.S. Government Printing Office.

Handbooks
Aljian, George W., ed. *Purchasing Handbook.* 3d ed. New York, McGraw-Hill, 1973.

Carson, Gordon B., Harold A. Bolz and Hewitt H. Young. *Production Handbook.* 3d ed. New York, Ronald, 1972.

Famularo, Joseph J., ed. *Handbook of Modern Personnel Administration.* New York, McGraw-Hill, 1972.

Riso, Ovid, ed. *The Dartnell Sales Manager's Handbook.* 12th ed. Chicago, Dartnell Corp. To be published in 1976.

Vancil, Richard F., ed. *Financial Executive's Handbook.* Homewood, Ill., Dow Jones-Irwin, 1970.

In addition, the collection should include one each of the following sets of two books:

Britt, Steuart H., ed. *The Dartnell Marketing Manager's Handbook.* Chicago, Dartnell Corp., 1973.

Buell, Victor P., ed. *Handbook of Modern Marketing.* New York, McGraw-Hill, 1970.

Davidson, Sidney, ed. *Handbook of Modern Accounting.* New York, McGraw-Hill, 1970.

Wixon, Rufus, Walter G. Kell and Norton M. Bedford, eds. *Accountants' Handbook.* 5th ed. New York, Ronald, 1970.

Handbooks are such useful compilations of concise data on specific management functions that any of those included in this book are worth considering for a small collection.

Periodicals and newspapers

Those periodicals that are starred (*) are of primary importance. Those designated with an (R) are included because their book review sections make them of special interest.

Accounting Review (R)
Bankers Magazine (R)
Barron's (*)
*Business and Society Review/
    Innovation* (R)
Business Week (*)
Dun's Review
Economist
Financial Executive
Forbes (*)
Fortune (*)
Harvard Business Review (*)

*Industrial and Labor Relations
    Review* (R)
*International Management
Journal of Marketing (*R)
Management Accounting
Management Review
Personnel Journal
Personnel Psychology (R)
Sales & Marketing Management (included primarily for its special issues)
Wall Street Journal (*)

A COMPANY LIBRARY

Once a firm has acquired this minimal collection it must make some arrangement to keep the periodicals and reference books up to date, since a "dead" collection is not of use for very long. A small collection can be managed by almost any bright, imaginative employee with a flair for organizing material and an interest in helping people. If this proves successful the collection may develop to the point where the company will consider a full-fledged library. When this point is reached the services of a trained librarian become important.

Although a good company library is not an inexpensive proposition, experience has proved it can result in a significant saving for the firm. The following guide will be of interest to company managers considering such a library:

Special Libraries Association. *Special Libraries: A Guide for Management.* With revisions through 1974. New York, 1975.

This is a useful pamphlet for individuals or organizations who need information or counsel on the establishment of information services, special libraries and information centers. It was written by 4 special librarians in the Illinois Chapter of SLA, and it discusses what a special library is, how to start one, what resources are required (staff, space and equipment, budget). There is a list of suggested readings on planning and operating a special library.

Thus one comes full circle in this guide to business information sources by returning to the library as the basic source for information and to the librarian as a knowledgeable, interested individual who wants to help people make the fullest use of the vast and varied materials being published.

INDEX

The letter "n" after a page number indicates that the author or title does not appear as a separate entry but rather is mentioned either in a general note or in an annotation to another book. With subjects, the "n" denotes a topic included in one or more of the books on that page.

When a specific book or subject is referred to on more than one page, the page number in boldface is the primary reference.